D1587160

EXPERIMENTS IN LIVING

EXPERIMENTS IN LIVING

*A study of the nature and foundation of ethics
or morals in the light of recent work
in Social Anthropology*

BY

A. MACBEATH

*Professor of Logic and Metaphysics
in the Queen's University
of Belfast*

THE GIFFORD LECTURES FOR 1948–1949
DELIVERED IN THE UNIVERSITY
OF ST. ANDREWS

LONDON
MACMILLAN & CO. LTD
1952

*This book is copyright in all countries which
are signatories to the Berne Convention*

PRINTED IN GREAT BRITAIN

PREFACE

THIS book is a study in comparative ethics. Its purpose is sufficiently explained in the first lecture, but certain features of the treatment require some further explanation. I was led to undertake a study of the experiments in living of primitive peoples because I found writers on ethics with the most divergent views about the nature of morality and the principle of moral judgement appealing for support for their theories to the moral ideas of primitive peoples. After I had spent several years reading anthropological literature, as opportunity offered, I decided to confine my attention to contemporary primitive peoples; for the number even of these is considerable and the literature about them extensive; and fuller and more accurate information is available about them than about the early ancestors of people who are now advanced. But even with this limitation, the problem of the form in which the results of my enquiries should be presented for publication troubled me not a little. The main difficulty was to decide how much detail about particular primitive peoples should be included; and the difficulty was aggravated when I tried to put the results in a form which would satisfy the requirements of the Gifford Foundation. For by the will of the founder the Gifford Lectures are ' public and popular ', which I take to mean that they should be intelligible to educated members of the general public who are not experts in ethics or anthropology. Such people could not be expected to read for themselves the accounts which anthropologists have given of the ways of life of primitive peoples, while the time at my disposal made it impossible for me to describe many of them in detail. In the end I decided to give a fairly full account of the ways of life of four representative primitive peoples, to use these as illustrations of the nature of primitive morality, and, where necessary, to supplement them by briefer references to other peoples. How far this compromise has been successful I must leave the reader to decide.

This method of treatment involved a certain amount of repetition, for some topics had to be dealt with on several occasions in different connections. In any case some repetition was inevitable in lectures to an audience in which some changes were liable to take place from week to week ; so that each lecture had to be relatively self-contained. It is true that most of the lectures as they now appear contain more material than could have been included in a one-hour discourse (though much of the additional material was discussed in seminars) ; but any attempt to eliminate all repetition would have involved so drastic a departure from the original treatment that the result would scarcely be recognisable as the lectures actually delivered, and in the end it might not be any more successful. I, therefore, decided to retain the lecture form and keep as near as possible to the spoken word.

I am unhappy about the term ' primitive ' which I have been obliged to use. As used by social anthropologists it is a purely descriptive term and does not imply a value judgement. It covers all peoples who have no written records and whose material culture is simple. But to the ordinary reader it is apt to suggest immaturity and crudity, if not even mental and moral inferiority ; and such a suggestion is not warranted. It is true that there are primitive peoples whose moral ideas and manner of life are in many ways crude and barbarous ; but there are others whose ways of life are gracious and dignified, and whose relations to one another compare favourably with those of peoples whose material culture is much more complex. I toyed for a time with various substitutes for the term ' primitive ', but the only alternatives which have been suggested or of which I could think were clumsy and inelegant, and in the end I came to the conclusion that the term is too firmly established to be dispensed with. I want, however, to make it clear that I use it in a purely descriptive and morally neutral sense ; for I am concerned to understand, not to evaluate.

In discussing contemporary ethical theories and considering how far they can be reconciled with what the anthropologists tell us about the moral judgements and ideals of primitive peoples, I have been mainly concerned with Intuitionism and Ideal Utilitarianism ; and this may be regarded as an anachronism. For though these were the main ethical theories current a decade or so ago when I began my enquiries and though they still have distinguished adherents, fashions in philosophy have been changing so rapidly in recent years that many of the younger generation of philosophers now show little interest in them. And it may be thought a serious omission in a work on the nature of ethics that it pays no attention to the latest developments of ethical theory according to which moral judgements are merely expressions of emotions, attitudes, preferences, decisions or what not : not judgements in the strict sense at all but something else which by a strange mistake has been put into the form of statements. It is with these latest developments of ethical theory, I may be told, that the contemporary writer on ethics has to make his account. My reason for not referring to them in this work is not any lack of respect for the people who propound them nor of appreciation of the importance of their theories ; it is rather that the moral ideas of primitive peoples do not seem specially relevant to the discussion of these theories and do not provide a special test of their adequacy. If these theories are a satisfactory account of the moral judgements of any people, they will apply to those of all peoples equally well ; and, therefore, comparative ethics is not relevant in considering them. They seem to me to give a partial account of all moral judgements, but not a complete account of any. They emphasise some important peculiarities of moral judgements and call attention to an aspect of such judgements which had been insufficiently recognised by earlier theories ; but they neglect or deny other elements in moral judgements which are equally important. So that they are right in what they assert, but wrong in what they deny. And their denial of the assertive element in moral judgements is the result not of an unprejudiced analysis of the deliverances of the moral consciousness, primitive or advanced, but of the presuppositions with which those who propounded them approached ethics. The advocates of the emotive and expressive theories had already come, on logical and epistemological grounds, to the conclusion that the only meaningful statements are either tautologies or empirical statements which are verifiable by an appeal to sense experience. Now moral judgements do not fall into either of these classes, but even advanced thinkers hesitated to class them, along with metaphysical and theological statements, as meaningless nonsense. Accordingly some other interpretation had to be found for them. This was done by concentrating attention on the non-assertive element in them and treating it as a complete account of their nature and function. If they do not assert anything, they are neither meaningful nor meaningless assertions. This, however, seems to me a drastic over-simplification; for while it emphasises an important and hitherto neglected characteristic of moral judgements, namely, the fact that at least most moral judgements and all original moral judgements express emotions and attitudes towards the acts and agents and states of affairs to which they refer, it neglects the equally important fact that they convey information about them as well. This, however, is not the place to discuss these important and highly controversial issues, and dogmatic assertions about them are undesirable. If there is one lesson which the study of the moral ideas and ideals of other peoples and my own reflection on morality have taught me, it is the bewildering complexity of the moral life and the unwisdom of dogmatism regarding it. There is no short-cut to moral infallibility, and simple theories about morality, however tidy and attractive they may be, are almost certain to be one-sided, the results of over-simplification. All I wish to do here is to explain why I have not discussed the recent controversies about the assertive or expressive character of moral judgements in this work. It is because the researches of anthropologists into the ways of life of primitive peoples do not seem to me particularly relevant to our attempts to resolve them.

It remains only to express my thanks to those who helped to make this book possible: to the University of St. Andrews for the honour which they did me in appointing me Gifford Lecturer; to my colleagues at St. Andrews for the warmth of their welcome and for their generous hospitality which made my stay among them one of the most pleasant periods of my life; to those who attended my seminars and by their questions and criticisms helped me to clarify my thinking on many topics; to my own University for two terms' leave of absence to enable me to pursue my enquiries; to Professor R. Firth of the London

School of Economics, Dr. R. O. Piddington of the University of Edinburgh and other anthropologists for advice about the relevant literature; to Mr. George E. Davie and Mr. John Faris, my colleagues in the Philosophy Department of this University, for assistance in proof-reading and many helpful suggestions; to my daughter Catriona for help in reading the proofs and preparing the index; to the University of Glasgow for permission to use in Lectures XI and XII some of the material which I used in the Frazer Lecture delivered in 1948 and published as a Glasgow University publication under the title *The Relationship between Primitive Morality and Religion*; and to the editor of *Philosophy* for permission to use in Lecture II two or three pages from an article on ' Duty ' which appeared in that journal in April 1948.

A. MACBEATH

The Queen's University of Belfast
July 1951

CONTENTS

" The best prophylactic against baseless speculation that man must believe this or do that is the actual knowledge that throughout a definite part of the globe he believes and does nothing of the kind."—R. H. Lowie.

" By dwelling mentally for a time among people of a much simpler culture than our own, we may be able to gain a new sense of proportion with regard to our own institutions, beliefs and customs."—B. Malinowski.

" There is no more liberal education than to consider how others are living."—Sir James Frazer.

" There is no arguing with history."—A. A. Golden-weiser.

ANTHROPOLOGY AND ETHICS

I APPRECIATE very highly the honour which you have done me by inviting me to join the ranks of the thinkers and scholars who have lectured on the Gifford Foundation ; but the feeling which is uppermost in my mind as I rise to address you is an overwhelming sense of insufficiency to the trust which you have so generously reposed in me. And this feeling is intensified by the recollection of the succession of illustrious philosophers who have taught in this place — Ferrier and Pringle-Pattison, Henry Jones and Bernard Bosanquet, Burnet and Taylor and Stout — men from whom I have tried to learn, but whose standards I cannot hope to maintain worthily.

In considering how I should try to carry out the duties of the lectureship, I thought that I could best repay your confidence by concentrating on one of the many topics pre-scribed by Lord Gifford rather than by attempting to construct a metaphysical system which would cover them all. In making my selection from these topics, I was guided by two considerations which Lord Gifford placed in the forefront of his require-ments : (1) that the lecturer should speak from genuine con-viction — that the knowledge which he seeks to impart should be ' true and felt, not merely nominal ' ; and (2) that it should contribute to human well-being. Now among the convictions to which I have been led by the experiences of a lifetime one stands out sharp and clear. It is that of the goods which can be achieved by man the greatest, indeed the only one which is absolutely and unconditionally good, is moral goodness — the goodness of doing that which he believes to be right because he believes it to be right. I might have started from this conviction, tried to work out its metaphysical and theological implications, and argued that moral goodness is the path to God ; but I have decided rather to consider the nature of our moral convictions themselves, to state them as clearly and simply as I can, and to examine their grounds with the sincerity and frankness which Lord Gifford rightly requires of those who lecture on the Foundation which he created. Accordingly, from among the topics which he prescribes, I have chosen as the subject which I wish to discuss with you, " The Knowledge of the Nature and Foundation of Ethics or Morals and of all Obligations and Duties thence Arising ". In dealing with this subject I shall try to take account of the relevant evidence from all sources ; but I propose to pay special attention to the light thrown on it by the researches and conclusions of recent social anthropologists. In this first lecture I want to indicate the nature of the problem, and to explain why, and in what ways, I regard the work of the anthropologists as relevant to the solution of it.

Our enquiry concerns the nature of morality, and in order to get the enquiry started, morality or moral conduct must be identified as a definite phenomenon. In practice this does not present any real difficulty. There are certain general characteristics of moral conduct which enable us to identify it sufficiently for our present purpose. No doubt these characteristics provide only a provisional and tentative description, which will have to be made more exact as our enquiry proceeds, but they will suffice to set our enquiry going.

In order that there may be morality, or that conduct may be regarded as moral, there must be not only behaviour or action or conduct. There must be reflection on behaviour, ideas about and attitudes towards action, and beliefs about conduct, which find expression in judgements that the actions are right or wrong, the conduct good or bad. Moral conduct then is the conduct of selves, self-conscious persons, beings who know what they are doing and have reasons for doing it ; conduct pervaded by ideas and ideals, motives and attitudes, in the light of which judgement can be passed on it.

There are at least three points of view from which we may look at any piece of conduct, and from each of them moral judgements may be passed on it. It involves the pursuit of certain ends or the initiation of certain states of affairs ; there are certain rules or principles with which it complies or fails to comply ; and it is the expression or manifestation of a certain spirit or attitude of mind. Many ethical theorists tend to regard one of these aspects as more fundamental, and try to express or explain the others in terms of it; but, in fact, not only the moral life as a whole but every piece of moral conduct has all three aspects. It is the pursuit of an end or ends, from a motive or motives, according to a rule or rules. These three aspects give us the three fundamental ethical concepts, the right, the good and the morally good. What these are and how they are related to one another is one of the main questions which ethics has to answer. Moreover, as we shall see later, the principles on which judgements are passed on ends as good or bad, on rules as right or wrong, on motives or attitudes of mind as morally good or bad, are different; and another of the main problems of ethics is to discover what these principles are, what authority they possess, and whence it is derived; how we get to know them, and what sort of knowledge we have of them. These, it seems to me, are some of the main questions which we have to discuss, if we would comply with Lord Gifford's request to consider the knowledge of the foundation of morals or ethics.

From the point of view of trying to discover the nature of morality, we may say then that a people's morality [1] is the way they think about, or the attitude they adopt towards conduct, the beliefs and convictions they entertain about actions as right or wrong, good or bad. But not all judgements about conduct as right or wrong are moral judgements; not all good ends are moral ends; not all right rules are moral rules. We have, therefore, to ask which of them are moral, and how they are to be distinguished from those which are not. For example, there are right and wrong ways of constructing a road, conducting an argument, carrying on a business, or playing a game; and there are good and bad roads, arguments, businesses and games. But however good a road may be, and however right

---

[1] The term ' a people's morality ' may be, and often is, used in another sense, to describe the extent to which the people realise their ideals, obey their moral rules and act from good motives, and this usage is quite legitimate; but however important this aspect of morality may be from the practical point of view, for an understanding of the nature and foundation of morality, it is the ideals, the rules and the motives themselves which we have to consider.

the method of constructing it, we may say that the conduct of those constructing it is morally bad if they are building it, let us say, as a means of invading the territory of a peaceful neighbouring people. However good a business may be, however well conducted from an economic point of view, however high the profits to its promoters, and the standard of living which it provides for its employees, however urgent even the demand for its products, we may say it is morally bad if it is engaged in, say, the manufacture of opium. However well a game is played, we may say that the conduct of those engaged in playing it is morally wrong, if in playing it they are amusing themselves at the expense of neglecting important duties. In other words, the goodness or rightness of such conduct, whether in engineering, industry or sport, is relative to a particular purpose or point of view, and the purpose itself may be morally wrong; the point of view may be too limited to give us a final judgement. The judgement which we pass may therefore have to be reconsidered and, it may be, reversed from a more inclusive point of view. Thus the rightness or goodness which we attribute to such conduct is conditional or hypothetical. The utmost we would be justified in saying is : if it is right to build a road, it should be made according to sound engineering principles; if it is right to carry on a business, it should be conducted on sound economic lines; if it is right to play a game, it should be done according to the proper rules and in the right spirit. But in certain circumstances it may not be right to do these things at all. Moreover, even if it is right to do them, considerations other than those dealt with by engineering or economics are relevant in deciding how they ought to be done.

Now the moral judgement differs from these hypothetical judgements of rightness or goodness in being absolute or categorical. It is not subject to review by any higher court; for there is no higher court to which appeal can be made against it. The end which is morally good is ultimately good; the judgement that a course of action is morally right is a final judgement. It may, of course, be mistaken and on further consideration it may have to be reversed, but only in favour of another moral judgement, that is, a judgement which appeals to or is based on the same ultimate principle, not in the sense in which the moral judgement overrides the economic or legal or other relative judgement. Other aspects of the relation between the moral and these other judgements we shall have to consider later. All I want to note at present is that the distinguishing characteristic of the moral judgement is that it is the final judgement, the principle to which it appeals the ultimate principle, the good in the light of which it is passed the ultimate good. The work of ethics is to discover and make explicit what good or system of goods is ultimately or morally good; what principles or rules are ultimately or morally right; what motives or attitudes of mind are morally good.

We may say, then, that a people's morality consists of the beliefs and convictions they entertain about conduct as ultimately or morally right or wrong, ultimately or morally good or bad. The judgements in which these beliefs and convictions find expression supply us with our data for the study of morality. Of such data there is no scarcity. We find them by introspection in the beliefs we ourselves entertain, the emotional attitudes we adopt and the judgements of approval or disapproval which we pass on our own and other people's actions. We find them also in the judgements passed and the attitudes adopted by those around us, and in the literature and laws and institutions of our people. It is true that even if we confine our study to such data, that is, to the deliverances of the moral consciousness as we find it among ourselves, the data of ethics are not so definite or precise as those of most other sciences. For some of our ordinary moral beliefs and convictions may be, and indeed often are, confused and inconsistent one with another; and the judgements in which they find expression can, therefore, be only partially true. Accordingly, we have to subject our moral judgements to critical scrutiny and only those which survive this scrutiny provide the real moral facts, by which ethical theories are suggested and by reference to which they are tested and either confirmed or disproved. No doubt, the distinction between facts or data and hypotheses or theories is difficult to draw in any field, but the difficulty is greater in the case of moral phenomena than it is in the case of the phenomena with which most other sciences are concerned; and it seems to me that many ethical theorists pay insufficient attention to the great importance and the real difficulty of this work of discovering moral facts. This work is a necessary preliminary to that of ethical science strictly so-called. The latter is concerned to make explicit the principle or principles on which considered moral judgements proceed, and to formulate a theory by which moral facts can be explained. A pre-condition of its work, therefore, is the possession of considered moral judgements or moral facts. It is the difficulty of getting these that seems to me insufficiently recognised, the difficulty of being sure that we have eliminated all influences due to local, environmental or cultural conditions, and so have an authentic deliverance of the moral consciousness.[1]

What I want to insist on at present, however, is that though it is natural to begin, and not unusual to end, enquiries into the nature of morality with the study of our own moral judgements and those of our neighbours, they are only part of the data of ethics ; and that, therefore, in view of the difficulty of being sure that any given moral judgement is an authentic deliverance of the moral consciousness, it is desirable not only to scrutinise our own moral judgements carefully, but also to make the widest possible survey of the moral judgements of men of different times and cultures, so that we may be able to check the authenticity of the moral judgements of some by those of others. For morality is a phenomenon which has appeared in a great variety of forms, of which the system of moral ideas and beliefs and attitudes of Western Europe or even of Western civilisation is only one. There are also, even at the present time, such moralities as those of India and China and contemporary primitive peoples. Each of these is, or at least contains, not merely certain kinds of conduct, but also certain systems of judgements about conduct and attitudes with regard to conduct, and these differ in many ways from one another and from our own. Moreover, morality is a historical phenomenon which has appeared in a large variety of forms in the

[1] I think it would be interesting and not unfruitful to consider how far the differences between writers on ethics are due to differences in their views about the facts rather than to differences in their interpretations of the same facts. For the way in which differences in their data tend to be obscured even from themselves, see below, pp. 363-9.

past, such, for example, as the morality of the Hebrews and Greeks, the Egyptians and Babylonians and Persians ; so that what we find is not morality but moralities.[1] And, when we consider the different moralities, we are impressed not only with how much they have in common, but also with how profoundly they differ.

Leaving for the moment the fundamental question to which this multiplicity of moralities gives rise, namely, how are we to discover morality among the moralities, what I want to emphasise is that all these moralities, past and present, and all the moral judgements in which they find expression, or at least all the considered moral judgements among them, are equally data of ethics, and that ethical theorists neglect any of them at their peril. For there are no men whose beliefs are known to history or anthropology who are not moral beings and members of social groups. They all pursue ends according to rules, distinguish some ends as good and some rules as right ; and they pass judgements on their own and other people's actions as morally good or bad, right or wrong. This is true both of contemporary primitive peoples and of the early ancestors of people who are now civilised or advanced. I am not suggesting that the moral beliefs of such people are more relevant to ethical enquiry than those of other people, past or present, still less that they alone are relevant. All I contend is that they are a relevant part of the data of ethics. Among my reasons for devoting special attention to the moral beliefs and judgements of primitive peoples are : (1) They have been largely neglected by recent and contemporary ethical theorists. (2) A great deal of information about them has recently become available, and much of it seems to me to be inconsistent with at least some contemporary ethical theories. (3) The ways of life of these people, their moral ideas and ideals, are the most radically different from our own that we can find ; and it is a commonplace in science that the severest test to which we can expose any theory is to consider how far it can explain the phenomena which differ most markedly from those which originally suggested it. (4) It has been not uncommon for moral and social

---

[1] Different moralities are not different theories about morality, but different attempts to embody the moral ideal or to realise the good life.

philosophers, from Plato onwards, to construct pictures of simple societies to show how people would behave and would feel they ought to behave under the simplest conditions. Now the study of the ways of life of primitive peoples provides us, not with speculative hypotheses as to what might happen, but with what in fact did happen and is happening today under such conditions. If, as these philosophers assume, conditions in such simple societies can throw any light on the nature of man and morality, it is wiser to draw our conclusions from societies which have in fact existed than from imaginary societies which are bound to be influenced by the preconceived ideas of their constructors. For, as Goldenweiser [1] says, there is no arguing with history.

There are, however, moral theories which, if we could accept them, would make enquiries into the different moralities of mankind, or indeed into any other than our own, unnecessary and even valueless. A consideration of them is perhaps the simplest way of showing the relevance of other moralities to the solution of our problem; for one way of testing the adequacy of these theories is to consider whether they are consistent with the moral judgements of men of other ages and civilisations. This itself might be regarded as sufficient to show the relevance of other moralities to our ethical problems. If we further find, as I think we shall, that at least some of these ethical theories cannot account for the moral judgements of all men everywhere, that should be conclusive evidence that the moral judgements of other men in other cultures are relevant to our problem. And there are, I think, other ways in which a consideration of these theories will bring to light the relevance of primitive morality, in particular, to our ethical enquiries. Let us, therefore, look briefly at one or two theories which profess to relieve us of the duty of examining moralities other than our own.

Some ethical theorists tell us that we can see or know that certain moral rules are right with the same certainty with which we see that two and two are four, or that the three angles of a triangle are together equal to two right angles. We do not,

[1] *Anthropology*, p. 474.

they contend, merely believe these propositions. We know that they are true. Similarly, they tell us, we immediately apprehend as self-evident truths the rightness of certain moral rules or the obligatoriness of certain acts or sorts of acts. Other ethical theorists tell us that we immediately apprehend or perceive by inspection that certain sorts of things or states of affairs are intrinsically good, in the same direct way in which we perceive that a rose is red or a primrose yellow; and that those actions are right which produce or promote, or are intended to produce or promote, such things.

According to these views, if a person does not immediately see that the rules in question are right or the ends good, the only advice that can be given to him is to look again and try to remove the obstacles and prejudices which prevent him from seeing; just as the only advice that can be given to the schoolboy who says that he does not see that the three angles of a triangle are together equal to two right angles is to look again, to follow the argument more carefully and with more concentrated attention. If he still does not see, there is nothing that can be done for him, except hope that providence will open his eyes. So if, after due attention, a person still fails to see the rightness of so-called self-evident moral rules or the goodness of so-called intrinsic goods, he must be regarded as in some way deficient in moral sense or moral reason.

Now I entirely agree that, if the obligatoriness of certain sorts of acts is genuinely self-evident,[1] the proposed method of procedure is the only one open to us. I agree also that the ultimate principle on which the moral agent proceeds in his judgements, that is, the moral criterion, must be of this kind — self-authenticating, unmediated, containing its evidence within itself — so that a person has only to grasp its nature to recognise its self-evidence. If, therefore, we were completely satisfied that the judgements in question had the self-evidence claimed for them by some theorists, we should have no alternative to accepting them as true, even if we were thereby forced

---

[1] In order not to complicate the argument unduly, in what follows I omit reference to ends or states of affairs which are claimed to be recognisable by inspection as intrinsically good. *Mutatis mutandis*, the same considerations apply to them as to sorts of acts.

to conclude that the moral consciousness of those who think otherwise is constituted in a different way from our own. Such a conclusion would in effect mean that the judgements of those who differ from us on this question are not expressions of the moral consciousness at all. For it is difficult to see any difference between a moral consciousness which operates on a different principle from ours and one which is not moral at all.

But, as I have already pointed out, it is by no means easy to be sure that in any given judgement we have an authentic deliverance of the moral consciousness, i.e. a deliverance uninfluenced by conditions which are peculiar to the agent who makes the judgement or to his people. And there are at least three reasons for doubting the claim that it is an authentic deliverance of the moral consciousness that the rightness of certain rules or the obligatoriness of certain sorts of acts is self-evident. (1) This character is claimed for the acts and rules in question when they are considered by themselves in isolation. But they never do occur in isolation; and it is difficult to be sure that the context in which they normally occur has nothing to do with their obligatoriness appearing to be self-evident. (2) As has often been pointed out, these acts are never described with the precision and freedom from ambiguity which are essential to the terms of a proposition which is to be recognised as self-evident. (3) We find little agreement, even among the most careful thinkers who claim that there are self-evident moral judgements, as to which moral judgements have this character. What seemed self-evident to Sidgwick is not accepted as such by Moore; and what Moore regards as self-evident is not accepted as even true by Ross. In view of these doubts, it is desirable to consider such judgements in different contexts, and especially in different cultural conditions, to discover whether they retain their apparent self-evidence in all contexts. If we find that they are not regarded as true by all men everywhere — let alone as self-evidently true — we should hesitate to accept their self-evidence as an authentic deliverance of the moral consciousness; for any judgement which is really self-evident should be recognised as such by all who have the capacity to grasp it and have paid sufficient attention to it. Accordingly, those who claim that certain moral rules are self-evident tend to minimise the differences between the moral judgements of different peoples, and attribute the failure of primitive peoples to recognise certain rules as self-evident either to their not having the capacity to grasp the terms involved in them or to their not having sufficiently attended to them.[1]   If the evidence compels us to reject this explanation, the only alternatives [2] open to us are either to reject their claim to self-evidence or to deny that the primitive moral consciousness functions according to the same principle as ours ; and the latter alternative amounts, as I have said, to a denial that primitive peoples are moral beings at all, in the sense in which we use the term.

Accordingly, in our attempts to test the adequacy of ethical theories which rely on what I shall call the method of isolation, that is the method which assumes that we can pass final moral judgements on acts or sorts of acts or ends or states of affairs in isolation from their context, the evidence about the moralities of primitive peoples is relevant in at least three ways. (1) It shows that some of the judgements which are regarded as self-evident by contemporary moralists are not even regarded as true by some primitive peoples. (2) It enables us to decide whether we can accept as adequate the explanation offered by contemporary moralists as to why some primitive peoples reject what are claimed to be self-evident moral judgements. As we shall show in detail later, the evidence of the anthropologists is all against the adequacy of this explanation. (3) It shows that some primitive peoples have moral rules of their own, which appear to them obviously right, but some of which are different from, and inconsistent with, those accepted by contemporary moralists.

But the relevance of the anthropological evidence to our ethical enquiries is not confined to providing examples of moral judgements which are difficult to reconcile with some of our ethical theories. It suggests and supports an alternative theory

[1] More often they simply ignore the moral judgements of other times and places, and the problem which the differences between the moral judgements of different peoples present for their theories.

[2] That is, on the assumption which is shared by the theories under consideration, that moral judgements are really statements, and are therefore true or false.

of the principle of moral judgement. It suggests that there are grounds for the judgements, whether about the rightness of acts or the goodness of states of affairs, which are regarded as obvious by a particular people; and that, therefore, they are not unmediated or self-authenticating. For, according to the considered and unanimous view of contemporary social anthropologists, we cannot understand why particular moral judgements are regarded as obvious, or even as true, by a primitive people unless we take account of the context of interrelated institutions which constitute their way of life and subject to the conditions of which their judgements on acts and agents and states of affairs are passed. Now, if this is true of the moral judgements of primitives, may it not be equally true of our own? May it not be that certain things seem good to us and certain rules right, because we consider them in the context of our own way of life? When different rules seem right and different ends seem good to men in different ages and civilisations, are we justified in concluding that in one case, namely in our own, the certainty or apparent self-evidence with which they are accepted is due to their intrinsic reasonableness, while in the case of all whose judgements differ from ours it is due to the mental and moral and social conditioning to which they have been subjected? Part of the value of the work of the social anthropologists and of its relevance to our ethical enquiries is that it forces us to raise such questions. It also supplies us with at least part of the evidence necessary to answer them.

All these considerations suggest that the ethical theories, which rely on the apparent self-evidence of certain moral judgements, whether about right or about good, do not make the study of primitive morality irrelevant to our ethical enquiries.

There is, however, another moral theory which seems, at first sight at any rate, to suggest that a consideration of primitive morality is, if not entirely irrelevant to, at least unnecessary for the solution of our problem. But a more detailed examination of this theory shows that, if it is accepted, the study of the moral judgements of other peoples becomes not only relevant, as providing facts by which the theory itself can be tested, but also important as making a positive contribution to our understanding of morality. This theory may be briefly stated as follows. Morality is a human phenomenon; it arises from the double nature of man as at once a creature of impulses and inclinations which have their origin in his animal instincts, and also a rational or self-conscious being, a being who is aware of himself as one amid the variety of his experiences, and as such capable of formulating, in a more or less coherent fashion, an ideal of a form of life which will satisfy his whole nature by satisfying its different aspects or elements in conformity with one another. Add to this the fact that man is social, a member of a group or society, the other members of which he is capable of recognising as rational or self-conscious and yet creatures of desire like himself, and therefore entitled to the same sort of satisfaction as himself; so that the ideal which he forms for himself and for them is at once personal and social, and so meant to provide for the satisfaction of all of them compatibly with one another. Granted all this it follows that, if we could discover what man, as a being at once self-conscious and social and a creature of desires, requires for the satisfaction of his nature, we would have an adequate account of the nature of morality. May we not, it is asked, discover this by examining the nature of man individual and social?

Now this is a theory with which, as the sequel will show, I have a great deal of sympathy, and the main contentions of which, with suitable reservations, I should be prepared to accept. But even if we accept this theory, it does not relieve us of the task of considering moralities other than our own; for, in our efforts to discover the nature of man and what he needs for his satisfaction, we meet precisely the same difficulties as we do in trying to discover morality among the moralities; and the anthropological evidence is equally relevant to both enquiries.

The reason for this is not far to seek. Human nature is not merely something given, but something which grows or develops, so that we never find pure or bare human nature, but that nature as it develops in interaction with one or another type of environment, an environment consisting largely of ideas and beliefs, customs and institutions. We never find human nature without a cultural environment, and in different environments it develops along different lines and it seems capable of satisfaction in different ways. It is difficult to discover in the resulting joint-product how much or which parts are due to human nature as such and how much to the particular kind of cultural environment. We are all too apt to assume that human nature is what it develops into among ourselves, under the cultural conditions of Western civilisation in the twentieth century, and that it needs for its satisfaction what it seems to need under our own conditions. Part of the importance of the work of the anthropologists is that it acts as a corrective to this assumption. It shows us how human nature expresses itself under different sets of cultural conditions, different from one another and from our own; and so it acts as a warning against predicating of human nature generally, what is true of white man under the cultural conditions of Western Europe.

I shall give one illustration,[1] the details of which are easily available, to show how misleading this assumption may be. Margaret Mead[2] found social workers and other serious-minded people in America concerned about the strains and stresses of adolescence, and the problems to which they give rise. They attributed these to human nature, and the crises which, as they thought, naturally and necessarily arise during adolescence. But it occurred to Margaret Mead that these difficulties might be peculiar to Western civilisation, or even to the particular form which it takes in America, rather than due to human nature as such. She, therefore, went and studied adolescence under entirely different conditions in Samoa, and found that it showed very few of the difficulties which perplexed her American friends.

But in order to avoid the hasty inference that the Americans could solve their difficulties by taking over one item of Samoan culture while leaving the rest of their way of life unchanged, it is necessary to add that the Samoan way of life fails to develop some of the values which we regard as among the most precious in our culture, and that its failure to do so is not unconnected with the conditions which explain the absence of the strains and

---

[1] This illustration was used by Professor Russell to make a similar point in the *Proceedings of the Aristotelian Society*, Supplementary Vol. xx, 61-2.

[2] *Coming of Age in Samoa.*

stresses of adolescence among its members.[1] The realisation of these values seems to require that the energies of some of the primary urges of human nature should be controlled and directed along certain lines or, as the psychologists say, that they should be sublimated, and it is this direction and control which give rise to crises. To give these energies free expression in adolescence, as the Samoans do, prevents strains, but it seems also to be inconsistent with sublimation and the values which are realised through sublimation. Whether the values can be realised without the strains and crises is a question to which neither the Samoan nor our own culture has yet provided the answer. Each of the cultures has its own values and disvalues, and the values and disvalues seem to be so inextricably bound together that we cannot remove the disvalues without endangering the values as well. Be this as it may, the Samoan culture shows that the crises of adolescence are the results not so much of human nature as of certain ways of dealing with it.

The evidence of other anthropologists, with whose views we shall be concerned later, shows that it is equally misleading to regard the development of some of the other primary urges of human nature, such as acquisitiveness or pugnacity, which we find under our own cultural conditions, as necessary expressions of human nature rather than as cultural products of our own civilisation. Such considerations show us the relevance of anthropological evidence to our attempts to discover what human nature is and what it requires for its satisfaction. What human nature needs for its satisfaction can only be discovered by experience, and experience proceeds by experiment. The people of Western Europe are not the only people who have made and are making experiments in trying to satisfy human nature and needs. The results of all these experiments are as relevant to our attempts to discover the good for man as they are to enquiries into the structure of human nature.

All the considerations which I have been urging in support of the view that a study of the moral ideas and ways of life of

[1] Cf. Mead, *Male and Female* (1950), pp. 118-19: "The price they pay for their smooth, even, generously gratifying system is . . . . There is no place in Samoa for the man or the woman capable of a great passion, of complicated aesthetic feeling, of deep religious devotion."

primitive peoples is relevant to our ethical enquiries, are based on two assumptions : (1) that the nature of primitive man is essentially the same as our own, that he is stirred by the same emotions, moved by the same desires and reasons according to the same principles as ourselves ; and (2) that his mind is sufficiently developed to grasp the nature of the acts which we regard as right and of the ends which we regard as good. But these assumptions have been questioned and I shall, therefore, have to defend them in the proper place. It has been held either that the primitive mind is constructed in a different way and acts according to different principles from our own, or that it is so undeveloped and immature as to be inferior to the civilised mind in ways which amount to a difference in kind, a difference which makes it incapable of grasping the rules which we regard as right and the ends which we regard as good. If either of these contentions is well grounded ; if, in particular, there are fundamental innate differences of kind either of con-stitution or of powers between the primitive and the civilised mind, that would prove the simplest and easiest way of explain-ing the differences between their moral beliefs and judgements and ours. It would also mean that the consideration of their moral ideas can throw no light on the nature of morality as we understand it, and that it is, therefore, entirely irrelevant to our present purpose. But, as I shall try to show in detail later, the overwhelming weight of anthropological evidence is against such a view. According to the available evidence, the primitive and the civilised child enter the world with substantially the same mental constitution and powers, and, therefore, we must regard primitive cultures with their moral and social institutions, their ideals and their rules, as the results of attempts, by people with interests and problems and powers of the same kind as our own, to discover the good for man, a way of life which will satisfy their aspirations for themselves and their fellows. No doubt their co-operative efforts at conceiving and realising the good for man, which I call their experiments in living, are at best only partially successful ; but may the same not be said of our own ? At any rate, each of these experiments throws some light on the nature of man ; the ways in which he seeks and, at least partially, finds expression and satisfaction for his moral aspirations; the kind of life which he regards as good; the ends which seem to him worthy of pursuit; and the rules which he has developed to guide him in the pursuit.

If the evidence compels us to conclude that the fundamental nature and powers of the human mind are the same among all men and that, therefore, the principle on which the moral consciousness proceeds is everywhere the same, that principle must be not only consistent with, but capable of explaining the enormous diversity of moral judgements which we find among different peoples. For whether or not we in the end discover some unity of principle underlying the moral judgements of the different sections of mankind, first appearances suggest not one morality but many, not unanimity but considerable diversity between the moral beliefs entertained and the moral judgements passed by men of different ages and civilisations. We find relative unanimity within a particular civilisation at a particular stage in its development, but great diversity between different civilisations and different stages of development. This diversity exists not only in judgements on particular acts but also in those on sorts of acts, that is on rules. For example, by one people suicide or infanticide is condemned as immoral; by another it is regarded with indifference; by still another it is regarded in certain circumstances as a sacred duty. If, then, the principle of moral judgement is the same everywhere, any account of it which is to be satisfactory must show that it is consistent with this diversity of moral judgements, that indeed the different moral judgements are really expressions of the same principle having regard to the different conditions and beliefs and cultures of those who pass them. This gives us two tests which we can apply to any ethical theory : consistency with the moral judgements of mankind everywhere, and capacity to explain the diverse moral judgements of different peoples and ages as expressions of the principle or principles which it propounds as the moral criterion or criteria. Among my reasons for considering primitive morality is the conviction that, when considered in the light of the moral judgements of primitives, some contemporary ethical theories will not survive these tests.

There is still another and, to my mind, a very important way in which the study of primitive ways of life is relevant to our moral enquiries. The tendency towards abstraction and atomism, which we find in the method of isolation applied by some recent ethical writers to acts and ends, is no less evident in the recent and contemporary treatment of other moral and social facts, such as the relation between moral and social theory or between the different social sciences. And the contention of the anthropologists that none of the judgements or beliefs or customs, none of the institutions or aspects of the life of a primitive people, can be understood without taking account of their whole way of life, provides a necessary corrective to all these tendencies. For if this contention is well grounded, it means that, whether in passing or in trying to understand moral judgements, we have to perform an integrating or synthesising activity in which we consider not only different ends and activities, but also the different aspects of life to which they refer, economic, legal, political, religious, and so on, in relation to one another and the way of life of which they form parts. This unifying, interrelating activity seems to me to be involved in all moral deliberation, and to be a condition of considered moral judgements. Our more serious and considered moral judgements seem to me to be passed, not on isolated acts, but on agents in respect of acts and on character as reflected in acts. Moreover, the agents in question are members of a community, and to understand either their actions or their judgements on them, we have to take account of their relations to others. Now on the subjective side, character and personality involve a certain unity and wholeness, a certain consistency of outlook based on formed habits and the building up of relatively permanent feeling attitudes. The self-conscious agent cannot help bringing some measure of such integration into his life. Similarly, on the objective side, we find a corresponding unity in more or less comprehensive plans and policies which manifest themselves in series of interconnected acts. These acts can be understood and judgements of value passed on them only in relation to the policies of which they are partial expressions and to the character of which the policies are the outward manifestations. But if the view of the anthropologists is sound we have to go further. We must not only consider acts and ends in relation to character and policies; we must also consider character and policies themselves in the context of the way of life which is the combination of both the inner and the outer aspects of conduct; we must consider the individual agent in the complexity of his social relationships; we must consider the moral ideal in relation to the social ideal, and the different aspects of life dealt with by the different social sciences in relation to one another and to the whole way of life whose aspects they are.

Now whether we look at moral and social facts from the subjective point of view of character and personality or from the objective point of view of plans and policies or from the point of view of the social sciences which provide the theoretical interpretation of these facts, we find in the modern world an emphasis on distinction, analysis and separation, with the result that unity and interconnection tend to disappear, or at any rate to fade into the background; and we are left with the unrelated elements or aspects on our hands. The structure of the modern civilised world is so loosely knit, the activities, industrial, social, political and religious, in which the modern man lives his life, are so heterogeneous, compartmentalised and apparently unconnected that it is difficult for himself or others to see his life as a whole, if indeed there is any whole to see; and the social sciences which deal with the different aspects of his life, economics and politics, law and social philosophy, ethics and theology, each goes its own separate way, within its own limited field, without paying more attention to its neighbours than an occasional nod of respectful recognition when they meet at the borders which divide their subjects. Even this is not infrequently accompanied by the warning, ' You had better keep to your own side of the border; only those who speak our language and accept our presuppositions are tolerated on this side '. This isolation of the different aspects of life and of the social sciences which deal with them seems to me one of the chief diseases of the modern world. Iron curtains are as disastrous in the realm of the spirit as they are in that of international politics. They result in a sense of frustration and moral bewilderment on the part of modern man, who has duties in all the different spheres, but finds it difficult to see how they are connected and on what principle he is to decide between them when their requirements clash. It seems to me that it is the business of the moral philosopher to break down these iron curtains, to provide a corrective to the method of isolation, to bring to light the unity underlying the differences, to try to see life as a whole, and to make explicit the principle on which its broken fragments can be united and the differences reconciled.

This is his business, not only because it is something which needs to be done and there is no one else to do it, nor merely because it is the traditional role of the moral philosopher to try to see life as a whole, but also because what is common to these different departments and to the sciences which deal with them is that they are all concerned with relations between persons ; and, whatever else may be said of relations between persons, they always have a moral aspect, and the final judgement on them is a moral judgement. An industrial policy may be economically efficient, but when the economist has told us all that can be said from his point of view, the question still remains : ' Is the pursuit of that policy morally right in its effect on the welfare of producers and consumers and the community as a whole ? ' And that is a moral question, one not for economics but for ethics, or better still for the two together. Similarly, a piece of legislation may be clear and consistent and impartially administered, but the question may still be asked : ' Is it just ? ' And justice is a moral notion to be dealt with by ethics.   Similar considerations apply to the other spheres of human activity and the relations between them.   Moral questions not only arise in all of them, but also concern the relations between them ; and it is the business of the moral philosopher to bring to light the principles on which they can be integrated into a consistent whole and the differences between their claims ultimately settled.

But few contemporary moral philosophers seem willing to undertake this task ; and some go so far as to say that the issues involved are not moral ; and that, therefore, the questions they raise are not questions for ethics at all.   One of the most recent writers on ethical theory, for example, tells us that students embark on the study of moral philosophy because they hope to get from it the answers to such questions as : ' What fiscal policy ought I to vote for ? ' And he gives this as an illustration of a mistaken approach to the subject, based on an inaccurate grasp of its nature. The answer to such a question, he contends, should be provided, not by moral philosophy but by economics. " That science ", he says, " will tell me how I am most likely to bring about prosperity or justice in my country." [1] But, surely, all that economic science can tell us is the economic consequences of different fiscal policies. It is true that without such knowledge we are not in a position to decide which policy we ought to vote for, but given that knowledge the moral question, the question of justice, still remains ; and that is a question for the moral philosopher, though in trying to solve it he needs the co-operation of the economist. It is in trying to discover his duties in relation to such questions which involve economic and social and political issues that contemporary modern man is most often baffled and perplexed. No doubt the issues involved in such questions are not merely moral, but the duties and obligations of individuals in regard to them are moral duties and obligations ; and if we respect Lord Gifford's wishes we must try to deal with them.

Now the researches of social anthropologists into the morality of primitive peoples seem to me highly relevant to our attempts to solve such problems ; for the members of a primitive community are few in number, most of them know one another, and all the relations between them, whether they be economic, political or legal, are recognised by them to be personal relations between individuals. Moreover, the different aspects of their lives are not so sharply separated and departmentalised as they are in the modern world. It is, therefore, much easier to see their lives as wholes, to see the interrelation between their different activities, than it is to do so when we are considering the large-scale and complex life of a modern society, where the relations between the different aspects of life and different groups of persons are very loosely integrated, and where relations between individuals are largely depersonalised. A consideration of the ways of life of such small and simple peoples should enable us to see more easily and clearly

---

[1] Carritt, *Ethical and Political Thinking*, p. 2.

C

how morality is concerned with the whole of life, without being the whole of it; how ethics is related to political and social organisation, to economics and law; how all these and the moral duties that arise in connection with them are related to one another, and how in their interrelation they constitute the unity of a way of life. It may also enable us to view such questions with greater objectivity and impartiality than if we were discussing controversial contemporary issues among ourselves, issues which are liable to arouse emotions which might cloud vision.

However relevant and important an understanding of primitive morality may be for our ethical enquiries, the study of it presents peculiar difficulties, for the subject has been largely neglected by recent and contemporary anthropologists. It is true that there is in their work much of the material required for such a study, but few of them have devoted any separate consideration to it. This is all the more remarkable when we consider that, during the present century, trained field workers have made intensive sociological studies of almost every other aspect of the lives of primitive peoples, their social organisation, their economic activities, their legal systems, their educational arrangements, their mentality, their art and their religion. The published results of these enquiries now constitute a considerable and growing body of literature. Many social scientists have recognised the relevance and the importance of this material for their own studies, and there has been a good deal of fruitful co-operation between field workers among primitives and specialists in some of the social sciences. But moral philosophers have been slower to recognise the relevance of such materials to their studies, and the social anthropologists have not helped them to realise it. For, as I have said, few of them have devoted any separate attention to primitive morality, and much of what they have to say about it has to be gathered from occasional remarks scattered throughout their treatment of other subjects. This state of affairs is unsatisfactory, both from the ethical and the anthropological points of view. Co-operation between the two would, I am confident, be fruitful for both. It is as an effort towards such co-operation that this study is undertaken; and I have found the anthropologists with whom it has brought me into contact most anxious to be helpful.

A brief consideration of the reasons for this neglect of primitive morality will bring to light some of the questions we shall have to discuss as well as the material which is available to answer them. No doubt the absence of any recent work on primitive morality is partly due to the intrinsic difficulties of the subject;[1] but it is probably much more due to changes which have taken place during the present century in the assumptions which anthropologists make, and in the conclusions at which they have arrived regarding primitive life as a whole. It is significant in this connection that the last serious treatment of primitive morality is to be found in the works of Westermarck[2] and Hobhouse,[3] who wrote some forty years ago before these changes took place. They dealt with primitive morality as part of a general treatment of comparative ethics, which in their accounts was concerned not only with the nature of morality but also with its origin and its development from the earliest times to the present day. Their treatment was necessarily based on the assumptions current among social anthropologists at the time when they wrote; but the intensive field work which has been carried out by trained experts in recent years has led to the rejection of some of these assumptions, and this rejection not only calls for a reconsideration of the work based on them, but also makes the treatment of comparative ethics in general and of primitive morality in particular much more difficult.

From our point of view, the most significant of these assumptions of the earlier anthropologists were: first, that not only did man develop progressively from the most primitive to the most advanced stage, but that in the course of this development every people passed through the same stages in the same order, and that these progressive stages can be traced in all the different aspects of their life, art and religion, social and political organisation, economic and industrial arrangements,

---

[1] For evidence that many social anthropologists are well aware of these difficulties, see below, p. 291, note 1.

[2] Westermarck, *Origin and Development of Moral Ideas* (1906).

[3] Hobhouse, *Morals in Evolution* (1906).

social customs and institutions, and so on; and second, that particular customs, forms of institutions, rites or other activities, can be understood without much reference to their context in the life of a particular people, and can, whenever found, be regarded as evidence of the same state of mind and stage of development. On these assumptions, once the general framework of the evolutionary development was determined, different customs, institutions, modes of belief or behaviour, gathered from different peoples, could be fitted into their place in the scheme and used to throw light on one another. The gaps in the evidence about a particular people, due to the absence of observation or any other cause, could then be filled from evidence collected from others who were believed to be at the same stage of development. According to this theory, most contemporary primitive peoples are still at stages of development through which our ancestors and those of other civilised peoples passed at or before the dawn of history; and, therefore, the evidence collected from them can be used to throw light on the ways of life of our early ancestors.

Now intensive surveys of particular primitive peoples by trained experts have led to the rejection of both these assumptions. They have conclusively demonstrated that, whatever criterion we apply, the different aspects of the way of life of the same people are seldom at the same stage of development; and that, whatever aspect of their life we consider, different peoples have not all passed through the same stages in the same order. And, what is more important from our point of view, they have also shown that what appears to the casual observer to be the same act or institution or custom may have an entirely different significance or function among different peoples. During the last thirty or forty years, social anthropologists have been demonstrating, in season and out of season with an insistence which is sometimes almost wearisome, that the different aspects of the way of life of a particular people, their ways of thinking and acting, their social and economic arrangements, their religious beliefs and ceremonies, their institutions and social organisation, dovetail, interconnect and interpenetrate in such a way that none of them can be understood in isolation from its context in the way of life of which it forms part. Now this makes the work of comparative ethics very much more difficult, for the units of comparison can no longer be isolated acts or judgements, rules or ends, but ways of life or at least groups of institutions as relatively integrated or unitary wholes. Indeed, some anthropologists have been so impressed with the uniqueness of each culture that they contend that there is no basis of comparison between them.[1]

But while these considerations may explain the recent neglect of comparative ethics in the sense and on the scale on which it was undertaken by Westermarck and Hobhouse, who worked under the influence, and on the assumptions[2] of the classical evolutionary theory, they will not explain the neglect of primitive morality by the large body of trained field workers who have given us so much and such accurate information about other aspects of primitive life. The explanation for this is, I think, to be found in a certain confusion in their views about the nature of morality itself, and especially about its relations to religion on the one hand, and to law and social organisation on the other.[3]

We may distinguish two main aspects of moral conduct. There is an inner or subjective or purely personal aspect, consisting of the motives, spirit or attitude of mind of the agent. There is also an outer or objective or visible aspect, consisting of activities and rules, ends and ideals. Now if we think only of the former aspect, and it is the specifically moral aspect, that to which moral goodness in the strict sense belongs, we may treat morality as a relatively separate part of life, one

[1] See pp. 90-91 below.

[2] It is true that Westermarck and Hobhouse themselves did not unconditionally accept the second assumption mentioned above. They recognised and indeed emphasised that their cultural context has to be taken into account in interpreting anthropological data and in their own work they tried as far as possible to do so. But the assumption is essential to the classical evolutionary hypothesis and it was accepted by those who collected and interpreted most of the materials which Westermarck and Hobhouse used in their work, and therefore it tended to affect the results which they drew from these materials more than they themselves seem to have recognised.

[3] It is difficult to blame social anthropologists if their views about the nature of morality are far from clear or consistent, when we consider the profound differences as to its nature which are to be found among professional writers on ethics.

among others. In the main, this is how most anthropologists seem to regard morality, but naturally they do not confine their attention to that aspect only : they also think and speak of moral rules and ideals ; and, therefore, confusion tends to arise, for what is true of the inner aspect does not always apply to the outer or visible aspect. Besides, the inner aspect of his morality is the most intangible and elusive thing about a man. The understanding of it requires a most intimate knowledge of him ; and even if we have such knowledge, it is not easy to formulate the results of it explicitly. It is much easier to describe a man's outward behaviour than his thoughts and judgements about conduct and the spirit which finds expression in them.

Moreover, this inner aspect of conduct does not vary from people to people. It is much the same everywhere and, therefore, there is not much for the anthropologist to say about it. Loyalty to the recognised ideal, doing what is right because it is right — such conduct is regarded as morally good everywhere. It is the ideals, the rules, the duties, the things which are regarded as good or right themselves, which vary from people to people. But looked at from this objective or outer side, morality is not a separate sphere of activities. It is concerned with the whole of life. For our moral duties in this sense, the things that are right or that we ought to do, may also be social or legal, economic or religious duties.[1] Accordingly much of what anthropologists describe under the headings of social organisation and law and economics is, in fact, a description of the outer aspect of the morality of the people concerned. The anthropologist who describes one aspect of a primitive community's way of life, whether the educational arrangements, the legal system or the economic organisation, recognises and indeed emphasises that, in order to understand the particular aspect in which he is interested, he has to give an account of the culture as a whole, of the way in which that aspect is related to the others and, in virtue of these relations, functions in the whole. In doing this, he is describing the things which the people in question

---

[1] This is specially obvious in the case of primitive communities, which are so small and closely integrated, and in which the relations between individuals are so intimate and personal.

think right, as well as the ways they think and feel about them, the motives and incentives by which they are moved, the ideals which they seek to realise, and the institutions and customs in which these find expression. Accordingly, there seems little left to be dealt with under the separate heading of morality, but to describe over again the way of life and the interrelated system of habits of thinking and feeling and acting which constitute it and show how the duties and rights of individuals and their conceptions of justice, distributive and corrective, are determined by them. In short, morality in this sense of the term, that is the outer or objective side of morality, is not a separate sphere of activities. Not only do moral issues arise in every sphere of life, in the sense that there are rights to be respected and duties to be fulfilled in relation to them, but these moral rights and duties are not merely moral. They are also social, economic, legal and religious rights and duties; and, therefore, they have to be described in describing these spheres.

Accordingly, the anthropologists tend to deal with most of what concerns the outer aspect of morality, the things which are regarded as right and the ends which are regarded as good, under the headings of social organisation and rules of primitive law, often without recognising that they are dealing with morality. Moreover, anthropologists are more concerned with why people do what they regard as right, especially when it is difficult and burdensome and not to their immediate advantage, than with why they regard it as right. In other words, they are concerned with the question of sanctions, and they are apt to regard sanctions not merely as incentives to follow a course of conduct, but also as its justification, the ground of its rightness. But it is necessary to distinguish between whether an act or course of conduct is right, and, if it is, what is the ground of its rightness, and what a person will get if he performs it or what will happen to him if he does not. This would be so even on the cynical view that men never do anything merely because it is right without an additional incentive for doing so. The anthropologists, however, seem to be more interested in the reasons which explain why people act in particular ways than in the reasons which justify the actions.

This, however, is not all. Not only are anthropologists apt to treat moral rules and principles, ends and ideals, as parts of social organisation, primitive law and economics, but they also tend to regard the inner aspect of morality, the spirit of goodwill, the attitude of mind in which morally good actions are performed, as either an effect or a part of religion; and, as this seems the only aspect of morality which they normally recognise as moral, they tend to regard morality as dependent on, and sanctioned by religion. They seem, therefore, to assume that what is to be said about morality should naturally come under the heading of religion. Yet when we consult works on primitive religion, of which there are many, what we find consists mainly of the views of primitive peoples about the supernatural and about their duties in the way of ritual in regard to it. They tell us little or nothing about the duties and obligations of men to one another.[1] We have to gather these as best we can from other sources.

Considering the extent of the field to be covered and how little work has been done recently on primitive morality, all I can hope to do in these lectures will be tentative and exploratory; and any conclusions at which I arrive will be provisional. What I am specially anxious to do is to call attention to what seems to me a rich and largely unexplored field of moral material, which I am satisfied is highly relevant to our ethical enquiries, and to express the hope that others, both moral philosophers and social anthropologists, will devote more attention to it, and either confirm or modify my tentative conclusions.

No doubt, the brief account which I have given of the treatment of morality by anthropologists is unduly simplified. It is an account of general tendencies rather than a precise statement of the views of any particular anthropologist. I gave it merely to explain why I have chosen the line of treatment which I propose to follow, and as an indication of the subjects which it will be necessary to discuss. I propose to begin with

[1] There are a few exceptions like Fortune's *Manus Religion*. The exceptions are to be found when the religion described is that of a people, like the Manus, whose moral code is sanctioned by their religion in the sense that either their moral code is believed to be prescribed or breaches of it punished by their gods.

a tentative and provisional account of the structure of the moral life and the relation of the moral and social ideals to one another and to life as a whole. This account, which will be sufficiently general to apply to all moralities whatever the detailed differences between them, should enable us to see in their interrelation the different problems which we shall have to discuss. In order to illustrate this account and provide a concrete filling for its general framework, I shall try to describe the ways of life of a few representative primitive peoples in sufficient detail to enable us to see their moral judgements on acts and ends and agents in their cultural context. I shall then consider the nature of primitive mentality and try to justify the assumption on which my argument is based that their minds are much the same as our own; and that, therefore, their moral beliefs and judgements are relevant to our ethical enquiries. Next, I shall discuss the relationship between primitive morality and religion, partly because, as I have indicated, there seems to me to be some confusion among anthropologists on the subject, and partly to justify my treatment of morality as an independent and autonomous sphere of activities — a sphere of activities which, no doubt, has theological and metaphysical implications, but whose main principles can be discerned and their authority justified by considering the nature of man as a person among persons. If this can be established we can claim the right to examine the moral beliefs and judgements of primitive peoples, without taking account of any aspect of their religion except its ethical content and its social consequences. Finally, I shall consider the implications for ethical theory of the facts which our account of primitive moralities will have brought to light. In doing so, I shall discuss, among other questions, the nature and authority of moral rules and their importance for the moral life, the content and structure of the moral ideal, and the nature and conditions of moral progress. This programme will still leave many questions regarding morality to which it will not be possible to make more than a passing reference, among them the theological and metaphysical implications of morality or what we might call the ethical interpretation of reality; but it is perhaps more than sufficient to occupy us during this course.

THE STRUCTURE OF THE MORAL LIFE

WE have seen that any piece of conduct may be looked at, and moral judgements passed on it, from three points of view — as the pursuit of an end, the observance of a rule, and the expression of an attitude of mind or motive. This gives us the three basic ethical concepts which, in their interrelation, constitute the framework of the moral life : the right, the good, and the morally good ; or the rule, the end and the motive. In this lecture, I want to indicate in outline the way in which these fundamental elements seem to me to be related within the structure of the moral life, and how that structure is related to the constitution of human nature. The account which I am going to give will be general and abstract, stating the pattern which seems to me to be common to all men and all morality, primitive and civilised alike. Later lectures will amplify this outline, and fill in the details and clothe the bare skeleton with flesh and blood. In so doing, I trust they will also confirm its accuracy and meet the objections that may be urged against it.

I trust, however, that the preliminary analysis which I am going to give here will commend itself to the reader as essentially sound, in harmony with the deliverances of the moral consciousness and with the conclusions of psychology and anthropology. To anyone who, at the end of the lecture, is still hesitating to accept its main contention, I would suggest that he regard it as a hypothesis to be further tested by reference to the material with which we shall be concerned in later lectures, a hypothesis to be accepted or rejected according as it succeeds or fails in enabling us to give an intelligible account of that material. I have adopted the procedure of stating the conclusion first, while most of the detailed evidence in support of it will be given later, because I think this should make it easier to follow the argument of the lectures as a whole. That argument as a whole contains the real evidence for the views which I am going to state here in a preliminary and provisional way. This procedure will have the further advantage of enabling me to explain at the outset the precise sense in which I shall use certain ethical terms in the sequel.

Let us begin then with the relation between the right and the good, or rules and ends in morals, one of the most controversial topics not only in contemporary ethics, but in the history of moral theory. For the most stubborn and deep-seated difference which divides writers on ethics is that between those who find in the attractiveness of the good the fundamental feature of the moral life and those who find the essence of morality in obedience to right rules. The contrasted concepts in terms of which this difference is expressed vary from writer to writer. We find it expressed not only in such antitheses as that between the right and the good, between rules and ends, but also in that between duty and the moral ideal, between standards and purposes, between principles of order and interests, between the good will and happiness, between social justice and ideal morality. Though the differences between the concepts contrasted in these different formulations are not unimportant, the principle on which all the antitheses are based seems to be essentially the same, and the affinities of a writer are disclosed by whichever of the two contrasted concepts he regards as supplying the key to the understanding of morality. To use the language of the schools, that affinity marks him as a teleological or deontological moralist.

But though most ethical theorists regard one of the contrasted concepts as more fundamental than the other, they all agree that the other is also important and that it is part of the business of ethics to explain both and to show the relation between them. This explanation takes one or other of two main forms, according as it is or is not held that one of the concepts is dependent on the other and that therefore its moral characteristics can be deduced from or expressed in terms of it. On the one hand, it may be held (as, for example, by Sir David Ross) that though one of the contrasted concepts is more fundamental, neither can be derived from or expressed in terms

of the other : that both stand for ultimate and irreducible, but
only externally related or altogether unrelated elements in the
moral life. This view has the merit of keeping close to the
facts of the moral life in which the contrasted elements seem
to be equally important and to exist without any sense of disharmony, now the one now the other receiving special emphasis ;
but it has the disadvantage of leaving us without any real unity
in the moral life — a disadvantage which is not only serious
from the point of view of theory but has the important practical
result of leaving the moral agent without any principle on which
he can decide what in particular circumstances he ought to do.[1]
On the other hand, it may be held, and this is the more common
view, that the contrasted concepts are not really unrelated :
that not only is one more fundamental but that the other is
dependent on it and can be deduced from it or expressed in
terms of it. Speaking generally and without going into refinements, this can be done in one of two ways. According to the
one, good is regarded as the fundamental concept, and right
acts are regarded as those which produce or promote good
ends. The duty of the moral agent is therefore to produce as
much good as he can, or to realise the best that is within his
power. Those who take this view emphasise ends, interests,
purposes, ideals, and explain the moral life mainly in terms of
such concepts. According to the other, the essence of morality
is to be found in the ought ; its fundamental concepts are right,
duty and obligation ; and good is explained in terms of obedience to rules or principles. Both these views have the theoretical
merit of achieving tidiness and unity of principle, but they are
apt to leave the impression that they have succeeded in doing
this at the cost of doing less than justice to one or other of the
main aspects of the moral life. The ordinary moral consciousness tends to offer a strong resistance when we try to formulate
all its judgements in terms of either of these theories. For
some acts seem to it to be morally significant primarily because
of the goods which are realised in or through them ; others

---

[1] Ross admits this result of his theory, but he does not regard the duality
to which it gives rise, or indeed the plurality of independent goods and rules,
as a serious or at least a fatal defect. Indeed he thinks that the demand for
system and unity of principle where he believes they do not exist has been
one of the snares of ethical theorists.

because of the rules with which they comply. Such resistance by the moral consciousness to an interpretation of its judgements should be regarded by the ethical theorist as a danger signal, a presumption, though not necessarily a proof, that he has missed something of importance.

I do not propose here to enter into a detailed examination of either the merits or the demerits of these views. I want rather to suggest and defend another way of regarding the relation between the contrasted concepts. According to it, the contrasted concepts are equally fundamental and irreducible in the sense that neither can be deduced from or expressed in terms of the other, but the relation between them is much more intimate than Ross suggests. Indeed, they are so intimately related that not only do they not interfere with the unity of the moral life, but they are both necessary to constitute that unity. For they enter into the moral life in different ways, as for example warp and woof, or form and matter, or structure and function. If this is so, the relation between them is not so much one of opposition as of mutual implication. Each is a different but necessary condition of living a good life or doing a morally good deed.

According to this view no isolated moral rule contains the grounds of its rightness, and no isolated end the grounds of its goodness within itself. Rather we find the grounds of the rightness of moral rules in a form of life which is also the realisation of a system of ends ; and we find the grounds of the goodness of good ends in the same form of life which also involves obedience to certain rules. That form of life is both unconditionally good and the source of moral obligation. All the acts which form part of it or in which it is being realised are both directed to ends and comply with rules ; but because of the way in which they function in the whole, the one or the other aspect may be more in evidence ; and so in the case of some acts we may think primarily of the rules with which they comply, and in the case of others of the goods which are being realised in and through them. But all have both characteristics ; and in passing a final moral judgement on them we have to take account of both.

As an approach to this way of regarding the matter, let us

look at some other spheres in which a similar state of affairs seems to prevail. The conditions in these other spheres, however, should be regarded as nothing more than suggestive analogies and the point of the analogies should not be pressed unduly.

Consider the activity of playing a game. We distinguish between the end or purpose which the players in a game have in view and the rules with which in playing the game they have to comply. Their end is to win the game and it is this end that gives zest and direction to their activities. But in their efforts to realise this end they have to comply with the rules of the game. They do not play in order to comply with the rules, but to win; and yet in order to win they have to comply with the rules. So that a good game is one in which the players wholeheartedly pursue their end according to the rules.[1] In order that there may be a game at all two conditions have to be fulfilled. An end must be pursued and rules must be observed.

Or take the nature of knowledge. In discussing the nature of knowledge, we distinguish between the given elements, sensa, percepts or whatever other name we call the elements of which knowledge consists, and principles of relation or categories, such as cause and effect, substance and attribute, etc., according to which they are organised. In order to have knowledge at all, we must have elements to organise and principles of organisation. The two have different but equally important functions to fulfil and one cannot be reduced to or take the place of the other. Neither by itself can give us knowledge. When we try to get knowledge in any sphere our purpose is not merely to comply with the categories or principles of thought, but in order to achieve our purpose, which is to get a knowledge of the facts, we have to order the elements according to these principles.

Or take again the nature of inference. In inference we argue from premises to a conclusion, but in doing so we have to comply with the principles or laws of inference. We don't

---

[1] A complete account of a game would have to take account of a third factor — the spirit in which the game is played. For even if two players obey the same rules and pursue the same end, the spirit in which they do so may be markedly different.

argue in order to comply with logical rules, but we cannot achieve our aim in arguing, which is to reach a valid conclusion, without complying with these rules.

Similarly, I suggest, in living the moral life, there are ends to be pursued, interests to be promoted, purposes to be fulfilled, ideals to be realised, such for example as building a house, writing a book, promoting a piece of social legislation, providing the means of happiness for an aged parent; and there are also rules to be observed, such for example as the rules of truth-telling and promise-keeping, the laws of copyright, the Corporation Byelaws about house-building.   We don't live our lives, any more than we play a game, in order to comply with such rules.   A man may comply with any code of rules, such for example as the rules implied in the list of prima facie duties given by Ross,[1] and yet his life may be empty and purposeless.   In order that his life may be worth living he must have ends to pursue.   It is they that supply its driving power and give it zest and direction.   He does not pursue them merely to obey the rules, but in pursuing them he has, in order to be moral, to observe the rules.[2]   This is at least part of the truth contained in the view that the end does not justify the means. This view emphasises the fact that the activities in which an end is realised have other morally significant characteristics in addition to their being the realisation of the end;   and these characteristics have to be taken into consideration in passing final judgement on them.   In other words, they are not mere means to an end;   and it is not the end alone which has value. In passing a value judgement on the end, we have to consider it as the end realised in and through activities which are elements in or parts of a form of life in relation to which they have other

---

[1] *The Right and the Good*, p. 21.   It is true that Ross includes in his list the duty of producing as much good as we can, but this seems to be a duty of an entirely different kind from the others.   It is a duty to pursue ends rather than to comply with rules.   If the distinction on which I am insisting is well-grounded, it is included in the list only as the result of a confusion. And the fact that it has to be included shows, so at least it seems to me, the difficulty of expressing the nature of the moral life in terms of the observance of rules alone.

[2] In the same way, a government imposes a tax, not for the sake of justice, but to raise money for specific purposes, but in its way of raising the money or levying the tax it should comply with the requirements of justice.

morally significant characteristics than being the realisation of the end.

In the moral life, then, there are ends to be pursued and rules to be observed, and moral goodness consists in pursuing the ends according to the rules.[1] Moral goodness is not itself one of the ends to be pursued, nor does it consist merely in obeying the rules. It is realised or manifested in pursuing the ends according to the rules. It is, in fact, like the spirit of a game in that, for its expression, it requires not one but two conditions — the observance of rules and the pursuit of ends. What gives a life moral worth, however, is neither the value of the ends pursued nor the observance of the rules obeyed, but the spirit shown in the pursuit and the observance. But in order that this spirit may have an opportunity of manifesting itself, there must be both ends and rules.

Now the purposes or ends which I have so far used as illustrations have only a relative or hypothetical goodness, and some, at any rate, of the rules which I have mentioned have only a conditional validity or authority. We have, therefore, to consider whether the same line of argument applies to all ends which the moral consciousness regards as good, including those which are said to have intrinsic goodness, and to all the rules which it regards as right, including those which are claimed to be self-evidently right. I believe the same line of argument does apply, but in order to show that it does, it is necessary to consider (1) the nature of the ends which we regard as good, the source from which they are derived, and the guarantee of their worth; (2) the nature of the rules which we regard as right, how we discover them, and the source of their authority; and (3) the relation of the different goods to one another, the relation of the different rules to one another, and the relation of the ends and rules to one another. These are very large questions, and here I can only sketch briefly the view which I should take regarding them consistent with the line of argument which I have been developing.

The view which I want to suggest is that if the moral spirit is to have an opportunity of manifesting itself, the ends pur-

---

[1] This is subject to the qualification explained below about the motive of morally good action.

sued and the rules obeyed by the moral agent must not be just any ends and rules. The ends must have a certain character, and the rules must be of a certain kind. And there must not be just a mere plurality of ends and rules. There must be a certain congruity between the ends, and the rules must be mutually adjusted. Otherwise different ends and different rules will conflict among themselves. Nor may there be a duality of unrelated elements, the good, the system of ends, on the one side, and the right, the system of rules, on the other. There must be a mutual affinity based on an underlying unity between the right and the good.

It is not easy to state the relation between the right and the good as I conceive it in terms of the relation between ends and rules because of what seem to me certain misleading implications in the latter terms, especially in the term 'end'. The term 'end' tends to suggest that the good or value which we call the end is a relatively static state of affairs and that the acts in and through which it is realised are means to this end and have value only as such; whereas, as I shall try to show later, many of the values or goods which we seek to realise exist only in the activities in and through which they are said to be realised. These activities are not means to the ends but the realisation of the ends. The term 'rule' as used in morals just describes certain characteristics which belong to acts, such, e.g., as being an act of truth-telling or promise-keeping; and in the acts which have such characteristics, ends are also being realised.

With this explanation, the view of the relation between ends and rules which I am suggesting might be stated as follows. The ends which are really good, as distinct from those which when considered in isolation seem to be good, are those which fit into a particular form or pattern of life; and the rules which are really right are statements of the characteristics of the acts, in which ends which are really good are realised, in virtue of which the acts and the ends which are realised in them constitute the pattern of this form of life. If this is the relation between them, when we try to discover which ends are really good we must take account of the structure of the pattern of life in which they are realised and of the characteristics of the acts which constitute it; and when we try to discover which rules are really right we must take account of the way in which the sorts of acts which are prescribed by the rules fit into the pattern of the form of life in which good ends are realised. In other words, the final guarantee of the goodness of ends and of the rightness of rules is to be found in a form of life in which not only are there content and structure, but within which content and structure mutually determine one another.

In order to show why this must be so, it is necessary to consider the second question which I mentioned at the beginning of this lecture — the relation of morality to the constitution of human nature. I do not think the two questions, the one about the structure of the moral life and the other about the relation of morality to human nature, can be kept separate in our attempts to answer them; for both the contents and the structure of the moral ideal derive from the constitution of human nature.

Let us look, then, at the constitution of human nature, and consider it first from the point of view of the ends which it prescribes, in order to show that we cannot discover which of them are really good without taking account of the structural pattern of the whole of which they form parts. It is difficult to describe human nature not only because of its complexity, but also because it is only partly given and partly to be realised. The realisation is perhaps always incomplete but it is more partial and imperfect in some persons than in others, and even in some aspects of one person's life than in others. Moreover, even of the relatively given elements some exercise a more or less controlling and directing influence on the development of others. In virtue of them man is an agent in his own development. Nevertheless, the factors in human nature which make man a moral being can be stated relatively shortly and simply. They are his possession of desires and interests or dispositions to desire, which are rooted in his instinctive nature; his intelligence or capacity to learn by experience; his power of imagination, which enables him to anticipate the results of his actions; his self-consciousness or awareness of himself as one amid the variety of his desires and experiences; his consequent capacity for reflection, which enables him to detach himself from the flow of his passing experiences and to view his life as a whole ; and his rationality or capacity to see things in their interrelations, which arouses in him a desire for some measure of consistency in his life.

Man, then, has certain natural needs which give rise to instinctive impulses, which in turn find expression in activities directed to satisfy the needs. The forms which these instinctive impulses take in a being which possesses imagination and self-consciousness we call desires. In man even the most specific of his needs, such as those for food or shelter, and the desires and activities to which they give rise, and the ends towards which they are directed, are relatively general. The ends which will satisfy the needs are not specific. They are sorts of things ; they can only be described in general terms. Accordingly, the desires for them are relatively plastic in the sense that they can be satisfied in different ways. But as each desire is a desire of a self-conscious individual who has other desires as well, one way of satisfying it may conflict with or contribute towards the satisfaction of other desires. Now considered by itself the end of each desire seems good. It makes a claim on the interest of the desiring self. But in the actual experience of the self which is also the subject of many other desires those ways of satisfying a particular desire which conflict with the satisfaction of other desires are regarded as so far bad ; and those which contribute to the satisfaction of other desires are regarded as good. Accordingly, as the result of experience, which may be more or less reflective and in which the exercise of constructive imagination may play a more or a less important part, the self-conscious agent builds up the idea of a system of ends or activities in which many desires can find compossible satisfaction. Moreover, not all desires are co-ordinate or of the same degree of generality or comprehensiveness. Some, as e.g. the desires for order and security and friendship, are more general, in the sense that if they are to be satisfied at all other desires must be satisfied in some ways and not in others. Thus the more general desires, the central desires or major interests as they are sometimes called, exercise a certain control over others and help to organise them into systems. Now the welfare of the self is more deeply implicated in these systems than in isolated desires. Their claims are, therefore, more imperative, and so the satisfaction of desires in ways which are required by them is regarded as right, and their satisfaction in ways which are inconsistent with them as wrong.

But the requirements even of these central desires or major interests may clash with one another, with the result that the self, to which they all belong, still remains unsatisfied. If, therefore, the self is to be satisfied, its major interests have to be reconciled under the control of a still more central interest which we may call the interest of the self as a whole or the policy of the will, which is just the self on its active side. The relation of the will to the desires and systems of desire is twofold. On the one hand, the will has no content but that of the desires. Therefore, it can only be satisfied through the satisfaction of the desires. On the other hand, not all satisfactions of desires satisfy the will or the self as a whole, but only their satisfaction at times and in ways which are consistent with its central policy. Thus the relation of the will to the particular desires is both positive and negative. Positively it reinforces those desires whose expression is required to further its central policy. Negatively it opposes any expression of a desire which is inconsistent with its policy with a ' not now ', or ' not in this way ', or, it may be, ' not at all '. In other words, it presents its demand, the demand of the unitary policy of the self, whether positive or negative, as an ought. The policy for which the will stands and in the name of which it enunciates its demands is not merely *a* good but *the* good, not a prima facie or seeming good but good unconditionally. We may, therefore, call it the personal moral ideal.

There are many other questions about the nature of this ideal and the factors which determine the degree of integration of an individual's interests and the comprehensiveness and consistency of his ideal which cannot be discussed here.[1] Some of them will engage us later. There are, however, two further considerations which should be mentioned at this stage. (1) Not only are the amount of integration of the self and the

---

[1] For a more detailed consideration of these questions see White and Macbeath, *The Moral Self*, chs. ii and iii.

adequacy of its ideal matters of degree, but the extent to which the ideal has been reflectively built up and is consciously before the mind also varies from individual to individual and from time to time in the life of the same individual. As far as an individual acts deliberately or as a moral agent at all, there must be some measure of integration of his interests ; and in order that he may realise his major interests, there must be a relatively high degree of integration ; but the process of integration may be more or less reflective and the unitary principle according to which it takes place may be operative in the mind of the individual rather than before it as an object of conscious reflection. (2) I mentioned that the needs of man and the desires to which they give rise are general and plastic in the sense that they can be satisfied in different ways. This is what makes it possible so to integrate them that they can find expression and satisfaction consistent with the policy of the will or the good of the self as a whole. Now if they were indefinitely plastic, they would, at least after a time, offer no resistance to their self-conscious direction and control by the will ; and one of the most characteristic features of the moral life would disappear, namely, the conflict between will and desire, between duty and interest, between ' the law of the mind ' and ' the law of the members '. But they are far from being indefinitely plastic. They rebel against certain ways of controlling and integrating them. However much they may be directed and controlled and certain expressions of them repressed, because they are rooted in our instinctive nature they will from time to time assert themselves with an urgency which, for most men at least, makes the conflict between them and the will a warfare from which there is no discharge. True the extent to which this is so in the case of what we may call the cruder and more isolated desires varies from individual to individual and depends on many factors, but especially on the extent to which and the ways in which they have been given expression in the past. But even for those who have brought their cruder passions into subjection, desires rooted in other partial interests tend to assert themselves in opposition to the will, and the conflict continues at another level.

What concerns us at present, however, is that the ideal of

the individual, the policy for which the will stands and which it is trying to realise, has a unitary character corresponding to the unity of the self as self-conscious. It is, indeed, the objective counterpart of that unity. Therefore, we cannot discover which desired ends are really good except by considering whether they fit into this unitary pattern.

So far I have described only one aspect of this pattern — its vertical or non-temporal aspect — the aspect which enables us to arrange desired ends or interests on a scale as more or less central or integral, and to reject as bad those which are inconsistent with the central policy of the will or the good of the self in its unitary character. But it has also a horizontal or temporal aspect; and the two aspects are intimately connected and can only be understood in relation to one another; for the moral ideal or the form of life in which the good of the self as a whole can find expression is not a static state of affairs which can be realised all at once. It consists of, and can only be realised in, and not merely as the result of, a series of activities. It has, therefore, a successive structure which determines the temporal order into which different goods must be fitted if they are to be realised at all. This horizontal or temporal structure is an essential aspect of the moral life, but its importance and its implications seem to be seldom realised by ethical writers.

It is, of course, generally recognised that there are entities which cannot exist all at once, like a song or a symphony. A purpose or an interest is an entity of this kind, and much more so a system of purposes or a form of life. Accordingly, the moral ideal, the system of ends or interests which constitute the good for man, must be conceived as having a temporal as well as a vertical pattern. For this reason, as I shall illustrate in detail later,[1] the vertical pattern, according to which interests are arranged in what we call their order of value, does not by itself enable us to decide what end or interest should be realised at a given moment. For conflicts take place between interests and a choice has to be made between ends, not merely or even mainly because one is higher and another lower or because the two are in principle incompatible, the manifestations of incompatible attitudes of mind. They take place much more

[1] See below, pp. 408-10.

frequently between ends and interests, like the production of food, the promotion of health, the pursuit of knowledge, and the enjoyment of beauty, which are not only all good and in principle quite compatible, but which are all necessary elements in the good life. The reason for these conflicts is our finite limitations which prevent us from doing more than one thing at a time. Therefore, we cannot realise all at once the goods which together constitute the good life or the moral ideal. They can only be realised over a period of time, though one or other of them may be being realised during every part of that period. But just because there are limits to what we can do at once, we have at a given moment to make a choice, and the choice often involves loss as well as gain, giving up something good as well as realising something good. Thus the good life has a negative aspect, an aspect of self-sacrifice, as well as a positive aspect, an aspect of self-realisation. Some of the implications of these facts and some of the difficulties which arise from neglecting them we shall have to consider later. All I want to note now is that if most of our interests are to be at all realised they must be realised one after another. Hence the importance of the temporal pattern which determines the order of their realisation. It is true that in realising a more specific end I may also be realising a more general end. It is also true that there are goods, such as keeping an appointment or helping the victim of an accident, which must be realised at a particular time or not at all. But even in such cases, in deciding whether or not a good should be realised, account must be taken of the temporal pattern of the way of life which is the good of the self as a whole.

In view of these considerations it is apt to be misleading to describe the moral ideal as the moral end or the ultimate end. Such a description tends to suggest that the moral ideal or the good for man is a state of affairs which can be realised all at once at some future date, and that present activities are means to this end and have value only as such ; whereas in fact they are parts of or elements in the realisation of the ideal. To avoid these misleading suggestions I prefer to speak of the moral ideal as a form or way of life. For a form of life exists only in being lived, and in being lived it is spread out in time ; and the activities in which it is lived are parts of it, not means either to it or to some other end beyond it.

What is important from the point of view of the present argument, however, is that the system of ends which constitutes the moral ideal and the activities in which they are realised has a structure or pattern. That pattern in virtue of its being the policy of the will, which is an attempt to embody the good of the self as a whole, presents itself to the individual, not merely as the good, but as an ought, a source of obligation that he should do and refrain from doing what it here and now requires for its realisation. Those ends which enter into it are really good; the sorts of acts in which it is realised are really right. The ends which are good are its content, the rules which are right are those which prescribe acts which fit into its structural pattern.

It is true that as long as we consider the individual by himself the principles connecting his different interests into the unitary system, which is the good of his self as a whole, and the rules which prescribe the sort of acts which fit into this pattern are not usually called moral rules. They are not included in ordinary moral codes. They tend to be regarded rather as maxims of prudence. But even from the point of view of enlightened self-interest, even when there is no question of the activities of the individual directly affecting others, what is required by the good of his self as a whole presents itself to him as an ought as against the solicitations and allurements of particular desires. And this ought is a moral ought; the acts and abstentions which it prescribes are moral duties; and they are accompanied by the same feeling of obligation as the duties which concern his relations with other people.[1] For it is not only with the interests of other people that a person's desires may conflict. They may also conflict with one another;[2] and it is the duty of the individual to realise those and only those which further his policy as a whole. If it is held that to do so is only

---

[1] Cf. Campbell, *Moral Intuition and the Principle of Self-realisation* (British Academy Lecture, 1948), pp. 29-30.

[2] Kant once said that man can get on neither with nor without his fellows; but the difficulty goes deeper: man cannot get on even with himself. His nature is divided against itself; and he has duties to himself as well as to others.

to be prudent, the answer seems to be that in some circumstances it is a moral duty to be prudent.

Nevertheless, from the moral point of view the isolated individual is an abstraction. Just as an end or an act has to be considered in relation to the other ends and acts of the individual whose it is, so the individual has to be considered in relation to other individuals who with him form the society or community of which he is a member. This is so not merely because every man known to history or anthropology, and therefore every man with whom ethics is concerned, is in fact a member of a society, and most of his duties arise out of his relations to others, but for the more fundamental reason that, as psychologists tell us,[1] self-consciousness, which is a condition of the possibility of morality, is itself a social product, a product which could only develop in a social medium. This, however, does not mean that, once self-consciousness has emerged, the moral agent has no duties which are not social duties, any more than it means that he ceases to be a moral being when he is alone. Moreover, for the satisfaction of most even of his non-social interests, such as his interest in food and shelter, knowledge and beauty, man is dependent on the co-operation of other people. Their satisfaction, therefore, requires at least a minimum of mutual trust and goodwill, and the observance of rules governing the relations between individuals which are necessary to make this co-operation possible.

Nor is this all. Co-operation with others and the observance of the rules which make it possible is not just a means to the realisation of other ends. The individual finds the co-operation itself good. For one of man's deepest needs is for friendly relations with at least some others; and the sorts of acts in which such relations find expression, i.e. the acts which comply with the rules which are the conditions of friendly co-operation, are not merely means to, or conditions of friendly relations. They are themselves expressions of, or elements in such friendship. They not only promote friendship; they are friendship. In thinking of friendship we normally dwell more on the inner attitude, the spirit of loyalty and mutual trust, than on the friendly actions in which it finds expression. And

[1] See, e.g., Stout, *Manual of Psychology*, 4th ed., pp. 583 ff.

it is true that without this spirit there is no friendship; but neither is there friendship unless that spirit finds expression in friendly actions. In all moral action there is both an inner and an outer side; but it is with the outward and visible forms in which the moral spirit manifests itself that we are at present concerned; and from that point of view co-operative action is not merely the means to, or the consequence of friendship; it is friendship itself.

Still more important, however, is the fact that man is social not only in the sense that he desires the co-operation and friendship of others but also in the sense that he has a natural interest in their welfare and a disposition to desire the realisation of their ends because they are theirs. This, indeed, is one of the most central and integral of all his desires; and if it is to find expression and realisation, his other desires must find realisation in some ways and not in others. Accordingly, the process of building up the personal ideal of the individual, his conception of the sort of life that is worth while, throughout involves the fitting of his ends into a system or pattern which includes the ends of others as well; so that the personal ideal of the individual is a social ideal, the idea of a way of life in which different people co-operate to realise the ends of all of them.[1] Thus the personal and the social ideal are not two ideals but two aspects of one ideal. There are important differences between them, with some of which we shall be concerned later, and for purposes of exposition it is desirable to treat them separately, but the one cannot be understood except in relation to the other.

Now the social character of the self introduces enormous complexity into its ideal.[2] It becomes a way of life in which different people co-operate and into which the ends of different people have to be fitted. But it still has the vertical and temporal structural pattern which we have described; only in this pattern the ends of different individuals have to be so

[1] Cf. Green, *Prolegomena to Ethics*, Sect. 199. " Man cannot contemplate himself as in a better state . . . without contemplating others, not merely as a means to that better state, but as sharing it with him."

[2] How complex this ideal is will become clearer in the next lecture, when we consider the way in which institutions and operative ideals mediate between the desires of the individual and the social ideal.

organised that they can find realisation consistently with each other. Among the most important links in this structure are the rules governing the relations between the individuals who co-operate, rules which are implied in the co-operation through which alone the system of ends can be realised. The observance of these rules — the rules which are embodied in moral codes — is not just a means to the co-operation, nor is the co-operation just a means to the realisation of ends. The activities which comply with the rules are themselves the co-operation, and the co-operation in accordance with them is the realisation of the ideal. It is the ends which fit into this structure which are really good; and it is the rules which are implied in it which are really right. It is in pursuing these ends in compliance with these rules that the individual realises his moral ideal — an ideal which presents itself to him as the good and his own good, the source of moral obligation and the ground of rightness. Despite its social character this ideal is sometimes, and I think not inappropriately, called the good of the self as a whole, that is, the good of a self which is not only self-conscious but social. But this description has been criticised on the ground that the demands which the social pattern makes on the individual, though he recognises them as right because they are the requirements of what he himself regards as the ideal form of life, sometimes involve the sacrifice not only of many of his major personal interests, but even of life itself — thus it would appear preventing the realisation of his personal ideal altogether.[1]

Now it is quite true that undoubtedly difficult practical problems arise from the conflict between the conditions of the personal development or personal happiness of the individual and the requirements of the social ideal.[2] Similar problems arise from the fact that the individual may be prevented,

[1] It has also been criticised on the ground that it savours of egoism, a criticism which I shall examine later. See pp. 416-19.

[2] This conflict appears even in the smallest and simplest societies, where there is little difference between the social pattern as it exists in the minds of different members, and where it is easy for the individual to see that the social good is his own good. But it is much more marked in the case of larger, more complex and less unified societies, where the individual is a member of many social groups, and it is much more difficult for him to see the whole pattern, or even that there is a pattern to see.

through no fault of his own, from realising the ends at which he aims. This may be due to the absence of intelligence or goodwill on the part of those on whose co-operation their realisation in part depends, or to some defect, for which he cannot be held responsible, in his grasp of the situation in relation to which he has to act, or to the hazards and accidents of a time-conditioned existence.[1] But however difficult these problems may prove in practice, the solution, in principle, seems to be contained in what has been said above. For, as I have already pointed out, though an action cannot be morally good unless the individual aims at such ends, the action does not derive its moral value from the ends at which it aims, much less from the actual achievement of these ends, but rather from the spirit or personality which finds expression in it. Now in doing what he believes to be required by his ideal, the individual always achieves the realisation and expression of his moral personality, the one thing which gives his life moral worth. No doubt it may appear rather paradoxical that while the actual ends at which an individual aims may not be achieved, his greatest good, the expression of his moral personality and the development of his character, is always achieved in the pursuit. But as far as morality is concerned this apparent paradox has to be accepted. Any attempt to consider the questions to which it gives rise would take us beyond ethics. The important consideration, however, from our present point of view is that, by whatever name we call it, an ideal such as we have described, which has both a personal and a social aspect, is the only form of life in which a being constituted as man is, a being who is not only a creature of desires but also self-conscious and social, can find the good which will satisfy his whole nature. However imperfect may be his conception of it, that conception determines, and provides the final justification

[1] It is facts of this kind, what Bosanquet called " the hazards and hardships of finite existence ", that suggest to many minds the idea of a future life, in which the balance of this can be redressed. If we accept this idea and the religious view of the world which usually goes with it, no doubt our final value judgements will be passed in the light of the pattern of the larger life which they imply. But such considerations fall outside the province of ethics. From the ethical point of view, all that can be said is that in the pursuit of ends, which he may not attain, the individual reveals and realises his moral personality, and his moral good is thereby attained.

for the ends which he should pursue and for the rules with which in pursuing them he should comply.

What we find then is this. When we consider the ends which men pursue, to discover which of them are really good, we find that we have to consider these ends, which have their origin in man's needs and the desires to which these needs give rise, as parts of a system of ends in which not only the ends of the individual but those of other individuals as well are so integrated that they can find realisation consistently with one another. Only the ends which fit into the structure of this system are really desirable; and they are desirable only in the form in which they fit into it. So that we cannot discover which ends are good without taking account of the structural pattern of the form of life in which they are realised; and this structural pattern finds expression in principles and rules determining the nature of the acts in which the ends are realised and the relations of particular ends and of the individuals whose the ends are to one another. In other words, in trying to discover which ends are good we have to take account of moral rules and principles. With these rules the individual in pursuing his ends has to comply. His duty is not simply to comply with the rules; but to pursue his ends in compliance with them. So that his duty always involves the pursuit of ends and the observance of rules.

We could arrive at the same conclusion regarding the mutual interdependence of good ends and right rules by beginning with the rules which are regarded as right, asking which of them are really right; and why, and subject to what conditions, they are right. But if my argument so far has been sound, to do so in general terms would be only to repeat from a different angle much of what has already been said. In my next lecture I shall give a more detailed account from another point of view of the rules which different societies regard as right, of the way in which in the course of experience they become adjusted to one another, and of the way in which their authority, within the limits within which they are binding, is to be found in such an ideal or form of life as I have described above. But even at the risk of repetition, some further consideration of the view of the nature and authority of moral rules and their relation to the moral ideal, to which the line of argument which I have been pursuing leads, and a comparison of it with some other views, may not be out of place here. It may help to make my position clearer; and it will indicate some of the questions with which it will be necessary to deal later.

With one possible exception — and that exception I should regard not as a rule but a principle — the ordinary moral rules which we regard as right, those which find expression in the institutions and customs and codes of different societies, are, according to the view which I am advocating, empirical generalisations based on the experience of mankind as to the conditions necessary for realising the form of life which is worth while. We have seen that this form of life — whether we call it the moral ideal, the good for man or the good of the self as a whole — consists of desired ends and acts, in and through which they are realised, organised into a pattern with a unity corresponding to the unity of the self as self-conscious. The final test of the rightness of acts is whether they both fit into this pattern and are the realisation of such ends. Now acts which have certain general characteristics or are of certain sorts, such as respecting life, telling the truth, helping others and so on, are normally found by experience, whether actual experience or ideal experiment, to satisfy this test. And still more clearly acts which have the opposite characteristics, such as not respecting life or not telling the truth, are usually found to be inconsistent with and to hinder the realisation of the pattern. However immediately satisfying the performance of such acts may be, they tend to leave behind them a growing conviction that they were not on the whole what we wanted. Now moral rules are just assertions that acts of the former kind are right, and that acts of the latter kind are wrong. They are, therefore, generalisations true for the most part but not universally so; and they do not contain the grounds of their rightness within themselves. Both they and the exceptions to them which are right derive their authority from the structure of the moral ideal, the form of life which is both good and the source of moral obligation.

Now it is generally agreed that this is true of many of the rules which we regard as right, such as the rules embodied in the institutions of particular peoples with regard to such things as the distribution and ownership of property, the relations between partners in an enterprise, between friends, between the sexes, between masters and men and so on. Such rules are the results of experiments in social co-operation in trying to conceive and live a good life, and they are retained or modified as men on the whole find or do not find the form of life to which they give rise acceptable. Modification of them may be called for, either because the resulting form of life is internally inconsistent, or because it fails to make adequate provision for the needs either of some or of all of those who co-operate in it. The final test as to the rightness of any of these rules is : Do the acts which it prescribes on the whole help or hinder men in their attempts to satisfy their whole nature as beings who are self-conscious and social ?

It is, however, often contended that this account does not apply to all rules which are regarded as right, but that some rules, such as the rules of truth-telling and promise-keeping, are self-evident intuitions, laws of reason or, as the Stoics called them, laws of nature, more like the categories of thought than the generalisations of science. According to this view such rules are self-authenticating, independent of the institutions of all societies, and not requiring any justification from any form of life, actual or ideal. Contemporary writers who take this view, however, recognise that such rules are unlike other rational principles in that they are not universally binding. The moral consciousness recognises exceptions to them which are not morally wrong. This happens both when the claims of different rules clash, as they sometimes do, and when much greater harm would result from observing a particular rule, as in such rare though not unimportant instances as refusing to endanger the life of a person who is ill by telling him the truth, or deceiving a would-be murderer as to the whereabouts of his intended victim, or misleading an enemy in war-time. The duties which such rules impose are, therefore, now generally regarded, even by those who claim that their obligatory character is self-evident, not as actual or absolute but only as prima facie obligations, that is, as constituting claims to consideration which are actually binding only in the absence of more urgent claims. The evidence which seems to me to show that even in this modified form these rules are not self-evident I shall consider later. All I need say here is that the fact that they admit of any exceptions suggests that, however important their general observance, and however fundamental they may be as conditions of individual and social well-being, they are not self-authenticating, but that both the rules and the exceptions to them require justification from some other source. The view which I am suggesting is that this justification is to be found in the way of life which I have called the moral ideal, a way of life whose conditions the rules are.

The one possible exception, to which I referred above, the one rule which seems to be not an empirical generalisation but a rational principle, which like the categories is true universally and admits of no exception which is not morally wrong, is the principle of justice or equity, which seems to be implied in one form or another in every moral code and in the ideal, if not always in the practice, of every society, from the *lex talionis* of an eye for an eye and a tooth for a tooth, to Kant's Kingdom of Ends and Bentham's each to count for one and no one for more than one, from the tit-for-tat of children and the Code of Hammurabi to the Confucian or Christian Golden Rule. This principle does not normally insist on absolute equality in the treatment of different individuals, though in its cruder forms it is apt to be a demand for simple equality. What it requires is that where people are treated differently there should be a relevant reason for the difference. From time to time and from people to people, men seeing differences of privileges and opportunities as between individuals or groups ask the reason for the difference of treatment and are dissatisfied unless a sufficient reason for the difference can be produced. It is true that the differences, such as differences of rank, wealth, capacity physical or mental, place of birth or residence, race, family, etc., which have seemed to men at different times and in different countries sufficient to justify difference of treatment, have varied enormously, but the persistence of the demand seems to show the operation in the minds of men of a principle, however imperfect may be their grasp of its full nature and implications. What they take to be the requirements of this principle determines the rules governing the relations between individuals which they try to embody in their customs and institutions and laws. But from time to time, men appeal from the accepted rules and existing institutions to the principle itself, and it is in the light of it or through its semi-conscious operation in their minds that they modify their social institutions and the rules which determine the respective rights and duties of different individuals.

Now the real basis of this principle — a basis which comes to light especially in its more developed forms — is the nature of personality and the recognition by the individual that others are personalities, manifestations of the moral consciousness, like himself. What precisely would be the effect of the full recognition of this principle of the fundamental moral equality of men as persons and of its embodiment in our moral and social institutions cannot yet be said with certainty. We have in principle recognised it in the legal and political spheres and we have tried to embody it in arrangements to ensure equality before the law and in political democracy. We have also made great concessions to it in the sphere of education and we have tried to use it as a criterion for modifications of the law of marriage and divorce, while its implications in the economic sphere are still a matter of keen controversy. With these implications we are not at present concerned. Their working-out is, I think, a matter of experience, and experience decides by experiment, not by *a priori* considerations. What we are concerned with is the principle itself, though, as I have already indicated, I should hold that we cannot fully understand any moral principle except in its detailed working-out in practice.

I have called this principle rational on the ground that, once the equality of men as persons is recognised as a fact, it seems unreasonable to treat them differently, unless there are differences between them to justify difference of treatment. The difficulty of applying the principle is due to the difficulty of being sure which differences between persons are morally significant, and so warrant difference of treatment.[1] The

---

[1] We might try to get over the difficulty referred to in the text by saying that in what we usually call justice there are at least two principles involved

negative requirements of the principle seem much clearer than the positive. If men are in fact persons, subjects of ends or ends in themselves, the principle of justice rules out as wrong certain ways of treating them, ways of treating them as if they were things not persons, mere means to the ends of others and not self-governing individuals with ends of their own. Perhaps these negative results are all that the principle of justice strictly interpreted will guarantee. It is true that its universal applica-

and that at least two criteria are applied in determining what treatment of individuals is just. The one principle, the principle of equality, demands absolute equality in the treatment of individuals in certain respects on the ground of their moral equality as persons. The other principle, the principle of equity or proportional equality, demands different treatment for individuals according, e.g., to some of the functions which they are called on to perform in the interests of the common good which requires that the functions in question should be efficiently discharged. According to this view, a complete analysis of justice would have to show in what respects individuals ought to be treated with absolute equality, e.g. before the law, in respect for life, in security for the person, in freedom of thought and expression, in educational opportunities, and so on, and what functions demand for their due performance differences of treatment for those who discharge them, e.g. the exercise of leadership, social, economic or political, and so on. But the two principles are not co-ordinate and we cannot maintain the distinction between them as simply as the above account suggests by delimiting their spheres of application ; for the performance of different functions may mean different opportunities for the development of the personalities of those who discharge them, and yet their discharge and the differences of treatment which it involves may be necessary for the maintenance of the common good which is itself a condition of securing even those rights or forms of treatment in respect of which individuals should, according to the principle of equality, be regarded as equal. The fact is that the rule of equality, like the other rules which we considered earlier, is too abstract to be regarded as final in any sphere. In the concrete context of the good life it has to give way to and, in those cases in which it is justified, find its justification in the principle of equity. And what the principle of equity requires can only be discovered by trying to embody it in a way of life in which respect for personality and the provision of opportunities for its development are the primary considerations. According to the view here suggested, the principle of equity is a rational principle, and the process of determining what is right or equitable in particular circumstances is a rational process, not only in the sense that it is a process which only a rational being can perform, but also in the sense that the conclusion as to what is right emerges from the consideration of the structure of the way of life in which the principle of equity is embodied as a conclusion follows from premises. But it has not the sort of rationality which we find in mathematics where each stage in the process and each subsidiary principle is, even when considered in isolation, self-evident, the result of an infallible intuition. For further discussion of this point see pp. 390 ff.

tion, even in this sense, would take us a long way towards the conception of a satisfactory moral and social order. Nevertheless, such an interpretation gives us only a negative conception of duty as the avoidance of that which is morally wrong. It does not give us the positive character of the moral ideal or the whole duty of man. To get the latter we have to add to the negative requirements of the principle of justice not only the recognition of the need for co-operation as a means to realising other ends, but also the desire of men for co-operative, friendly relations as good in themselves, and especially the direct desire for the welfare of others, which is one of the most deep-rooted interests of man, though it is often prevented from getting free expression by the pressure of other interests. When we add to these social desires the recognition of other men as persons — the basis of the principle of justice — we see that the ideal required to satisfy a being who is the subject of such desires involves the positive promotion of the ends of other people as theirs ; and that whatever further rules or sorts of acts are involved in doing this are not only justified but obligatory.

This positive ideal which gives us the whole duty of man is, however, merely formal. Its full requirements can be expressed only in very general terms. Attempts to give it concrete form in the conception of a detailed way of life embodied in rules and institutions are only partially successful. At best they are only imperfect approximations to its requirements. The distinction between the formal ideal — the objective counterpart of the unity of a self which is self-conscious and social — and what I shall call the operative ideals — the detailed forms of life in which different peoples have tried, more or less successfully, to articulate its requirements — is the basis of the distinction often drawn by writers on ethics [1] between ideal morality and the morality of social justice, or between the morality of perfection and the morality of my station and its duties. The latter are attempts, only partially successful, to give concrete expression to the requirements of the former.

The formal ideal not only requires compliance with the more or less negative demands of the principle of justice strictly

---

[1] See, e.g., Bradley, *Ethical Studies*, Essays v and vi ; Lindsay, *The Two Moralities* ; Lamont, *The Principles of Moral Judgement*, ch. vi.

interpreted, but it has, as we have seen, a further positive character which makes additional demands on the agent. The operative ideals are only partial embodiments either of these positive requirements or even of the more negative demands of the principle of justice. The duties which they prescribe are only the minimum of morality. They are what others have a right to expect of us. But they are not merely negative. They do not just require that we leave other people alone to pursue their own ends within the limits of the accepted social pattern. They also at times require that we assist them or co-operate with them in their attempts to realise their ends. On the other hand, the maximum of morality, the whole duty of man, the demand of the morality of perfection, is to comply with the requirements of the formal ideal. This is the demand which in our best moments we make on ourselves, even though others have no right to expect it of us. These requirements, as I have said, are only inadequately expressed in existing institutions and ways of life. It is in the light of them that we try to improve institutions and operative ideals. It has indeed been contended,[1] and not without justification, that the full demands of the formal ideal do not admit of being completely expressed in rules, that rules belong to the sphere where rights and duties are reciprocal, " the world of claims and counterclaims "; distinct from the sphere of ideal morality, " the world of spiritual membership ", to use Bosanquet's phrases.[2]

Be this as it may, it is the demands of the formal ideal, which the systems of rules regarded as right by particular peoples, and the institutions and forms of life in which they are embodied, are trying to express. And the relation of the rules to the form of life, whose requirements they are attempts to express, seems to provide the explanation of what intuitionists have called the greater stringency of certain rules, in virtue of which their claims take precedence over those of less stringent rules. Though the intuitionists find this characteristic of moral rules useful in solving the difficulties which clashes between the requirements of different rules, whose rightness they claim to be self-evident, create for their theory, they do not find it easy

---

[1] See, e.g., Lindsay, *op. cit.* p. 99.
[2] *The Value and Destiny of the Individual*, Lect. v.

to explain it. Indeed, important though it is for their theory, they say very little about it, and what they say is hesitating and unconvincing. In the end they seem driven to account for it in terms of a greater sense or feeling of urgency which, they say, some rules produce in the moral agent. According to the view urged here, the more stringent rules are those which are more fundamental to the form of life whose conditions they are in the sense that, if breaches of them became general, the way of life would collapse more completely.

We may now sum up the results of our enquiry so far. We considered the moral ideal as the pursuit of ends, and tried to discover what ends are really good, and what are the conditions of their realisation. And we found that those ends are really good which fit into the pattern of a form of life in which different people co-operate to realise the ends of all of them; and that moral principles and rules are the principles according to which this form of life is organised and the conditions of the co-operation between individuals which are involved in living it. We next considered the moral ideal as the observance of rules, and tried to discover what rules are really right, and what are the grounds of their rightness. And we found that right rules are statements of the characteristics in virtue of which acts fit into, or are expressions of, the structural principle of the form of life in which good ends are realised, and more particularly statements of the conditions of co-operation between individuals involved in living such a form of life. In other words, we found that, when we try to understand moral ends, we have to introduce the idea of moral rules; and when we try to understand moral rules, we have to introduce the idea of moral ends. We are, therefore, driven to the conclusion that the moral ideal or the good for man cannot be explained in terms of either the pursuit of ends or the application of rules alone. Its explanation requires both.

Thus an action is capable of fitting into, or failing to fit into, the pattern of a way of life in two different but interconnected ways. On the one hand it is forward-looking; it is an attempt to bring about a certain state of affairs; and this state of affairs may or may not fit into the pattern of the ideal way of life. On the other hand, whether or not it succeeds in bringing about the state of affairs at which it aims, it has characteristics which belong to it as an act in virtue of which it is or is not appropriate to its context in a way of life. These two aspects of the act — its intended consequences and its relation to its context — are interconnected, and in passing moral judgement on it we have to take account of its fittingness in both respects. An act is morally obligatory if, and only if, in virtue of all its characteristics or its whole nature, it fits into or is required by the pattern of the way of life which is the moral ideal.

But while living a morally good life involves both the pursuit of ends and the observance of rules, moral goodness is neither one of the ends which we pursue or directly aim at, nor yet is it merely the observance of rules. It is achieved or realised in the conscious pursuit of those ends which fit into the form of life which is the moral ideal, in compliance with those rules which are involved in the structural pattern of this form of life. The development of character is a by-product of this pursuit and compliance; and a morally good character is the permanent disposition to act in this way.[1]

Now this means that there is no such thing as a duty to be moral in the sense of a duty whose end is the development of character, or which directly aims at producing or promoting moral goodness. Every duty is a moral duty and, in that sense, a duty to be moral. But every duty is also a duty to do a particular act, such as visiting a sick friend, relieving the victim of a road accident, keeping an appointment, promoting knowledge or producing food. Each of these acts is the pursuit of an end or the initiation of a state of affairs, and it also complies with a certain rule or rules. The act is one of a series of

---

[1] In a complete account of the moral life as here conceived, it would be necessary to distinguish between those actions which have and those which have not moral merit. The distinction is not relevant to the present argument, but it is mentioned here to avoid misunderstanding. There are actions which are right in the sense that they comply with the requirements of morality but the ends at which they aim are in the line of the agent's natural inclinations. They are not done from a sense of duty and they require no effort. Therefore, while they form part of a morally good life they have no moral merit. Moral merit, in the strict sense, belongs only to actions the doing of which is contrary to our natural inclinations, and their moral merit varies with the effort of will which it cost the agent.

interconnected acts; the end or good which it seeks to realise
is one of a system of ends which are the ends of the series of
acts; and the rule or rules with which it complies are members
of a system of rules which are the principles of interconnection
of the ends and acts. Now the acts which it is our duty to do
are the acts which fit into, and are the realisation of, the form
of life which is the moral ideal, i.e. the acts which aim at ends
which are really good, and comply with rules which are really
right. In doing these acts, character is developed and moral
goodness is realised. But the development of character and the
production of moral goodness are not themselves among the
ends aimed at. They are realised in and through the doing of
acts which aim at other ends and directly seek to realise other
goods. The ends which are pursued in such acts are the ends
which I earlier described as the ends of desires which are rooted
in human nature and required to satisfy its needs — ends such
as food and shelter, health and freedom, knowledge and beauty
and friendship. But it is these ends as ordered and unified into
the pattern required to satisfy the self as a whole. Strictly
speaking, all these ends are non-moral ends; but because they
are the constituent elements of the moral ideal or the moral good,
and because for that reason it is our duty to realise them, they
are often referred to as moral ends or moral goods; but this
is apt to cause confusion. The fact is that the terms ' moral '
and ' moral good ' are used in a large number of different
senses; and if we are to avoid confusion, we must distinguish
carefully between some of these senses.

For example, we use the term ' moral ' to describe, among
other things, both the different constituents of the moral ideal
and the moral ideal itself which these elements in their interrelation constitute. But however useful this usage may be for
certain purposes, it is liable to cause confusion. For as used
of the constituent elements of the moral ideal, the term ' moral '
is a relational property, indicating that the things to which it is
applied are elements in the moral ideal, and that their moral
significance, the reason why it is our duty to pursue and realise
them, cannot be understood without reference to the whole in
which they are elements. But these elements which in their
interrelation constitute the moral ideal are all non-moral goods,

the ends of desire. The moral ideal has in fact no contents but these non-moral goods, the ends of desire, and therefore it can be realised only through their being realised. Therefore it is our duty to realise them, not in their own right, but as elements in the moral ideal, i.e. because in doing so we are realising the moral ideal.

What, however, is more liable to cause confusion and has, I think, in fact done so, is the use of the term ' moral good ' to describe both the quality of mind or motives of the moral agent and also the character of the moral ideal, the system of goods which will satisfy the whole nature of man. Let us see how the two things which are thus described are distinguished from and related to one another. The constituent elements of the moral ideal are, as has just been said, particular non-moral goods, the ends of desire or of systems of desires. But we call the whole system in which they are so integrated as to satisfy the whole nature of man the moral good, in order to distinguish it from the particular goods — the non-moral goods — which constitute it. But the moral good in this sense is not itself another good in addition to the non-moral goods of which it consists. It has no content but the non-moral goods ; but it is not a mere aggregate of non-moral goods, but an integrated system in which some ends of desire are subordinated to others, and some have to be realised in certain ways and at certain times, and some repressed altogether. Thus the moral good or ideal makes a demand on the moral agent that he do or refrain from doing those acts, and realise or repress those ends, which are here and now required for its realisation. It is this demand which is experienced as the sense of duty or obligation. The acts which are thus demanded we call morally right. They are the acts which fit into the moral ideal and comply with the rules which are implied in it. Now when we do the acts which we believe to be right in this sense from a sense of duty, or because we believe them to be right, we are said to be morally good. In doing them we are developing and expressing our moral character, and realising or revealing our moral goodness. Here we are using the term ' moral good ' or ' moral goodness ' to describe a quality of the moral agent himself ; and it is important that we should not confuse moral good or moral goodness in this sense, i.e. as a quality of the moral agent, with the moral good as the system of ends or goods which is the moral ideal.

The moral goodness of the agent is not one of the ends pursued by the agent, and, therefore, it is neither the whole nor any part of the moral good as a system of ends. Moreover it does not derive its character of moral goodness from the goodness of the ends of which it is the pursuit. Yet it cannot exist except in the pursuit and realisation of such ends. It belongs to the attitude of mind or the spirit which finds expression in this pursuit and realisation. Moral goodness, then, or goodness of character is not an end at which it is our duty to aim directly in any of our actions. Yet it is realised or manifested only in the pursuit of the ends and the performance of the actions which are required by the moral ideal. Accordingly, the relation of moral goodness to the moral ideal, the good for man, is quite different from the relation of other or non-moral goods to that ideal. The latter form a part of the ideal or the good for man, the former is realised in the pursuit of the latter as elements in the good for man.

This view of the relation of the different elements in the moral life to one another seems to me not only to account for the main facts of the moral life in a way which avoids difficulties and paradoxes which embarrass many other theories ; it even helps us to see the sources of these difficulties and paradoxes. In the first place, it enables us to avoid the vicious circle which has often been pointed out in the teaching of Kant and Green and many idealists, who hold that the object of the good will is the good will, or that the moral ideal is the pursuit of the moral ideal, or that moral goodness or goodness of character is the end pursued in morally good actions. As against this position, I suggest that the good will finds expression in the pursuit of non-moral goods, when these are pursued as elements in the moral ideal or the good for man. To repeat : there is a sense in which it is our duty to be morally good, but we cannot be morally good in the abstract. To be morally good is to perform our particular duties in the spirit of duty. In other words, to be morally good is to manifest a good will ; and a good will is manifested in setting oneself to initiate the particular state of affairs which the moral ideal here and now requires. It may be an act of kindness, the fulfilment of a promise, the pursuit of knowledge, the relief of distress, the production of food, the promotion of beauty, or whatever else the ideal here and now requires.

In the second place, this view gives to moral goodness the unique position claimed for it by the moral consciousness and by most ethical writers; for, according to it, moral goodness not being part of the end aimed at, but rather realised in the pursuit of other ends, does not come into conflict with other goods. We are not called upon to choose between the pursuit of knowledge or beauty or pleasure and moral goodness. We are called upon to choose between the different non-moral goods, that is, to choose between the different goods other than moral goodness; and when we choose whichever is required by the moral ideal, and pursue it for that reason, we realise or express our moral goodness in the pursuit, and the pursuit is morally good.

There are, in fact, no duties which are not moral duties but there are no duties which are merely moral duties, that is, duties to be moral and nothing more. Our moral duties are also duties to do particular acts. This explains why a theory, like Intuitionism, which insists on comparing moral goodness with other forms of good, as if we had to choose between the different kinds, gets into the paradoxical situations to which Ross calls attention [1] but from which on his theory we cannot escape. The paradoxes arise from the fact that, according to such a theory, it is necessary to ask such questions as " whether in any given situation it is rather our duty to promote some good moral activity or some good intellectual activity in ourselves ".[2] On the view which I am defending, such a question is not legitimate, for it never in practice arises. If in any given situation it is my duty to promote some good intellectual activity, it is my moral duty to do so; and, therefore, in promoting a good intellectual activity I am in the same act promoting a good moral activity. So that there can be no conflict between the two. The alternatives with which actual life

[1] *Foundations of Ethics*, p. 284.   [2] *Ibid.*

presents us are, for example, between a good intellectual activity and doing an act of kindness or a piece of social service or taking a rest in the interests of our health, that is between different non-moral goods. The alternatives are never between any of these and doing our moral duty. If in particular circumstances it is my duty to engage in some intellectual activity, then it is my moral duty to do so, and in doing it I am expressing my moral goodness and promoting my moral character. The other so-called duties between which and it I am called on to choose are not my actual duties at all but what would be my duties, if the circumstances were different and if it were not here and now my duty to engage in intellectual activity.

It seems to me no small advantage of the theory I am advocating that it saves us from unreal paradoxes of this kind, paradoxes which arise from theories which regard moral goodness as one among several goods between which we may be called on to choose. According to such theories, moral goodness must be comparable, if not even commensurable, with other goods; and yet, as the theorists themselves admit, the deliverance of the moral consciousness compels them to regard it as ' infinitely superior ' to all other goods.[1] The present theory takes the view that no conflicts between moral goodness and other goods arise; so that no choice or comparison between it and them is necessary. It is good in a different sense or a good of a different order from all other goods. This is so because it enters into the moral life in a different way from them.

In the third place, this theory enables us to reconcile two convictions of the moral consciousness which many theories seem to find in conflict. The one is that in the good life there are other goods besides moral goodness, that it includes, for example, such goods as knowledge, aesthetic experience, happiness, friendship, freedom, health and other non-moral goods. The other is that morality is concerned with the whole of life and has jurisdiction over all of it. According to the present theory, moral goodness and these other goods enter into the good life in different ways and not only do not conflict but are necessary to one another. The latter are the ends to which it is directed, the former is realised in the pursuit of them. On

[1] See, e.g., Ross, *The Right and the Good*, pp. 151-2.

the other hand, in any set of circumstances in which we are called upon to act there is something good to be realised in order to meet the demands of the moral ideal, and the good will is revealed in the pursuit of that, whatever in detail it happens to be ; so that there is no situation in which the good will cannot be realised.

In the fourth place, in the conception of the moral ideal as the objective counterpart of the unity of the self as self-conscious, this theory provides a unitary principle for the determination of our duties. No doubt, as we have seen, in order that this principle may prescribe particular duties, it must be embodied in plans and policies and systems of institutions. But above all such detailed embodiments of the ideal, which at best are only imperfect realisations of it, there is the formal ideal itself to be used in our original moral reflection as the standard in the light of which we can pass judgement, not only on particular acts but also on institutions and ways of life ; and its unitary nature, however indefinite when expressed in general terms, and however difficult it may be to apply in particular situations, gives a guarantee that the more we reflect the more likely we are to discover what our duties are.

Finally, this theory enables us to see how the possibility of moral progress can be reconciled with the possibility of genuine or absolute moral goodness for all men in all societies, whatever their stage of development or degree of enlightenment ; for, according to it, moral goodness consists in loyalty to the requirements of one's own conception of the ideal, whatever in detail that conception and its requirements may be, and this is possible for all men, that is for all beings who have any ideal of conduct and are not mere animals ruled by each instinctive impulse as it arises. However crude and unenlightened men may be, they can do what they believe to be right, because they believe it to be right. Progress in moral goodness, therefore, consists in increasing loyalty to one's own ideal. On the other hand, we can get progress in moral insight or enlightenment, that is, in our grasp of the nature and needs of man and what he requires for his satisfaction, both as regards the ends which they prescribe and the rules which are necessary for their realisation. In other words, while moral goodness in the sense of devotion to one's own conception of the ideal is possible at all stages of development, the conceptions of the ideal which men entertain, the operative ideals in the light of which they decide their duties and obligations, vary from age to age and from individual to individual and even from time to time in the life of the same individual. They grow in worth and adequacy, in consistency and comprehensiveness, as they approximate more closely to the formal ideal. If we call progress in this latter sense progress in enlightenment, we see that progress in moral goodness and progress in enlightenment need not keep pace with one another.

According to this theory, moral goodness alone is good absolutely and to be realised always. Other goods are relative in two senses. The whole system of goods which constitutes the moral ideal is relative to the constitution of human nature ; and its constituent elements, the non-moral goods which enter into it, are not only relative to the needs of human nature, but they are also relative to one another in the sense that none of them is to be pursued always. Any one of them may at times have to give place to another, according to the requirements of the pattern of life which is the moral ideal. Moral rules are generalisations regarding the sorts of acts and the relations between individuals which either mankind as a whole or particular peoples have found to be involved in the realisation of that ideal or the living of that form of life. Their nature is determined by, and their authority is derived from, the structure of the ideal. This ideal, which is both the moral and the social ideal, is the standard by which ends and rules, policies and patterns, have to be tested ; but it is abstract and formal apart from the detailed forms of living in which different societies have tried to give it concrete expression. These expressions, however, are all partial and imperfect, and the formal ideal is always above them as the critic of their incompleteness and imperfections.

If these contentions are sound, the aspect of morality to which a consideration of the moralities of people other than ourselves is relevant is the outward and visible aspect, that which is concerned with the ends which are good and the rules which are right and the pattern of the form of life which in their interrelation they constitute.   It is men's ideas about these which vary from age to age and from people to people, while moral goodness is the same in all ages and among all peoples.   It is to them, therefore, that the researches of social anthropologists are specially relevant ; and it is with them that we shall be mainly concerned in the sequel.

OPERATIVE IDEALS

In my last lecture I tried to give an account in general terms of the framework of the moral life and of the way in which the main ethical notions are related to one another and to the constitution of human nature. We saw that the raw material of the moral life consists of the interests and inclinations, impulses and desires which have their roots in man's animal nature, and that its goal is the production of a way of life in which this material would be so adjusted and ordered that the persons, whose the interests and desires are, will find the maximum expression and satisfaction of their nature. We also saw how, in the process of trying to conceive and realise this ideal, systems of ends and rules of conduct come to be formulated, and how they are related to one another within the life of the moral agent and the pattern of the moral ideal.

I spoke of this process as if individuals or groups of individuals arrived at their conception of the good life as the result of the slow and painful process which has been called the dialectic of experience, that is, the process by which men arrive, as the result of trial and error, through failure and disappointment and partial success, at their idea of what will satisfy their nature and its needs. But while I believe this is what has happened in the history of the race, it certainly has not happened in the experience of any man known to history or anthropology. Men are not born adults into a community with no history, a community in which they would have to start with the raw material of human nature, and, without guidance or direction, discover their own rules for integrating this material into a coherent whole or personality. Each of us found in existence and embodied in the institutions and behaviour patterns which constitute the way of life of his people, the accumulated results of the slowly garnered wisdom of his ancestors, who have for many ages been engaged in trying to solve the moral problems with which every son of Adam is called on to deal anew. The individual arrives on the scene after many of the problems have already received partial and tentative solutions, and these solutions have been embodied in a way of life which is imposed upon him and recommended to him with the authority of those whom he respects most, and perhaps with the authority of a divine sanction as well. Moreover, as embodied in the institutions and customs of the social environment in which his mind develops, they mould his habits of thinking and feeling about certain matters, and largely contribute to make him the individual that he is, before he is in a position to think these matters out for himself; so that to the demands that the way of life of his people makes on him there is an answering echo in his own conscience.

What we find, then, is that the raw material of human nature which has to be organised into conformity with the moral and social ideal is the same everywhere and for all people; and the formal ideal at which they aim, that which gives direction to their moral and social efforts, when conceived in quite general terms, is also the same for all men. In other words, the starting-point, the problem and the goal are the same for all. But between the starting-point and the goal there are the solutions at which different peoples have arrived in their attempts to give concrete expression to the ideal, and to embody it in a way of life. It is these concrete and detailed articulations of the formal ideal, that is operative or embodied ideals, which provide practical guidance and prescribe the detailed duties and obligations of the moral agent.

Thus, in considering the moral life, we have (1) to look back to human nature and its needs as that which sets our problem; we have (2) to look forward to the formal ideal conceived in abstract and general terms, such as the good for man, the greatest good of the greatest number, the good of the self as a whole, the system of moral rules, or whatever other term we use to describe the standard of moral judgement. In between these we have (3) the embodied or operative ideals, which are attempts to bring (1) into line with (2), or to embody (2) in (1). But as we saw in the last lecture, we have to deal not merely with needs or desires but with persons, and to pass judgement not merely on acts but on agents; and the persons are related to other persons, the agents members of a community. Therefore the embodied or operative ideal has both a personal and a social aspect; and, while the two can and should be distinguished, they cannot be separated or understood apart from one another.

It is with these embodiments of the moral and social ideal that I shall be largely concerned in these lectures. Their importance for ethical theory seems to me considerable and largely neglected. Apart from them, the formal ideal, in whatever terms we conceive it, is apt to remain nebulous and abstract, and gives little practical guidance to the moral agent. Indeed, until we try to embody an ideal in a detailed way of life, we do not really grasp its nature or requirements. In our attempts to embody it, we may find that we have to modify our conception of it, not because it is too ideal but because it is not ideal enough, because, e.g., its elements are mutually incompatible in the sense that the realisation of one is inconsistent with the realisation of another. So that we discover whether an ideal is really a good ideal only in our efforts to realise it through trying to embody it in a relatively coherent way of life.

No doubt all embodiments of the moral ideal are partial and imperfect, and point beyond themselves to something more complete in the light of which they can be criticised and improved. They all lack the coherence and rationality of the neat and tidy pattern which I tried to put before you in general terms in my last lecture. They are efforts after unity and coherence rather than their complete achievement. Progress in moral insight or in enlightenment consists largely in seeing that the requirements of the formal ideal, which different people are trying to express in their ways of life, are only incompletely embodied in their systems of institutions, and therefore point beyond them and demand their modification. For it is what people find good but incomplete and so pointing beyond itself that suggests the line of advance towards a more adequate operative ideal. But before we can get beyond existing ideals, we must make our own the spirit which finds expression in them. Even the moral hero, let alone the ordinary man, is the child of his age, and how far he gets depends on the

F

point from which he starts.   Newton once said that he could not have done what he did if he had not stood on the shoulders of giants.   The work and insight of the moral giants of the past are embodied, partially and imperfectly no doubt, in the operative ideals of their peoples.   Before we can hope to stand on their shoulders we must sit at their feet, and learn what they have to teach us, as it has been formulated, not in vague general terms, but in the detailed arrangements of moral and social institutions with their rights and duties and obligations.

The ways of life of different peoples I regard as experiments, more or less successful, at giving concrete embodiment to the formal moral ideal.   Each of them is the result of a co-operative effort on the part of a group of people related by bonds of neighbourhood, and often of kinship, to work out a way of living which will satisfy the main needs of man, his needs as a moral and social and rational being, as well as his material needs.   I call these ways of life or operative ideals with which we shall be concerned experiments in living, in conceiving and living the good life, because they seem to be the nearest approach we can get to experiments in moral and social science. From the nature of the case we can never get genuine experiments in the social sciences, but in the variety of the operative ideals or ways of life, which different people have worked out, we get as good a substitute for experiments as the nature of moral and social facts will permit.[1]   Whether we say that God or nature has been experimenting with different ways of life, or that different people have been left alone to experiment for

---

[1] It is true that during the present century some attempts have been made to test ethical theories or at least to provide data for ethics by what might be regarded as an approach to experimental methods.   For example, Sharp and a number of his colleagues at Wisconsin University constructed imaginary situations in which individuals are called on to make moral decisions, and got specially selected groups of individuals to give their reactions to these situations first in writing and later in oral discussions.   (See Sharp, *Ethics* ; and *The Influence of Custom on Moral Judgement.*)   These and other similar enquiries seem to me to have considerable value, but they have also serious limitations from which the ' experiments ' described in the text are free.   For a short account of the nature of such experiments and a balanced judgement regarding their value and limitations see Lamont, *The Principles of Moral Judgement*, pp. 25 ff.   I shall have occasion to refer later to ways in which some of the results of these experiments corroborate some of the conclusions of the present work.

themselves, to work out their own salvation, we find many peoples who have been isolated or relatively isolated from outside contact for long periods — it may be generations, it may be centuries, it may be millennia — working out their own conception of the good life. The results of their efforts should be of interest and value to all students of the social sciences, but especially to students of psychology and ethics. As I have already suggested, they seem to me to provide important data for moral and social theory, and to be worthy of much more serious consideration than they usually receive.

It is true that these experiments are largely blind in the sense that they have not been deliberately planned or consciously thought out. That does not mean that they are not rational, but their rationality is implicit and unreflective rather than conscious or reflective. No doubt outstanding individuals from time to time played their part in developing them, and they contain no idea or ideal which has not originated in some mind, and all modifications of them are also the work of individual minds. But these modifications often come about because the frustration to which existing conditions give rise removes the incentives which keep certain institutions going, rather than because the new state of affairs is consciously before the minds of those who help to bring it about. It is indeed probable that the requirements of the formal ideal are more often present in the minds of men negatively as a dissatisfaction with their existing way of life rather than positively as a consciously entertained ideal.

It is also true that the good life, as a particular people conceive it and articulate it in their operative ideal, is never lived fully or completely realised in practice. I am concerned, however, not with their actual conduct or the extent to which they realise their ideal of the good life in their actual living, but rather with their conception of the good life, with their operative ideal itself, the ideal in the light of which they pass moral judgements and think of their duties and obligations.

Operative ideals, the results of the experiments of particular peoples in conceiving the good life and embodying their conceptions in the detailed structures of ways of life, thus act as links between the formal ideal and the particular desires and interests of human nature which provide its constituent elements. They serve the double purpose of giving concrete form to the demands which the requirements of the ideal make on the desires, and of moulding and organising the desires into some partial conformity to the requirements of the ideal. But between the separate desires and interests of individuals on the one hand, and the operative ideals on the other, there is interposed yet another link, namely institutions. They too perform a mediating function. They help to mould the particular desires of individuals into harmony with the pattern of the operative ideal and to interpret its requirements to the desires rooted in man's instinctive nature. They are better able to perform these functions because they are relatively permanent and usually handed on from one generation to another. They help to mould the desiring nature of man and to provide for its satisfaction as so moulded; while they are themselves modified through their interaction with one another within the framework of the operative ideal. Institutions also mediate between the individual and the society of which he is a member. The main impact of society on the individual is seldom direct. It is mediated through institutions which are the simplest forms of the co-operation between individuals which man's social nature makes essential. Operative ideals find expression in systems of interrelated and mutually adjusted institutions, so that most of the demands which the operative ideal makes on the individual come to him through the medium of institutions.

Thus between the formal ideal and the particular desires and interests of men there are two intermediate links, institutions and operative ideals. Accordingly, before giving illustrations of the operative ideals or experiments in living of different primitive peoples, I propose to devote this lecture to considering the nature and functions of institutions and operative ideals, and the importance for our understanding of morality of the way in which they mediate between human nature and needs, on the one side, and the moral ideal conceived in general terms, on the other. This should enable us to realise what we should look for as relevant to our ethical enquiries when we come to consider particular ways of life in detail. It should also help to give concreteness to our discussion of moral questions, and to show us how intimate is the relation between the moral and the social ideals as they operate in practice in the lives of men and societies.

Let us begin our analysis of the structure of operative ideals by considering the nature of institutions and their relation to human needs and interests. An institution is a pattern or framework of personal relationships within which a number of people co-operate, over a period of time and subject to certain rules, to satisfy a need, fulfil a purpose or realise a value.[1] Examples of such institutions are a family, a canoe crew, a hunting expedition, a war party, a religious society. Some of the needs which these institutions are intended to satisfy are recurrent and some continuous. Some are transitory and some permanent. And of the institutions themselves some are organised on the basis of kinship, others on the basis of neighbourhood and others on the basis of common interests. Some are permanent and compulsory: one is born into them and can leave them only by death. Others are voluntary and temporary, and so on. Each of these institutions lays down an ideal pattern of behaviour, determining the rights and duties of the individuals who take part in it, what they must do and what they must refrain from doing, and what benefits they can claim. In some simple institutions in which the number of people who co-operate is small, the relation between the welfare of all and the good of each is specially obvious. Moreover, the members are often bound together by ties of loyalty and affection; and rules are usually not very much in evidence; for most members are prepared to do more and to exact less than the rules strictly interpreted would require of them. Thus though rules are involved in the structure of such institutions

---

[1] Some sociologists use the term ' institutions ' with a more restricted meaning, namely to describe only the more fundamental and more permanent types of social organisation, those " which are found generally in a large number of cultures and which have existed through long periods of time ". Minor types they describe as group habits, associations, etc. (Ogburn and Nimkoff, *A Handbook of Sociology*, p. 365). For my purposes it is not necessary to distinguish the different kinds of organisation and it is convenient to have one term to describe them all. I have therefore followed the usage of Malinowski, Radcliffe-Brown and other anthropologists who use the term in the more general sense.

and though their observance is necessary for their effective functioning, they state the minimum which is required to keep the institutions going rather than the maximum which the members are prepared to do.

In the simpler conditions of primitive life, if not always in the more complex conditions of advanced societies, all who co-operate in an institution know the purpose or value which it fulfils, as well as the rules which govern the relations between the individuals who take part in it, and which determine the rights and duties of each. The purpose is a common or conjoint purpose in the sense that each of the individuals concerned expects some satisfaction from the successful working of the institution and some disappointment from its failure. But the satisfactions which different individuals expect need not necessarily be identical. While some of the values to be realised may be common to all the individuals, others may be enjoyed by some only; so that the duties of one become the privileges of another. For example, the values which husband and wife derive from the family may be in part common, such as a common interest in the children and home, and in part different but complementary, like their mutual interest in and services to one another. Similarly, chief and commoner, leader and follower in a war party, owner and hand in a canoe crew, priest and layman in a religious society have different duties to perform and expect somewhat different advantages in return. But each recognises that it is his interest as well as that of others that the institution should function successfully, though it may be his interest mainly or even only because he has a direct interest in the welfare of others. The driving force which keeps an institution going is the desires and interests of those who take part in it. It is necessary, therefore, that each of them should recognise it as good, and this involves that it should give him something which he wants in return for the duties and restrictions it imposes on him. If he is to play his part, a part which he and others recognise as necessary to the successful working of the institution, he must regard the whole arrangement, including the price paid in the way of restrictions and duties and the benefits received in the way of satisfactions and privileges, as worth while.

Now the individual finds institutions already in existence among his people. They serve to stimulate his interests and awaken his powers. They set before him ideals to pursue and ways in which to pursue them. Thus they at once control and direct human nature and try to shape it to their requirements. They point out to the individual how his desires must find expression if they are to be satisfied at all. If, for example, a man wants to have a wife and family and the status and satisfactions and services which go with them, the required pattern, which shows him how to proceed, is available in the marriage regulations and family arrangements which his people have developed. These socially approved and prescribed patterns make clear to him the duties and obligations which he must accept, as well as the rights and privileges which he may claim. In the same way, there are ideal patterns indicating how his other needs and interests, whether for agricultural produce, for taking vengeance on his enemy or for conciliating or controlling supernatural powers, are to be realised and satisfied — the things which he must do and which he must not do, the obligations to others which he must undertake and the rights which he must respect, as well as the rewards and compensations which he may claim if he complies with the prescribed regulations.

In a primitive society, at any rate, most of a man's duties and obligations and the rules which impose them are laid down in the ideal patterns of behaviour determining the co-operation of individuals in institutions; and what gives the rules their authority and what makes the duties obligatory is that they are necessary if the institutions are to function effectively, that is, if the needs, individual and social, are to be satisfied and the values realised. There are, no doubt, in every society individuals so constituted that they do not fit easily or well into the institutions of their people. Most societies have evolved roles which they assign to the more pronounced of these misfits. Otherwise they just become rebels against the established order and have to be dealt with as such. But there are many degrees between being ideally suited to and completely happy in a station and being a complete misfit. Unless the institutions of a people supply the great majority of its members with stations and ideals to which they can, without too great discomfort and too much frustration, adapt themselves, it contains the seeds of disintegration within itself.

In any relatively stable society, the majority of the citizens must find the way of life of their people on the whole good. This does not mean that they regard it as completely satisfactory or incapable of further improvement, or that it does not involve a great deal of preventable human misery and unhappiness. What it does mean is that they believe that, if all or even the great majority of the members of the society were to carry out their duties, pursue their ends and reap their rewards according to the spirit of their institutions, the resulting state of affairs would be worth while. It is true that an individual finds the institutions and way of life of his people good partly because he has been brought up under them and his habits have been formed by them. He may never have thought of any other; and he may regard many of their defects and the resultant evils and frustrations as inevitable, part of the human lot, due to causes which are beyond human control. But this by itself is not a sufficient explanation for his acceptance of their demands. He must also find that they work, in the sense that they provide some satisfaction for his main needs. It is because he in this sense finds the institutions of his people on the whole good, that he accepts the demands they make on him as right, and the duties they impose as obligatory : he recognises them as conditions or parts of a scheme which he regards as good both for himself and for his people.

Let us look briefly at some of the main needs or classes of needs which are at the basis of the most fundamental institutions — the needs for which some provision must be made in any way of life which is to be reasonably satisfactory. To begin with, man has certain biological needs which must be satisfied if he is to survive and prosper. These include the need for a place in which to reside and work, for food and shelter and safety, and for a mate. For the satisfaction of these needs the individual requires the co-operation of others ; and, in order that this co-operation may be effective, certain conditions must be fulfilled. There must be a certain amount of goodwill and mutual trust between those who co-operate. They must submit to certain restraints and restrictions, recognise certain rights on the part of others and fulfil certain duties. In other words, there must be rules governing the behaviour of those who co-operate. If, e.g., all or even a considerable number of them were to allow their acquisitive or pugnacious tendencies or their sex impulses to express themselves without restraint, or if they did not respect the life and property of their fellows, and made no efforts to fulfil their part in joint-undertakings, the possibility of co-operation would be at an end. Accordingly, round the attempts to satisfy these needs there has grown up a network of institutions in which what are regarded by the people concerned as the rules of the sort of co-operation necessary to satisfy the needs are embodied. Some of these rules are peculiar to particular institutions; others are more general conditions of the possibility of any form of co-operation; but even the more general rules seem to have been accepted in the first instance as conditions of particular forms of co-operation and the functioning of particular institutions, and to have been gradually extended to other relations and wider circles. Moreover, they may continue for a long time to be recognised as right in the service of one institution or in one set of relations and not in another in which their observance would have equally desirable results.

But even if we had a society with a system of institutions which made provision for the biological needs of man, i.e. for food and shelter, protection and reproduction, and such harmony among its members as would enable them to co-operate sufficiently to realise these provisions, it would be much nearer the merely animal level than any society known among men. For man has many needs and interests other than the merely biological. The satisfaction of these other needs may be less necessary for mere survival, but it is no less necessary if man is to be satisfied. For these other needs are no less deep-seated in human nature. It is indeed difficult in practice to separate these additional needs sharply from the merely biological; for some of them help to determine the forms which the satisfaction of the biological needs takes, because they can be satisfied at all only if the biological needs are satisfied in some ways and not in others. For example, man, however primitive, is not satisfied by getting sufficient nourishment to keep him alive and healthy. He wants food cooked and seasoned and served with some order and decency; and he may refuse food which is wholesome enough, if these other requirements are not satisfied. Moreover he may want company to enjoy it with him; he may desire to offer hospitality to friend or stranger; he may also want to offer some of his food to his gods. Such and many others are the needs which food may help to satisfy; and if they are not satisfied, not only does the individual remain unsatisfied, but he may even refuse the food however wholesome it may be. This means that the appetite for food, as it exists in man, cannot be satisfied by mere food; and that if the appetite is to be fully satisfied many other needs have to be satisfied too. What has to be satisfied is not a need but a person, a person with other needs besides that for mere food. Similar considerations apply to the satisfaction of the other biological and non-biological needs and their relations to one another.[1]

It is for this reason that it is so difficult to discover what a particular need requires for its satisfaction. We are apt to think that it requires what it seems to require among ourselves, under the institutions and cultural conditions of our own people. But other men with needs and natures like our own have found and are finding satisfaction for them in many other and very different ways, and all of them believe that their own way of satisfying them is what the needs require. We cannot say on *a priori* grounds that human nature or any of its needs can be satisfied only in a particular way, when there are men and societies scattered throughout the world supplying evidence that this is not so.[2] What will finally and fully satisfy human nature and its needs can be learned only by experience, and experience works by experiment, actual and ideal, and not by *a priori* considerations. Hence the value of studying the experiments which men have actually made, and the institutions and ways of life which they have developed and found good.

[1] It would be a great mistake to think that contemporary primitive peoples or any men known to history or anthropology are concerned exclusively with the satisfaction of the lower or merely biological needs.

[2] Cf. Lowie, *Primitive Society*, p. 161.

Let me mention just a few of the more fundamental non-biological needs which are common to all men, and specially relevant to our problem. We have seen that man needs the co-operation of his fellows to satisfy even his biological needs, but he also finds their companionship and friendship good in itself. He wants their esteem and approval, their assent to his views, and their favourable emotional reaction to his conduct. Whether this is due, as some think, to his having been brought up in a family in intimate relations with others, or whether, as others think, it is an innate characteristic, we need not enquire. In either case, it is so urgent a need that to be deprived of its satisfaction, whether by being driven away from the company of his fellows or being treated by them with scorn or ridicule, is one of the most cruel forms of punishment.[1] Among primitives, the need for the company and the favourable attitude of his fellows is one of the strongest weapons which society has against the individual who refuses to comply with the pattern of their way of life. It becomes even more powerful when the community of which he considers himself a member includes not only his contemporaries but also their dead ancestors. In such circumstances, expulsion from the society of the living members of his people may carry with it sentence of exclusion from their company in the afterworld as well, a fate which in the opinion of some tribes is worse than death itself. Among all peoples, however, whether civilised or primitive, man desires the companionship, the fellowship and the friendship of others as one of the conditions of any life which is worth while. It is, of course, true that a man may trust his own insight against the considered opinion of his fellows, and may go his own way despite their disapproval, but he is discontented unless he can persuade them, or at least some of them, to share his beliefs and value judgements.

But, as we have already noted, man not only needs the co-operation, and desires the favourable attitude of his fellows, he has also a natural interest in their welfare and happiness. Other things being equal, he desires the good of those with whom he comes in contact. This spontaneous urge of man to promote the well-being of others, which is recognised by

[1] Cf. James, *Principles of Psychology*, i. 293-4.

Aristotle and Butler, Hume and Green, McDougall and Campbell [1] and many others, has to compete with his other interests and is at times overwhelmed by them. Its expression is apt to be controlled and directed by social forces, which stimulate its expression along certain lines and repress it along others. Its range may be circumscribed by ignorance, lack of imagination and of opportunities for contact, but it is always there ready to assert itself whenever the conditions are favourable for its expression. All that we know of primitive man goes to confirm that this is as true of him as of civilised man. Observers are agreed that altruism is as natural to the primitive as egoism. A recognition of man's natural or disinterested desire to promote the good of those with whom he comes in contact seems to me essential for the understanding of many moral and social facts.

From our present point of view the importance of these social desires and interests is not so much that they form the bases of specific institutions as that they tend to manifest themselves in every institution. Wherever men are brought into close contact with one another, they tend to develop social sentiments and mutual helpfulness and loyalty. It is true that these are often more in evidence in some institutions than in others, even within the same society. But in all of them they serve a double purpose. On the one hand, so far as they assert themselves at all, they tend to modify institutions into line with their requirements, thus eliminating their harsher aspects. On the other hand, they help to produce a cohesion and solidarity, a mutual trust and goodwill, which enable institutions to function effectively.

All men also desire security; and this desire expresses itself in two main forms which give rise to two different types of institution. The one is concerned with protection from our fellow-men both within and outside our community; and it gives rise to institutions to maintain internal order and to provide protection from external enemies. The other is con-

<hr>

[1] Aristotle, *Nicomachean Ethics*, 1155 a; Butler, *Sermons* (ed. Gladstone), pp. 38-9; Hume, *Enquiry Concerning the Principles of Morals* (ed. Selby-Bigge), p. 226; Green, *Prolegomena to Ethics*, Sect. 199; McDougall, *An Introduction to Social Psychology*, 18th Ed., pp. 75-81, 276; Campbell, *Moral Intuition and the Principle of Self-realisation* (British Academy Lecture, 1948), p. 32.

cerned with protection against the hazards and hardships which are, or are believed to be, due to causes beyond human control; and it gives rise to institutions which express man's attitude to the powers that rule his world. Men in all societies known to us feel a need for at-one-ment with these powers. However they conceive them and by whatever means they try to conciliate or control them, they are never a matter of indifference to them.

Another need which is common to all societies and finds expression in institutions, which may be specially designed to meet the need or which may be intended primarily to serve other purposes, is education. No society allows its young to grow up without guidance. They all desire to pass on to the new generation the accumulated skill and wisdom of their ancestors.

Again, the men of every age and civilisation of which we have knowledge have some interest in order and beauty. Even the most primitive men embellish their stone implements. They decorate their canoes and spears and spades. They enjoy song and dance and rhythm. They are capable of being bored, and to find refreshment they resort to games and other forms of amusement. In fact, even the most primitive people pay so much attention to what Linton calls ' non-utilitarian embroideries ' that he justly concludes that, whatever else we may say of them, we cannot describe them as utilitarians.[1]

Moreover, all men have a desire for knowledge, a desire to explore and understand the things with which they come in contact. True it is sometimes held that primitive men are pragmatists and have no interest in knowledge for its own sake; but this is difficult to reconcile with the fact that many of them take a keen interest in observing plants which they do not use for food, and animals which they neither use nor fear. They want explanations of events and happenings, however crude from our point of view may be some of the explanations which will satisfy their curiosity. Some of them take an intense interest in trying to discover how new things work, and all of them have an interest in gossip. They want to know what other people are thinking and feeling and doing; and they seem to derive a

[1] *The Study of Society*, pp. 88-90, 440.

satisfaction from this knowledge, even when it has no further or utilitarian value.[1]

Now round these and many other social and spiritual needs and aspirations, as well as round the merely biological, there have grown up institutions, ideal patterns of behaviour to be followed, to ensure their satisfaction and fulfilment. The needs which I have been describing are common to all men; and, therefore, if we defined an institution with reference to the need which it satisfies, the basic institutions of mankind would be everywhere the same. But there is no one-to-one correspondence between institutions and needs or interests. One institution may and often does satisfy more than one need, and the same need may be satisfied at least in part by more than one institution. Moreover, when a new need arises there is a tendency to attach the provision for meeting it to an existing institution rather than create a new one; and so the same need may be provided for by different institutions in different societies. Therefore, while all peoples have institutions to satisfy all their basic needs, the same institutions do not satisfy the same needs everywhere. An institution as a rule also involves not only overt activities but also the manipulation of part of the natural environment, the use of tools and implements. It has, therefore, a visible and external aspect; but it exists not so much in such external arrangements as in habits of thinking and feeling, and in the attitudes of individuals to their fellows and their external environment.

But though the institutions of different peoples vary considerably in the bases of their organisation, in the ideal patterns of behaviour which they prescribe and in the external arrangements to which they give rise, every people has developed institutions to fulfil the different functions which I have indicated, to meet their biological, their social and their spiritual needs. They have all been faced with the same basic problems. They have solved them well or ill, but solve them they must, some on pain of extinction, others on pain of major unhappiness.

[1] Cf. Stout, *Analytic Psychology*, ii. 100: " The first strong development of pure curiosity arises in connection with social relations. It consists in the felt need to know what those around him are doing or thinking. The greater part of all ordinary conversation, both among the civilised and the uncivilised, illustrates this primary social impulse."

And, however much the institution which satisfies a particular need may differ in details from people to people, and whatever be the purpose of the institution, whether economic advantage, protection from enemies or religious peace of mind, all institutions involve co-operation between individuals, and, among primitive people at any rate, the relations between the individuals who co-operate are, and are recognised as being personal relations, and the demands which an institution makes on him are regarded by the individual as duties which he owes to the others.

Now no operative ideal or way of life is a mere aggregate of institutions or unrelated patterns of behaviour; just as no personality is a mere aggregate of needs and desires. Accordingly, the most fundamental question which has to be con sidered in trying to understand the nature of a way of life concerns the manner in which institutions and the patterns of behaviour which they involve are related to one another within the framework of the social order, just as the most important question in considering the personal ideal of an individual concerns the way in which different values and interests are related to one another within it. As we have seen, if the different needs of men are to be satisfied, if their different interests are to be realised, they must be fitted into a pattern. Similarly, the institutions of a society must be interwoven into a relatively coherent way of life.

The need for this adjustment of institutions, the forms which it takes, and the way in which it takes place, follow from conditions which we have already described. The function of institutions is to provide for the satisfaction of the needs and desires of men. These needs and desires can find expression and satisfaction in many different ways. Some ways of satisfying one need conflict with, others are compatible with and may even help towards, the satisfaction of other needs. Therefore, the requirements of the institutions which have been developed to satisfy them may conflict with or may reinforce one another. Accordingly, if the individuals whose the needs are, are to be on the whole satisfied, the institutions which provide for their satisfaction must be mutually adjusted, so as to avoid major clashes between their requirements. This adjustment takes the form partly of fitting the incompatible requirements of different institutions into a temporal pattern, so that the demands of the institutions concerned with, e.g., the need for food, for protection, for revenge, for religious peace of mind, give rise to a time sequence of activities which will at least not clash with one another and may reinforce one another; and partly of arranging institutions and the needs which they serve in an order of precedence whereby the relative importance of their requirements may be determined, if they clash with one another. In the course of these adjustments institutions develop other and still more intimate connections which make them interdependent in ways which we shall consider later.

The mutual interaction of institutions within the framework of an operative ideal or way of life is not the only factor which helps to determine the forms which they take. We also find a process of mutual interaction between human needs, which as we have seen are not entirely plastic, and the institutions which provide for their satisfaction. And both these forms of interaction, between different institutions and between institutions and needs, are not only going on all the time and mutually modifying one another, but they also take place in interaction with the natural environment of the society concerned. Accordingly, the forms which institutions take are determined partly by the needs which they satisfy, partly by the natural environment to which they are responses, and partly by the way of life in which they are elements. It is the fact that, within limits, human nature and needs are plastic and modifiable which makes this mutual adjustment of institutions possible. The fact that they are modifiable only within limits makes the adjustment difficult, and helps to determine the part which institutions play in the structure of operative ideals. Progress in the operative ideal of a people, therefore, consists mainly in the growing coherence of the pattern which results from the interaction within it of the three factors : human nature, natural environment and institutions. This adjustment, however, is never perfect nor is the resulting pattern of the operative ideal completely coherent. The friction and consequent frustration which remain point the way to further progress and fresh adjustments.

. How then does this adjustment of institutions take place ? It takes place through the interaction of their requirements in the minds of individuals. Institutions, as we have seen, exist primarily as habits of thinking and feeling and acting in the minds of individuals. This is their common meeting-ground where they mutually modify one another. It is the requirements of individuals which they meet more or less adequately, and it is the appeal which they make to individuals which keeps them going. The same individual takes part in the working of many institutions, and they all make demands on him which have somehow to be adjusted. It is true that the normal human being has a great capacity for entertaining inconsistent beliefs, adopting inconsistent attitudes and behaving in inconsistent ways in different contexts and connections, especially as long as the inconsistent elements can be kept in water-tight compartments and do not come into open and conscious conflict. But though the average man, whether primitive or civilised, is only partially and intermittently rational, he is still aware of himself as one amid the variety of his beliefs and attitudes and activities, and there are therefore limits to the inconsistencies which he can harbour. Accordingly, though institutions may in the first instance develop independently, if in practice the requirements of one frustrate those of another, or if two require incompatible lines of conduct in the same situation, some adjustment of their claims is necessary in the interests both of peace of mind and of effective action. Moreover, the individual who forms certain habits of thinking and feeling and acting in the service of one institution has a tendency to carry them with him when he behaves as a member of others ; so that there tends to be a certain affinity or congruity of spirit between the different institutions of a particular people. In other words, the mutual adjustment of institutions takes place in the same way and for the same reason as the ends desired by an individual tend to become integrated into systems or patterns, that is because men are self-conscious, aware of themselves as one amid the variety of their experiences and activities, and therefore desire some measure of consistency in their way of life ; and the ideal towards which this mutual adjustment tends both in the case of institutions and the desires which they serve

G

is a form of life with a unitary pattern corresponding to the unity of the self as self-conscious.

Accordingly, if the individuals who co-operate in them are to be on the whole satisfied, institutions must be at least so adjusted as to be compossible. But this adjustment does not normally take place at the conscious or reflective level, much less as the result of deliberate planning. Among most peoples there is much uncritical acceptance of and unquestioning allegiance to traditional ways of life ; and the individuals who are frustrated by traditional institutions seldom think out the causes of their condition. Nevertheless, they feel the discomfort and the frustration, and in time these undermine the incentives which keep the institutions going, and so lead to their modification or decay. Moreover, as we shall see in detail later, institutions are so connected that the satisfactions gained in one provide the incentives necessary to do the duties required by another or others ; and therefore changes in one indirectly produce changes in others. It is true that people do not normally think out these interconnections between their institutions, and that even when they deliberately change one they seldom realise the indirect effects which this will produce in others. Still less is this so, when the changes come about unconsciously as the result of the frustration to which a particular institution leads. Nevertheless, the interconnections are there and operative, and as a result changes in one institution lead to changes in others which are neither foreseen nor desired. The clearest evidence of this is to be found in the effects produced on the ways of life of primitive peoples by their contact with more advanced civilisations, but it can be illustrated from the way of life of any people. As a result of these interconnections of institutions, we cannot understand the ways in which they work or the incentives which keep them going, the responses which they evoke or the judgements which are passed on them, unless we consider them in their relations to one another within the context of the way of life of which they form parts.

In recent years a great deal has been written about the way in which institutions, and especially the institutions of primitive peoples, are integrated into structural patterns constituting ways of life or patterns of culture. But different authorities are apt to mean different things by such terms as the ' pattern of a culture ' or the ' integration of a way of life ', and it is essential that we should distinguish between these different meanings ; for their implications for moral and social theory are different, and the evidence in support of them seems to vary in cogency.

Functional anthropologists, like Malinowski and Radcliffe-Brown, mean by the integration or unity of a culture that its different institutions interlock and interpenetrate in the sense that the satisfactions gained in one provide incentives to the performance of the duties required by others. For example, the requirements of a family and the satisfactions it provides may be the motives for performing the duties of economic or agricultural institutions ; or participation in religious cere-monies may foster the spirit of goodwill which is necessary for performing the duties required by social institutions. In this way, the different institutions of a particular people interweave and support one another, with the result that we cannot under-stand one without taking account of others and it may be of the whole of which they are parts. The evidence in support of this contention seems to me overwhelming and conclusive. We shall find many examples of it in our account of primitive societies ; and, as the way in which this interlocking takes place varies from people to people, I shall postpone further illustration of it till we meet actual instances of it in their concrete context. Meantime, I want to consider what precisely is involved in the concept of this integration or interpenetration of institutions, and to distinguish it from other and, as it seems to me, less cogent conceptions regarding patterns of culture.

The integration of institutions in a way of life to which the functional anthropologists call attention does not necessarily mean that the parts of a way of life are all different expressions of one principle, or that they are logically connected, or even that a particular institution might not fit equally well into another pattern or way of life. It means only that they are psychologically connected in the minds of the individual mem-bers of the society, in the habits of thinking and feeling and acting which have grown up in relation to them ; and that as a result they have become so adjusted that their requirements are not only compatible, but that they mutually support one another. It means in fact that the pattern of the way of life is the objective counterpart of the unity of the minds or personalities of the individual members who share it. Neither is usually, or perhaps ever, completely coherent, and such unity as they have is usually below the conscious or reflective level, but the one is the measure of the other.

Other anthropologists, like Benedict and Mead, regard the unity or integration of a pattern of culture as meaning that the culture is the consistent expression of a particular attitude of mind or spirit, or of the dominance of one or a particular set of values. I do not think that they distinguish clearly between these two grounds of integration. For instance, of the three examples of ' patterns of culture ' given by Miss Benedict in her book with that title, one — that of the Pueblo — has as its unifying principle the spirit of moderation. Miss Benedict traces in detail how this spirit or attitude finds expression in every sphere of their life and modifies the nature of institutions, which they have in common with or have even borrowed from their neighbours who are much more given to excesses. But while this attitude, the high value which they attach to self-restraint and moderation, gives a certain unity and consistency to their culture, it neither determines what their institutions should be nor what duties they should require. All that it demands is that, whatever they do, they should not carry it to excess nor get too excited about it. Now this is quite different from the functional interdependence whereby the different institutions of a people dovetail into and support one another in the way described by Malinowski and Radcliffe-Brown ; and it still leaves unanswered the question with which we are primarily concerned, namely : What determines the particular duties of individuals ? For what the spirit of moderation determines is not so much what people should do as certain characteristics of how they should do it. It is true that a dominant spirit or attitude leaves its mark on all the institutions of a people. It may even rule out certain institutions as being inconsistent with it ;[1] but it is a common characteristic rather

---

[1] It is, however, significant in this connection that the spirit of moderation of the Pueblo does not rule out the practice of scalp-collecting and

than an interconnecting principle, an abstract rather than a concrete universal; and, therefore, it does not bring to light the principle by which duties are determined, the principle which guides the choice of the moral agent.

Another of the cultures examined by Miss Benedict is characterised not so much by a dominant attitude like moderation, as by an exaggerated and one-sided emphasis on one of man's primary interests or impulses, that of self-assertion. This emphasis leads to an attitude of self-reliant individualism, competition and even aggressiveness. This exaggerated value placed on one interest gives some consistency to a culture, but it also may express itself in many different ways of life, or through many different institutions among different peoples. It may reveal itself, for example, in the warlike activities of some Indian tribes or the acquisitive tendencies of some capitalistic societies, as well as in the accumulation of wealth to be destroyed in self-glorification and the discomfiture of one's neighbour, as among the Kwakiutl.[1] But, like the dominant attitude of the Pueblo, it does not determine what the institutions of a people should be, or what duties they should require, but only the spirit in which the duties should be performed.

Nevertheless, this dominance of one interest differs from the attitude of moderation which characterises the Pueblo culture in one important respect. The latter is quite consistent with the satisfaction of all the main human interests, as long as this is done with moderation, but the dominance of one interest like self-assertion is not. If the latter is carried to its extreme or ideal limit, it becomes destructive of any way of life. As Miss Benedict herself points out, it is only the chieftain class who could pursue it in Kwakiutl, and they could do it only because the conditions under which the community found themselves made living easy and provided a surplus of wealth in addition to what was required for normal consumption. What is more important, even they could only carry it out within limits which were consistent with some satisfaction of other

witch-hunting among them, though it has no doubt eliminated the worst excesses which are often connected with them. This seems to show that their way of life is not so coherent as Miss Benedict suggests.

[1] The people whose way of life is chosen by Miss Benedict to illustrate it.

interests. If they exceeded these limits, their followers would not provide them with the wherewithal to continue their destructive pastime. The same considerations apply to an even more marked degree to the natives of Dobu, the third people whose way of life is analysed by Miss Benedict.

I dwell on these considerations for three reasons. First, I want to point out the difference between such patterns of culture, whether they result from a dominant attitude or from the special position given to one interest, and those which are due to the functional interdependence of the institutions of a society and which result from an attempt to satisfy human nature as a whole.

Secondly, Miss Benedict and those who share her view hold that different societies are not engaged in doing or trying to do the same thing. There are, they contend, so many different possible interests or values, any one of which may be given the dominant position, that no society can pursue them all. Each society has therefore to make a selection and seek to realise the particular values which it has chosen. According to this view, different societies do not just arrive at different solutions of the same problem. Even their problems are different. As Miss Benedict puts it, " they are travelling along different roads in pursuit of different ends ",[1] and therefore the results of their efforts are " incommensurable ".

Now this seems to me a mistaken conception. All societies seem to me to be trying to satisfy human nature as a whole, and, therefore, trying to go in the same direction towards the same goal. Of course, the results of their efforts are different, but the nature and needs of man provide a basis of comparison between them. It may well be that this nature and those needs may be satisfied in more than one form of life, and certainly we are not in a position today to say that any one form of life which has been worked out in detail is just right, and all others merely wrong. Therefore, those anthropologists who emphasise this aspect are justified in insisting on the desirability of tolerance towards those who have made, or are making, social experiments, and on the need for an empirical attitude which would learn from the experiments which have been made, as against

[1] *Patterns of Culture*, p. 161.

a priori speculation, as to the ways in which it is or is not possible to satisfy human nature.

There are, however, ways in which we may test the adequacy of ways of life which have the kind of unity described by Miss Benedict. We may, e.g., consider whether a way of life whose unity is based on the dominance of a particular attitude or interest contains the seeds of disintegration within itself in the sense that its principle is incapable of being universalised without disastrous consequences.[1] This is true, e.g., of the exaggerated self-assertion of the Kwakiutl. A particular personality may be integrated on this principle, but the result is liable to be unstable, because it fails to satisfy the whole nature of the individual. It is even more unsatisfactory as the basis of a social order; for a society in which everybody consistently acted on it would disintegrate in anarchy. When it is applied to the relations between societies, as it unfortunately so often still is, the results are no less disastrous. Moreover, while we get a few societies to whose ways of life one dominant attitude or major interest gives a certain unity and consistency, even Miss Benedict admits[2] that this is probably not true of all; and to get the measure of consistency, which she attributes to the ways of life of the peoples whom she describes with such charm, Miss Benedict, as Boas points out in his introduction to her book,[3] chose a few rather extreme examples; and even these she presents in a somewhat one-sided way.[4] The impression which is apt to be left by her presentation is that primitive societies are more consistent than any societies in fact are.

Thirdly, when all allowance has been made for these considerations, views such as Miss Benedict's emphasise an important point of principle, namely, that there is a spirit or an attitude of mind which pervades the institutions or the way of life of a particular people, and that they cannot be understood unless we enter into and appreciate this inner attitude. There is a certain affinity between the institutions of a particular people which makes them different from what they would be

---

[1] I shall return to this point when I consider the nature of moral progress in Lecture XV.

[2] *Patterns of Culture*, pp. 161 ff.　　　　[3] *Ibid.* pp. x-xi.

[4] See above, p. 88, note 1.

among other peoples however much their external arrangements may resemble one another.[1] Nevertheless, the network of institutions which constitutes the way of life of a people is seldom the expression of one principle or a logically consistent whole. It is more often a compromise based on the limitation and mutual adjustment of different principles, a psychological unity which is the result of the dovetailing and interlocking of interests rather than a logically coherent whole. Its unity or adequacy can only be considered in the light of the nature of man for which it is an attempt to provide.

It is of course easy, either for an individual or a society, to get consistency by subordinating every other consideration to one particular interest or value; but this will not give the comprehensiveness necessary to satisfy all the needs of the individual, much less those of all the individuals who constitute a society. Accordingly, the mutual adjustment of institutions while a necessary is not a sufficient condition of a satisfactory form of life. All the institutions in which a form of life is embodied may be perfectly adjusted, but it may nevertheless fail to make adequate provision for some or even for many of the most fundamental needs of man. And therefore, as I have said, the interaction between human needs and institutions is as important for the development of a satisfactory social order as is the interaction of institutions with one another; for if the way of life which the institutions of a society constitute fails either to make adequate provision for the main needs of its members or imposes on them, or on too many of them, such restraints and restrictions as leave them frustrated and unhappy, it contains a source of contradiction within itself which makes its permanence unlikely. This is specially so among the smaller and simpler peoples who have little political authority or organised force which would enable them to impose a way of life on recalcitrant members. If, therefore, the pattern of their way of life is to be complied with, it must provide compensations and rewards which are obvious and attractive to the majority of their members.

These considerations, no doubt, also explain why we sometimes find institutions which are not so much consistent with

[1] Cf. Lowie, *Primitive Religion*, ch. ix; and Hogbin, *Experiments in Civilisation*, ch. x, especially pp. 227-8.

the other institutions of the people whose they are, in the sense of being based on the same principles with them, as complementary to them in the sense that they provide an outlet for impulses and desires which are frustrated by, or given inadequate expression in their main institutions. For example, we sometimes find as a regular institution periods of licence, occasions when the usual restraints of ordinary life are removed. Such institutions cannot be integrated with the other institutions of the people concerned as parts of one consistent whole. Open conflict can only be prevented by keeping such activities to stated periods. This, however, does not reconcile them with the requirements of other institutions whose rules have to be suspended while these activities are taking place; and this is not integration but failure to integrate.

The integration or mutual adjustment of institutions is so important because it is the incompatible demands which institutions make on individuals that give rise to the most acute conflicts of duties and clashes of loyalties. These conflicts give rise to moral perplexity, perplexity as to what is right, what ought to be done. These are quite different from the ordinary moral conflicts in which a man has no doubt what his duty is, but finds it so opposed to his inclinations that he is tempted not to do it. Conflicts of duties are common enough among all peoples whether primitive or civilised. They arise, e.g., between what a man regards as his duty to the family which he has created, his wife and children, and his duty to the family to which he originally belonged, his kin by blood; or between his duty to his friend, to whom he has sworn lifelong loyalty, and that to his clan or group, who may be at war with those of his friend. Sometimes, indeed, we find conflicting principles at the very core of a way of life, between its most fundamental institutions;[1] and unless some adjustments were made, some compromise arrived at, the very foundations of the society would crumble. But despite such adjustments, conflicts do from time to time occur, and they are a source of weakness to the society and of unhappiness to its members. For conflicts between the institutions of a society tend to be repeated in the personalities of its members. They are due to inconsistencies

[1] For examples of such conflicts see below, pp. 113-15, 144-5.

not only in the social pattern, but also in the personal ideals and minds of its individual members ; for, as we have seen, the one is the counterpart of the other.

If the adjustments in the way of life of a society were regarded as perfect, there would be no stimulus to or hope of further progress, except as the result of outside interference, whether in the way of contact with other people or a change in the natural environment. But while such outside influences have often proved an effective stimulus to change in the way of life of a people, whether in the way of progress or regress, there are at least two other factors which tend to bring about such changes. One is the pressure of the needs and interests of human nature which are inadequately provided for by existing institutions ; the other is the conflict of the requirements of different institutions which are based on principles inadequately adjusted to one another. Both these forces are probably operative all the time in every society. It is true that in some primitive societies they operate slowly and imperceptibly ; but we are assured on good authority [1] that there is no society, regarding whose condition over any length of time we have reliable evidence, in which such changes are not found to be taking place.

In every society, then, we find ideal patterns of behaviour embodied in working institutions. The institutions are part fact, part idea ; for none of them ever in practice completely embodies its ideal. These institutions are mutually adjusted through their interaction in the minds of the individual members of the society, but again this adjustment is never perfect. The way of life which they constitute, therefore, points to an ideal which it only partially embodies. We can thus distinguish between the formal ideal which cannot be described in detail but only in such general terms as the good for man, or the greatest good of the greatest number, or the good of the self as a whole, and an operative ideal which is embodied in the system of institutions of a particular people.

Even within the embodied or operative ideal and its constituent institutions, the form of life which has been conceived in detail, there are still further distinctions to be drawn. We

[1] Linton, *The Study of Society*, p. 296.

may distinguish between the spirit and the letter of a way of life or an institution; for the spirit can never completely find expression in rules or patterns of behaviour. Indeed if men as a whole were not prepared to act in the spirit of an institution, and do more than the rules require from them, it is doubtful if any institution would function effectively. We may thus distinguish between the minimum requirements of an institution or way of life in the sense of that short of which the individual is regarded as blameworthy, and the ideal demands of the best that the individual can conceive, or that for which his fellows would regard him as praiseworthy; and there are many stages between these limits. Moreover, individuals enter some more some less into the spirit of their institutions. There is a great difference between the requirements of an institution or operative ideal as it is conceived by the best men in their best moments and as it is conceived by ordinary men in their average moments. There is also a wide variety in the powers of mind and imagination of the different members of any society, and, therefore, some see much further and appreciate more clearly the relation between what is required of them in particular circumstances and the good of their society as a whole.

If the view which I have been suggesting is sound in principle, it follows that the personal and the social ideal, and moral and social theory, should not be so sharply separated as is often done. But though it seems to me important to recognise the intimate relation between them, it is no less important not to confuse them.

What, then, is the difference between the points of view of moral and social theory? To any way of life or any piece of conduct, there are, as we have seen, two sides: an inner and spiritual side, a side of motives, beliefs and attitudes of mind, and an outer and visible side of rules and ends and patterns of behaviour. Though the two sides are inseparable, they can and should be distinguished. Morality is concerned with both sides. It is concerned both with the actions or courses of conduct which are right and with the motives from which they should be done. Social theory is concerned mainly with the outer aspect, the structure of society, its ideal patterns of behaviour, systems of rights and duties, considered in abstraction from the spirit or attitude or motives of the individuals who fulfil the duties and claim the rights. Thus the concern of morality with the outer side, the side of rightness, of rules and ideal patterns, brings it into close connection with social theory; but its emphasis on the inner side, the side of motives, distinguishes it from social theory. Its concern with the inner side is the distinguishing characteristic of morality; and it is to the inner side that moral goodness in the strict sense belongs. In these lectures I am mainly concerned with the outer aspect, the ideals which different peoples consider good and the rules which they regard as right. It is, therefore, all the more necessary to insist here that no ideal pattern, no rules, no system of rights and duties will give us the whole of what is morally required of us. It is also required of us that we should adopt certain attitudes and act from certain motives. Even if a man knows what is right, and in that sense what his duty is, he may do it, if he does it at all, in a spirit of generosity and goodwill, perhaps even doing more and exacting less than others have a right to expect; or he may do it in a halting and niggardly manner, doing the minimum which he can without being blameworthy, and doing even that from fear of unpleasant consequences. While this makes no difference to the outer aspect or to what is regarded as right, it makes all the difference to the moral value of the actions and the agent.

It is of course true that it is the inner aspect, the motives of individuals, which makes a way of life a reality and keeps its institutions functioning; and, therefore, no complete account can be given of them without reference to this inner side. Nevertheless, not only may we for certain purposes consider the structural pattern of a way of life by itself in abstraction from the motives which keep it going, as is done by social theory, but we have to do so when we are trying to discover or understand what is right. But while insisting that this is only one aspect of the ethical problem, and that there is another aspect which distinguishes ethical from social theory, it is no less important to recognise that morality has this outer and visible aspect, that it is concerned with the principles on which we discover what is right, and that this brings it into a very intimate relationship to social theory.

Even from the outer aspect, the point of view of what is right or what ought to be done, there is a difference between the individual and the social ideal. It is true that the social ideal exists only in the minds of individuals, in their habits of thinking and feeling, in the judgements they pass and the ideals they entertain, but the whole of it does not normally exist in any one mind. The parts of it which exist in different minds overlap in all sorts of intricate ways, but normally no individual has sufficient knowledge and experience to cover the whole social pattern. And even if he had, it would not be his duty to realise it all. As far as its requirements from him are concerned, the individual sees the social ideal from a particular point of view, a point of view determined by his station and his gifts. No doubt in the simple conditions of many primitive societies there is less difference between the ideal as it is conceived by different individuals and, therefore, less difference between the personal and the social ideal than there is in the more complex and advanced societies. The members of a primitive or any small society normally recognise the identity of their own good and that of their people, even though they may find the requirements of their society very much opposed to their inclinations or their immediate advantage. Nevertheless, even in the simplest and least complex societies, there is sufficient differentiation of function to make some variation in the ideals of different individuals inevitable. For example, the ideal for a war leader d.ffers from that for his followers; where there is a difference of rank, the ideal for a commoner is not the same as that for a chief; and in no case is the ideal the same for a man and a woman.

Moreover, the social ideal involves elements which are not necessary for the realisation of the personal ideals of many of its members. For example, the needs of at least some adults could be met and their ideals realised without any reference to the coming into being, the education and training of other individuals who will carry on the society; but the needs of the society could not be met nor the social ideal realised without such a reference.

Acceptance of such a close connection as is here suggested between the moral and social ideals and between moral and social theory would, no doubt, have the effect of making moral philosophy more difficult and perhaps more controversial, or at least controversial in a different sense; for on this view there may not be so much unanimity about the judgements of value which constitute its data as many writers on ethics are apt to take for granted. It would, however, make it more concrete and less academic and perhaps more helpful to the moral agent, especially in a society like our own, which is not only rapidly changing but trying consciously to reconstruct many of its institutions; and which, therefore, presents the individual with moral problems which mere goodwill, however necessary and important, will not alone enable him to solve.

It may be objected, however, that the primary business of ethics is not to give practical guidance to the moral agent, but to understand and explain the nature of morality. With this contention I am in entire agreement. Ethics is a theoretical enquiry. It is not its business to tell the moral agent what his duties are, or on what principles he should base his moral judgements. Its business is rather to bring to light the principle or principles on which he does in fact base his most considered moral judgements and, if there is more than one principle, to show the relation between them. Nothing which I have said is inconsistent with this. What I am contending is that the principle or principles on which the moral agent bases his judgements must be principles which give practical guidance. Otherwise they would not serve his purpose, which is to discover what he ought to do in particular circumstances. Unless the moral agent's procedure, even in his most reflective moments and his most considered judgements, is irrational and arbitrary, unless, that is, the moral life is a chaos of unrelated particular judgements, it must involve or proceed according to some principle or principles, even though these may at times be operative in the mind of the moral agent rather than consciously before it. My contention is that these principles are principles which give practical guidance, and that, therefore, unless the principles brought to light by ethical theory are principles which supply such guidance, the theorist has not done his work thoroughly. It seems to me that much recent ethical writing and many recent ethical theories are too abstract and general, too remote from the concrete facts of the moral life as it is lived from day to day. This is one of the reasons why I want to bring it into closer relation to social theory and to social institutions in connection with which men have, and recognise that they have, particular rights and duties, privileges and responsibilities. But I am concerned with the social ideal and social structure, not for their own intrinsic interest, but because they set the individual his moral duties and obligations.

Do I suggest, then, I may be asked, that there are no moral rules which have a general application, rules which are the conditions of the functioning of all institutions or ways of life, rules which apply to all relations between persons, and which therefore do not derive their justification or authority from any particular institution or way of life or specific relation between persons? I shall return to the nature of moral rules and their place in the moral life after I have considered the ways of life of some representative primitive peoples. Meantime I shall confine myself to four observations. (1) There are general rules which are the conditions of effective co-operation anywhere, and they tend to be recognised as right by all peoples; but the limits within which they are recognised, the interpretation which is placed on them, and the exceptions to them which are regarded as right, vary from people to people. The forms which these variations take not only find expression in, but tend to be determined by, institutions and the interrelation of institutions within ways of life. What in practice constitutes the most difficult and perplexing problem is not so much what rules should be generally recognised, but which should give way when their requirements clash, and in what circumstances it is right to make exceptions to them; and this cannot be understood by considering the rules in general terms by themselves, but by reference to the way of life in which they are embodied. It is their relation to the institutions which constitute this way of life which gives the rules concreteness, and explains how they function in determining the duties and obligations which are regarded as binding. (2) Even the more general moral rules are recognised as right in the first instance in the relations between those who co-operate in particular institutions; and it is only when the form of life to which they give rise is found good in the working of these institutions that the rules are gradually extended to other institutions and relations, and in the end to all relations between persons. This seems to be the way in which mankind arrived at the rules which are regarded as generally binding. (3) Not only among the less enlightened peoples, but at all stages of moral development, higher ideals and more stringent rules tend to be regarded as binding in the relations between members of small and simple institutions. Every new step in moral enlightenment seems to take place within such groups; and much progress in moral insight consists in the recognition that the ideals and rules which are binding within the narrower group not only admit of, but demand a wider application; and with this recognition comes a truer grasp of the ideals and rules themselves. But once they are recognised as binding in one set of relations, a powerful lever is provided which can be used to enforce recognition of them in other relations. (4) In view of these considerations, while I have no wish to belittle, much less to deny, the importance of rules in the moral life, I am not at all satisfied that, in our original moral reflection, we think in terms of general rules to anything like the extent which some writers on ethics suggest. It seems to me that we think much more often in terms of the relations between individuals who co-operate in institutions, and the conditions which are necessary for the development of their personalities and the realisation of their purposes; and, while the working of these institutions and the satisfaction of these conditions presuppose rules, and can be expressed largely, if not entirely, in terms of rules, it is they themselves which justify both the rules and the exceptions to them which are considered right.

Accordingly, I think the most fruitful way of approaching moral rules is through considering the nature of institutions and the rules which their functioning requires, and seeing how institutions and their rules are related to one another in a way of life. This will enable us to see how the ways of life, which their institutions in their interrelation constitute, explain and justify both the rules and the exceptions to them which different peoples regard as right. I propose, therefore, to devote the next few lectures to describing the institutions and ways of life of some representative primitive peoples in order to show how they explain and justify the rules which they regard as right and the form of the ends which they regard as good.

Before beginning this description I want to sum up the results of this lecture so as to bring out the characteristics of the ways of life of different peoples which are specially relevant to our ethical enquiries. A way of life or an operative ideal is an exceedingly complex system of interrelated and mutually adjusted elements. Looked at from the outside, it is embodied in a system of institutions which dovetail into and mutually modify and support one another. Looked at from the inside, it is the expression of a certain spirit or attitude of mind. And there is an affinity between the inner and the outer aspects. For a system of institutions both expresses and encourages a certain type of character or personality; and a spirit or attitude of mind finds expression more naturally and more adequately in certain types of institutions. But while the inner and the outer aspects are the subjective and the objective counterparts of one another, it is on the inner side that the connections and the mutual adjustment of the factors take place. To such a way of life we may apply the double test of comprehensiveness and consistency, i.e. adequacy to provide for the main needs or interests of those who share it, and freedom from internal disharmony. Moreover, the conception of such a way of life is developed in relation to the natural and supernatural environment of those who entertain it, and therefore the ideas which they entertain about their environment help to determine their operative ideal.

If these contentions are sound, no element in a way of life, whether end or act, interest or rule, plan or policy, can be completely understood or have final judgement of value passed on it except in its context. It does not contain the ground of its goodness or its rightness within itself. The work of moral deliberation consists in placing the possible alternatives open to the individual in the widest possible context to discover which of them is best fitted to maintain or promote the way of

H

life which is his operative ideal. An end is morally good not because considered in isolation it seems to be so, but because it fits into, and is an expression of the spirit of, this way of life. A rule is morally right not because considered in abstraction it seems to be so, but because it is a condition of realising and maintaining this way of life. The way of life itself stands for the good which is the source of moral obligations ; and we accept its demands as binding because, our nature being constituted as it is, we cannot do otherwise. When we carefully contemplate the form of life which we take to be the good for man, we cannot help recognising its requirements as obligatory on us. I cannot seriously think that on careful consideration we can regard anything as obligatory unless it seems to us on the whole better than any possible alternative would be. But what is on the whole better is determined not by the characteristics or consequences of particular acts in abstraction or isolation, but by their place in the context of the form of life of which they are parts.

THE WAY OF LIFE OF THE
TROBRIAND ISLANDERS

WE have now seen the structure of the moral life and its relation to human nature and the social order. We have also seen that the detailed nature and requirements of the moral and social ideal become clear only in the light of the efforts which men have made to embody them in concrete forms of living or systems of institutions. No doubt there may be conditions which any form of life which is a reasonably adequate expression of the ideal must satisfy, but there is no evidence that these conditions can be fulfilled only in one way or through one system of institutions. At any rate, the ways of life of every people, their operative ideals which are partially embodied in their institutions and yet point beyond them, are attempts, more or less successful, to give concrete expression to the formal ideal of the moral and social life. They are attempts to reconcile and satisfy the claims of the different desires and interests of different individuals, and to indicate in detail the conditions which must be fulfilled, if the individuals are to get what they value most, to realise themselves, to find satisfaction or happiness or whatever else we take to be the moral ideal or the good for man. The moral end or ideal conceived in general terms is absolute, but formal and abstract. The embodiments of it in ways of life are relative but concrete. It is the latter which give men detailed guidance about their particular duties and obligations,[1] and all duties and obligations are particular.

[1] There is also the duty of making the operative ideal as adequate an embodiment as possible of the formal ideal; but this duty is seldom recognised as a separate duty or consciously undertaken as such. The formal ideal is usually operative in the mind of the individual as a dissatisfaction with certain aspects of its embodiment, and so driving him to modify the operative ideal into line with the requirements of the formal ideal rather than consciously before it as a positive ideal.

Now if the account which I have given in my last lecture of these operative or embodied ideals is sound, we cannot understand any part of the morality of a people, any of their judgements of value, whether on acts or ends or rules or states of affairs, except in the context of their way of life as a whole. This does not, of course, mean that the moral agent who makes a judgement of value normally has this context consciously before his mind. When habits have been formed, a personality built up, rules formulated and institutions developed, the individual who is passing moral judgement does not usually need to look beyond the immediate situation with which he is faced. His judgement is the result of applying his total state of mind as so far formed to this situation, and the resulting judgement is immediate or intuitive though not infallible. But the context of the way of life is there as the background of the immediate situation, and it has played its part in building up the total state of mind that results in the judgement. We cannot, therefore, understand the judgement without reference to it; and, in our original and considered moral thinking, the immediate situation is considered in its relation to this wider context, and the judgement of value passed on it accordingly. And, as we have seen, the context of the way of life, in relation to which alone moral judgements can be understood, includes not merely the whole network of institutions but also beliefs about non-ethical matters of fact. It includes, in fact, all the beliefs, convictions and value-judgements of the people concerned about their natural and social and supernatural environment. As far at any rate as the ways of life of primitive peoples are concerned, this, as we have already partly seen and shall see in more detail later, is the considered and unanimous and oft-repeated contention of contemporary social anthropologists.

Now this makes our task in considering the morality of primitive peoples very onerous. Even if the facts were available and I had mastered them, it would be impossible within reasonable limits, and certainly within the limits of these lectures, to give an account which would enable us to understand the whole way of life of every primitive people to whose ideas and beliefs and value judgements I shall have occasion to refer by way of illustrating and supporting the conclusions which I propose to submit for your consideration — much less all that have led me to arrive at these conclusions. On the other hand, the easier alternative, which has been more commonly followed, of taking a number of isolated moral convictions and judgements from a considerable number of primitive peoples must be ruled out as not only valueless but misleading. It would omit, in the case of each people, the context of which the particular facts considered form part, and in relation to which alone we can understand either themselves or the judgements passed on them. What I propose to do, therefore, is first to describe the way of life of one primitive people in sufficient detail to enable us both to understand their moral ideas and the way in which they are related to the rest of their way of life, and to appreciate the conclusions at which recent and contemporary social anthropologists have arrived about the ways of life of such peoples, and especially about the intimate manner in which the different parts of their cultures are related to one another. I shall then give a briefer account of the moral ideas and ways of life of three other peoples ; and in doing so I shall emphasise particularly those features in which they differ from the way of life which I have chosen for more detailed description. This will prevent us from regarding the latter as typical in respects in which it is not so. In order to make my account as representative as possible I have chosen people from different continents, and I have included among them some of the less advanced and some of the more advanced of primitive peoples.[1] In this account I shall not be concerned with the origin or development of their ideas, beliefs and institutions, moral or other. I shall try rather to describe them as an interconnected whole as they were at the time when they were observed by our authorities. I shall, therefore, be concerned mainly not with isolated beliefs or institutions much less with quaint and sensa-

[1] According to the principle of classification generally accepted by anthropologists (Hobhouse, Wheeler and Ginsberg, *The Material Culture and Social Institutions of the Simpler Peoples*, pp. 29 ff.), the four peoples with whom I shall be concerned are graded in an ascending order as follows :

The Australian Aborigines	.	Lower Hunters
The Crow Indians	.	Higher Hunters
The Trobriand Islanders	.	Agriculturists (2)
The Bantu .	. .	Agriculturists (3)

tional customs, though these undoubtedly exist among them, nor with acts of romantic idealism or sublime heroism, though these also are to be found among primitives, but with the interconnected series of ideas and ideals, judgements and actions, which make up the way of life of the ordinary man and the typical citizen. For the moral life, whether among primitives or civilised peoples, consists mainly of unexciting events and humdrum activities like the neighbourly kindness of the Good Samaritan, or the giving of a cup of water in the spirit of service.

Even this programme, however, presents sufficient difficulties. In describing the way of life of a people, especially a people whose culture differs radically from our own, it is relatively easy to describe its different aspects one by one. It is more difficult to convey an accurate impression of the way in which the different aspects are interwoven to constitute a more or less integrated whole. It is still more difficult so to present it that we can see it as the native sees it from the inside, and appreciate what we may call the spirit of the way of life, the attitude of mind, the sentiments, the scale of values which find expression in it, and which give both to the parts and to the whole their significance. None of the aspects, whether institutions, magico-religious beliefs and practices or principles of social organisation, can really be understood by itself, in separation from the others. They all interpenetrate and modify and support one another. Even within each of these aspects we are met by the same difficulty of presentation. Thus, for example, in considering the social organisation of a particular people, we have to describe the principles which find expression in it one at a time and in general terms; but as they actually operate in practice they limit and restrict as well as support one another in all sorts of intricate ways. Thus we cannot really understand any of them until we have seen them all in relation and realised the modifications and exceptions to which each is subject in practice as it functions in relation to the others.

We might compare our method of approach to these ways of life with that of a person who is learning a foreign language and begins with the rules of grammar stated in general terms. He does not really grasp the rules till he sees how they operate in the living language in which they are related to one another and in which they are subject to all sorts of exceptions and limitations. The method of approach of the field worker, on the other hand, is more like that of the child learning his mother tongue. He finds people behaving in certain ways in particular situations and passing judgement on their own and other people's actions. From these actions and judgements and the reasons given for them he has to formulate for himself their moral and social rules and principles and the exceptions to them. But however we approach a way of life, we can understand the moral and social principles embodied in it only when we discover how they operate in particular actions and situations, and see how they illumine and interconnect the details of the way of life. Much discussion of moral rules and principles seems to me too abstract and general. It takes too little account of the way in which they operate in practice in the context of ordinary life and concrete circumstances. And if greater concreteness is desirable even when we are discussing our own moral rules, which we see against the background of a common way of life, it is essential when we are dealing with those of primitive peoples, where the background is so different from our own. If we are to understand any of their rules or principles, their institutions or their value judgements, we must consider them in their relation to one another within the context of their way of life, and not against the background of our own beliefs and scales of value. I fully realise the difficulty of conveying in one lecture the nature of a way of life very different from our own in such a manner as to enable you to see its different aspects and principles in their relation to one another and to the whole, and to enter into its spirit with real appreciation of what either the parts or the whole mean to those who live the life and find it worth while. But I must make the effort.

The people whose way of life I have chosen for detailed analysis and description is the Trobriand Islanders.[1] I propose

---

[1] I have not thought it necessary to burden the text with detailed references for every statement which I make about the peoples whose ways of life I describe. I propose merely to give my main authorities for each people, and to confine specific references to actual quotations and to points which are specially important to my argument.

My authorities for the Trobriand Islanders are Malinowski's *Argonauts* in this lecture to describe their social structure, their magico-religious beliefs and some of their typical institutions. In the next lecture I shall try to show how these in their interrelation help to determine their moral ideas and ideals, their duties and obligations. But the two subjects are so intimately connected that I shall not try to separate them sharply and references to both will be made in each lecture.

I have chosen the way of life of the Trobriand Islanders for special study for three reasons. First, their pattern of culture consists of institutions and is based on principles of social organisation which are as radically different from our own as we can find anywhere. Second, the necessary material is available in rich profusion in the writings of Malinowski, one of the most distinguished anthropologists of the present century, who lived among them for several years, learned their language, lived their life, gained their confidence, took part in the working of their institutions and then devoted the rest of his life to describing and interpreting their way of life and its system of values. Third, and most important, we have in their case, to an extent which is rare in the records of primitive peoples, an account of their inner or personal attitudes, their thoughts and emotions, their motives and purposes, as these find expression in the utterances of the natives themselves and their commentaries on their life and its values — an account in the light of which we can see the spirit in which their life is lived and the values which for them make it worth while. Malinowski is not content merely to describe their customs and institutions and the way they are related to one another and together constitute their cultural pattern. He tries to discover the human needs which they are intended to satisfy, the purposes they are meant to serve and the incentives which keep them going. Moreover he does this, not in general terms by reference to the ideas and

of the Western Pacific; Coral Gardens and their Magic; The Sexual Life of Savages; Crime and Custom in Savage Society; The Foundations of Faith and Morals; Sex and Repression in Savage Society; " Magic, Science and Religion " in Science, Religion and Reality (ed. Needham); " Myth in Primitive Psychology " in Frazer Lectures, 1922–32.

I have also used Malinowski's numerous articles and his more general works on different aspects of social anthropology. They are largely illustrated by materials from his work among the Trobrianders, and so provide a commentary on their way of life.

attitudes and purposes of the community as a whole, but by showing how they arise from the interaction of the thoughts and purposes of individual men and women — individuals who, however much they may have in common, are each moved by interests and ideas of his own — interests selfish and unselfish, ideas mean and noble.

In our study of the Trobrianders, then, we have the guidance of an experienced observer who interprets their way of life for us with sympathy and understanding, and yet with the cautious and critical eye of the trained scientist. He has described in detail their social organisation, their economic system, their marriage arrangements, their magico - religious beliefs and practices, and most of their more important institutions. Curiously enough, almost the only aspect of their life to which he has given no separate consideration and to which he makes few explicit references is their morality. He might have remedied this defect, if his premature death had not prevented him from completing his final interpretation of their way of life as a whole in the way which he at one time contemplated.[1] I suspect, however, that his failure to give us a fuller account of Trobriand morality is in part due to a certain lack of clearness in his own view of the nature of morality which led him to regard it as either a part or an effect of religion. But it is also partly due to the fact that he was interested, not so much in why the Trobrianders regard their rules of conduct as right and their institutions and ideals as good, as in the sanctions and social machinery which provide them with incentives to do what they believe to be right, even when it proves irksome and difficult to do it. In other words, he was interested in the legal rather than in the moral aspect of their institutions and way of living. At times, indeed, he does not seem to distinguish clearly between the two ; he writes as if the sanctions which enforced their rules also provided their justification, the ground of their rightness. Despite this lack of clearness in his own conception of morality, a subject to which I shall have to return later,[2] Malinowski provides us with the data from which we can construct the main outlines of the Trobriand morality for ourselves. For in his description we can see the virtues they

[1] See, e.g., *Coral Gardens*, i. 455-6.   [2] See Lecture XI.

approve, the vices they condemn, and the characters they admire, their principles of distributive and corrective justice, and their rules of conduct which govern the relations of individuals and groups to one another and which determine the rights they recognise and the duties they regard as binding. Let us address ourselves then to his account of them.

The Trobrianders inhabit an archipelago of coral islands about 120 miles north of Eastern New Guinea. The islands are flat and fertile and densely populated. The natives live by agriculture and fishing and the fruit of certain trees. Among them there are good craftsmen and expert sailors, and they have developed an extensive system of trading not only among themselves but also with neighbouring islands; but everybody — chief and commoner, men and women, old and young — takes part in agriculture. So that they are, first and foremost, gardeners, and all their other activities take place in the intervals during which work in the gardens is not necessary.

The population is divided into four clans, each of which has numerous subclans.[1] According to their traditional mythology, each subclan is descended from a woman who emerged from the ground at a point in the territory which the subclan occupies. A sacred grove, a hole in the ground, a creek or a crevice can still be pointed out as the spot from which the original ancestress emerged. The myths give significance to these spots, while the existence of the spots and the efficacy of the magic which the original ancestress brought with her and handed on to her descendants tend, to the native mind, to confirm the myths. Each member of each subclan can claim the right of residence in the district from which his ancestress emerged and he is entitled to part of the produce of its soil. There also he must be buried, and thither he will from time to time return after death still to partake of the fruits of its soil. Thus the relation of the Trobriander to the soil of his district is very close and intimate, and he sees it in the light of the halo

[1] This arrangement into clans is totemic. Each subclan has its totem, that is, an animal with which it is specially associated; and the totems of the different subclans of one clan are linked into a series, and the series is different for each clan. But our authority does not suggest that totemism plays any really important part in the beliefs or practices of the Trobrianders.

which has been cast over it by the myths and legends which constitute the sacred tradition of his people.

The structure of Trobriand society is based on four main principles, kinship by blood and by marriage, rank and neighbourhood. (1) Kinship by blood, on which the unity of the clan is based, is reckoned in the female line. This means that a child belongs to his mother's clan and inherits her rank and social status, while the inheritance of goods and other privileges such as the knowledge of myths and magical lore is from the mother's brother to her son, that is, his nephew. But while privileges, status and authority are transmitted through the mother, she herself does not directly exercise them. This is done by the senior male member of her family, that is, her maternal uncle, her brother and her son in turn, but not by her husband who belongs to another clan and is, therefore, treated as an outsider.

This emphasis on the matrilineal principle and on the intimate connection between children and their maternal kinsfolk is all the more natural for the Trobrianders, for they are entirely ignorant of the part which the father plays in the coming into being of children. For them fatherhood is a social, not a biological relationship. Children, they believe, enter the mother's womb as the result of the activities of some of their female ancestors. The father, therefore, is merely the mother's husband and has nothing to do with the procreation of the children. Nevertheless, the ties of friendship and affection which bind Trobriand fathers and children are very strong — stronger than is usual among many or even most other peoples. The father assists in nursing the children in their early years, takes part in their early play, helps to carry them when their mother is tired, apprentices the boys to gardening and fishing and the other activities which they will have to undertake, and remains throughout life their close companion and friend. But " he is not the head of the family ; he does not transmit his lineage to the children ; nor is he the main provider of their food ".[1] These are the privileges and responsibilities of their maternal uncle or their nearest male relative on their mother's side. For it is not only at death that a man's wealth passes to his sister's

[1] *Sex and Repression in Savage Society*, p. 30.

family. He has to provide for their maintenance during his lifetime. Each year the greater part and the choicest products of the fruits of his agricultural labours must be handed over to her and her family, or rather to her husband on their behalf, while her brother and his family themselves look to his relatives-in-law for similar provision for their own needs.

The reasons which make this state of affairs appear to them right and reasonable we shall see later. But I want to call attention here to one of its implications. It is that in his main economic activities the Trobriander's incentive is not his own self-interest or that of his wife and family, but the welfare of his sister and her family and the prestige that comes to him as a good gardener and a dutiful brother. The principle which we find operating here is very important for our understanding of the outlook and institutions of the Trobrianders, and we shall meet it again and again in their so-called economic activities. The motives which induce them to undertake such activities and which sustain them in their performance are, like those of the rest of mankind, complex and many-sided, but the interesting point about them is that they are mostly non-utilitarian. Indeed, Malinowski goes so far as to say that with the Trobriander personal economic gain is never the stimulus to work.[1] And if, under the influence of nineteenth-century economic individualism, we imagine that under such circumstances the native will not put forth his best efforts, we are greatly mistaken. " The truth is ", Malinowski writes,[2] " that the native can and . . . does work hard and work systematically, with endurance and purpose, nor does he wait till he is forced to work by his immediate needs." Nor can we infer from this that the acquisitive instinct or the desire to possess, which is at the basis of the sense of ownership and the institution of property, is less strong among the Trobrianders than among other peoples. It shows only the powerful influence of the institutions and cultural pattern of a people in moulding even the strongest impulses of human nature.

(2) The principle of kinship by marriage on which the unity of the individual family, father, mother and children, is based cuts right across that of kinship by blood which underlies

[1] *Argonauts of the Western Pacific*, p. 156.   [2] *Ibid*. p. 58.

the unity of the clan. For among the Trobrianders no person may marry anyone within his own clan. He must find his consort within one of the other three. Along with this clan exogamy goes a strict brother-sister taboo. From their earliest years, the relations between brother and sister are stiff and formal, devoid of the intimate friendship and confidence which we associate with the relationship. In particular, neither may speak to the other about his or her relations to the opposite sex. Nor may either mention the sexual affairs, whether matrimonial or illicit, of the other to anyone else or show any interest in them.

It is true that none of their principles of social organisation is strictly universal; and, therefore, though clan exogamy is the theoretical ideal, the strict requirement of tribal law, we shall see that, in practice, marriage within the clan, provided the degree of consanguinity is not too close, is tolerated. It is not even regarded as wrong. It has the authority of what Malinowski calls legalised usage. But at present we are concerned with the full demands of the ideal, and according to that sexual relations within the clan are forbidden.

The normal Trobriand family is almost invariably monogamous, except among the chiefs, in whose case polygamy performs important social and political functions. Their marriages are patrilocal, that is, the wife goes to live in her husband's village, among his people; but the children belong to their mother's village as well as clan; and their maternal uncle, who is the real head of their family, is responsible for their education in all ceremonial and traditional matters connected with the clan.

The matrilineal principle, based on kinship in the female line, and the unity of the individual family, based on mutual affection, give rise to opposing interests and conflicting loyalties. Thus the loyalties of the child are divided between his father and his mother's brother. To the former he is united by ties of affection based on mutual service and a common life lived together during his formative years. To the latter he is bound by ties of blood and kinship and mutual duties and privileges based on tribal law and custom. The loyalties of a husband are divided between his own children, or rather as he believes his wife's children, for whom he feels the tender regard and affection which the helpless young with whom he has lived and whom he has nursed and nurtured evoke in the normal human being, and his sister's children, his relatives and heirs by blood, for whose welfare he is according to tribal law in duty bound to labour while he lives, and to whom he leaves his name and possessions when he dies. The mother's loyalties are divided between her husband, whom she loves with an affection which normally increases and ripens with the passage of the years, and her brother, with whom her relations are always strictly formal and her contacts few and far from intimate, but who is by traditional custom the head of her family, who provides for their sustenance and to whom and to whose family she is expected to turn in adversity and in all the major crises of life.

But while the two principles stated absolutely would give rise to clashes of interests and while conflicts of loyalties do in practice sometimes arise, the natives do not think of the principles or their requirements in abstract and general terms. Their institutions lay down in detail and quite explicitly what the duties of children and parents, husbands and wives and paternal and maternal kin are to one another. They think of their duties not in terms of general principles but in relation to particular situations and the requirements of their institutions; and in the detailed working of their institutions the demands of the principles are adjusted and reconciled. Thus a compromise is arrived at which works with reasonable smoothness. It is true that, in strict legal theory, kinship in the mother's line should prevail, but in the operative ideal, what Malinowski calls legalised usage, which finds expression in their network of detailed institutions, the requirements of this principle are curbed and modified by other principles. The result is a scheme which taken as a whole is workable, intelligible and not unreasonable. To make the position clearer it should be added that among these people marriage is a contract, not merely between the two individuals primarily concerned, but also between their families and kinsfolk. It brings into existence a whole system of new rights and duties and mutual obligations. These find expression not only in periodic exchanges of gifts, but in specific duties in connection with their agricultural and fishing and economic activities, their constructing and sailing of canoes, their arrangements for dealing with the education of children, with ill health, with death and so on.

(3) The third principle which underlies their social organisation and modifies further the operation of the principles we have been considering is rank and status. Rank is determined by the subclan to which an individual belongs, the subclans being graded in rank according to immemorial custom; and, being a clan privilege, rank is transmitted in the female line. Rank " consists in personal prestige and titles ".[1]   A person of rank is entitled to wear certain ornaments, varying with his rank; he has to be addressed in certain specified ways; he is subject to certain taboos — for example, there are certain foods that he must not eat; and in his presence people have to behave in a prescribed manner. But rank not only confers privileges; it also imposes duties, some of them quite onerous. Most of these duties and privileges, however, belong to the person of rank, not as such, but as the holder of specific offices which he is entitled, and even bound, to hold in virtue of his rank. The nature of these and the way in which rank acts as a determining principle of social organisation, we shall see in the light of the fourth principle of their social structure, namely neighbourhood, on which their local, territorial or political organisation is based.

(4) For many purposes the unit of territorial organisation is the village. This consists of a number of houses, some for dwelling, some for storing produce, ranged round an open space which is used for meetings and ceremonial and festive purposes. The inhabitants of a village consist sometimes of members of one, at other times of members of two or more subclans, in addition of course to women from other clans who have married into it. Each village has its headman who usually belongs to a family of rank. He is, in fact, the senior member of the subclan of highest rank in the village. His authority merely as headman is not great. He is just *primus inter pares* among the village elders. But when he is a man of substantial rank he may be, as well as headman of his own village, the chief of a wider district, all the villages in which owe him allegiance.

[1] *Coral Gardens*, i. 33.

The village is normally the agricultural unit. Its members form the gardening team.[1] Their gardens are together. They do some of the agricultural work communally under the direction, as we shall see, of the magician, who is either the headman himself or one of his relatives whom he delegates to act in his place and who performs the main magical rites, which in their opinion are essential to the growth of the crops, on behalf of the village as a whole. For many ceremonial and festive purposes, for mortuary ritual and for purposes of waging war, the unit is usually a wider district consisting of several villages under a chief. The chief, one of whose privileges, as we have seen, is the right of polygamy, marries a woman from each of the villages under his jurisdiction ; so that the number of his wives varies with his rank. From the relatives of each of his wives he receives, according to the ordinary marriage custom, annual gifts of produce, to which not merely his brothers-in-law but all the members of their villages contribute. This is the main source of the chief's wealth, and he uses and is obliged to use this wealth mostly for communal purposes, such the payment for services which in virtue of his position he organises on behalf of the community of which he is the leader and representative. Thus the polygamy of the chief binds the villages more closely to one another and to the chief, and acts not only as the medium through which what we would call taxes are collected but also as a justification for levying them. It is true that the chief or headman is entitled to call on those under his jurisdiction to perform specific services, either on all of them or on specific individuals according to the nature of the task, and they are in duty bound to comply with his request. But for every such service, whether to himself or the community, he is expected to pay them either by distributions of food or presents or both ; so that the relations between chief and commoner are, like most of their other institutions, based on the principle of reciprocity or mutuality of services, a principle which, as we shall see, is at once moral, legal and economic.

These, then, are the main principles on which the organisation of Trobriand society rests — clan unity based on kinship

[1] In some villages, however, there are two or more gardening teams.

reckoned through the mother, patrilocal marriage, brother-sister taboo, clan exogamy and political power based on a hierarchy of rank determined by birth. Before considering the system of institutions which they have built within this structure, institutions in the working of which we see how the principles we have discussed mutually modify one another and help to determine the rights and duties of individuals, I want to look at their magico-religious beliefs which not only provide the background against which their life is lived, but interpenetrate all their institutions and help to explain many of their features.

The most fundamental feature of their view of the supernatural and the most illuminating for our understanding of their views about themselves and their environment is their belief in magic. This belief plays an essential part in all their major undertakings such as gardening, fishing, overseas expeditions and the construction and sailing of canoes, and in their attitude to all the important crises of life such as illness and death, love and war.

Let me give one or two illustrations. Agriculture, as we have seen, is their most vital interest. Most of their time is occupied in it and much of their thought and many of their ambitions centre round it. Now every stage in the agricultural process, from the first consecration of the garden site to what we might call the final harvest thanksgiving, is accompanied by and, from the native point of view, dependent for its success on its appropriate rites and spells. These magical activities contribute to the success of the gardening work in two ways. They inspire the workers with confidence that their efforts will succeed, that the rain will fall in due season, that vermin and pests will not destroy the crops and so on ; and this confidence is an important factor in maintaining morale on which in part at least depend the efforts which a man will put forth in any of his activities.[1] Moreover, the magical ceremonies initiate the

[1] Some anthropologists think that Malinowski tends to over-estimate the importance of magic as a source of confidence (e.g. Goldenweiser, *Anthropology*, p. 210). Firth doubts if Malinowski's view is true of the Tikopians, who seem to experience little emotion in connection with the performance of their magical rites (*Primitive Polynesian Economy*, pp. 184 ff.) ; and Radcliffe-Brown suggests that magic is a source of anxiety and concern

I

different stages of the agricultural process and so help to organise and direct the work of those who engage in it ; for at each stage in the proceedings the magician takes the lead, announces during which periods the workers should rest and when the next stage will begin — the allocation of the plots, the cutting and burning of the scrub, the building of the fence, the planting of the crops and so on right up to the final gathering of the harvest. In this work of leadership and organisation of work, the magician performs an important economic function ; but he does more. When he publicly announces that the time has come to go on to the next stage he will, if circumstances require it, call attention publicly and by name to any who have been lazy and are lagging behind either with the work of their own gardens or with their share of a common task, such as the building of the fence round the plots. He thus brings moral and social pressure to bear on the defaulters. It should be added that the gardening arrangements are relatively flexible, and that the organising activities of the magician still leave scope for individual and group initiative. Some parts of the work, such as the cutting of the scrub, are done communally. Other parts, like the planting of the crops, are normally done individually, or rather by the family working as a unit. But for almost any part of the work a number of individuals or families may organise themselves into a team and do the work on different plots in turn.

In the same way every stage in the process of constructing a deep-sea canoe, from the felling of the tree to the final launching, is punctuated by rites and ceremonies designed to make it safe and speedy and seaworthy, and this helps to organise the work and to inspire confidence in those who will sail the vessel ; and so on, with their other major activities.

Magic plays so important a part in the life and thought not only of the Trobrianders but of many other primitive people

rather than of confidence (*Taboo*, Frazer Lecture, 1939, pp. 37 ff.). It may well be, as Firth suggests (*op. cit.* p. 185), that the belief in magic is itself the source of some of the anxiety which its rites are designed to remove ; but Malinowski does show in detail that the Trobrianders appeal to magic mainly, if not only, in situations which are naturally dangerous or in which the issue is important but uncertain, i.e. situations which naturally give rise to anxiety.

that it is essential to have a clear idea of their attitude to it and of their belief as to what it can and cannot do. However necessary magical operations may be to the success of their gardening or canoe-building or other activities, the natives do not regard them as a substitute for hard work and technical skill. No magic will cut the scrub or build the fence or make crops grow on unprepared or unsuitable soil. Of this the Trobriander is as well aware as we are. He recognises that accurate knowledge and honest toil are necessary, and that all that they can do must be done to ensure success. But experience has taught him that even this may not suffice. Periods of drought which he cannot control, the onset of diseases and the ravages of pests, the causes of which he does not understand, may destroy the best crop in what may seem the most favourable season. Or again the best native expert may build a canoe of the best wood, according to the best design, and the most experienced sailor may navigate it in strict accord with accepted principles of seamanship, but a sudden storm may mean shipwreck and death to its crew. Similarly, a man is felling a tree when, for no reason that he can discover, his axe slips and cuts his leg or kills his neighbour. Now it is to guard against such unseen evils due to causes which he does not understand and cannot control that the Trobriander relies on magic. It is a supplement to, not a substitute for, skill and energy.

For the Trobriander, magic is a power exercised entirely by human agents. Its use does not, except in very rare instances and indirect ways, involve any appeal to non-human agents; and when he does appeal to such agents the native asks not for assistance to make the magic effective but only to enable himself to do his part correctly. The appropriate spell and the prescribed rite, which have been handed down from his original ancestors, will, when duly performed by the human agent, automatically and directly produce the desired effect. Why, then, do we call this power supernatural? How does its exercise differ from that of any technical skill? The answer is to be found in the way in which it acts and in the emotional attitude of the native, who according to our authority never confuses the natural and the supernatural.[1] The exercise of magic is

---

[1] *Foundations of Faith and Morals*, pp. 20 ff.

accompanied by the sense of the uncanny, the sense that mysterious forces are in operation. It evokes a profound and peculiar emotional thrill. Therefore the power involved, though it is controlled by human agents, is itself supernatural.

This power is in itself morally neutral, neither good nor bad. It can be used either for good or for evil ends according to the purposes of the agent who uses it. So far we have illustrated its use for good purposes only. But, to take just one of the principal uses of black magic, the Trobrianders believe that all serious illness and all deaths, except perhaps those due to suicide and murder, and death in battle, are due to magic; and only magic can cure illness. Thus in the Trobriands magical power is believed to be used for both good and evil purposes; for the common good, as in the ritual of rain-making and gardening and canoe-building; for the support of law and order, as in bringing disease or death on those who break the laws or endanger the public welfare; for evil and wicked purposes, as in killing an innocent fellow-citizen or in enticing a neighbour's wife away from her husband.

To the question, Why does the native continue to believe in the efficacy of magic in the light of the mass of empirical evidence that the desired results do not follow from its application? I shall return later.[1] For the answer to it is not peculiar to the Trobrianders, but applies equally to all who practise it. Meantime we just note that in the Trobriands magic performs useful social functions, though it has also serious disadvantages for those who practise it. The useful function which it serves is, as we have seen, twofold. (1) It gives confidence to the natives in the face of difficulties and obstacles and unknown dangers. In the strength which it gives him the Trobriander will brave the perils of a long overseas expedition, through stormy, shark-infested seas where strong currents run, in a relatively frail canoe which can sail only with and not against the wind. (2) The magician who wields this power often acts, through the exercise of it, as the leader, director and organiser of important enterprises vital to the welfare of the community. If we accept, as I think we may, the principle laid down by Frazer [2] and endorsed by Malinowski and other anthropologists, that no

[1] See below, pp. 265-6. [2] *Psyche's Task*, p. 4.

institution will continue to survive unless it performs some useful function,[1] these advantages might be regarded as sufficient to account for the continued practice of magic. But obviously they are not the reasons why the natives continue to believe in it; for they apply only in the case of a people who independently believe in its efficacy.

But though magic has its uses, it has also grave disadvantages. Apart from the fact that the belief in it is unfounded, the practices which it enjoins, as for example in canoe-building, involve a considerable waste of time and energy. More serious is the fact that the belief in its efficacy at times prevents the natives from trying to discover and control the real operative causes, as we see, for example, in their attitude to human diseases or in the way in which their belief in rain-magic discourages them from undertaking schemes of irrigation. Still more serious is the fact that the belief in black magic or sorcery, especially when it is pronounced as we find it, for example, among the natives of Dobu or in some African tribes, has a peculiarly disturbing and unsettling effect on the minds of those who believe in it and introduces an element of fear and suspicion and sometimes of hatred into the relations between individuals and families and clans.

Compared with the fundamental importance of his belief in magic the Trobriander's belief in personal supernatural agents is relatively insignificant. He believes that the spirits of the dead go to the island of Tuma, north-west of the Trobriands. There they carry on a life not unlike that which they lived before they died. From Tuma they return once a year to partake of the food offered to them at a great festival held in their honour. Apart from this annual visit they play little part for better or for worse in the lives of the natives. They are objects neither of fear nor of worship. They neither reward virtue nor punish vice, though there seem to be traces of a vague belief that they will be displeased at breaches of tribal custom and that disasters may result from their displeasure.[2] The Trobrianders believe in the existence of one or two

---

[1] But the function which it serves at a given time may not be that for the sake of which it was originally established.

[2] *Coral Gardens*, i. 468.

non-human spirits, one of whom causes minor ailments and another of whom is responsible for epidemic diseases; but the part which they play in the life and thought of the natives is relatively insignificant. "The Trobriander worships nothing",[1] and he has no conception of any supernatural agent or power whose favour he could win by doing right or whose displeasure he would incur by doing wrong.

There is another consideration which may be mentioned here. It is the high value the Trobrianders attach, and the time and energy they devote, to aesthetic considerations. The keenness of their aesthetic sense might be illustrated from almost any aspect of their life such, for example, as the beauty of some of the products of their craftsmanship, but here I need only quote what Malinowski has to say about their gardening. "Much time and labour", he tells us,[2] "is given up to aesthetic purposes, to making the gardens tidy, clean, cleared of all debris; to building fine solid fences; to providing specially big and strong yam-poles. All these things are to some extent required for the growth of the plants; but there can be no doubt that the natives push their conscientiousness far beyond the limit of the purely necessary. . . . Various tasks they carry out entirely for the sake of ornamentation . . . in order to make the gardens look neat. No self-respecting man would dream of omitting this."

We have now before us in bare outline the framework of the social structure of the Trobrianders and their view of the world as determined by magico-religious beliefs. That framework and those beliefs are inextricably intertwined with the network of other institutions which in their interrelation constitute their way of life and determine their particular duties and obligations. I want now to consider some of their typical moral and social institutions, the ways in which they are related to one another and the ways in which the principles and beliefs we have been considering enter into them, and in their actual operation determine and are determined by them. We shall thus be able to appreciate the parts which they play in the native's ideas of individual and social well-being, the rights

[1] *Argonauts of the Western Pacific*, p. 513.   [2] *Ibid.* pp. 58-9.

which their operation establishes and the duties it imposes, and the justification for claiming the rights and accepting the duties as binding.

An institution, as we have seen in my last lecture and as Malinowski is continually reminding us, is a framework or structural pattern of relationships between a group of individuals, determining the ways in which they should behave towards one another. The structure of the institution remains more or less permanent while the individuals who enter into it and play the different parts required by it come and go. Its purpose is to realise certain values or achieve certain ends of the individuals concerned. In the institutions of primitive people, at least, each individual sees the part which he must play, and recognises that it is essential if the institutions are to run smoothly. He also sees the values which he will realise or at least can claim, if he fulfils his duties. It is because individuals recognise these values as worth while at the price that they regard the pattern of behaviour as good and the duties it requires as binding. But the different institutions are not independent or self-contained. They are interconnected not only in the structural pattern of the society as seen by the outside observer, but also in the minds of the individual participants; for the values realised in one may be the justification of and the incentive to the performance of the duties required by another. These values are complex. They are always in part and often wholly non-utilitarian; and if they were not there, or if they ceased to appeal, the institutions would cease to function. One or two illustrations will enable us to see more clearly the nature of Trobriand institutions, the general principle of reciprocity on which they are based as well as the particular rules which find expression in them, the way in which they operate in practice in moulding as well as satisfying even the strongest impulses of human nature, the way in which they are related to one another, and the natives' scale of values which in their interrelation embody the things which for them make life worth while.

One of the Trobrianders' most characteristic institutions is concerned with the interchange of fish and agricultural produce between the coastal and the inland villages. In all their main ceremonial and festive activities, distributions of food play a prominent part. For these the people of the inland villages use fish and those of the coastal villages use agricultural produce. This custom makes each dependent on the other. When such an occasion has been arranged, the people of the inland village inform their coastal partners of the fact. The latter put to sea as soon as the weather is favourable to get the necessary fish. On their return they find their inland partners waiting for them. The fish is handed over and immediately carried inland to be used in the ceremonies there. The reverse process takes place when the coastal villagers need additional agricultural produce for their festivities and ceremonies.

Though these exchanges are organised between villages they are really individual and not communal exchanges; for each man in the coastal village has his partner in the inland village, and all exchanges take place between these partners. In these exchanges there is no bargaining or barter. The amount and value of the gifts and counter-gifts are left to the giver. Not that these people cannot barter or haggle. They can do so as keenly as any in cases where it seems appropriate to do so. But in any of the major exchanges it would be thought unworthy of a Trobriander to bargain. The way to win prestige among them is to give more than one receives. They regard generosity as the highest virtue and meanness as the lowest vice. Nevertheless, they normally keep a careful eye on the exchanges and are disappointed, and find ways of expressing their disappointment, if in the long run gifts and counter-gifts do not even up. What concerns us at the moment, however, is that in these exchanges it is a recognised duty to give generously, and that the prestige and social standing of the giver as well as his relations to his partner depend on his so doing.

But to return to the exchanges of food and vegetable produce, the rules governing the exchanges are not rigid or inelastic. They make due allowance for motives and circumstances. If, for example, the sea is rough or the catch small or if the harvest is poor, a lavish gift is not expected. As long as a man honestly does his best and shows a generous spirit in giving, he is credited with having done his duty. How seriously these duties are regarded by the natives and how much there enters into them in addition to mere hope of personal gain or economic advantage, can be gathered from the fact that as soon as they learn that their inland partners have sent word that they want fish, the coastal natives will immediately leave pearl-diving for a white trader, in which, with less exertion, they will earn ten to twenty times the value of their catch of fish, in order to comply with their obligations.

We might take as other illustrations of the operation of the principle of reciprocity what might seem to us more purely economic relations, such as the relations between the members of a canoe crew or a gardening team or between those who take part in constructing an overseas canoe — all of which Malinowski describes as typical Trobriand institutions. These are all systems of personal relations in which each individual has definite duties and specific rights. While they have an economic aspect, that aspect is just the expression in economic terms of the system of rights and duties which arise out of the personal relations of individuals, and the duties are regarded as duties which the individual owes to the other members.

Take, for example, the crew of a fishing canoe. One man is responsible for making and repairing it. He is the nearest approach to what we would call the owner. But even in this work he has a right to call on the other members for their co-operation in specific tasks. Similarly, they have their right to their place in the boat and their share of the catch. If the owner is unable to go to sea on a particular occasion, the others have a right to use the boat without him. In the boat each has his allotted task with its specific duties. Often the performance of these duties is a highly pleasurable activity, for the Trobrianders are fond of the sea, and sailing in the lagoon is often a pleasant activity. But whether they regard it as pleasurable or burdensome, they recognise the performance of their duties as something owed by them to and rightly expected of them by the others. Here again the rules are not rigid or based on merely economic considerations. Motives and circumstances are taken into consideration and exceptions made in the light of them. If, for example, a member fails to be in his place because he is unwell or his wife has developed fever, he is not only excused but given his share of the catch. But if he absents himself from laziness or disinclination the result is different. Thus their so-called economic relations are never merely a question of the cash nexus. They are one aspect of or element within a nexus of personal relations, a system in which the individuals are not so many hands or so much labour or productive power but human beings, men and women who recognise that they have duties and obligations towards one another.

Perhaps the most characteristic of Trobriand institutions, both in the light which it throws on their attitude to life and in the way in which it integrates so many of their other activities into an interdependent whole, is the system of semi-ceremonial and semi-economic exchanges called the Kula. This is one of the most remarkable systems of exchange known in the primitive world. It provides one of the main interests of the Trobriander's life, and Malinowski describes it as " the highest and most dramatic expression of the native's conception of value ".[1] In this system the main objects of exchange have only a sentimental and aesthetic, not a utilitarian value. They consist of armbands of white shell and necklaces of red shell exchanged against one another round a ring of islands several hundred miles in circumference. Each ' valuable ' is exchanged in one direction only — the one travelling clockwise, the other counter-clockwise round the Kula ring. The exchanges take place both between individuals in one island and between the inhabitants of different islands, but I am going to confine my account to the overseas exchanges. They will illustrate sufficiently the principles involved. In these exchanges, though the overseas expeditions to carry them out are communally arranged, each individual who takes part has his partners in the neighbouring islands. From one partner or set of partners he receives the one type of article and he passes it on to the other, while in the case of the other article the process is reversed. But all exchanges are between individual partners, and these partners have other duties and obligations to each other in addition to taking part in the Kula exchanges. They act as hosts, patrons and allies to one another in a land of danger and insecurity, and this creates social ties and establishes a system

[1] *Argonauts*, p. 176.

of friendly relations both between individuals in different districts within an island and also between neighbouring islands.

The articles exchanged vary in size and value. They are carried from one island to another in large fleets of canoes at more or less regular intervals of which due notice is given. The exchanges are made publicly and with great ceremony. Both they and the expeditions are accompanied by the performance of much ritual and many magical rites. Round the exchanges has gathered much intertribal trading which is conducted on ordinary barter lines. But Kula partners have no purely commercial transactions with one another. Any exchanges that take place between them, even when the objects concerned are not Kula valuables, take the form of gifts.

For one of these expeditions extensive preparations are made which affect many aspects of native life and extend over many months. Thus the Kula exchanges provide the incentive to many of their other activities and help to unify them into an ordered whole. For example, their main programme of building and overhauling deep-sea canoes takes place when one of these expeditions is in prospect; the activities of gardeners and craftsmen are intensified and much trading between coastal and inland villages takes place, in order to provide provisions for the voyage, and goods and produce to barter with their overseas neighbours under cover of the Kula exchanges; and their magico-religious beliefs are also closely bound up with the exchanges, which form the theme of many of their myths and much of their folk-lore. Nevertheless, the articles which form the core of this complex system of activities are without any utilitarian value. They are seldom worn even as ornaments, and no one can keep them for long without being accused of meanness — the most despised of all the vices. They are, however, very highly prized not only by the individuals who are their temporary possessors, but by the whole community of which they are members.

In the Kula exchanges, like the other major exchanges we have already considered, the equivalence of the return gift is left entirely to the recipient of the original gift. The original giver can neither barter nor even claim the return gift, much less can he enforce his claim. Moreover, the return gift is never made at the same time as the original gift, but on the return visit, usually many months later. If a gift is very valuable, it may be a year or two before a suitable return can be made. In such cases, however, a token gift is made as an earnest of good faith. But while an individual who feels himself aggrieved cannot directly complain to his partner of his negligence or niggardliness or of the value of the return gift, he may vent his feelings to others and thus bring indirect pressure on his partner. This sometimes results in bitterness and resentment. It may even lead to open quarrels and brawls.

But I am concerned not so much with the details of the working of the scheme as to call attention to certain features of it which seem highly significant for our understanding of the Trobriand way of life. These are : (1) the principle of reciprocity on which it is based and according to which it is the duty of a partner to make a return gift of equal value with no direct sanction to enforce the claim but public approval, a sense of duty to his partner and what Malinowski [1] calls his sense of his own dignity ; (2) the element of credit and commercial integrity involved in the transactions ; (3) the way in which the Kula system intertwines with and helps to interconnect and encourage almost every aspect of their life from religion to economics, from canoe-building to agriculture, from magic to rank and social status ; and the dependence is not one-sided but mutual ; for one of the incentives to undertake the Kula expeditions is the desire to engage in the commercial transactions with their overseas neighbours which take place under the cover of the Kula exchanges ; and (4) most significant, the native attitude to wealth and ownership which it reveals. Among the Trobrianders, as among other peoples, power and prestige are associated with wealth. But their ideas about wealth and the way in which it confers power and prestige are radically different from ours. They do not mean by wealth the ownership and accumulation of goods but rather the right to use them, and the use they make of them is mainly to give them away. Prestige is acquired by giving wealth away generously and with good grace ; and the higher a person's status, the more rigid the obligation to give liberally. But though generosity is

[1] *Argonauts*, p. 511.

for them the greatest good, the highest value in their moral code, the Kula system provides that the recipient of a gift should make an appropriate return, and in its detailed working it indirectly provides a sanction which helps to enforce the claim. This sanction, however, is not what makes the claim just. It is rather, as Malinowski puts it, " a stimulus to moral steadfastness " [1] which helps a man to do what he recognises as right when he has a strong temptation to do otherwise.

Malinowski repeatedly tells us that the institutions which I have been describing, and in fact all the relations between these people, are expressions of the principle of reciprocity, that indeed without the operation of this principle no primitive community could exist.[2] What account, then, does he give of this principle, and why does he attach so much importance to it ? What is its nature ? What precisely does it determine ? And what part does it play in the life and thought of the natives ?

Malinowski describes the principle on different occasions as a moral, an economic or semi-economic, and a legal principle ; but he does not make clear why the same principle should be regarded in these different ways or what the relations between its different aspects are. But taking his account as a whole into consideration, the illustrations he gives and the facts which he quotes, I think we may say that the principle may be looked at from three points of view, that it performs three functions in the life of the natives, and that its requirements may be complied with from three different sorts of motives. (1) The natives recognise the forms of life in which it operates as good, the principle itself as right and its requirements as morally obligatory. (2) The principle finds expression in a system of exchanges partly of goods and partly of services and satisfactions, and the individual recognises that, in the long run at least, it is to his own advantage or interest that he should comply with its requirements. Malinowski sometimes puts it that it is to his own ' economic ' interest ; but he uses the term ' economic ' in a very wide sense to include not merely goods and services but anything which satisfies a desire, even a desire for prestige or security, for the recognition of his fellows or the

---

[1] *Argonauts*, p. 157.   [2] *Crime and Custom*, p. 25.

good of others. (3) The individual recognises that, if he does not comply with its requirements, unpleasant consequences are likely to follow; and Malinowski holds that these are essentially of the nature of, or that they perform the same function as, legal sanctions.

Thus the Trobriander recognises the principle of reciprocity as morally right; he has positive extra-moral incentives to comply with its requirements; and its working brings home to him the consequences to himself of any neglect on his part to comply with it, and fear of these consequences acts as a deterrent against breaches of it. As the principle may be looked at from these different points of view and as people have these different incentives to comply with it, it is difficult, in the case of any particular act which complies with it, to be sure whether or how far it is the result of moral motives, such as sense of duty or regard for the rights of others, or of economic or semi-economic motives, such as hope of advantage, economic or other, to himself, or of fear of ' legal ' consequences. Malinowski seems to describe the principle as moral, economic or legal, according as he is thinking of one or another of these motives as the main incentive for complying with its requirements. It is, however, with the third of these aspects that he is specially concerned, for in it he finds what among the Trobrianders fulfils the functions which law fulfils in more advanced societies; but the second, and to a less extent the first, also enters into his account; and he does not distinguish as clearly between them as one would wish; nor indeed is it easy to do so.

Now the principle of reciprocity does not itself determine all the details of the patterns of behaviour which the institutions of the Trobrianders prescribe, the particular rules which govern the relations of individuals within them, the detailed duties which they require and the rights which they confer. Most of these details are determined by their principles of social organisation, their beliefs about nature and man and super-nature, the past experience of their people and their own needs and purposes. Thus as far as the principle of reciprocity is concerned, there is a certain arbitrariness about many of these details. E.g. the exchanges of goods and services might equally well have been between different individuals or have taken different forms, and yet be in accordance with the requirements of the principle.

What, then, does the principle determine and what is its moral significance ? It requires that the rights and duties which institutions based on it prescribe should be mutual, in the sense that each member has both rights and duties, instead of some having only rights and others only duties. This implies that the individuals whose relations are governed by it regard one another as persons, subjects of rights and objects of duties, self-governing individuals with desires and purposes of their own which are entitled to consideration, subjects to be persuaded and induced, not objects to be used or coerced. The natives find co-operation based on this principle good, they regard the principle as right, the institutions in which it finds expression as just, and the duties which they prescribe as binding. They find such co-operation good both as a means and in itself. In such co-operation they develop social sentiments, their natural interest in one another's welfare finds expression, and they recognise one another as persons. As this recognition takes place and this interest finds scope for exercise, the co-operation becomes more effective. It is difficult to assign any priority to one of these over the others : to say, e.g., that the natives recognise one another as persons and then develop an interest in one another's welfare or co-operate more effectively or vice versa. All three tend to develop *pari passu*, and the development of each is a condition of the fuller development of the others.

Thus the moral significance of the principle of reciprocity is that it is an expression of the principle of justice or equity based on a recognition of the moral equality as persons of those who co-operate in certain ways. However much the details of Trobriand institutions are determined by the experience of their people, it is the fact that they comply with this principle which makes them right or just ; and it is the fact that the natives recognise them as expressions of this principle which makes them recognise the duties they impose as morally binding.

Malinowski is concerned not so much with the moral as with the legal and economic aspects of the principle of reciprocity.

The reason for this is that, when he is discussing the principle,[1] his main purpose is to expose certain misconceptions commonly entertained about primitive peoples, in particular the view that they obey the customs of their people spontaneously or automatically, and that there is nothing among them corresponding to law among ourselves. He is anxious to show, therefore, (1) that the Trobrianders perform their duties or conform to the requirements of the principle of reciprocity, so far as they do so, not merely from respect for custom or from fear of supernatural sanctions or from threat of force, but because they recognise the arrangements of which they form parts as good, and good not only for the community but for themselves individually; and (2) that no society can afford to leave the doing of irksome and unpleasant duties to the mere goodwill of its members; and that, though the Trobrianders have no *ad hoc* authority, such as courts and constables, to enforce the provisions which among them correspond to our civil and criminal law, the working of their social institutions based on the principle of reciprocity calls into operation psychological motives and a social mechanism which sanction and enforce their requirements on those who might feel inclined to ignore their obligations. This mechanism, he contends, enables the individual to see not only that his own good is bound up with the effective functioning of the institutions, but also that failure on his part to perform his duties will not only interfere with the working of the scheme, and so bring on him the disapproval of his partners, but that in the end it will be to his disadvantage in more material ways as well.

In his insistence that it pays the individual to do his duty, and that the native sees that this is so, Malinowski is apt to leave the impression that the Trobriander never does his duty except from considerations of enlightened self-interest or even of economic advantage. But, as we have seen, in other connections he is equally emphatic that, even in his so-called economic activities, the native is not moved merely or even mainly by purely utilitarian considerations. So that, despite the ambiguity of some of his expressions, his insistence on the economic aspect of the principle of reciprocity is intended merely to

[1] *Op. cit.*, especially Pt. I, chs. iv, viii and ix.

emphasise the fact that the performance of certain duties is so important for the smooth working of any way of life that they must normally be carried out, and that there exists among the Trobrianders a social machinery which ensures that this will normally happen. For the fact is — and Malinowski's account brings it out quite clearly — that it does not always, at least in the short run and in economic terms, necessarily pay the individual to respect his obligations; and it is certainly not always clear to him that it will. It will only do so if others also do their duties. What he does in fact see is that if everyone, including himself, did what the scheme requires of him, everyone, including himself, would benefit; and if other people did their duty he would benefit; but he cannot have a guarantee in advance that they will; and without such a guarantee he still recognises it as his duty to do his part. Without so much mutual trust and faith in other people, no institution or social order would be possible. On the other hand he sees that if he habitually abuses other people's trust, their faith in him will be undermined and they will cease to do their duties towards him. So that his failure to do his duty will not only interfere with the working of the scheme but it will tend in the end to bring unpleasant consequences on himself; and fear of such consequences, which the operation of the principle of reciprocity is likely to bring on him, may act as a deterrent against neglecting his duties, when he finds them burdensome and feels inclined to evade them.

It is true that such a sanction cannot guarantee that obligations are fulfilled from moral motives; but Malinowski insists that some rules are so important for the maintenance of the social order that it is better that they should be complied with from any motive than that they should not be complied with at all. The rules of which this is true are those which he calls legal. But the fact that they are legal in this sense does not prevent them from being moral rules as well, nor from being obeyed often from moral motives. Mere compliance is the minimum which can be enforced, but it is not the maximum which is morally required. Among primitive people, like the Trobrianders, who have no special authority or machinery for enforcing law, it is not easy to draw a clear distinction between

K

law and morality; and Malinowski makes it specially difficult to do so by the very wide meaning which he gives to the term ' law '. He defines it as " the forces which make for order, uniformity and cohesion " in a society.[1] But he admits that the rules of social justice of the Trobrianders, what he calls their rules of law, are " not exclusively legal ".[2]

To some of these considerations we shall have to return. It is sufficient to note here that though Malinowski is mainly interested in the legal aspect of the principle of reciprocity, he does state explicitly that it is a moral principle; [3] that among the motives for complying with its requirements he mentions " a sense of duty and the recognition of the need for co-operation . . . side by side with a realisation of self-interest, privilege, and benefit "; [4] that he writes of " the sense of what is right . . . as a strong psychological incentive " to the native to do his duty to his sister's husband; [5] of " regard for the rights of others " as " always prominent in the minds of the natives "; [6] of the sense of duty as operative in connection with Kula exchanges; [7] and so on. In other words, the requirements of the principle of reciprocity are regarded as morally right whatever other sanctions may be attached to them, and however mixed may be the motives of individuals who comply with them; and they are regarded as morally right because the native recognises the form of life in which they are complied with as good, good both for himself and for the community of which he is a member.

[1] *Crime and Custom*, p. 2; cf. p. 122.
[2] *Ibid.* p. 61; cf. p. 98.
[3] *Foundations of Faith and Morals*, pp. 28, 43.
[4] *Crime and Custom*, p. 20.
[5] *Sexual Life of Savages*, p. 119.
[6] *Crime and Custom*, p. 28.
[7] *Argonauts*, p. 353.

THE WAY OF LIFE OF THE
TROBRIAND ISLANDERS (*continued*)

IN my last lecture I explained the principles which are embodied in the Trobriand social structure, the magico-religious beliefs in the light of which they interpret their environment, and some of the institutions in which these beliefs and principles find concrete expression. These institutions are adjusted to one another and in their interrelation constitute the framework of their way of life. That framework moulds the thoughts and feelings of the native, and prescribes for him the conditions under which he can satisfy his needs and realise his ideals. I have already illustrated the effects of this process of conditioning by reference to their attitude to wealth, but the subject is so important for our understanding of the nature of man and morality that it is desirable to give another illustration of it. We can find no better example of it than the Trobriand pattern of sexual morality which is closely inter-woven with their economic arrangements. I want, therefore, to describe briefly some of the closely related network of institutions which are concerned with the relations between the sexes and the laws of marriage. These show us how they deal with another of the basic urges of human nature; and, as we shall see, their attitude to sex is as different from ours as is their attitude to wealth. We have already seen some aspects of their marriage arrangements, such as clan exogamy, patrilocal marriage, brother-sister taboo, and the intricate economic relations between the husband and his brother-in-law. There are other aspects which I have no time to describe, such as the division of labour between the parents in caring for the children and in the work of the house and the gardens; and their educational arrangements, according to which father and mother and maternal uncle have well-defined duties in the instruction of the young.

The Trobrianders, even as adults, go about almost naked. They have no reticence about the physiological facts of sex, nor do they feel any sense of guilt in connection with them. Accordingly they do not in any way discourage children's interest in them. As a result, in the playful activities of boys and girls, sexual practices begin to play a part at a very early age, and premarital chastity in either sex is practically unknown. Out of ' this promiscuous free love of early youth ' there gradually grow more permanent attachments, and marriage follows. From the time of marriage the partners are expected to be faithful to one another, but our authority reports that even this rule is not very strictly enforced.

Unlike most primitive peoples, the Trobrianders do not mark the crises of puberty by any initiatory rites. Nor is marriage among them accompanied by any special ceremony public or private. The wife just goes to live with her husband's people, but she must get her parents' consent. Later an exchange of gifts takes place between the families of the bride and bridegroom and more permanent semi-economic arrangements are established between them. The most important of these is the obligation, to which I have already referred, on the part of the bride's brother or brothers to supply the main provision not only for herself but also for her husband and children. None of these economic arrangements can be regarded as a purchase of or a dowry for the bride. But they tend to strengthen the family bond and give it greater permanence. They also make marriage a bond of connection not only between bride and bridegroom but also between their respective families.

In thinking of their marriage arrangements we must also remember the peculiar position of the father, which, as we saw, is partly at least due to their ignorance of the part which he plays in the coming into being of the children. This tends to give the mother a higher status and a greater measure of independence. Her husband, we are told, " will seldom quarrel with her, hardly ever attempt to brutalise her, and he will never be able to exercise a permanent tyranny " over her.[1] Nevertheless she needs a husband as much as he needs a wife,

---

[1] *Sex and Repression in Savage Society*, p. 30.

and not just for sexual satisfaction, nor even for his services to herself and the children, but to give herself and her children approved social status. For despite the sexual freedom of the unmarried girl, pregnancy and childbirth on her part " are invariably regarded as a disgrace ".[1] This ' postulate of legitimacy ', as it has been called, seems to be universal in all human societies, however much their ideas about sexual morality may differ in other respects. " I know of no single instance, in the whole of anthropological literature," Malinowski writes, " of a community where illegitimate children, that is, children of unmarried girls, would enjoy the same social treatment and have the same social status as legitimate ones." [2] To this rule the Trobriand Islanders are no exception.

Some people might imagine that, however their pattern of sexual morality originated, the Trobrianders now accept it only because they have no knowledge of any other. But this is far from being the case. They are well acquainted with the ways of life of the natives of neighbouring islands with whom they take part in Kula and other exchanges ; and some of these, like the natives of the Amphletts and Dobu, have as strict a code of sexual morals as the mid-Victorians. What their approval of their own code of sexual morals shows is the influence of cultural conditions in moulding even the most powerful urges of man. For their attitude to sex is so intimately connected with many of their other institutions that it could not be altered without changing these institutions as well, and so revolutionising their whole way of life.

In order to bring out the influence of this cultural conditioning we have only to compare their pattern of sexual morality with our own, from which it differs so radically. In their way of life and in ours there are both opportunities for the satisfaction of the sexual urge and regulations which forbid its expression under other conditions. But the conditions for its expression and for its repression differ in the two ways of life. In their case there is free expression before marriage though no children may result, and there are rules not only of incest but also of exogamy which forbid either sexual relations or marriage between certain people, and the group to which these refer is

[1] *Ibid.* p. 212.　　　　[2] *Ibid.* pp. 212-13.

much larger in their case than in ours. Moreover, they have many rules which forbid sexual relations even between husbands and wives under certain conditions; for example, before or during important expeditions such as the Kula or war parties, or in or near gardens and so on. The fact is that no society can afford to allow its members unlimited scope for the exercise of their most powerful impulses, while no society can completely repress them. All societies therefore have rules governing the conditions in which they may find expression, and these rules differ from people to people. Yet within wide limits which are not easily ascertainable, human nature seems to be so plastic, so easily moulded by cultural conditions, that it settles down not unhappily under many different kinds of regulations. What we find, therefore, in any of the different ways of life is the expression not of pure or bare human nature, but of human nature as moulded or conditioned by different cultural environments. Accordingly, it is difficult to say what the sex impulse or any other impulse requires for its satisfaction. We are apt to assume that it requires what it seems to require under our own system of institutions, but the Trobrianders are satisfied that it requires what their system of institutions provides.

We have, however, to remember that what has to be satisfied is not particular impulses or urges or desires, but persons, and persons who are members of societies, and that what they require is a way of life in which their different impulses find expression and satisfactions in ways which are compatible with one another and with similar satisfactions by other people. This is what the systems of institutions of different peoples are trying to provide. As we have repeatedly pointed out, the institutions in these systems are so interdependent that we cannot alter one which seems to us undesirable without also affecting others which we would be glad to leave as they are; for no custom or institution is self-contained or intelligible by itself alone. To appreciate its form or its function or the judgement of value passed on it by those who live under it, we have to see it as part of a complex pattern which includes many, and it may be all, of the other institutions of the people concerned; for other institutions help to determine its form and to provide the incentives which keep it going. Accordingly, if we take the institution by itself or against the background of our way of life, it may appear to us stupid or wasteful or even absurd. But if we take it in its relations to the other institutions and beliefs of the people who approve of it, it becomes intelligible even if we still refuse to regard it as right.

We have already met with examples of the way in which the institutions of the Trobrianders are interrelated and the light which their interrelation throws on their nature. We have seen, for example, how marriage regulations and agricultural arrangements, agriculture and magic, magic and canoe-building, canoe-building and Kula expeditions dovetail into and mutually support each other. I want to give one more illustration of the way in which their institutions interpenetrate and to show how their interpenetration renders intelligible a custom which on the surface is apt to seem to us the most absurd of all their institutions — the arrangement whereby a man is obliged to work for his sister's household while his brother-in-law provides for the man's own family. This arrangement seems to us not only wasteful of effort but grossly unfair. To realise how wasteful it is we have to remember that, owing to clan exogamy and patrilocal marriage, a man and his married sister live in different villages and so do a man and his wife's brother. Therefore, under this arrangement, every man's storehouse is filled from the gardens of a village other than his own. As a result, produce has to be carried at harvest time longish distances from village to village in a strange criss-cross kind of pattern. Nor is this all. The arrangements are carried out with great public display and ceremony which might seem mere waste of time and effort. The produce is first erected into neat conical heaps in the original garden where it is exposed to the criticism and appreciation of the whole community. It is then carried ceremonially to the other village, there to be again displayed for some days in front of the storehouse. Finally those who grew it, harvested it and carried it to the village return to store it away for safe-keeping, while those for whose benefit all this is done look on with apparent indifference. Could any arrangement be more wasteful or absurd from the point of view of those who tend to think of work as an evil performed only for economic advantage ? And the arrangement seems as unfair as it is nonsensical. For when a person works hard and reaps a good harvest the best fruits of his labour go to others, while he and his family may suffer because their welfare is at the mercy of someone else who may be lazy or inefficient or in indifferent health.

That is how the situation appears to us. But when we consider these arrangements not in the context of our ideas and values, but as they appear to the natives in the context of their beliefs and cultural conditions, we not only understand them ; we see why they approve of them as right and reasonable and accept as binding obligations the duties they impose.

To appreciate the situation as they see it, we have to take account of the following among other factors : (1) The woman to whom and to whose family the produce is sent has a claim on the land in which it was grown. The village in the gardens of which it was grown is her village, though for the present, as the result of patrilocal marriage, she lives elsewhere ; and the magic by which it was blessed is that of her people — her subclan. (2) Her children also belong to that subclan, and when her sons reach maturity they will go to live in her village and help her brothers to grow the produce which is sent to their parents. (3) The man who sends the produce is sending it to his kin, those who are according to tribal law his heirs, those who will associate with him and be on his side in all the important crises of life, at mortuary ceremonies, during ritual performances, in a fight or in war. (4) According to the native theory of procreation, a man's wife's children are not his flesh and blood. To the land and produce of their father's village, therefore, they have no claim. (5) Though the father is, from the point of view of his wife's clan, an outsider and as such not entitled to any part of the produce, he receives his share in recognition of his services to his wife and children and through them to their clan. (6) Not all the produce of a man's gardens goes to his sister's family, but rather more than half. The part which is thus sent, however, contains the choicest produce, the only part which is ceremonially displayed, made the subject of public comment and used for special festive occasions. The remainder, less what goes as tribute to the chief under the polygamous arrangement which we already noticed, is taken quietly and without ostentation to the man's own subsidiary storehouse to be used partly as seed and partly to meet the day-to-day requirements of his family. (7) The ceremonial display of the part which is sent to his sister's family earns for a man renown and public approval if he is a good gardener and a generous giver, and contempt and loss of caste if he is inefficient or niggardly. The social prestige which comes as the result of the public recognition of his generosity, his efficiency as a gardener and his dutifulness as a member of his clan, is to the Trobriander one of the highest values which life can offer. It therefore provides him with a further incentive, in addition to clan loyalty and respect for tribal law, to do his duty in a generous way. Moreover he receives from his brother-in-law a return gift, but its economic value is insignificant compared to that of the original gift. Its main value is as an acknowledgement of services rendered and an expression of friendly feeling. Whether or not such a return gift is made, makes no difference, in the view of the natives, to the stringency of a man's obligation to continue his annual gifts to his sister's family.

Taking all these considerations together, we see that, to understand the attitude of the Trobrianders to the final disposal of the produce of their gardens, we have to take account not merely of economic considerations but of their relation to the soil as determined by their magico-religious beliefs, the matrilineal principle on which clan unity is based, the principle of legitimacy, the position of the father, the laws of marriage such as clan exogamy and patrilocal marriage, and the status of all the individuals concerned. In fact these arrangements are largely an expression in economic terms of the principles of social organisation and magico-religious beliefs which I described in the last lecture; and the economic arrangements cannot be understood without taking account of these principles and beliefs. Into a man's motives for carrying out his duties to his sister's family there enter, no doubt in varying proportions in the case of different individuals, sense of duty, devotion to his clan, sentiments of affection to his sister, regard for the rights of his brother-in-law, vanity and ambition, a desire to win the applause of the public and the commendation of the magician, rather than economic self-interest. But whatever be his motives for performing his duties, it is the factors which I have mentioned, not in isolation but conjointly, which make him regard the whole arrangement as good and the duties which it imposes as binding obligations.

From this account we can see the important functions which the arrangement fulfils in the life of the Trobrianders. It not only provides for the satisfaction of economic and other needs, but it helps to give greater stability to marriage, and it provides the mechanism whereby the chief collects tribute and his justification for exacting it. We see, in fact, how intimately interrelated their different institutions and beliefs and customs are, and how they interpenetrate and support one another. For example, the arrangement which I have been describing not only receives support from the magico-religious beliefs of the natives and from the principle of inheritance through the mother, but it also supports them. Or again, Kula expeditions provide the incentive to construct and repair canoes, which are used for many other purposes, and an additional incentive to internal trade and agriculture, while the desire for other forms of trade and for the exchange of agricultural produce with their overseas neighbours is part of the incentive to undertake Kula expeditions. Thus if we interfere with one institution, we take away, or at least decrease, the incentives which keep others going.

It is this interdependence of its institutions, whereby they mutually support one another, to which functional anthropologists refer when they speak of the pattern of the culture of a particular people. It does not mean that the institutions are logically connected or rationally coherent, but only that they are so connected in the minds and motives and purposes of the people that the satisfactions provided by one act as incentives to perform the duties required by another. When we say that they are consistent, all that is meant is that they are not inconsistent: that they are so adjusted that the duties required by one do not conflict with those required by another, but rather act as incentives for performing them. It is a long road from such functional interdependence to rational coherence, and there are many intermediate stages on the way.

We have now seen the way in which some of the institutions of the Trobrianders are related within the framework of their way of life. This framework, the institutions which constitute it, the principles which are embodied in them and the behaviour patterns which they prescribe, are to be found not in written laws or codes but in the attitudes and beliefs and mental habits of the natives, in their habits of thinking and feeling, in the attitudes they adopt to one another, in the judgements which they pass on their own and other people's conduct, and in the reasons which they give for these judgements. The natives do not normally formulate in abstract terms even the rules and principles which are embodied in particular institutions, let alone the interrelation of principles which finds expression in the whole pattern of their way of life. They are too near and familiar to be held at arm's length and reflected on objectively as they are by us when we describe the cultural pattern of the Trobrianders — if not usually when we think of our own. Like most members of most communities, primitive and advanced, they realise what the operation of a principle, or an institution in which it operates, requires of them in particular concrete situations, and they see how their rights and duties dovetail into those of their neighbours. But most of them do not see beyond this. Among them, as among ourselves, there are individual differences. Some minds have a wider, some a narrower range. Some individuals enter more deeply into the spirit of their institutions and have a firmer grasp of their structure and purpose. Malinowski tells us of native sociologists who not only understand the nature and functions of some of their institutions but can explain them to the anthropologist.[1] But they are rare exceptions, though, we are told,[2] some are to be found among all primitive peoples.

Before considering the attitude of the natives to the principles and rules and behaviour patterns which are embodied in their institutions to see how far and in what ways they appreciate their interrelations and the reasons which for them are the grounds of their rightness, I want to illustrate from their moral ideas and way of life a point which I made earlier in general terms and which seems to me important for our understanding of morality, Trobriand or other. It concerns the

[1] *Science, Religion and Reality* (ed. Needham), p. 36.   [2] *Ibid.*

distinction between different kinds or levels of ideals entertained by the same individual or people, and especially the
distinction between a theoretical ideal, that is a principle or
set of principles or ideal accepted in abstract and general terms
and an operative ideal, that is a principle or set of principles
embodied in working institutions. A consideration of this distinction will enable us to see how different institutions and
principles interact and mutually modify one another, and how
progress in moral ideas or moral enlightenment takes place
even among primitives.

Malinowski repeatedly calls attention to the difference
between the strict letter of tribal law, as a native will explain
it — that is, the theoretical ideal — and what he calls legalised
usage, that is, the operative ideal embodied in their interrelated
institutions. The theoretical ideal insists on the consistent
application of one principle or set of principles. In the operative ideal, principles are so adjusted to one another and the
needs of human nature as to admit of many exceptions which
are not only tolerated but regarded as right by the ordinary
member of the society. For example, according to the letter
of tribal law a man should leave all his possessions to his
nephew, but in practice many men give to their sons during
their lifetime things which should according to the strict ideal
go to their nephews. Now this, though resented by the legitimate heirs, is regarded by their fellows as right and reasonable.
It has, therefore, become part of the tradition which Malinowski calls legalised usage, and social institutions have been
established which embody this legalised usage. These institutions, such as cross-cousin marriage and the keeping of a chief's
son after maturity in his father's village, are traditional and
institutionalised ways of evading the requirements of clan
unity based on matrilineal descent. And Malinowski reports
that the natives understand and can explain the reasons for such
institutions.[1] The institutions have been established and
continue to flourish because the natives regard the purposes
which they serve as right and reasonable. As long as this is
the case, the Trobrianders are not over-much troubled about
their abstract consistency with some of the principles embodied

[1] *Sexual Life of Savages*, p. 86.

in their other institutions. They are fitted into the pattern and the other institutions are adjusted accordingly. During the period of adjustment, before the new institution is fully established, acute clashes sometimes take place. They involve conflicts of loyalties and perplexity as to what is right. Malinowski reports several of them from the Trobriands.[1]

Take another example. The tribal law requires strict exogamy, that is, no marriage within the clan. And this law has a supernatural sanction. A breach of it is not only regarded as shameful, it is believed to cause illness and perhaps even death. Yet when the relation between the spouses is not one of near consanguinity, public opinion tolerates such marriages and regards them as reasonable. There is even a series of traditional magical rites and spells which are believed to counteract the harmful consequences which would otherwise follow. Here we have a traditional and legalised way — supported by magico-religious ceremonies — of evading one of the most stringent of tribal laws. Or again when an individual is killed by a member of another subclan, tribal law demands that his kin should undertake a vendetta against the murderer and his kin, but when it is recognised that the murdered man was clearly in the wrong it is not thought necessary nor even right to undertake the vendetta.[2]

In this way even the most rigid rules, those which have a supernatural sanction, can be evaded or circumvented not only with the connivance but with the backing of public opinion and legalised usage, when the exceptions are in conformity with the people's sense of what is right. The fact is that none of their principles of social organisation and none of the rules embodied in their institutions is strictly universal. But the exceptions to them which are recognised as right are not usually thought of as exceptions, because they are normally not thought of in relation to the rules at all, but in relation to the institutions, such, for example, as cross-cousin marriage, which have been established to embody the behaviour pattern which constitutes the exception. In the same way, among ourselves we do not think of killing an enemy in war-time as a breach of the sixth commandment, because we do not think of such killing

---

[1] See, e.g., *Crime and Custom*, pp. 100-111.   [2] *Ibid.* p. 118.

in relation to that commandment at all, but in relation to the behaviour pattern prescribed by the institution of war. Thus we see how the institutions of a people determine the interpretation which they put on rules which they in general accept, and how they justify the exceptions to them which they regard as right.

Accordingly, the operative ideal of the Trobriander is not the coherent expression of one principle, but rather the result of the joint operation of several principles which are liable to conflict both with one another and with the requirements of human nature. The operative ideal is thus a balance or equilibrium in which different rules or principles mutually modify one another; and this equilibrium is not static but dynamic. Progress in moral enlightenment consists largely in adjusting the requirements of different rules and principles in the interests both of greater consistency and greater adequacy to the needs of human nature. We see evidence of this progress among the Trobrianders in the growth of institutions embodying legalised usage and the consequent modifications of tribal law.

Now this phenomenon of professing allegiance to a principle or theoretical ideal conceived in general terms — an ideal which we keep, as it were, for Sunday use — while determining our particular duties and passing judgement on our own and other people's conduct in the light of a nearer and less consistent operative ideal which makes many concessions to other principles and considerations, is by no means confined to primitives. Among ourselves, for example, the code of conduct of even the best Christians is perhaps a compromise between the teaching of the Sermon on the Mount and the operative ideal embodied in our moral and social institutions; while the latter itself, the operative ideal of the average member of a Christian community, is a compromise between the code of conduct of the best Christians and the natural desires and inclinations of human nature. To note this contrast between the theoretical ideal, to which we pay a homage which is more than lip service, and the operative ideal of our average moments, is easier for the outsider, whether primitive or advanced, than for the person who entertains both and does not usually pay much attention to the conflict between them. The result of failure to recognise this conflict for what it is in the case of primitives is that we often accuse them of inconsistency or hypocrisy ; and they, seeing the same conflict in our own case, pass on us exactly the same judgement as we pass on them. Malinowski gives an interesting illustration from his own experience among the Trobrianders during World War I, which shows that they see us in much the same light as we see them. " Many of my Melanesian friends," he writes,[1] " taking at its face value the doctrine of ' brotherly love ' preached by Christian missionaries and the taboo on warfare and killing preached and promulgated by Government officials, were unable to reconcile the stories about the Great War, reaching the remotest Melanesian or Papuan village. They were really puzzled at hearing that in one day white men were wiping out as many of their own kind as would make up several of the biggest Melanesian tribes. They forcibly concluded that the white man was a tremendous liar, but they were not certain at which end the lie lay — whether in the moral pretence or in his bragging about war achievements."

Thus, whether among savages or civilised, it is one thing to accept an ideal or principle in a vague general way as worthy of our allegiance. It is quite another thing to embody it in our moral and social institutions. But we do not really grasp the nature of a moral ideal or principle till we see how it is going to operate in practice and what it requires, and what exceptions will have to be made to it, in particular concrete situations, that is, till we have so worked out its detailed requirements in terms of our actual life and institutions that it becomes what I have called an operative ideal. In our accounts of the ways of life of other primitive peoples we shall come across further illustrations of this difference between a theoretical and an operative ideal, between accepting principles or rules in general terms and embodying them in a way of life in which they are adjusted to other principles and rules and admit of many exceptions, though the exceptions are not usually thought of in relation to the rules and therefore not as exceptions to them. I shall consider the implications of this for ethics later when we have before us more evidence about its detailed working.

[1] *Crime and Custom*, p. 83, note.

So far we have been considering characteristics common to all the Trobriand institutions and all the rules of conduct which find expression in them. But the rules and the forms of conduct which they prescribe are of different kinds, not all of which are moral. Some are merely economic or ritual or legal or technical. The acts which are supernaturally prescribed or demanded by law or economically advantageous or technically correct may also be morally right, but they need not be ; and even if they are, it is only when they are recognised as morally right and done for that reason that the doing of them has moral value. The distinguishing characteristic of moral rules and conduct is their categorical or final character, whereas other rules and forms of conduct have as such only a hypothetical rightness. They are the means to certain ends or the conditions of certain states of affairs, and their rightness is conditional on the obligation to realise the latter. Moral rules directly evoke the sense of duty or unconditional obligation, the other rules as such do not. We have now to consider to what extent, if at all, the Trobriander distinguishes between different rules and forms of conduct, to see his attitude to each and the reasons why he regards it as right ; or, if the same form of conduct is both morally right and ritually prescribed or economically advantageous or demanded by law, how far he distinguishes between its different characteristics. We have, in particular, to consider how far, if at all, his attitude to moral rules or the moral aspect of conduct differs from that which he adopts towards other rules and other aspects.

Primitive man has a profound respect for custom in which is embodied the accumulated wisdom of his ancestors ; and he accepts all rules as right in the first instance because they are the customs of his people. Until the ways of life of primitive peoples had been intensively studied by trained experts, it was generally believed that their attitude to all rules was the same, that they accepted them as right merely out of respect for custom. The group was thought so to dominate the individual that he more or less spontaneously or automatically obeyed all the traditional rules of his people — the operative causes or motives being partly mental inertia and partly a superstitious fear of supernatural agencies which would punish him if he did not. But careful observation has shown this view to be entirely without foundation; and no one has done more to discredit it than Malinowski.[1] The position as he found it among the Trobrianders is this: (1) Under normal conditions (when they are obeyed and not defied) the observance of their rules is " at best partial, conditional and subject to evasion ".[2] (2) Few of their rules of conduct have supernatural sanctions of any kind. And (3) their attitude to different kinds of rules is quite different both as regards their reasons for regarding them as right and their motives for complying with them when they do so.

In considering Malinowski's attempt to distinguish the different kinds or classes of rules of conduct to be found among the Trobrianders and the attitude which they adopt towards each, it is desirable to distinguish carefully between two questions: (1) Why do they believe that certain rules are right, that is, what do they regard as the moral authority of the rules, the grounds of their rightness? (2) What motives and incentives does their society provide to individuals to obey the rules which they recognise as right, in addition to the fact that they are regarded as right, and what happens to them if they do not obey them, that is, what are the sanctions attached to the different rules? No doubt the two questions are very closely connected and Malinowski does not explicitly distinguish them; nor was it necessary for his purpose to do so. Indeed some of his statements suggest that he confused them; for he sometimes speaks of sanctions as not merely enforcing rules, but as making them valid. This confusion, which is not confined to Malinowski, seems to be in part due to an ambiguity in the term ' sanctions '. Sometimes it seems to mean nonmoral or extra-moral, e.g. legal, supernatural or economic, sanctions. At other times it seems to include the strictly moral sanction of moral approval and disapproval, whether by the individual himself or by his fellows who usually share his

---

[1] *Crime and Custom*, pp. 3, 15 *et passim.* Cf. Goldenweiser, *Anthropology*, p. 231; Radin, *Primitive Man as Philosopher*, pp. 37-8, 79; Firth, *We, The Tikopia*, pp. 564-5; Driberg, *At Home with the Savage*, p. 11; Linton, *The Study of Man*, pp. 95, 278; Hogbin, *Law and Order in Polynesia*, pp. 82 ff.; Culwick, *British Journal of Psychology* (1935-6), p. 189.

[2] *Op. cit.* p. 15.

L

judgement. But the confusion seems to be partly due to the fact that in the case of the rules with which Malinowski is specially concerned the main incentives for obedience are provided by the operation of the form of life, whose goodness is also the ground of their rightness. Be this as it may, in his most explicit and detailed treatment of the Trobriand rules of conduct Malinowski is mainly concerned with extramoral sanctions and incentives, with the social machinery which ensures that what he calls legal rules are normally obeyed, with what he elsewhere calls " stimuli to moral steadfastness ". We, on the other hand, are primarily concerned with what the Trobrianders regard as the moral authority of their rules, the grounds of their rightness ; for this is what brings to light the foundations of their morality.

In distinguishing the different kinds or classes of rules of conduct recognised as right by the Trobrianders, Malinowski takes as his principle of classification the sanctions which are attached to them. This is in fact the principle of division used by practically all anthropologists who deal with the subject. But however useful it may be for Malinowski's purpose, and though it serves to bring out certain facts which have a bearing on our problem, this principle of division is from our point of view very unsatisfactory, for the different classes of rules at which we arrive by the use of it are not mutually exclusive. The same rule of conduct may have several different sanctions. Among ourselves murder, e.g., is morally wrong, legally a crime, and from the religious point of view a sin. In other words, among us the rule against killing has moral, legal and religious sanctions. Therefore from the point of view of a classification based on sanctions it is at once a moral, a legal and a religious rule. But if a rule is morally right, the fact that non-moral sanctions are attached to it does not make it cease to be a moral rule ; nor, of course, does the fact that any or all of the non-moral sanctions are given to it make it morally right, if it is not so independently. Accordingly, the treatment of moral rules by those who use sanctions as a principle of classification of rules tends to be very unsatisfactory. Some of them do not include moral rules at all as a separate item on their lists, no doubt because they are to be found in more than one class. Others arrive at their list of moral rules by a process of elimination. Thus Diamond,[1] using Austin's definition, describes moral rules as " rules prescribing conduct between man and man, not being rules of law or of religion "; a description according to which the sixth commandment cannot be regarded as a moral rule, because it was promulgated in the name of God and legal penalties are attached to breaches of it.

Thus whatever value such classifications may have from the point of view of those interested in non-moral rules, their treatment of moral rules is not only unhelpful but misleading. What is more important from our point of view, however, is that a classification of rules based on sanctions ignores the characteristics which make right rules right, and which explain and justify the exceptions to them which are regarded as right, and which determine the relative urgency of different rules when their requirements clash. It ignores the functional analysis of ways of life into systems of interdependent institutions and the relation of rules to institutions and ways of life. It suggests that rules which are regarded as right are regarded as right in general, that is, as applicable to all relations or situations of a certain sort; whereas, as we shall see, among primitives no rules are regarded as binding in their relations to all men; and even those rules which are generally accepted as binding between the members of the group are often differently interpreted within different institutions or in relation to different people. Nor is this confined to primitives. We ourselves interpret the rule of truth-telling differently, e.g. in the family in relation to our friends, in business in relation to our competitors, and in war in relation to our enemies. The requirements of this rule, the extent to which it is considered obligatory to tell the whole truth, varies from one institution to another, and in some institutions, such as war, deliberately to mislead others may be considered morally indifferent, if not even praiseworthy. Now such differences of interpretation of what may seem in abstract terms the same rule, and such limitations of, and approved exceptions to rules, which in some connections they regard as right, are more common among primitives; and we cannot understand the reasons for them without

[1] *Ancient Law*, p. 50.

taking account of their institutions and the ways of life which these institutions constitute.

Despite the defects of a classification of rules of conduct by reference to the sanctions attached to them, I propose to begin with it, partly because it brings out certain facts which are important for our understanding of primitive morality, and partly because it is used not only by Malinowski but also by the field workers who describe the other primitive peoples with whom I shall be concerned; and I want at present to keep as near my authorities as possible. Using this principle of division, Malinowski distinguishes the following main classes of rules of conduct among the Trobrianders:

(1) *Rules with a magico-religious or supernatural sanction.* These include all magical and ritual rules, rules regarding incest and exogamy and perhaps some of the principles at the basis of the constitution of their society, such as matrilineal descent and chieftainship. These rules rest merely on tradition or authority. The Trobriander does not understand and does not profess to understand why they should be as they are. But they are not merely customs, they are sacred customs. Justified by mythology and backed by supernatural sanctions, they are part of the sacred tradition of his people. They give rise to the religious thrill, the sense of the supernatural. The native obeys them partly out of respect for custom, partly because he regards them as sacred and partly because of fear of the consequences for himself and his people which he believes would follow any violation of them. These motives are no doubt at times reinforced by others, such as spontaneous horror of incest or the piety and love of parents that enter into mortuary rites. The observance of these magico-religious rules is, however, also a moral duty. Even if there is no idea of a supernatural agent to whom they are owed as sacred duties, they are social obligations to one's fellows. For the good of the community, including one's own as well as one's neighbour's, is believed to depend on their performance. Any breach of them, therefore, arouses strong social disapproval as well as, or because of, fear of supernatural consequences.

(2) *Rules of manners and conventions.* These rest entirely on tradition and the conservatism of custom. They are followed

more or less automatically because there is no inducement to depart from them. They do not involve any sacrifice or concession that runs counter to the desires or self-interest of the natives. On the other hand, they have a strong inducement to comply with them; for any deviation from them would make " a man feel and look in the eyes of others ridiculous, clumsy, socially uncouth ".[1]

(3) *Technical rules, rules of skill and craftsmanship.* To these the same considerations apply as to the last class, but there is an important difference: " their practical utility ", as Malinowski puts it, " is recognised by reason and testified by experience ".[2] Accordingly, while the natives adhere very closely to the traditional technical rules, whether in agriculture or fishing or craftsmanship, they understand and can explain why it is necessary to do so. They recognise them as the natural means to certain ends which they desire.

(4) *Rules of secular morality, individual and social.* These include almost all rules governing the relations of a man to his neighbours, rules of social justice, distributive and corrective, rules regarding respect for person and property, rules about truth-telling and promise-keeping and so on. They are, therefore, the rules with which we are specially concerned. These rules differ from magico-religious rules on the one hand and rules of manners on the other. Unlike the former " they have in no way the character of religious commandments ",[3] they " are not endowed with any mystical character, not set forth in the name of God, not enforced by any supernatural sanction but provided with a purely social binding force ".[4] Unlike the latter, many of them are felt to be burdensome and irksome restraints. Their requirements, positive and negative, are often opposed to man's natural inclinations and his immediate self-interest.

What, then, gives these rules their moral authority? Why do the natives regard them as right? Or, as Malinowski puts it, what are " the forces which make them binding " ?[5] The natives regard them as right because they recognise them as the conditions on which the smooth working of their institutions

---

[1] *Crime and Custom*, pp. 52-3. [2] *Ibid.* p. 52. [3] *Ibid.* p. 31.
[4] *Ibid.* p. 50 ; cf. p. 66. [5] *Ibid.* p. 67.

and the effective functioning of the common life of the group depend. These institutions and that life they find good, good not only for the group but also for themselves. They provide for the satisfaction of their needs, material and spiritual. The natives therefore regard compliance with the conditions which are necessary for their maintenance and functioning as right and reasonable. They regard the duties which they impose as binding, not out of respect for custom or tradition but because they recognise them as the conditions of individual and social well-being.

No doubt the extent to which the Trobrianders recognise the way in which the rules of their moral code are conditions on which the smooth working of their way of life depends varies considerably from one individual to another. Few, if any, of them think of these rules and their functions in the abstract or in relation to their way of life as a whole, as the social anthropologist or the moral philosopher does. But they recognise quite clearly in particular circumstances what benefits will accrue to themselves and to others if the rules are observed, and what consequences to themselves and to others will result from breaches of them. There is among them, as there is among the ordinary members of most communities, a great deal of uncritical and unquestioning acceptance of customs, the reasons for which they do not clearly understand. But Malinowski assures us that the Trobrianders recognise the need for and the conditions of co-operation as clearly as we do. As their rules are embodied in concrete institutions with their systems of rights and duties, the individual not only realises what is required of him in a particular situation, and that what is required of him is essential for the working of the system; he also realises that it is good for him as well as for others that he should perform it. Thus Malinowski writes of " the rational appreciation by the native " [1] of the requirements of the system, and of his " understanding " of " the social forces which maintain it as rational and necessary ".[2] In case these statements should leave the impression that Malinowski represents the moral beliefs or the way of life of the Trobrianders as a more coherent whole, or the attitude of the natives towards them as

---

[1] *Crime and Custom*, p. 58.   [2] *Ibid.* p. 74.

more rational, than in fact he does, I should explain that, when we take his account as a whole into consideration, what he seems to be trying to convey by them is that to the natives their different institutions or the different parts of their way of life belong together or are intelligible, in the sense that they understand how the values and satisfactions which they give are connected with the duties and obligations which they impose.[1] Elsewhere Malinowski himself puts the matter thus : " Though no native . . . can formulate this state of affairs (i.e. the detailed and elaborate working of the whole system of mutual rights and duties which constitutes their way of life) in a general abstract manner . . . yet everyone is well aware of its existence and in any concrete case he can foresee its consequences ".[2] And he sees that, taken as a whole, it is good, good for himself as well as for the community with which his welfare is so closely bound up.

Here we see the main difference between the attitude of the native to magico-religious rules and to rules of secular morality. He understands the reasons for the latter in a way in which he does not understand the reasons for the former. In this respect his attitude to moral rules is like his attitude to technical rules. While both of them belong to the traditions of his people, they belong to the secular not the sacred part of that tradition, that part which is not merely accepted on authority, but " recognised by reason and testified by experience " to be right. But the Trobrianders do not think of their moral rules in abstract or general terms, nor do they recognise them as right in isolation but as they enter into and are required by the co-operative framework of personal relations which we find in their different institutions and, still more, in the interrelation of institutions which constitutes the pattern of their way of life. Malinowski reminds us again and again that " the real problem " for our understanding of the morality or the way of life of a primitive people is " not a bald enumeration of rules " but a recognition of the way in which they operate in practice ; and he contends that " the study by direct observation of the rules . . . as they

---

[1] We saw in the last lecture the importance which Malinowski attaches to the principle of reciprocity as a means of bringing this home to the native.

[2] *Crime and Custom*, p. 42.

function in actual life . . . reveals that they are always organic-ally connected and not isolated ; that their very nature consists in the many tentacles which they throw out into the context of social life ; that they only exist in the chain of social trans-actions in which they are but a link ".[1]

In discussing the moral rules of the Trobrianders I have been referring to all their rules of individual and social morality ; but, as I have said, Malinowski is specially interested in those of their moral rules to which extra-moral, secular sanctions are attached, sanctions which encourage the native to do what he believes to be right. Some at least of these rules, Malinowski contends, are so important to the welfare of the community that conformity to them cannot be left to the mere goodwill of the individual. He calls them rules of law, and many of the statements which I have quoted from him refer specially to them. Whether they include all the secular moral rules of the Trobrianders is not clear from Malinowski's account ; but if they do not, he draws no distinction between them and other moral rules. Nor would it be easy for him to do so. For as the Trobrianders have neither courts nor constables to enforce such rules, the sanctions, positive and negative, which are attached to them and which in their case serve the same purpose as legal sanctions among ourselves, are the results of the working of their system of institutions which, as we have seen, are based on the principle of reciprocity or exchanges of goods and services. These sanctions are both economic and non-economic. Among the latter we find, e.g., the satisfaction of social impulses, of vanity and ambition, of desires for the approval of their fellows and so on. These sanctions, whether economic or non-economic, provide additional incentives to the Trobrianders to comply with their rules when their sense of duty and regard for the rights of others are not by themselves strong enough. And for those for whom these positive incentives are not a sufficient inducement there is the fear of economic consequences to themselves to act as a deterrent against breaches of the rules. This fear is evoked by the economic aspect of the principle of reciprocity. That is why Malinowski lays so much emphasis on it. It is these positive extra-moral incentives to

[1] *Crime and Custom*, p. 125 ; cf. *Coral Gardens*, i. 338.

obey their rules and these deterrents against breaches of them which, among the Trobrianders, fulfil most of the functions which law fulfils in more advanced societies. They do not guarantee that rules are obeyed from moral motives, any more than our laws do, but they encourage people to fulfil obligations which they might otherwise feel inclined to disregard.

Now Malinowski is at considerable pains to distinguish these rules, the rules of primitive law, from the other three classes which he describes, i.e. ritual, conventional and technical rules. And the distinction applies both to the sanctions which attach to them and to the attitude of the natives towards them. But he does not try to distinguish those which he calls the rules of primitive law from other moral rules, if there are any others. The reason for this is, I think, that most of what he says about them applies to all secular moral rules. This seems to be so even as regards the extra-moral sanctions attached to them. For among all small closely knit groups of people who are dependent on one another for all goods and services, all moral and social approval and disapproval tend to find expression in ways which are apt to affect the satisfaction of the needs of the people concerned, i.e. in economic or semi-economic ways ; and so the sanctions which Malinowski calls legal tend to be attached to all moral rules. It is of course true that when a man complies with a rule which he regards as right from non-moral motives, his action is not morally good. But Malinowski makes it plain that, even in the case of the rules which he calls legal, mere external conformity, which is all that non-moral sanctions can ensure, is not all that the Trobrianders expect from the good man or all that they normally get from one another. They often obey their rules, we are told, from sense of duty or regard for the rights of others as well as from more self-interested and less creditable motives. But a person's motives for complying with a rule, if he does comply with it, are irrelevant when we are considering the grounds on which he recognises it as right. And as regards the grounds on which they recognise them as right, Malinowski's account of the rules which he calls legal applies to all Trobriand moral rules.

It might be thought possible to distinguish what Malinowski calls rules of primitive law from other moral rules in a different way. But when we consider this way of distinguishing them we find that it is not so clear as it seems on the surface, and that it has little relevance either to the grounds on which the rules are considered right or to the sanctions which are attached to them. The rules with which Malinowski is specially concerned are mainly those of social justice, distributive and corrective. They find expression in the particular forms of co-operation which we find in the social institutions of the Trobrianders, such as Kula exchanges, marriage arrangements, the relations between the members of a canoe crew or a hunting expedition, and so on. About these particular forms of co-operation there is, as we have seen, something arbitrary. Though the principle of reciprocity which finds expression in them is not arbitrary, it might equally well find expression in other forms of co-operation based on other rules. But there are other moral rules such as those about respect for life and property, truth-telling and promise-keeping, which have nothing arbitrary about them. They are general conditions of any form of co-operation, even of the minimum of co-operation involved in being members of one community. We might, therefore, say that these more general conditions of co-operation, which apply to all communities and to the working of all institutions, are the strictly moral rules; but, among the Trobrianders at any rate, the distinction between them and the more specific rules which vary from institution to institution is not so important or so clear as it might at first appear.

When Malinowski says that the Trobrianders realise that co-operation is necessary and desirable and that they therefore recognise as obligatory the conditions which make it effective, his account makes it clear that the conditions which they recognise as right include both the particular expressions of the principle of reciprocity which we find in their social institutions and also the more general conditions of any form of co-operation. So that the grounds on which they regard the rules as right apply equally to the two classes; they are both conditions of a form of life which they regard as good. But the main reason why the distinction between the two kinds of rules is not so clear as it might at first appear is that we cannot understand the interpretation which they put on the more general conditions of co-operation, the extent to which they regard them as right or the exceptions to them which they admit, without taking account of their particular institutions. We may say that any form of co-operation or of orderly social life requires that, in general, truth should be told, promises kept, theft condemned and life respected. Such rules, therefore, seem to be of general application to every form of life. But stated in such general terms these rules seem to mean only that the specific rules respecting life, property, truth-telling and promise-keeping, which are embodied in the institutions of the people concerned and necessary for their working, should be obeyed. For when we ask to whom should the truth be told, how much should be told, and in what circumstances it should be told, we cannot answer without taking account of the particular institutions which make up the way of life of the people concerned. Among the Trobrianders it is a condition of the working of some of their institutions that one should not tell the truth about certain things. E.g. they believe that no man should tell the truth about his contribution to his brother-in-law's family,[1] or about the contents of his own storehouse ;[2] and there is no obligation at all to tell the truth to a foreigner. In the same way among ourselves whether the truth should be told, and if so how much should be told, depends on whether we are dealing with family and friends, with business competitors, or with an enemy in war-time. Similar considerations apply to any other rule we care to take, at least among the Trobrianders.

The fact is that as their rules are embodied in their institutions and operate in practice, none of them is strictly universal. They all admit of exceptions which are regarded as right. But as the rules are neither taught to them in their youth nor thought of by them as adults in abstract general terms, and as the exceptions as well as the rules are embodied in institutions, the exceptions are not usually thought of in relation to the rules but as the requirements of particular institutions. Therefore, they are not usually thought of as exceptions. What may seem to us the same rule, e.g. the rule to tell the truth, or not to steal

[1] *Coral Gardens*, i. 175-6.
[2] For other instances of situations in which the truth should not be told see *ibid*. i. 173 and 185-6.

or to kill, may be a condition of the working of one of their institutions but not of another. But as their institutions are adjusted to one another so that conflicts between their requirements do not normally arise, and as the rule is not thought of in the abstract, the conflict between the rule and the exception may not be recognised by them as such, any more than it always is by us when we are living our own way of life. The exceptions and the rules are regarded by them as right for the same reason, because they seem to them the conditions of a form of life which they find on the whole good.

The only rule which they regard as strictly universal is the rule that duties should be performed, obligations fulfilled, rights respected.[1] Particular moral rules as to what are duties, obligations and rights are universal only in the sense that they are not respecters of persons or at least of personal identity; for, in some connections, the Trobrianders regard differences of rank and social status as morally relevant. Their moral rules are universal in the sense that what is right for me to do in a given situation would be right for anyone of my rank and status in similar circumstances. They are not universal in the sense that if it is not right for me in a particular situation to make a deliberately misleading statement, to kill a man or to take the property of another, it is never right either for myself or for anyone else to do these things in any circumstances.

There is still another sense in which their moral rules are not universal. They do not apply outside the group, whether this be a village, a district, a clan, a tribe or a group of tribes. There is always a limit beyond which the outsider has no rights. In other words, they do not recognise any rules which apply to men as such, or even to all men or all natives with whom they come in contact. What they recognise as good is the maintenance of the common life of the group whose members alone they regard as objects of duties and subjects of rights. It is the values embodied in the institutions which constitute this common life which for them make life worth while. They therefore accept as binding the rules and duties which the maintenance of this life and the realisation of its values seem to them to imply. But they regard them as binding only so far

[1] This is not so much a rule as a statement of the nature of morality.

as they are thus implied. It is their conception of this form of life that for them gives validity and authority to their rules, in those cases in which they are recognised as binding, and that justifies the exceptions to them which are regarded as right. But as we have already seen, their conception of this life is not vague and nebulous. It is embodied in a system of concrete institutions. Through the working of these and the principle of reciprocity on which they are based, they recognise both what particular duties it requires of them and how their own good and the realisation of the values which they cherish are bound up with it and with the performance of their duties.

Three other comments remain to be made before we take leave of the Trobrianders :

(1) I have been mainly concerned in trying to discover what for them gives their rules moral authority, but needless to say the recognition of rules as right and duties as obligatory does not of itself ensure that the natives will fulfil them ; and, when they do, they do not necessarily do it from moral motives. Their motives for obeying their rules, when they do obey them, are usually mixed and vary from individual to individual and from time to time in the life of the same individual : sense of duty, respect for the rights of others, loyalty and devotion to the group, desire of social approval or fear of disapproval and self-interest all enter.

(2) In his detailed treatment of their moral rules, Malinowski is primarily concerned with the extra-moral incentives and sanctions which help the Trobriander to do what he believes to be right. But he tells us that, in the moral judgements which they pass on one another, they take account not only of whether people do their duties but also of the spirit in which they do them. A man may comply with the requirements of their moral code from unworthy motives. He may do his duties in a mean and niggardly spirit, or again with ostentation and boastfulness. Both these attitudes are condemned by the Trobrianders. They regard as the good man, the man who carries out his duties quietly and generously, without too much regard for his own selfish interests — he who resists temptation, has a proper regard for the rights of others, and gives more than he

takes. What we are not told is how far they attain to the highest reaches of the moral life, where the individual not only struggles against his own weaker nature, but in a lonely venture of faith trusts his own moral insight against the accepted moral beliefs and code of his people, when his fellows, and perhaps many of us, might say that he was playing the fool. But we are told that they sometimes complain that some of the accepted customs of their people are not right,[1] and we have already quoted instances of ways in which they change them.

(3) I have quoted from Malinowski statements to show that most of the moral rules of the Trobrianders have no super-natural sanctions in the sense either of being promulgated in the name of supernatural agents or of having supernatural rewards or punishments attached to them, but this does not mean that their magico-religious beliefs and practices have no influence on their morality. Malinowski is quite explicit and emphatic that their magico-religious beliefs, and especially the performance of the practices which they enjoin, exercise a profound influence both on the character of the individual and on his relations to his fellows. They help to produce in those who take part in them an unselfishness, a respect for the common good, and a spirit of goodwill and mutual trust which makes it more likely that they will perform their duties to one another. To this aspect of the relation between their morality and religion I shall have to return later.

[1] See, e.g., *Sexual Life of Savages*, p. 272.

A BANTU TRIBE [1]

I TAKE as my second illustration of experiments in living, the way of life of the Bantu tribes of South East Africa. My main reasons for this choice are : (1) The pattern of Bantu culture rests on a number of principles of social organisation and contains a number of institutions which are common among primitive people but which are not found among the Trobrianders. For example, they reckon kinship through the male, they practise polygamy, they worship their ancestors, they have initiation rites and they pay the bride price or bride wealth. (2) Not only is there an extensive literature about them, but Junod, on whose account I shall mainly rely, has given a more detailed description of their moral ideas than we usually get from field workers among primitive peoples. (3) A comparison between their culture and that of the Trobrianders illustrates a truth to which I have already called attention, namely that the different aspects of a people's culture do not develop uniformly, for neither the Bantu commerce, which is exceedingly primitive, nor their industrial development will bear comparison with the Kula arrangements and the high craftsmanship of the Trobrianders. Yet they have a keener sense of justice, and they have developed a very remarkable system for its administration. They have also a more developed form of religion, and it plays a greater part in their lives. We shall, therefore, be able to see more clearly in their case the relation between primitive morality and religion strictly so called. (4) They have been in contact with Western civilisation for more than a century, though it is only in the past two or three generations that it has exerted any marked influence on

[1] My main authorities for this account are : Junod, *The Life of a South African Tribe* ; *The Bantu-speaking Tribes of South Africa* (collective work), ed. Schapera ; Willoughby, *The Soul of the Bantu* ; Culwick, *Good Out of Africa*.

them. The results of these contacts will enable us to see the close interdependence between their institutions ; for external interference with one tends to affect others as well.

The principles which determine the fundamental structure of the ways of living of all the Bantu tribes are much the same, but there are differences of detail in the way in which different tribes apply and combine them. Accordingly, while the main outline of the following account applies to all Bantu tribes, and while some of its details will be illustrated by reference to other tribes, it is concerned specially with the Tonga [1] group of tribes described by Junod in his *Life of a South African Tribe*.

The Bantu practise a mixed form of agriculture, partly arable, partly grazing. Much of the land which they occupy is covered by rocks and sand-dunes and forests. It is, therefore, sparsely populated, the households or kraals being usually a mile or more apart. This comparative isolation and relative economic independence of the villages has, as we shall see, an important significance for certain aspects of their way of life.

What, then, are the principles which determine the framework of their social structure ?

(1) The principle of kinship is at least as important among them as among the Trobrianders, but the Bantu reckon kinship through the father. The father is head of the family. He is the source of authority, to whom obedience is due. From him status and goods are inherited. The attitude to him and his kin is, therefore, more like that adopted towards the maternal uncle and his kin among the Trobrianders — an attitude of deference to authority and dutifulness to the source of discipline and legality. But this attitude is partly softened by the natural affection between parents and children. The attitude to the mother and her kin is much less restrained. Indeed " the deepest bond of affection known to these people " [2] is that between mother and children.

(2) The second principle of the Bantu social organisation is seniority. In the family the older brother takes precedence,

---

[1] The spelling used by Junod is ' Thonga ' or ' Bathonga ', but the spelling used in the text is recommended by the Inter-University Committee for African Studies as the more correct (Schapera, *op. cit.* p. xv).

[2] Schapera, *op. cit.* p. 71.

and the others follow in order of age. The same principle applies between sisters, between the children of different brothers, between families within the clan, and between clans within a tribe. On it status everywhere depends.

(3) The principle of seniority also underlies the third feature of their social structure — the chieftainship. While the tribe generally is believed to consist mainly of descendants in the male line of one ancestor, the chief is supposed to be the most direct descendant, that is, through the eldest son of the eldest son, and so on.[1] The chief occupies a position of pre-eminent importance. He is responsible for the maintenance of law and order. To him all members of the tribe owe allegiance, and he can call on them for various services in peace and war. He has also the largest herd of cattle. But though the chief has much more wealth at his disposal, there is very little difference between his standard of living and that of a commoner. They both eat the same sort of food, wear the same sort of clothes and live in the same kind of hut. The possession of greater wealth merely offers an opportunity and imposes an obligation to provide more hospitality and to give more generously. The personal prestige which this confers ranks in the estimation of the Bantu higher than personal comfort. But the chief's prestige does not rest merely on riches and power. He is also the chief priest. He has the most powerful magic, and he acts as mediator between his people and their ancestral gods. He is in fact the symbol of the unity of the tribe, and this is no mere empty symbolism. The unity of the tribe finally rests on allegiance to him rather than on kinship from a common ancestor. For when a tribe has a popular chief, members of other tribes, individually and in groups, ask to be allowed to join it. They are allowed to do so and to enjoy all the privileges which membership involves on condition that they declare their allegiance to the chief and undertake the various duties which he requires from his tribesmen. Despite such transfers, however, the clan based on kinship retains its unity, especially for ritual purposes and the regulation of marriage.

[1] This, however, is partly legal fiction. In actual fact there are many exceptions to it. See pp. 167-8.

M

(4) The relationship of husband and wife, on which the unity of the individual family rests, cuts across the clan unity reckoned in the patrilineal line. But among the Bantu kinship by marriage is a much weaker bond not only in legal theory, but in actual fact than kinship by blood. Among us, the tie of mutual affection which binds man and wife is regarded as the strongest of all ties and takes precedence over all others, including ties binding a person to his brothers and sisters. Among the Bantu the position is reversed. They reckon the tie of blood the strongest of all bonds. This is the key to many of their institutions and much of their behaviour, and in particular to many of their marriage customs. Among them marriage is patrilocal, that is, the wife goes to live at her husband's village; and polygamous, that is, one man may have and usually has several wives. Each wife, with her children, occupies a separate hut, and has a separate field allotted to her. Among wives and children the principle of seniority holds. The first or great wife has precedence over all the others, and the others have precedence according to the order of their marriage; while the status of children follows that of their mother. In general, among the Tonga group of tribes, there is clan exogamy to the eighth degree, but there are minor differences in this respect not only between different groups of tribes but even within the same group. On the mother's side, a man may marry anyone beyond his first cousin. Subject to these conditions, a man may marry anyone within the tribe, but it is considered desirable that his wives should be taken from people who are already known to his kinsmen. A man may even marry certain persons within the prohibited relationship, provided a special ceremony is performed as a safeguard against untoward consequences.[1] There are also women, such as his wife's younger sister or his brother-in-law's daughter, whom it is considered specially suitable for a man to marry. It is not obligatory on him to do so or on them or their families to agree, even if he wants to, but there is a feeling that such unions are specially appropriate.

[1] Here we have again the phenomenon which we met among the Trobrianders, namely, that legalised usage with a magico-religious sanction may enable the native to evade the strict letter of tribal law.

(5) Among the Bantu the territorial unit is the village or kraal. This normally consists of a man with his wives and children, his brothers and their wives and children, and other relatives in the patrilineal line, such as unmarried brothers and unmarried, divorced or widowed sisters. The senior male member acts as head of the village. He maintains order in the kraal and acts as its representative to the outside world. A group of such villages usually connected by kinship constitute a sub-district, and several sub-districts constitute a district, and so on up to the area ruled over by the paramount chief.

We have now before us the main principles which constitute the structure of Bantu society : kinship reckoned through the father, family exogamy, polygyny, patrilocal marriage and seniority with a hierarchy of status culminating in the paramount chief. In the eyes of the natives this structure derives its authority from its antiquity. Indeed its main lines are believed to have been already laid down when their first ancestors emerged from reeds, with many of the present characteristics of their descendants, including much of their knowledge and skill and many of their customs. And as their ancestors are their principal gods, whose goodwill is ensured by the observance of certain tribal customs, this confers on the principles of the hierarchy a semi-religious sanction. But while this guarantees a high degree of stability to the social structure, changes do from time to time take place, and these sometimes amount to considerable reorganisation. For example, though the antiquity of the principle of seniority and the institution of the chieftainship is sufficient to compensate for minor faults of character or of administrative ability in the holders of positions of authority, it does not render them immune from criticism nor does it enable them to use their power for personal ends. The headman or even the chief may be deposed for incompetence or maladministration ; and there are other ways in which his position may be undermined. For example, a reigning chief may appoint his brothers or other relatives as sub-chiefs of districts and such positions tend to become hereditary. As we have seen in the case of the chief, families or groups may transfer their allegiance from one sub-chief or headman to another. Consequently, a descendant of one of these sub-chiefs may by force of personality and reputation for just administration so enhance his position and increase the number of his people as to threaten the position of the legal chief. Open conflict may then result, and if the sub-chief is victorious, he may transfer the chieftainship to his own family, and reduce the legal chief to a subordinate position; and the change may be accepted by the tribe as a whole. This is why I described the seniority of the reigning chief as in part a legal fiction.

Consider next the Tonga view of the supernatural, the unseen forces, personal and impersonal, which operate in their environment and which provide the background of all their thinking and acting. They believe that after death their ancestors continue to live and behave more or less as they did during their lifetime. They regard them as still members of the clan, able and willing to exercise an influence on its affairs; so that their religion has been not inappropriately described as the extension of the principles of family life based on seniority into the next world. The ancestors of a particular family are worshipped only by the living members of that family, and their powers for good or evil are limited to the members of their own family. On the other hand the ancestors of the chief, who during their lifetime were expected to take an interest in the welfare of the whole tribe, are still publicly appealed to on behalf of the whole people in times of crises or disaster. What these gods expect from their worshippers is merely a continuance of the respect and deference which, on the basis of their seniority, was regarded as their due in their lifetime. The Bantu religious ritual lays down the ways in which this deference is to be shown. In accordance with its requirements, offerings are made to the ancestors and they are appealed to for prosperity on certain stated occasions, as well as in all the crises of life. Such occasions include marriage,[1] death,[2] removal to a new village,[3] drought,[4] harvest festivals [5] and so on. If the proper ceremonies are performed, the ancestors are believed to be as

---

[1] Junod, *op. cit.* i. 134.   [2] *Ibid.* i. 142.   [3] *Ibid.* i. 323.
[4] *Ibid.* ii. 421.   [5] *Ibid.* i. 396.

much under an obligation to look after the interests of their
descendants as they were during their lifetime. Accordingly,
when disaster overtakes the devout Bantu, he sometimes scolds
his ancestors for neglecting their duties,[1] so that his prayers are
sometimes as much protests as petitions.[2] But while these
ancestor gods are believed to be keenly interested in the correct
performance of tribal ritual and in the payment of due respect
to themselves, they do not seem to pay much regard to the
spirit in which the worship is given, and still less to the conduct
of their worshippers towards one another in the ordinary affairs
of life. But though Bantu worship consists largely of ritual
without reverence, and though their religion does not demand
that they should behave morally towards one another, there are,
as we shall see, ways in which their magico-religious beliefs
indirectly affect their conduct to their fellows ; and the ritual
practices in which they lead them to engage profoundly influence
their attitude to one another.

The Bantu do not draw a very clear distinction between
supernatural forces which operate directly and impersonally
and those which involve the intervention of personal agents.
Most of the ceremonies which they perform at the main crises
of life are magical rather than religious. Only in the case of
marriage and death is there a direct appeal to the ancestors,
and even these appeals are accompanied by ritual practices,
the due performance of which is believed to produce the
desired results directly and automatically.

The impersonal supernatural forces operate in two main
ways. On the one hand, certain things or happenings have in
themselves properties or powers which, without the intervention of any agency, human or superhuman, produce certain
effects, mostly harmful. Such powers are possessed, for
example, by menstrual blood, abortion, the birth of twins,
lightning and so on ; and appropriate action has to be taken
if these untoward consequences are to be prevented. For
example, one of each pair of twins has to be killed and purifying
rites performed. On the other hand, there are things like
magical medicines or formulae which require a human agent

---

[1] Junod, *op. cit.* ii. 423.
[2] Cf. Willoughby, *The Soul of the Bantu*, pp. 277-8.

to use them. When so used they directly produce the appropriate results. Some of them may be used by anybody, others only by a properly trained expert, the magician.

The belief in magic pervades every aspect of Bantu life, but it is specially prominent in relation to agriculture, ill-health and the main transitions of life. The failure of agriculture is to them the greatest of calamities for it threatens their very existence. Accordingly, every step in the agricultural process is accompanied by its appropriate magical rite, and the natives sincerely believe that this is essential to the success of the crop. The main rites in connection with agriculture are performed by the husbandman himself, and appeals to the ancestors are often mixed with them. Thus they do not play so important a part in organising and timing the agricultural process as they do among the Trobrianders. Among the Bantu the organising work is done by the chief and the hierarchy. Similar magical rites are necessary to ensure the success of hunting and fishing and all other activities which are dangerous or of uncertain issue. Ill-health, especially serious illness which threatens or causes death, is believed to be mainly due to magic, and only by magical means can illness be cured. In all cases the power of magic is morally neutral. It can be used either for good or for evil purposes. In other words, there is among the Bantu both a white and a black magic. Black magic is greatly feared, and when it is discovered it is the most severely punished of all crimes.

The Bantu divide the life of man into a series of well-marked stages and they regard the transition from one state to the next as fraught with danger. To get over these critical periods the individual has to be supported and protected by a number of magico-religious rites. We find such rites performed, for example, at birth, when a child gets his first tooth, when he begins to crawl, when he is weaned, at puberty, at marriage and at death. The rites at the more important transitions serve to introduce the individual to a new status, and some of them help to impress on him his new duties and responsibilities. For example, the ceremony at crawling is intended to make the child a full member of the clan. Till it is performed he is not regarded as fully human, and if he dies his mother buries him without assistance or ceremony.[1]   Until the ceremonies at weaning, which takes place about the age of three, are performed, the mother must not again become pregnant, a restriction which is rendered less onerous by the institution of polygyny.   The ceremonies at death are designed not only as an expression of affectionate remembrance of the deceased but also as a means of helping them on their way to the next stage of their life story, where they join the elder members and ancestors of the clan who are also the family gods.   But the most important of the transition rites are the initiation ceremonies which take place at puberty, somewhere between the ages of ten and sixteen. These ceremonies constitute the youth's introduction to real manhood and they are meant to impress upon him his new status as an adult member of the tribe.   They occur every four or five years.   They take place at a lodge in the wilderness where the boys are secluded for a period of three months. There they are exposed to a severe discipline and a series of hardships in order to teach them " endurance, obedience and manliness ".[2]   They are also taught magico-religious formulae, but among the Tonga at any rate they are not given much moral instruction.   Such instruction as they receive is indirect, by means of symbolism rather than precepts.   Many of the formulae which they have to learn " may appear to the observer or reader, unaware of their setting and significance, as crude ; but ", we are assured, that " to the native they do not appear so. Out of their context they might convey to the native mind some obscenity, corresponding somewhat to the translation into licentious language by indiscriminate use in ordinary social relations of the scientific terminology of a professor in physiology.   But . . . they are taught in an atmosphere of such awe and respect for the school, and all it stands for, that their psychological effect cannot be otherwise than to emphasise the importance of the things that are taught."   And among the things which the schools succeed in inculcating are " obedience, discipline and general good behaviour, qualities that make many a European employer prefer ' boys ' that have been through the schools to others ".[3]

[1] Cf. Junod, *op. cit.* ii. 373.   [2] *Ibid.* i. 85.
[3] Schapera, *op. cit.* p. 107.

Those who pass through these schools together tend to become united for life by bonds of friendship and mutual service — thus strengthening the cohesion and solidarity of the tribe — and, among some tribes, these groupings provide the organisation on the basis of which are arranged military service and other forms of communal work, such as the labour required by the chief for working his fields or building or repairing his huts.

What we find, then, is that among the Bantu magico-religious performances are regarded as necessary at every point at which failure, danger or disaster threatens the native from causes which he does not understand, and which he has not learned to control; and they serve the purpose of inspiring confidence and strengthening morale. But we need not enter further into the details of these magico-religious rites, for they contain no principle which we have not already met among the Trobrianders. While the details of the ritual performed and the points at which it is applied differ from people to people, according to their history and experience and the points at which the environment seems to threaten their welfare, the belief in and the appeal to unseen powers, personal and impersonal, and the functions which this appeal performs in their lives, remain much the same.

In addition to their belief in impersonal supernatural power, the efficacy of magic, and the power of their ancestral gods, the Bantu also believe in the existence both of minor spirits who were never incarnate, at least in human form, and in a supreme spiritual power. Their conception of this supreme power is vague and indefinite, and our authorities are uncertain as to how far they conceive it as personal. But whether personal or not, it is regarded as remote from and little interested in the affairs of men. There is no suggestion among the Bantu that any supernatural agent will call them to judgement after death, or that their happiness hereafter is in any way determined by their conduct to their fellow-men in this life.[1]

Against the background of their magico-religious ideas regarding the nature of the universe, natural and supernatural,

[1] Junod, *op. cit.* ii. 366.

and their own destiny as part of it, and within the general framework of the social structure which I have described, the Bantu have developed moral and social institutions for satisfying their fundamental human needs. It is in the detailed working of these institutions that the principles and beliefs which we have been considering find concrete expression, and help to determine the rights and duties of individuals. What, then, are these institutions ? On what principles do they operate ? How do they dovetail into one another so as to constitute the characteristic Bantu way of life ?

I am not suggesting that the institutions of the Bantu are the only ones which could function within the structure which I have described, or that all their details are determined by it; but only that it helps to make them what they are and that many of their special features cannot be understood without reference to it; that, in short, even if the parts of their way of life are not in their own nature necessarily connected, they are so interwoven in the habits of thinking and feeling and acting of the natives as to form a relatively integrated pattern. It is the nature of this pattern and the relations of a man to his fellows within it which determine his rights and duties, his privileges and responsibilities.

It would be impossible in the time at my disposal to give a detailed description of all Bantu institutions and the ways in which they are related. I propose, therefore, to give one main illustration, the series of interrelated institutions which centre round the nature and functioning of the Bantu family, and to explain more briefly some of their economic arrangements and some aspects of their system of legal administration. These are among their most characteristic institutions. They contain their provision for the satisfaction of some of their most fundamental needs. And they provide typical examples of the interdependence of their institutions, as well as of the way in which the principles of their social structure and their magico-religious ideas penetrate into their social institutions, and help to make them what they are. In trying to understand the Bantu family, e.g., and the duties and obligations that arise in connection with it, we shall find it necessary to take account of their ideas of kinship, seniority and clan solidarity, their economic arrangements, their ancestor worship and their ritual practices. Without a grasp of these, we cannot hope to understand the nature and functioning of their family life.

Among the Bantu, marriage is a complex, protracted and costly process ; but it is necessary to give a man full status as an adult member of the community. When a young man decides that he wants to marry, he does not go to the girl of his choice and propose marriage. For, owing to the operation of the principle of kinship, marriage among these people is a contract between families or groups, at least as much as between individuals. The young man, therefore, informs his father of his desire. If the father, usually after consultation with other members of the group, approves, he opens negotiations, through an intermediary, with the girl's parents. If they and their group are satisfied that an alliance is desirable, the girl is consulted. If she consents, protracted negotiations follow between the families regarding the *lobola* — the bride wealth or bride price, as it is sometimes rather inaccurately called. This is one of the most characteristic of Bantu institutions, and it shows how their marriage arrangements and their economic affairs are inextricably interwoven. The bride wealth consists of payments, sometimes spread over a period of years, made by the bridegroom, or rather by his father, sometimes with the assistance of his kinsmen, to the father of the bride. It takes many different forms : so many head of cattle, so many hoes, or more recently so much money, and so on.

These payments are not regarded by the natives as a price for which the girl is sold to her husband's family, but it is often referred to as compensation to the girl's family for the loss of a member, and the payment is often used to get a wife for the bride's brother. If it is not a price paid for the bride, much less is it a dowry given to her, for it goes to her father's family in their village, while she goes to live with her husband in his. But whatever its origin or early significance, *lobola* is " what constitutes legal marriage, which to the Bantu is inconceivable without it ".[1] No doubt the ordinary marriage ceremony also comprises many ritual performances, much festivity and many exchanges of gifts, but *lobola* is marriage in the sense that unless

[1] Schapera, *op. cit.* p. 113.

it has been paid any children of the union are illegitimate, that is, without social status, and belong to the family of the mother, not that of the father. Moreover if, as sometimes happens, a poor man, who or whose family cannot raise the necessary payment, runs away with a girl, the children are illegitimate unless negotiations are opened with the wife's family and payment promised and in due course made. This is the normal ending to runaway Bantu marriages.

In addition to making marriage legal, *lobola* serves many other purposes. It gives social standing and a certain security to the wife ; for if she is badly treated, and has in consequence to leave her husband, he cannot claim the return of the payment. It gives stability to the marriage ; for if a wife leaves her husband without due cause, or is divorced for legitimate reasons, the bride wealth has to be returned by her people.[1] It emphasises the solidarity of the family and clan ; for other members besides the father are liable to be called on to contribute towards the payment. It cements the bonds between brother and sister, and gives the sister an additional claim on the brother for whom her *lobola* provided a wife, and on the children who result from his marriage. It also helps to unite by bonds of lifelong friendship and mutual service the two groups to which the husband and wife belong. To begin with, there is apt to be a certain suspicion and mutual distrust between the two groups. This no doubt partly accounts for the formal correctness, often amounting to a taboo on any intimate personal relations, between the spouses and their relatives-in-law, especially between the husband and his mother-in-law and the bride and her father-in-law. But when the union has proved harmonious and the alliance has been fully established, especially by the birth of children, this distrust lessens and the taboos and avoidances may be considerably mitigated ; but, despite many exchanges of gifts and other mutual services, the relations between the two groups tend always to remain somewhat strained and formal.

[1] This often causes serious complications ; for the original payment may have been used years earlier to get a bride for the wife's brother, and any attempt to return it may seriously affect the brother's domestic arrangements.

Nevertheless, the *lobola* arrangement has its disadvantages from the wife's point of view. Under it her children are not her own, but belong to her husband and his family. She is at times in danger of being regarded as an outsider, for whose services her husband and his family have paid. This is seen, for example, in the Bantu attitude towards adultery. Adultery with a wife is regarded not as a crime against her, but against her husband, the theft of that for which he has paid. Accordingly, the adulterer has to pay compensation to the husband. It should be added, however, that this is only one aspect of the native attitude towards adultery. For they also believe that there is a magico-religious sanction against it. An illegitimate baby causes a difficult and protracted birth,[1] and adultery produces undesirable physical effects on men.[2]

Thus marriage to the Bantu is mainly a secular contract, validated by economic exchanges and mutual services; but it is also accompanied by magico-religious ceremonies. The principle ceremony takes place before the bride leaves her father's house, when sacrifices are made to the ancestral gods, and a prayer is offered not only for her material prosperity but also for her moral welfare in her new home. But what specially strikes us about the Bantu thought of marriage is that all the emphasis is laid on the mutual services of the spouses to one another, while nothing is said or thought about mutual affection or regard. The woman has done her duty by her husband if she cultivates his fields, cooks his food and rears his children, while he has done his duty by her if he supplies her with a hut and cattle and other amenities. In their view the tie of blood is stronger than the tie of marriage, and the duties which it imposes are more stringent. The husband tends to reserve his friendship for his male companions and his affection for his sisters and the other members of his father's family. The wife bestows her affection on her children and her brothers, and her companionship on her female friends. She continues to worship the gods of her father's family, and it is to her brothers and her other near kin that she turns for advice in perplexity, and flees for help and protection if she finds life too difficult. This does not mean that married life among them is not often

---

[1] Junod, *op. cit.* i. 40.   [2] *Ibid.* i. 198.

happy and harmonious, or that tender affection between the spouses does not sometimes develop. But their whole conception of marriage and the values which are realised in it are different from ours, and affection is not one of the values expected from it.

We might bring out the difference between their conception of marriage and ours in this way. Man needs companionship and affection, and he also needs a mate and other personal services. In our way of life, the family provides all these — sexual satisfaction and intimate personal services on the one hand, and the deepest bond of friendship and the tenderest affection on the other. In the Bantu way of life, the satisfaction of these different needs is provided by separate institutions, the former through the family, the latter through other channels. As Culwick puts it, " in Bantu society physical attraction, affection and companionship usually follow quite different channels, a man desiring his wife, loving his sister and seeking companionship among his male relations and friends. The same is true for the woman. The most important object of her affections is usually one of her brothers, while her female relatives and friends provide her with companionship. If she is in trouble she invariably goes to her male clansmen, not to her husband. He is from another group and is therefore not to be trusted as one would one's brother." [1] As a result, not only is divorce among them relatively easy, but it is neither regarded as a disaster nor does it usually leave such a legacy of bitterness and frustration as it does among us.[2]

In our way of life, however, the family performs another function. It provides for the care and the early training of children. How, then, does Bantu divorce affect the children for whose sake, even more than for the parents', stability of marriage seems to us essential ? To discover the answer to this question, we must consider other aspects of their married life, especially polygyny. The ambition of every Bantu is to have several wives and many children as well as much cattle. This will enable him to be generous and hospitable to his friends, and on the

[1] *Op. cit.* p. 36.
[2] For the account of the Bantu family in this and the following paragraphs, I am specially indebted to Culwick, *Good Out of Africa*, ch. v.

extent of his generosity, in large part, depends his social standing among his fellows. Accordingly, " to have a large harem is to have succeeded in life ".[1]

Among the co-wives the principle of seniority holds, and each has her place in the hierarchy. They are said to be so free from sexual jealousy that the first wife sometimes indicates to the husband a woman who might be suitable as an additional partner. To their husband's affairs with unmarried girls they seem to be entirely indifferent. This does not mean that jealousy is absent from their nature or that it never appears, but only that their way of life discourages it and that their institutions provide little scope for its expression. Relations between the co-wives, though sometimes strained, are usually fairly harmonious and there is much co-operation and mutual help between them. Though each is responsible for the cultivation of her own field, and has her own storehouse, they often arrange to work together and cultivate the different fields in turn. Though each is complete mistress within her own hut, there is much co-operation in cooking and looking after the children. Though each hut has its own cooking arrangements where food from its own storehouse is prepared, at the main meal of the day — the evening meal — no household cooks merely for itself. Each prepares a portion for the husband and his male friends and any visitors who may be with him. It also sends a portion to every other household, to wives and children alike. Thus, while the system cannot be regarded as communal, it means that everyone within the kraal gets his share of what is going and that no one is left destitute. Junod describes the profound impression of the unity and solidarity of the kraal which this meal leaves on the observer.[2]

This co-operative community of women which makes up the female section of the kraal includes not only the co-wives of the same husband but also the wives of his brothers, and it may be others, such as grandmothers, young unmarried sisters and divorced or widowed sisters who have returned to the village. These unattached women occupy a separate hut and play their part in the work of the kraal, including looking after the children. Accordingly, children are from their earliest

---

[1] Junod, *op. cit.* i. 284.   [2] *Ibid.* i. 317-18.

years accustomed to the care and protection of several women, to all of whom under the classificatory system they apply the same term — 'mother' or 'grandmother' according to their age. They also stay at times for longish periods with their grandparents or their maternal uncle in their mother's village. Thus they have a right of entry into several huts on more or less equal terms; and it is equally natural for them to stay in any one of them.[1] Wherever they are, they associate freely with the other children of their own age group who are related to them by blood, whether through the father or the mother, and they are expected to take their share in the work of herding the goats, caring for the cattle, and performing various domestic duties. Consequently, when the original hut is broken up, owing to the divorce of their mother, either on her own or her husband's initiative, they continue to live much the same life, cared for by much the same seniors and doing much the same work: only they have one fewer home that they can call their own. In these circumstances the break-up of the marriage of their father and mother is not for the children the major catastrophe which it is in our form of society.[2] If there are young children, they continue to live with their mother who is still responsible for their care; and even the older children may still visit her and her family, and may even stay for longish periods with them in the village to which she has returned. For, provided certain formalities regarding the *lobola* have been complied with, there is usually little bitterness between the divorced parents or their families.

What we find then is that, subject to the general framework of their social structure and their magico-religious ideas, marriage is for the Bantu a secular contract based on a reciprocity of mutual services. Each partner has his or her duties to perform and rights to claim. Each recognises that the

---

[1] Culwick, *op. cit.* p. 35.

[2] It must not, however, be assumed that as compared with our form of family the Bantu form has all the advantages; for even if the break-up of a Bantu marriage is not the major catastrophe which divorce among us is apt to be, the Bantu marriage is usually regarded as less satisfying emotionally, and those who are reared in the enlarged Bantu family are said to be incapable of experiencing great intensity of feeling. For the advantages and disadvantages of the two forms, see Linton, *The Study of Man*, ch. x.

performance of his duties is a condition of his claim to the reciprocal services being satisfied. They recognise the arrangement as good in that it provides the means to satisfy important needs, and therefore they recognise its duties as binding. When they cease so to regard it, they bring the arrangement to an end, the conditions under which this can be done being also socially prescribed by law and morals. Once they withdraw from the arrangement or fail to fulfil its requirements, they can no longer claim their rights under it.

The principle of reciprocity of mutual services, of which their marriage arrangements are a typical example, supplies the key to most of their other institutions and to the way in which they think of their duties and obligations to one another — always granting the principles which determine the framework of their constitution, principles which enter into and, in all sorts of subtle ways, condition the detailed working of all their institutions. This principle is the basis of all their rules of distributive justice, the rules according to which land and its products and other privileges and amenities are distributed among them. But though the principle and the rules in which it finds expression are, like their family arrangements, partly concerned with the interchange of goods and services and thus have an economic aspect, they are primarily moral; and the duties and obligations which arise in connection with them are, and are recognised as being, moral duties and obligations; for among the Bantu there is no sharp distinction drawn between economic and moral relations. Economic relations are regarded by them as relations between persons, and therefore their moral aspect, the part which they play in promoting the welfare of individuals and so in contributing to social well-being, is clear to them. They seem to have no notion which exactly corresponds to our conception of ownership, and therefore any attempt to describe the economic aspect of their institutions in any of our terms which imply the concept is apt to be misleading. If we are to understand their attitude to such matters, we must consider what functions such goods and services perform in their way of life and what rights and duties devolve on individuals and groups in connection with them.

As another illustration of the way in which the economic and the moral aspects of the principle of reciprocity are bound together and affected by the principles of their social organisation, we may take their system of land tenure.[1] The land occupied by the tribe is all subject to the jurisdiction of the chief in a twofold sense : (1) no new individual can occupy any part of it or derive any benefit from it without his consent ; and (2) he requires certain services and payments in kind from those who reside within this territory. But it is not his in the sense that he could sell any of it or otherwise alienate it from the tribe, nor yet in the sense that he could dispossess any member of the tribe or his heirs from the part which has been allocated to him, except as punishment for some serious offence for which they might be driven out of the tribe altogether.

The detailed arrangements by which land is allocated to individuals or groups are not carried out directly by the chief himself, but through the hierarchy of sub-chiefs and headmen. So that the principle of seniority on which the hierarchy rests as well as the institution of chieftainship enters into the system of land tenure. The principle of tribal unity also enters ; for all members of the tribe are entitled to land to be cultivated. But though, subject to their continued allegiance and services to the chief or to the community whose representative the chief is, neither they nor their heirs can be dispossessed, they can neither sell the land nor give it away to anyone else ; and, if they leave it, it reverts to the chief or the tribe. In the same way when a husband gives land and cattle to one of his wives and her children, he cannot take them away from them or their heirs as long as they continue to use them ; but they have from the produce to provide food for him and the other members of his village or kraal. Thus in order completely to understand the Bantu system of land tenure, we have to consider all these and other principles, including their laws of marriage and inheritance.

Similar considerations apply to their other economic arrangements. Putting the matter generally we may say that to the Bantu the value of wealth consists not so much in its possession or accumulation as in its use ; and much of this use consists in

[1] Junod, op. cit. ii. 6 ff.

N

giving it away, i.e. in applying it to promote the good of others rather than the individual's own selfish pleasure. The personal prestige which this brings to him ranks higher with the Bantu than his own personal comfort. As we have already seen, there is very little difference between the standard of living of the chief and the commoner; and the fact that the higher status of the former gives him command over more wealth merely imposes on him a greater responsibility to be generous in giving it away. Nevertheless, wealth is not communally owned. Different people have definite rights in regard to the use and disposal of different forms of property. These rights are clearly defined and other people are expected to respect them; and, whether or not they in fact do so, they recognise an obligation to do it.

What applies to the economic aspect of their institutions applies equally to their other relations and duties to one another. They are all expressions of the principle of reciprocity. And though some of the details of the way in which the principle works in their institutions are due to the other principles which I have described and which the Bantu regard with the respect due to the customs of their people, its operation makes it easy for the individual member of such small groups to see that the smooth working of their institutions is for his own good as well as that of his fellows. Each sees what the main rights and duties of every individual within the group are; and he recognises that the due discharge of all of them is for the general good. He sees that it is to his advantage that everyone else should do what the system requires of him, however burdensome he may find his own duties and however much he may at times want to evade them. When he does try to evade them, others are not slow to remind him of them; and if he persists in his evasion, they are likely to express their disapproval, among other ways, through the weapon of reciprocity which their interdependence has placed in their hands. But though fear of such consequences, economic or other, may provide an additional stimulus to the individual to do his duties, it is not what makes them duties or even what makes the native recognise that they are his duties. They are his duties because they are necessary for the effective functioning of the institutions which constitute the way of life of his people; and he recognises them as duties and as binding on him because he recognises that way of life as good. The Bantu's sense of duty is probably neither stronger nor less variable than that of the rest of mankind; and while he often, perhaps usually, does what he believes to be his duty, his motives for doing it are usually mixed. But it is important to distinguish between his motives for doing his duty, when he does it, and his recognition that certain actions are right and that it is his duty to do them. The evidence suggests that he regards them as his duties, not out of respect for custom or fear of consequences, but because he sees that they are required for the smooth functioning of a form of life which he believes to be on the whole good both for himself and for his people.

So far I have been mainly concerned with Bantu rules of distributive justice and the grounds on which the natives regard them as right. It is on much the same grounds that he regards as right the other moral rules which he recognises as binding. But before considering the detailed evidence for this conclusion, I want to consider briefly the Bantu system of corrective justice. They do not rely on the working of the principle of reciprocity alone to maintain the equilibrium of their way of life or to restore it when it is disturbed. They have also developed a complex system of legal administration for dealing not only with crime but also with civil disputes. This consists of a series of courts, with a uniform procedure, involving the calling of witnesses and the giving of evidence, and the right of appeal from lower to higher courts. Thus they have made for themselves the distinction between the legal and the merely moral aspects of the rules which they regard as right, the distinction which Malinowski is at such pains to insist on in the case of people like the Trobrianders who have no *ad hoc* machinery for enforcing law, or indeed any laws in the strict sense.

The senior member of a kraal tries to maintain law and order within his own village; but the lowest court is really that of the headman of a sub-district. He deals with minor disputes mainly between members of different kraals. The need for legal machinery is more necessary in dealing with such disputes because the relative self-sufficiency of each kraal makes economic sanctions less effective in relation to them. But the sub-district headman has no means of enforcing his decision, if the law-breaker should prove recalcitrant. Cases in which this happens, as well as all major disputes, are referred to the headman of the district, to whose court there is also the right of appeal against the verdict of the sub-district head. From the district court again cases may be referred, and there is a right of appeal, to the chief's court.

The chief's court deals not only with appeals from the lower courts but also with all serious disputes and all crimes involving capital charges. It consists of the chief's counsellors, mainly his senior male relatives, sometimes under the presidency of the chief himself and sometimes not. The proceedings are in public, though the court usually retires to consider its verdict. Once the main evidence has been heard, anyone present may take part in the discussion, but not in the decision. In passing sentence the court takes the demeanour of the accused into consideration. If, e.g., the guilty person confesses and shows signs of contrition, the sentence is less severe. The court may also, when considering its verdict, take account of the conduct of witnesses in the case; and, if it is satisfied that any of them has been guilty of gross perjury, it may punish him by the imposition of a fine. There is usually no difficulty in enforcing the decision of the court once it is confirmed by the chief; for the alternative to submission is to flee the tribe. The laws which the courts administer and the penalties which they impose we shall consider below, for they throw a great deal of light on the moral ideas of the Bantu.

We have now seen the Bantu magico-religious ideas about themselves, their fellows and their natural and supernatural environment, the main principles of the social structure which they have built up against this background, some typical examples of the institutions by which, within this framework, they try to satisfy their nature and needs, and the machinery by which they try to maintain law and order. Bearing this complex structure in mind, and remembering that none of their rules of conduct can be understood except as it functions within, and subject to the conditions of, this general framework, let us try to distinguish the different rules or classes of rules which they consider right and the reasons why they consider them right. In considering the grounds of the obligations which they recognise, we should remember that some of their rules may be regarded as right for more than one reason, and that the natives themselves do not always distinguish clearly between these different grounds of obligation. Much less do they distinguish between what makes a rule right and what makes them believe that it is right. These distinctions we have to try to make for ourselves, and the effort to make them is rendered more difficult by the fact that few of our authorities themselves make such distinctions. Nevertheless, our authorities make it clear that some forms of conduct are believed by the natives to be obligatory without any clear understanding on their part as to why they should be as they are. They are accepted on authority and enforced by supernatural sanctions, but they are not seen to be right in any other sense. But, as we have already seen in part, there are other forms of conduct which, while they are in the first instance accepted on authority, are regarded as right in the sense that they are, and are seen by the natives to be, in- volved in a way of life or a system of institutions whose working they understand and find good. They see the reasons for such forms of conduct, they understand why they are right. No doubt they seldom reflect on these reasons or consciously formulate them in abstract terms ; and when asked for them they may be at a loss to state them. In this, however, they do not greatly differ from the majority of the members of civilised communities. Such difference as there is, is one of degree rather than of kind.

What kinds or classes of rules of conduct, then, are recog- nised by them as right, and what do they regard as the grounds of their obligatoriness ? First, there are rules which, as we have seen, are regarded as obligatory because they have a magico- religious sanction. Among these we may distinguish two classes, although the natives do not always distinguish clearly between them. Breaches of the one class evoke the displeasure of per- sonal supernatural agents, principally their dead ancestors, and they are believed to be punished through the active inter- vention of these agents. Breaches of the other class are believed to produce disastrous consequences either for the individual or the group, directly and automatically, without the intervention of any personal agent.

To the first class belong all rules regarding ritual observances and respect for the ancestors, including such things as the offering of the first fruits of the harvest of which the ancestors are believed to partake, and what I might call the principles of the constitution, such as respect for the hierarchy and the chief, and the rules about exogamy. Non-observance of these rules evokes the displeasure of the family gods, and so brings misfortune and disaster on their descendants. The ancestral gods also punish with death those who lose all restraint in sexual matters, " but to other sins ", we are told, " they are quite indifferent ".[1]

Even the rules thus sanctioned are not inflexible. There are exceptions to them which are recognised as right, and even supported by magico-religious sanctions. For example, there are recognised exceptions to the principle of seniority and to the principle of exogamy. These illustrate the distinction which we considered among the Trobrianders between tribal law and legalised usage. A detailed discussion of them would show both how changes in their institutions and customs come about and the way in which the principle of the conceived good of the group determines these changes.

To give one example. The heir presumptive to the chieftainship may marry and may indeed have several wives before he succeeds to the office. The first of his wives has all the prerogatives of the great wife and she continues, according to tribal law and for ritual purposes, to occupy this position after her husband becomes chief. But for certain other purposes she does not remain the great wife, and her children do not succeed their father in the chieftainship. This honour is reserved for a wife chosen for the chief by his counsellors — a wife whose *lobola* is paid not by the chief or his father, but by the tribe as a whole. This royal consort takes precedence in practically everything except ritual over the original great wife. Here we see both the relative inflexibility of ritual requirements and the way in which modifications in other rules and institutions come about, when they are considered desirable in the interests of the community.

[1] Junod, *op. cit.* ii. 426-7.

To the second class of supernaturally sanctioned rules belong all taboos and all magical requirements. Certain acts or occurrences as well as magical rites and spells are believed to have a peculiar potency for good or evil, and these results follow automatically unless steps are taken to counteract them. Many of these taboos refer to sexual intercourse, which under certain circumstances is regarded as essential for the welfare of the community and at other times is forbidden as liable to produce disastrous consequences. For example, sexual relations, mostly of a ritual kind, have to be performed for the good of the community on such occasions as after settling in a new kraal or at the completion of the period of mourning for the dead; while such relations are forbidden during the period of moving to a new village or during hunting expeditions. Failure to observe these taboos is believed to bring misfortune not merely on the individuals themselves, indeed sometimes not at all on them, but on the group as a whole or on the headman. There are also occurrences for which no one is responsible, like abortion or the birth of twins, which are fraught with danger unless proper magical steps are taken to deal with them.

Junod is satisfied that the Bantu distinguish between an act which is taboo because it is dangerous, i.e. liable to cause misfortune, and one which is morally wrong, even though some acts are both taboo and morally wrong. A person who commits some of the tabooed acts may, as we have seen, be protected by magico-religious means against the danger to which he has exposed himself or others, but in the case of some acts the natives say that though the danger or taboo has been removed, the ' badness ', the moral evil, of the act still remains.[1] Thus though there are some acts that are both tabooed and morally wrong, the native does not confuse the two characteristics.

Most of the Bantu moral rules, however, have no supernatural sanction. On this the testimony of our authorities is explicit and unanimous. Junod's testimony is particularly valuable in this connection not only because he was a keen and sympathetic observer, and knew the Bantu very intimately over a long period of years, but also because he himself thought the absence of such a sanction the gravest defect in Bantu

[1] *Ibid.* ii. 580.

morality. " Bantu religion ", he tells us, " is a non-moral religion, by which I do not mean that it is immoral, that is, opposed to the law of morality, but that it has no, or at least very little, connection with the moral conduct of the individual. It has no moral prescriptions except those that ensure the hierarchical order in the family. It neither promises rewards nor threatens punishment after death." [1] And at the end of his account of their morality he concludes : their " religion is non-moral ; the ancestor gods themselves are non-moral. . . . If the great fault of Bantu religion is that it is non-moral, that of Bantu morality is that it is non-religious. No supreme legislator has ordained it. Hence the want of the idea of the absolute in the dictates of the Bantu conscience. Nevertheless, the rudiments of morality are present in the Tongan conscience, the feeling of duty, the sense of right and wrong. These are independent of the essentially self-interested idea of taboo." [2] Junod's testimony in this respect is confirmed by Eiselen and Schapera [3] and Willoughby.[4]

Why, then, do the Bantu regard the rules of their secular morality, the rules which have no supernatural sanction, as right ? Junod, who, as we have just seen, considers the secular character of their morality its chief weakness, puts the answer thus : " For the Bantu, the (moral) law is the *interest of the clan*.[5] Theft is bad because it ruins individual property, and it is necessary to respect property otherwise collective life becomes impossible. So theft, blows, murder and witchcraft are condemned and punished because these actions endanger society and its recognised modes of life." [6] Such are the reasons given by the natives themselves why they regard certain actions as obligatory, certain rules as right. Respect for custom, fear of punishment, human or divine, economic or legal sanc-

---

[1] Junod, *op. cit.* ii. 427-8.   [2] *Ibid.* ii. 582-3.
[3] Schapera, *op. cit.* p. 270.   [4] *The Soul of the Bantu*, pp. 382-3.
[5] While this statement is substantially correct, it is not quite accurate, as, e.g., Junod's own account of the Bantu attitude to lying shows (see p. 191 below). According to that account they regard certain actions as wrong primarily because they harm particular individuals. No doubt by so doing they indirectly interfere with the good of the group ; but the latter is not the reason which the natives actually give for regarding them as wrong.
[6] Junod, *op. cit.* ii. 582 (italics in text).

tions, may provide powerful motives and strong incentives for doing what they believe to be right. But before these motives can begin to operate, rules have to be recognised as right. What makes the rules right and the duties obligatory, is the fact that the rules are implied in their conception of the good life, and the duties required for the smooth working of its institutions, and that they are recognised by the natives to be so. No doubt there is much uncritical and unquestioning acceptance of tradition, much passive acquiescence in the customs of their ancestors, as well as much merely outward conformity to traditional requirements. There is much intolerance of change and criticism, an absence of the pioneering spirit and the experimental approach. Their conception of ' the interest of the clan ' may, from our point of view, be narrow or mistaken, mixed up as it is with much superstition, but it is their conception of the good of the group, as that good is embodied in their institutions, that sets them their duties and prescribes their obligations. It requires of them that they subordinate their personal advantage and private inclinations to the larger good, the good of the group as a whole, a good which they also recognise as their own.

The fact that the Bantu not only find their own way of life good, but that they sometimes reflect on their rules and customs and institutions, and compare them with those of other people, with a degree of objectivity and impartiality which is not common even among those who pride themselves on their higher civilisation, appears from the reprimand given by a native woman to a missionary who had preached a sermon against the Bantu custom of allowing the women to do all the heavy carrying. She said : " You observe us and you wonder at certain things. We also on our side are observing you, and we see things that we also do not understand. When your wife does the washing you remain standing by and do not help her. With us it is the men who do the washing. Again we have seen your wife sewing and mending your clothes and the clothes of the children, and you beside her not thinking of helping her. With us, it is the men who make the clothes." Having spoken thus, she put her two hands joined together on the mat, as if she were cutting something in two, and said : " That is the way your forefathers distributed the work, a little heap here and another little heap there, and they said, ' This is the work of men and that is the work of women '. Our fore-fathers proceeded in the same way, and said, ' This is men's work and that is women's work '. . . . We must leave it so. The gospel has no concern with these matters. We do not wish to have the reputation of being lazy, and you do not wish it either." [1]

Stated in general terms many of the Bantu moral rules are much the same as our own — not to steal, not to kill, not to bear false witness; [2] but the ways in which they interpret these rules and the exceptions which they make to them are determined by their particular institutions. Our authorities make it quite clear that the natives do not regard their rules as having an independent authority in their own right. They do not regard them as what some contemporary ethical writers call self-evident obligations, even of the prima facie sort, that is, as rules which contain the grounds of their rightness within themselves and which, therefore, neither admit of nor require any justification or reason beyond themselves. The Bantu regard their rules as the conditions of effective co-operation, on which corporate well-being depends, and as binding only because and in so far as they are required by such co-operation. The conditions of effective co-operation between any group of people are much the same everywhere and most of them are clear enough even to the least imaginative. Within the small community of the Bantu kraal or district or even tribe, the individual both finds co-operation good and recognises that it is a necessary condition of realising his major interests and chief values. It is equally clear to him that co-operation requires a minimum of mutual trust and goodwill which finds expression in the observance of certain rules between those who co-operate. Beyond the limits of the group, whose good they identify with their own, the Bantu do not recognise any rules as binding; and even within the group they recognise them as binding only so far as they are expressions of, or required by, the co-operation on which individual and corporate well-being,

[1] Junod, *op. cit.* i. 340, note 1.
[2] The Bantu, however, distinguish between bearing false witness and telling lies ; and it is only the former which they regard as wrong.

as they conceive it and as it finds expression in their institutions, depends.

We may illustrate this from their attitude to lying and theft. " To tell lies ", Junod writes, " they regard as mere play . . . if the lies are not intended to harm your fellow-men." [1] On the other hand, they regard perjury on the part of a witness in court as a punishable offence, because it does harm to others and interferes with the administration of justice. They also treat defamation of character as a punishable offence. Of their attitude to theft we are told : " Theft is universally condemned, not so much for its immoral [2] character as for the fact that it renders a normal social life impossible ".[3]

The attitude of the Bantu to their moral rules and their reasons for regarding them as right, and their non-observance as wrong, might quite well be expressed in words recently used by the Speaker of the British House of Commons in reprimanding a member who had been found guilty of " corruptly accepting payment for the disclosure of secret information ". He said : " If other members acted as you did, it would be impossible to maintain mutual confidence. The system under which we work would break down." [4] The Bantu, like the British House of Commons, find their institutions on the whole good. The forms of conduct which are required for their maintenance and proper functioning they regard as obligatory. Neither their institutions nor ours are such perfect instruments for carrying out their purposes that no improvement in them is possible ; but as long as they are accepted as good, they provide the grounds of the obligation of certain forms of conduct, the reasons which make certain things right and certain duties binding.

Among the rules of conduct which they recognise as right and which are not subject to supernatural sanctions, the Bantu distinguish three main classes :

(1) There are social conventions and customs regarding such matters as dress and greeting, respect to parents-in-law,

---

[1] Junod, *op. cit.* ii. 582.
[2] By ' immoral ' Junod seems to mean ' opposed to the will of God '.
[3] Junod, *op. cit.* i. 446.   [4] *Hansard*, 30th October 1947.

attitude to pre-marital sex relations or to the bathing of men
and women in different places. These are regarded as right
because they are the traditional customs of the people. The
native conforms to them because others do so, and he has no
special inducement to do otherwise. He would feel ill at ease
if he behaved differently from his neighbours in such matters.
The natives do not believe that any harm would follow from the
non-observance of such customs, but they say it would not be
' decent ' or ' respectful '.[1]

(2) From such actions they distinguish actions which are
morally right or wrong, actions which they regard as obligatory
though they often find them difficult and burdensome and
sometimes feel inclined to evade them. To describe their
attitudes to this class of actions the Bantu have an unusually
rich vocabulary. They not only have terms for duty, right
and conscience, terms which, according to Junod, show " a
clear and deep sense of right-doing "; [2] they also distinguish
within what is bad between what is morally wrong, " bad in
the heart ", and what is aesthetically ugly, " ugly as regards
the face ".[3] As " clear evidence " of their " developed moral
ideas ", Junod quotes, not only his own conversations with the
natives, but also their folk-lore, in which vice is punished and
virtue rewarded, and " the pangs of conscience are depicted in
a wonderful manner ".[4] In this folk-lore we find " punishment
following on such faults as jealousy, obstinacy, unkindness,
presumption, disobedience, self-will, laziness and selfishness,
and we find kindness and pity rewarded ".[5] Such accounts emphasise the importance which the natives attach to the inner
aspect of moral conduct as distinct from mere outward conformity.

The duties which are thus regarded as morally obligatory
include mutual services both in the way of assistance and gifts
between kin by blood and marriage, duties of hospitality and
many other duties towards individuals and groups which are
involved in the working of their institutions. They also include
the duty of complying with more general rules, such as promise-
keeping and respect for life and property, which express the

                ¹ Junod, *op. cit.* ii. 579.   ² *Ibid.* ii. 581.   ³ *Ibid.* ii. 580.
                        ⁴ *Ibid.* ii. 581.   ⁵ *Ibid.* ii. 222.

minimum of mutual trust and goodwill necessary to make any form of social life possible. The working of the principle of reciprocity, the desire for prestige and fear of loss of esteem or of ridicule and contempt, and many other motives may act as additional inducements to the native to perform such duties, but many of them are not legally binding and their performance cannot be directly enforced.

(3) Some of these duties, however, are so important for the welfare of the community, and especially for safeguarding the rights of others, that their fulfilment, from whatever motive, is better than their not being fulfilled at all. The Bantu do not leave the enforcement of these to the incentives provided by the principle of reciprocity and the normal working of social forces. They have, as we have seen, established legal machinery to enforce them. But the rules which are thus enforced do not derive their rightness from the fact that the courts enforce them; rather the courts enforce them because they are already recognised as right.

No doubt the fact that society has attached legal sanctions to a course of conduct helps to bring its rightness or wrongness home to the individual. As a result of it, he may come to regard as right some things which he had not so recognised before. The social disapproval which finds expression in the sanctions attached to certain forms of conduct may find an answering echo in his own conscience; and he may come to condemn such conduct not only in others but in himself. He may then avoid it because he believes it to be wrong and not just because it is forbidden or punished.[1] But whatever value legal sanctions may have in helping the individual to recognise what is morally right, the sanctions neither make the rules to which they are attached right nor can they ensure more than external conformity to them. As regards the grounds of their rightness, the rules to which such sanctions are attached among the Bantu do not differ from other moral rules. We are, in fact, explicitly told that " the courts do not create or even confirm the rule: they merely recognise it " [2] and enforce it. The rules which are thus enforced " are inherent in the social

---

[1] Cf. Rashdall, *The Theory of Good and Evil*, i. 299.
[2] Schapera, *op. cit.* p. 198.

system of the people ". They are accepted " as binding and obligatory " because " they satisfy the more fundamental and common needs of life in society ".[1] But the work of the courts helps to clarify these rules and gives them greater precision. " Their decisions afford a precedent for . . . the future. When there is any dispute regarding the nature or validity of the law, it is settled by discussion among the old men . . . appeal being made to what has been decided in similar cases in the past. . . . It is only when no precedent can be found that the court feels called upon to supply one in the form of an *ad hoc* decision. . . . Bantu law has undoubtedly grown and expanded in the form of such decisions, so that it has become very largely a system of oral ' case law '."[2]

Some of the obligations which are enforceable at law arise out of the specific position of a man as a member of a particular institution ; others, such as respect for life and property, apply to all members of the tribe irrespective of status. The large majority of the civil cases coming before the courts are concerned with marriage arrangements, especially *lobola* and divorce. Others concern cattle and so on. The court " may force a man to carry out the obligations he has neglected to fulfil, or to make restitution or pay compensation for the damage he has done or to suffer punishment for the offence he has committed ".[3] " The most common form of punishment is the imposition of a fine ", the amount of which varies " according to the position of the offender, the enormity of his offence, his previous record and his ability to pay ".[4]

The following may be quoted as illustrating the crimes dealt with and the relative heinousness which the natives attach to them.[5] Witchcraft is considered the most serious of all crimes. It is punished with a cruel death, by hanging, impaling or drowning. Of old the punishment for murder was death, but it has now been reduced to a fine ; but even after the fine has been paid, the murderer is scorned and despised and treated as unclean. Like most primitive people, the Bantu do not regard any occurrence as an accident. They therefore tend to attribute to a person some intention to produce even the

---

[1] Schapera, *op. cit.* p. 197.   [2] *Ibid.* p. 198.   [3] *Ibid.*
[4] *Ibid.* p. 200.   [5] Junod, *op. cit.* i. 440 ff.

accidental results of his actions. Accordingly, while they distinguish between murder and what we would call accidental manslaughter, a person who is found guilty of the latter does not get off scot-free. He or his family have to give to the family of the dead man a girl and ten hoes or an ox. Other crimes and their usual punishments are adultery, a fine equivalent to the *lobola*; ' fighting which ends in blows and wounds ', eight pounds; theft, fines of varying amounts; ignoring a court order, two pounds.

Though the Bantu have such a keen sense of justice, and have provided so adequately for its administration, their ideas regarding it differ in certain respects from ours. E.g., they still accept the principle of collective responsibility in cases in which we would not be prepared to do so; as we have seen, though they distinguish between murder and accidental man-slaughter, they do not allow the latter to go entirely unpunished; when a man does damage or commits a crime with a borrowed tool such as an axe or a spade, the owner, though entirely ignorant of what has happened, is regarded as in part respon-sible; and a breach of their law committed by an outsider, i.e. a member of the tribe but of another group or district or clan, is punished more severely than a breach by a member of the group. On the other hand, not only is the vendetta not practised among them, but there is no tradition of its ever having been practised. And even in the case of those rules to which legal sanctions are attached, they regard mere external conformity as the minimum which can be enforced, not as the maximum which is morally required of the good citizen. As regards both the demands which they make and the grounds of their rightness, these rules do not differ from other moral rules. They are enforced by the courts because they are first recognised as right, not regarded as right because they are enforced; and they are regarded as right because they are recognised as con-ditions of the forms of co-operation on which the working of their institutions and their way of life as a whole depends.

There are three other points about Bantu moral ideas which should be noted here, though I propose to defer consideration of their implications till a later stage in my argument.

(1) Their moral horizon does not extend beyond the limits of the tribe or, at most, the group of tribes. Those beyond these limits have no rights, and moral conceptions and considerations do not apply to them. This is no doubt partly due to ignorance and fear, especially fear of the unknown. It is significant in this connection that even so developed a primitive people as the Bantu believe that white people are cannibals.[1]

(2) Instances are given by our authorities of individuals who have a private conscience in the sense that they do not always regard as right some of the customs approved by their people. Junod,[2] for example, mentions a young man who refused to indulge in pre-marital sexual relations which are customary among the Bantu, not because he did not feel inclined to, but because he did not regard the practice as right. They also give instances of serious moral deliberation and conflicts of loyalties. These are not cases of ordinary moral struggle in which a man who knows his duty may find it difficult to do it, but cases in which a man, after serious reflection, finds it difficult to discover what his duty is. Culwick,[3] for example, quotes cases of young chieftains who after serious moral deliberation refused to accept Christianity on moral grounds or from a sense of duty. They were much attracted by the teaching of the missions and accepted what they took to be the main ethical teaching of the gospels, but they found some aspects of the requirements of the church inconsistent with the duties and responsibilities which they had undertaken, not only responsibilities for the welfare of their tribe, but duties to particular individuals, which these individuals had a right to expect them to fulfil. Junod [4] refers to a similar dilemma on the part of the heir to a chieftainship, which was resolved by a refusal to accept the responsibilities of the position.

(3) I have quoted our authorities to the effect that Bantu morality is secular and that their religion is non-moral and does not help to make them morally better; but while their religion does not tell them what their duties to their neighbours are, and while it does not in the main directly encourage them to perform them, or discourage them from neglecting them,

---

[1] Junod, *op. cit.* ii. 353-4.   [2] *Ibid.* ii. 582, note 1.
[3] *Good Out of Africa*, p. 30.   [4] *Op. cit.* i. 408.

nevertheless their magico-religious beliefs and practices indirectly provide an added incentive to perform those duties which they independently regard as obligatory. There are indeed instances in which they seem to encourage them directly to behave morally.

To take the indirect effects first. Common ritual and worship make for the social cohesion and solidarity of those who engage in them. When the common worship is that of the recent ancestors of the family who are still regarded as its senior members, it is a powerful influence in fostering social sentiments, and it provides a strong stimulus to the individual to obey the laws of the group and do his duties to his fellow members. As regards the direct effects, we find instances in which a high level of moral conduct and, sometimes, the performance of difficult moral duties are required either as a pre-condition or a part or an accompaniment of ritual performances. To give just one example of each : If brothers, or even other members of families, have become estranged, they have, before approaching their ancestral gods for certain benefits, to be genuinely and publicly and ritually reconciled.[1] Part of the ritual ceremonies in connection with mourning consists in members of the family who have, or believe they have, grievances against the others airing them publicly, thus removing a cause of bitterness and hatred.[2] A similar reconciliation is required as part of the ritual when a new village is being established.[3] Finally, no quarrels between co-wives at home are permitted during the three months of the initiation ceremonies at the lodge in the wilderness.[4] Whether or not such practices were introduced into the magico-religious ritual with this end in view, their beneficial moral effect is unquestionable and considerable.

[1] Junod, op. cit. ii. 398-9. [2] Ibid. i. 161.
[3] Ibid. i. 323. [4] Ibid. i. 80.

THE AUSTRALIAN ABORIGINES [1]

THE Australian Aborigines are usually regarded as one of the most primitive, if not the most primitive, of contemporary peoples. Certainly their material culture is much simpler and more rudimentary than that of the Trobrianders or the Bantu. Nevertheless their social organisation is exceedingly complex, and their initiation rites protracted and intricate. But the most profound difference between them and the peoples we have so far considered is that their view of nature and man is based on totemism and a belief in reincarnation.[2] Moreover they have no rank or chieftainship, and they do not worship their ancestors. So that among them we have not only a very primitive but a highly distinctive way of living or pattern of culture ; and perhaps no culture illustrates more clearly the interweaving of customs and beliefs and institutions into a closely knit system, in which each supports others and cannot be understood without reference to them.

These considerations apply to all Australian tribes, but as there are important differences of detail between the cultures of different groups I propose to devote special attention to one group — those of the Central and Northern Central district. But as the fundamental social structure is similar throughout Australia I shall from time to time illustrate their way of life by reference to the beliefs and practices of other tribes.

The Australian Aborigines are a nomadic people, but the territory within which each tribe, and each local group within

---

[1] The main authorities for this lecture are : Elkin, *The Australian Aborigines* ; Spencer and Gillen, *The Arunta* ; do. *The Northern Tribes of Central Australia* ; Radcliffe-Brown, *The Social Organisation of Australian Tribes* ; Ashley - Montagu, *Coming into Being among the Australian Aborigines.*

[2] It is true that the classification of clans among the Trobrianders is totemic and that totemic beliefs exist among some Bantu tribes ; but totemism does not have among them the important place which it has among the Australian natives.

a tribe, roams has well-defined boundaries. These are respected by their neighbours and the groups do not normally tend to stray beyond them. They neither cultivate the soil nor rear cattle. They just hunt and collect food ; so that they are entirely dependent on unaided nature's bounty. And as much of the country which they occupy is arid and infertile, many groups are separated by long distances from their neighbours. Such windscreens and rude shelters as they build for themselves can scarcely be called huts,[1] and they prefer to sleep in the open, even in places where the temperature sometimes falls below freezing-point. They do not wear any clothes for warmth, and very little for concealment.[2] Thus their provision for their creature comforts is of the most meagre kind.

I shall not attempt to give a detailed description of all aspects of their way of life. I can only give such an account of their main, and especially their most characteristic institutions as will enable us to see how they dovetail into one another and how the resulting pattern determines the duties and obligations of individuals, and the way they think of their own and other people's conduct, together with some indication of how changes in what they believe to be right take place.

The social structure of the Australian Aborigines and their beliefs about the way in which individuals should behave towards one another within it are largely determined by considerations of kinship. Fortunately it is not necessary for our purpose to describe their extraordinarily complex system of kinship in detail. All we need note is :

(1) Their kinship system is all-embracing.[3] Not only is everybody with whom the native is likely to come in contact within the local group, or even within the tribe, related to him by blood or marriage or tribal fiction, but he knows or can discover what the relation to each is ; and these relations determine how he should behave in any company, or towards any individuals — whether, for example, he should show special respect

---

[1] Elkin, *The Australian Aborigines*, p. 18.
[2] Spencer and Gillen, *The Northern Tribes of Central Australia*, p. 693 ; cf. *Arunta*, p. 510.
[3] Elkin, *op. cit.* pp. 45-6.

to them, whether he should offer them assistance or protection or hospitality, whether he can count on their co-operation, whether, and if so to what extent, he should share with them anything which he has or receives, such, for example, as the produce of his hunting, whether it is legitimate, and if it is legitimate whether it is specially desirable, to marry one of them, and so on.

(2) They classify relations of kinship in a different way from us ; and it is this method of classification which enables their kinship system to perform the function which it does in their social system without impossible complexity. For example, a man uses the same term to describe his father and his father's brother. Now if his father's brothers are also ' fathers ', their wives are also ' mothers ', and their children ' brothers ' and ' sisters '. On the other hand, the mother's brother is not a ' father ' but an uncle, his wife an aunt, and his children cousins. Moreover, the mother's brother belongs to a different local group ; for the different local groups are exogamous, and marriage is patrilocal. In other words, a man takes his wife from another group, and she lives with him in his. Thus the terms ' brother ' and ' sister ' are extended to include what we would call one group of cousins — those who are reckoned through the father and therefore belong to one's own local group ; while the term cousin covers the other set — those who are reckoned through the mother and belong to another group. Moreover, the father's brothers or the mother's brothers may marry persons from yet other groups, and so may the father's or the mother's sisters. And so the relationships extend and ramify until the whole tribe is included within the network.

Now as the result of this extension and this method of classification, the same term, brother, sister, cousin, aunt, etc., is applied to a group of individuals whose blood relationships are quite different, and some of whom are not related to others by blood relationships at all. But an individual is expected to behave in the same way towards all who bear the same name, whether their relationships to him be a blood relationship or only a tribal one.[1]

[1] Spencer and Gillen, *op. cit.* p. 95.

This does not mean that the Aborigines do not distinguish between blood and tribal relations. A man does distinguish between his own and his brother's children, though they are both described by the same term.[1] What it does mean is that there is a pattern of behaviour which applies equally to all who bear the same name, or belong to the same class, however different the exact relationship to them may be. Accordingly, when an individual visits a group other than his own, the first point to be considered is his relationship to the members of that group. This having been determined, his standing and his rights and his duties are at once known. If, as sometimes happens, he does not himself know, and the elders of the group are unable to trace, the exact relationship necessary to place the visitor in his proper class, they treat him as the ' brother ' of the man who introduced him. Then he is treated as if he belonged to the same class as the latter, and behaviour to him is determined accordingly.

Thus the principle of kinship is a source of social order and a determinant of social behaviour both within the local group and also in the relations between groups, and most of the individual's rights and duties depend on it. Its value in this respect is specially obvious at intergroup or intertribal meetings. The position of individuals and classes, as determined by this principle within their own group or tribe, enables them to know how to behave towards, and what behaviour to expect from, individuals and classes of the other tribe, some of whom they may never have met before. This makes for smoother and more harmonious relationships at such meetings.

The actual operation of the principle of kinship is, however, conditioned by a number of other principles ; and the functioning of the resultant organisation is rendered easier and more effective by its intimate connection with the magico-religious beliefs of the natives. Let us, therefore, try to see what these principles and beliefs are, and how they combine together to produce the native pattern of culture.

The local group or horde, to use Radcliffe-Brown's term, is the unit of political or territorial organisation. This horde

[1] Radcliffe-Brown, *The Social Organisation of Australian Tribes*, p. 151.

is an enlarged family. While the individual family consists of a man, his wife or wives and children, the horde consists of several such families, the heads of which are related in the male line, together, it may be, with other dependent relatives. The horde is patrilineal and exogamous, that is, a child belongs to his father's local group, while his mother belongs to another local group. Thus, apart from the married women, who are in it but not of it, the horde is a biological unit based on descent in the male line. But the horde is also a spiritual unity based on magico-religious considerations. Indeed, the spiritual bond is probably stronger than the biological one ; for the Australian Aborigines, like the Trobrianders, have no idea of the part which the father plays in the coming into being of children. It is true that some, at least, of the tribes attribute to the father some part in ' discovering ' the spirit of the child, and directing it to the woman into whom it should enter, but this has nothing to do with intercourse with the mother. The natives also believe in pre-existence and reincarnation. According to their traditional mythology, their early ancestors left in certain spots in the territory which they now occupy the spirits which become incarnate as the men and women of the horde. From these spots, the spirits, from time to time, come and enter into married women and are born as children ; and to these spots they again return at death to await another incarnation. In this way, the relation of the native to the territory occupied by his horde is much more intimate than can be conveyed by saying that it is his home or the home of his fathers. This relationship not only binds him by a mystic bond to the other members of the horde, but it also explains why he does not want to go far, or for long, away from his home ; and why although there are quarrels and wars between groups, they never fight for or desire one another's territory.[1]

The Aborigines do not recognise any distinction of rank, but they pay great respect to age and the experience and wisdom which age normally brings with it. The control of the affairs of the horde is, therefore, in the hands of the senior elders, who discuss matters informally among themselves before any decision is arrived at. Among them the senior in years normally

[1] Elkin, *op. cit.* p. 26.

acts as *primus inter pares*, until he gets too old, when he hands over to the next senior. But the position of this ' headman ' is neither official nor hereditary ; [1] and it requires qualifications other than mere age, such as ability and knowledge of tribal customs.[2]

The tribe, as distinct from the horde, has no political organisation and no chief or headman ; and it seldom, if ever, functions as a unit.[3] The main source of tribal unity is the intricate network of kinship ties between the members of the different hordes which constitute it ; but in the case of the tribe, as in that of the horde, the social bonds based on kinship are strengthened by the spiritual unity of the members as connected by magico-religious ties to the territory which they occupy. These bonds are further strengthened by a close similarity of customs, beliefs and language. But the unity of the tribe does not find concrete expression in any individual or council of individuals to manage its affairs, nor in any tribal political machinery. Nevertheless, when groups meet together for ritual or ceremonial or other purposes, the chief elders of the different hordes take counsel together and settle disputes between their groups. In these councils, which are quite in-formal, men of character and ability exert an important influence on their fellow elders. Sometimes they succeed in bringing about changes in practices and institutions within the general framework of the social structure which is common to them all.[4] Such changes sometimes come about, in the first instance, within one group ; and then, after discussion at intergroup meetings, they are extended to other groups ; and, it may be, to other tribes. But as there is no machinery by which un-welcome changes can be enforced, such changes as take place come about after they have been " discussed, understood and adopted " [5] by the people concerned.

There are other social groupings, other divisions of the tribe, which cut across the unity of the horde. These divisions serve at least as much to connect as to divide the members of

---

[1] *Ibid.* p. 75.
[2] Spencer and Gillen, *op. cit.* p. 13 ; *Arunta*, p. 9.
[3] *Ibid.* p. 20.   [4] *Ibid.* pp. 26-7 ; *Arunta*, p. 224.
[5] Elkin, *op. cit.* p. 30.

the tribe. Thus tribes are divided into moieties, sections and sub-sections. The principles of division are mainly based on kinship, by blood or marriage; but they are also bound up with, and reinforced by magico-religious considerations. In some of these groupings, as, for example, in sub-sections, different members of one horde, even parents and children, not only may, but must be in different groups; while members of different hordes may belong to one group. This intricate network of interconnection helps to strengthen the unity of the tribe as a whole.

The details of these divisions and groupings are so complex that no useful purpose would be served by trying to describe them here. Suffice it to say that the division into moieties is mainly for ceremonial purposes. People group themselves in these ways, for example, at initiation rites, totemic ceremonies and burial ritual. Sections and sub-sections, on the other hand, are convenient ways of describing groups of relatives, determined by kinship. They provide a shorthand way of stating the relationships between individuals without having in each case to find one's way through the complexities of the kinship system. This is specially useful on such occasions as intertribal meetings.

These divisions and groupings are sometimes regarded as intended to regulate marriage, and they do often serve this secondary purpose; but they are neither necessary nor by themselves sufficient to do so. Kinship by itself is sufficient for the purpose; and so far as sections or sub-sections are used to do it, they can serve the purpose only because they are groupings of natives on the basis of kin. Moreover the attempt to regulate marriage by such groups, sometimes, so restricts the field of choice of partners that it becomes necessary to provide for marriages which do not comply with their requirements; and the custom of doing so is socially approved so long as the kinship rules of exogamy are not infringed.

My main reason for mentioning these groupings is their intimate connection with the magico-religious beliefs of the natives. Whether their purpose is social or ceremonial, most of the groups are totemic. What then are totemic groups, and what function does totemism fulfil in the life of the Aborigines? Totemism is usually defined as " a relationship between an individual or a group of individuals on the one hand, and a natural object or species on the other " [1] — a relationship which is denoted by the individual or group bearing the name of the totem. This definition, however, does not take us very far; for it leaves undefined the nature of the relationship between the totem and the individual or the group whose totem it is. The fact is, as Elkin points out, that there are many varieties of totemism and many kinds of totemic group; so that the relationship concerned is not necessarily the same in all cases. To say, therefore, that a group is totemic does not tell us either the principle on which it is formed or the function which it fulfils in the life of the society. If, for example, a group is based on kinship and has a ceremonial function, neither its nature nor its function is altered by its being a totemic group. But if a group is totemic, that may give it greater cohesion and so enable it to perform its function more effectively. For a group to be totemic means at least that the members have in the totem a badge or symbol of membership by which they can recognise one another. But it usually means much more than this. It connects a group with the past history of their people, and thus, in a way, gives it a sort of mystical character. Moreover, the totem binds the members not only to one another, but also to some aspect of nature; and the bond of connection is not only a peculiarly intimate one but also one which cannot be severed, and which imposes duties and obligations and confers rights and privileges. Totemism, in short, is a way of expressing the unity of men with one another, the unity of past and present, and the unity of men and nature or at any rate the unity of the men who live in a particular territory and their natural environment.

Totemism connects the past and present in two ways — on the one hand, through myths regarding the activities of culture heroes and the relics which they left behind, especially the sacred places where the ceremonies for the increase of the totem take place; and on the other, by stressing the identity of substance, through direct descent, between those who now exist and those heroes of bygone days who sometimes appeared in the form of the totem and at other times in human form.

[1] Elkin, *op. cit.* p. 127.

The doctrine of reincarnation further emphasises this connection, for according to it the same spirits appear in past ancestors, present members and future children.

Totemism also expresses the unity and co-partnership of man and nature in two ways. On the one hand, man has to co-operate with nature in order to enable nature to do its work. This is seen in the increase ceremonies, the *intichiuma*, which are so prominent a feature of the ritual of the Aborigines; without the performance of these ceremonies the totemic animals would die out. On the other hand, nature has to provide for man's needs, and to protect and help him. This is specially obvious to a people who do nothing to help themselves except gather the fruits, animal and vegetable, which nature provides for their use. Totemism thus stands for or expresses a large number of relations. In the case of one totemic group, one bond of connection may be more prominent, in another group a different one. The membership of one totemic group is transmitted through the father, that of another through the mother, while membership of another is determined by place of birth or conception. Moreover, the same individual may be a member of more than one totemic group.

Without entering into further detail, or raising the question on which so much has been written, whether totemism is a philosophy of nature, or a religion, or a feature of social organisation, or perhaps, as I think, a rudimentary form of all three, I trust enough has been said to enable us to understand the light which it throws on the mentality of the natives, and the influence which it exercises on their views of the relation between individuals and groups of individuals.

To take the former first. The belief in totemism and the way in which the member of a totemic group thinks of the relation between himself and his totem, is part of the evidence put forward in support of the view that the primitive mind is pre-logical, and works in a different way or according to different principles from our own. I propose to delay consideration of this view till I am discussing the nature of primitive mentality, when totemic beliefs will be considered along with the other evidence submitted in support of it.[1] But one or two further

[1] See Lecture IX.

remarks on the relation between the native and his totem seem called for here, not only because of their relevance to the fundamental issue with which we shall be concerned later, but also because a clear idea of the way in which the native thinks of his relation to his totem is necessary for an understanding of many of his beliefs and practices. This relation the native himself often describes as one of identity. He *is* a crow or a cockatoo, an emu or a witchetty grub. What, then, does he mean by this ? We already saw that there are different kinds of totemic groups, and that the relation of their members to one another and to the totem, the principle of identity of the group, need not be the same in all of them. Sometimes the native specifies the principle of identity more precisely as being an identity of substance or flesh. In relation to certain totemic groupings, the meaning of such language is clear enough. There are, for example, certain social groups, membership of which is transmitted through the mother. In their case, identity of flesh obviously refers to descent in the matrilineal line from a common ancestor. That is the only identity of flesh recognised by a people for whom fatherhood is a social rather than a biological relation. Now the animal or other species which is the totem is not only the symbol of this identity of substance, but itself shares in it, because it shares in the common ancestry.

There are, however, instances in which the principle of identity is not at all clear to us, as, for example, when the native asserts not only that he is descended from an emu, or that he will become an emu after death, but that he is an emu now, and still more when he says that " lightning is crow, and so are thunder, rain, clouds, hail and winter, that the moon and stars are black cockatoo, that fish, eels and seals are karato (a non-poisonous snake) ".[1] Now this does not mean that he regards himself as in all respects identical with an emu, or that he does not see any difference between his fellow members of the totemic group and the emus which roam in his territory. But it does mean that he does not draw the sharp distinction which we do between men and animals or between either of them and inanimate objects. It is not that the native begins by regarding men and animals and natural events as different,

[1] Elkin, *op. cit.* p. 147.

and then finding certain powers such as desires, intentions and inclinations operative in his own experience, projects them into nature, animate and inanimate, and thus reinterprets nature in the light of his own experience. It is rather that he has not yet learned to draw such clear distinctions as we do between these different regions, and that he thinks of all of them in animistic and personalistic terms. He has not yet developed the idea of the natural or inanimate nor yet of personality in our sense of these terms. Consequently he finds no more difficulty in thinking of animals and natural objects as thinking and behaving like human beings than the little girl does when she talks to her doll, or tries to lull it to sleep. But he would be as terrified if the object or animal were, in his presence, to turn into a man or behave like one as the little girl would be if her doll were to answer back.

It is true that the most primitive people that we know have learned by experience what to expect under certain circumstances, and how to behave in relation to it. There are certain regularities about the behaviour of events and animals and fellow-men which they observe as accurately as we do, and to which they respond in appropriate ways, as, for example, in preparing their tools or pursuing their prey or co-operating with their fellows. Without such learning by experience neither man nor animal could survive. But even of the environment to which primitive man thus responds, his understanding is imperfect and his mastery incomplete. Not only is it surrounded by forces and powers which he does not understand and cannot control, but these forces and powers make incursions into his workaday world in such forms as rain or drought, birth or death, famine or plenty, forms which affect his welfare and that of his group in the most intimate ways. Accordingly he tends to regard everything with which he is in contact or which affects his welfare, whether in the heavens or on the earth, as parts of his social order. He classifies them according to the principles which operate in that order, especially the principles of kinship and totemic grouping; and he thinks of their behaviour in terms of motives and powers derived from his experience of himself and his fellows. Hence his magico-religious beliefs about them, and his attempts at conciliating and controlling them.

What, then, are the social consequences of totemism, the ways in which it influences man's relations to his fellows? (1) By emphasising the identity of the totemic group, it fosters strong social sentiments between its members whether the group be a local horde or one which cuts across territorial frontiers. It thus increases the individual's sense of loyalty to the group, and provides him with an additional incentive for performing his duties to his fellow members. (2) The members of the totemic group have duties in the way of assistance and protection and hospitality to one another, and this is very important, especially when members of one local group visit another. (3) Still more important, totemism emphasises the dependence of all the hordes within a tribe and even of different tribes on one another. This interdependence is specially emphasised by the *intichiuma* ceremonies which take place for the increase of the totem. The sacred spots at which the ceremonies for the increase of a particular animal or other natural species have to be performed and the secret of the necessary rites belong to a particular totemic group.[1] If they fail to perform the appropriate ceremonies, the supply of that animal, for example the emu or kangaroo, will cease. This will be a catastrophe, not so much to the group concerned, because they do not normally eat their own totem, as to the rest of the tribe. Thus, according to their beliefs, each group is dependent for its livelihood and welfare on all the others duly performing their duties for the increase of their own totems. Thus totemism not only connects man with nature and his fellow-men, but it imposes on each of them duties for the welfare of all. How seriously they take these duties and what effects their performance produces on them is thus described by Elkin: " When they return (from their ceremonies) to the world of secular affairs they are refreshed in mind and spirit. They now face the vicissitudes of everyday life with a new courage and strength gained from the common participation in the rites, with a fresh appreciation of their social and moral ideals and patterns of life, and an assurance that having performed the rites well and truly, all will be well with themselves and with that part of nature with which their lives are intimately linked." [2]

[1] Spencer and Gillen, *Arunta*, p. 145.   [2] *Ibid.* pp. 155-6.

One further remark about the attitude of the native to his totem is necessary to complete our survey of their magico-religious beliefs. The native has certain taboos against killing or eating his totem except on ceremonial occasions; and even then he eats of it sparingly. But he does not worship it, nor does he appeal to it for aid in any of his difficulties; nor does he worship or pray to his ancestors or culture heroes with whom totemism connects him. Ancestral worship seems to be precluded by the belief in reincarnation. In fact, among the group of tribes with which we are specially concerned there is no idea of a personal supernatural agent whom they could worship, or to whom they could turn for aid in their difficulties and perplexities.[1]

We have now before us the main principles of the Aborigines' social structure: kinship, horde exogamy, patrilocal marriage, respect for age, totemic groupings and the magico-religious beliefs which are intimately bound up with them. From our account of them, it should be clear, as our authorities are never tired of telling us, that " the different aspects of Aboriginal life are almost inextricably intertwined, and that to explain one of them fully demands almost a complete understanding of the whole culture ".[2] Begin where we will, in our attempts to understand what we find we soon discover that we are involved in all the other aspects. If, for example, we try to understand the Aborigines' social groupings, we find we have to consider their ideas about kinship; but we soon find that these can only be grasped in the light of their beliefs about totemism and reincarnation, and these in turn prove to be intimately bound up both with their past history and their economic welfare. In short the different aspects are interlinked, and to explain one we must understand all.

While the principles which we have so far considered provide not only the conditions within which the Aborigine must pursue his ends and seek the satisfaction of his needs, but also much of the content of his ideal, they do not precisely determine

---

[1] To this statement there is one exception, but the supernatural agent concerned has no interest in the moral conduct of the natives. See Spencer and Gillen, *Northern Tribes*, p. 496.

[2] Elkin, *op. cit.* p. 41 ; cf. also pp. 16, 100, 181-2.

all his duties. When, however, we turn to consider the code of
morality or the system of rights and duties which the Aborigines
have built up within the framework of these principles, we find
our authorities less detailed and explicit than we could wish.
They are explicit and emphatic enough that the Aborigines
have a code of morals and that it has no direct supernatural
sanction. Spencer and Gillen write : " The Central Australian
natives . . . have no idea whatever of the existence of any
supreme being who is pleased if they follow a certain line of
what we call moral conduct and displeased if they do not do
so. They have not the vaguest idea of a personal individual
other than an actual living member of the tribe who approves
or disapproves of their conduct, so far as anything like what we
call morality is concerned." [1] And again : " So far as the in-
culcation of anything like moral ideas is concerned . . . it is
never associated with the mention of the name of any individual
who is supposed in any way whatever to sanction any moral
precepts. . . . We have searched carefully in the hope of
finding traces of a belief in such a being, but the more we got
to know of the details of the native beliefs, the more evident it
became that they have not the faintest conception of any (such)
individual." [2]

But, they continue, " it must not however be imagined that
the Central Australian native has nothing in the nature of a
moral code. As a matter of fact, he has a very strict one, and
during the initiation ceremonies the youth is told that there are
certain things he must do and certain things he must not do.
But he quite understands that any punishment for the infringement of these rules of conduct which are thus laid down
for him will come from the older men and not at all from any
supreme being of whom he hears nothing whatever." [3]

Now all that this means is that the natives have a secular
morality devoid of any direct supernatural sanction and that
this morality is taught by the elders to the youths during the
initiation ceremonies. It does not mean that their magico-
religious ideas, which in the form of totemism and magic pervade the whole of their life, do not influence the way in which
they think of and behave towards their fellows. While it is

---

[1] *Northern Tribes*, p. 491.   [2] *Ibid.* pp. 502-3.   [3] *Ibid.* pp. 491-2.

true that the main content of their morality, their ideas regarding their duties to their neighbours, are not determined by magico-religious beliefs, it is also true, as we have already seen, that, given the belief that they have these duties to their neighbours, magico-religious considerations have a great deal to do with the loyalty with which they are carried out. We can even go further and say that some parts of their magico-religious ritual provide an indirect, if not a direct sanction for some of their duties — whether or not they were consciously intended to do so. Thus we are told that at some of the great intertribal gatherings, before the ceremonies begin, " all grudges and complaints must be expressed and cleared up, and all disputes settled ".[1] Again, we hear that " there must be no quarrelling while the ceremonies are in progress or while the churinga (that is, one of their sacred objects) are being kept near by ".[2] We are also told of ritual practices which form part of some of their magico-religious ceremonies, the purpose of which is to prevent a man from being " hard-hearted and greedy ", so that he might be " ready to divide what he secures with others who may not have been as successful as himself ".[3] In this way, forgiveness, friendship and generosity are directly encouraged, partly no doubt because they are independently recognised as good, but also because they are felt to harmonise with the unity of purpose, the solemnity and the reverential awe which observers [4] tell us characterise these ritual ceremonies on which the life and welfare of the people as a whole are believed to depend.

Before considering the moral ideas which the youths are taught during initiation it is desirable to refer to the initiation ceremonies which occupy such an important place in the life and thought of the natives. For in order to understand the way in which they think of their duties and obligations, we must know not only the content of the moral instruction they receive, but also the circumstances under which they receive it.

[1] Elkin, *op. cit.* p. 161.
[2] *Ibid.* p. 172, note 9.
[3] Spencer and Gillen, *Northern Tribes*, pp. 266-7 ; cf. *Arunta*, p. 143.
[4] *Ibid.* pp. 179, 253 ; Elkin, *op. cit.* pp. 167, 176 ; *Arunta*, pp. 122, 190.

For the native, initiation is the doorway to manhood, to full adult status as a member of his tribe. It is a necessary preliminary to marriage and to entrance into the council of those who settle the affairs of the horde ; and it is the way of entry into the secret and sacred life of his people, such as the mysteries connected with the increase ceremonies, on which their continued welfare depends. It is in fact the door to everything to which the native youth looks forward as the things which make life worth while.

The hardships to which he is subjected, the discipline of mind and body which he has to undergo, the atmosphere which surrounds many of the ceremonies and especially the sacred awe with which the elders approach their ritual objects and reveal to him their secrets, are all calculated to impress the novice with a sense of the importance of the step which he is taking and of the teaching which he receives. He ceases to be a child, spending most of his time with the women and children, and becomes a man with the status and privileges and responsibilities which this involves. He dies [1] to the frailties and weaknesses of childhood and is born a new being whose conduct should be characterised by courage, strength and manliness. Above all he ceases to be an outsider : the group mysteries are revealed to him and he is allowed first to see and then to take part in the sacred ceremonies of his people.

The physical preparation of the initiate consists of such things as circumcision and subincision, knocking out a tooth, marking the body and other trying and painful processes. The details and the intensity of this preparation vary from tribe to tribe, but the general pattern is the same for all. Then follows a period of seclusion, during which the initiate is cut off from the rest of the group, especially from the women and children, and submitted to many food taboos and other forms of discipline. At intervals during this prolonged period the elders, with due rite and ceremony, relate to him the mythology regarding their totemic or culture heroes. They also reveal to him their sacred symbols, the churinga, the bull-roarers, the sacred spots, and they instruct him in the ritual to be used in

[1] Part of the ritual is intended to symbolise this death and rebirth. Cf. Elkin, *op. cit.* pp. 165-6.

connection with them.   In the course of this revelation, he
learns that the noise which he had hitherto regarded as the
voice of an all powerful supernatural being is only a bogy to
frighten the women and children.[1]   It is in fact the noise of a
bull-roarer whirled by one of the initiated.

The instruction given to the novice, however, is not confined
to religion and ritual.   He is also given moral instruction as to
how he should behave to his fellow-men, and probably there is
no very clear distinction drawn between the two ; for the ceremonial duties are also, in part at least, social obligations.   On
their due performance the welfare of the tribe is believed to
depend.   Loyalty to the group, sense of duty to his fellows and
even self-interest as well as magico-religious ideas and feelings
may, therefore, enter into his motives for performing them ;
so intimately are the social, moral, economic and religious
aspects of the life of the native bound together.   Moreover,
the feelings of respect and awe associated with the ritual ceremonies tend to be extended to the moral instruction.   This
helps to impress it more forcibly on the mind of the initiate,
and gives it, in his view, an added authority.

What, then, is the content of the moral instruction given
during initiation and on what authority does it rest ?   It is in
our attempts to answer this question that we find our authorities
least helpful.   They tend to be more concerned with the native
principles of social organisation than with the life and personal
relations of individuals within the society ; and so far as they
deal with the latter at all, they tend to describe the details of
native practices rather than the way the natives think about
them, and the reasons why they consider them right.   Certain
things, however, are clear.   Much of the instruction consists in
emphasising the importance of complying with tribal customs
and fulfilling the duties which these customs impose.   With
many of these customs the novice is already acquainted before
initiation.   Many of the duties, both positive and negative,
which they require are determined by the principles of their
social organisation which we have already described.   They
include such duties as co-operation and mutual helpfulness

[1] Spencer and Gillen, *Northern Tribes*, p. 492.

between the members of the horde ; protection, hospitality and assistance between members of totemic groups ; and exchanges of gifts and services between persons who are related by kinship ties, in accordance with " the principle of reciprocity which ", we are told, " runs through all native life ".[1] Thus elders should make gifts to youths during initiation and the youths are expected to bring food to them later. A man's maternal uncle has duties in connection with his betrothal and marriage, and he in turn makes a gift to his uncle. A man receives a wife from his parents-in-law and he is expected to make gifts to them in return,[2] and so on. The performance of such duties is, and is seen by the native to be, for the good of the group, and no doubt this aspect is brought home to him during initiation. Doubtless, also, the working of the principle of reciprocity in the long run ensures that the individual recognises their performance as being for his own good as well ; and in a small community, where all duties involve personal relations between people who all know one another, the long run is much shorter than in a large and complex modern society. Accordingly, when an individual is asked why he should behave in a particular way, he sometimes points to the return service which he expects, but he may equally well answer that it is the custom of his people, or that other people have a right to expect him to do so. In a given situation or in the case of a given individual, no doubt one of these may be more prominent ; but it would be unwise to treat immediate self-interest or respect for custom or regard for the rights of others alone, either as his motive for the action or as his ground for considering the action obligatory. It is true that he does not normally ask why the particular institutions and customs of his people are as they are.[3] To him they are parts of the traditional way of life of his people, and he does not seem to ask for further reasons. Nevertheless, the mere fact that they are the customs of his people is not by itself sufficient to make them continue to be accepted as obligatory. If the native did not in fact see that the performance of the duties required of him by custom was on the whole for his own good and that of the group, the custom would lose its binding

---

[1] Elkin, *op. cit.* p. 103.   [2] Spencer and Gillen, *Arunta*, pp. 491-2.
[3] Elkin, *op. cit.* p. 121.

force and the native would cease to consider its requirements as right and reasonable. This does not mean that the natives would consciously try to change it, though, as we have seen, they are reported to do this at times, but only that the incentives which keep it going would cease to function, and that therefore it would gradually disappear. Accordingly, we are justified in saying that while the natives are not moved merely by self-interest, it is only because and so far as the customs of their people appear to them to be parts of a form of life which seems to them worth while that they continue to consider the duties which they impose as obligatory. And if they do not regard these duties as binding merely because they are customary, still less do they do so because some supernatural authority has ordered them, and will be displeased if they are not complied with; or because they believe that untoward consequences will follow, through the operation of natural or supernatural causes, from neglecting them. There are, of course, taboos and ritual duties which have supernatural sanctions of this sort; but such sanctions do not apply to their secular duties to their neighbours.

The attitude of the natives to such questions may be gathered from the rules which are taught to the youths during initiation, and especially from the way in which these rules are interpreted and the exceptions to them which are regarded as right. Among these rules our authorities mention the follow-ing:[1] (1) to obey the elders and not to quarrel, especially with the elders; (2) not to eat certain foods; (3) to give food to those who are related to them in certain ways and especially to the elders; (4) not to commit adultery; and (5) not to reveal to the uninitiated any of the secrets of the ceremonies. Among these, (2) and (5) may be regarded as magico-religious or ritual duties, though (5) at least is also in the interests of the group as conceived by the elders. The other three concern the interests of the horde and especially those of the adult men. One requires obedience to tribal law, of which the elders are the guardians; another requires the generous fulfilment of economic duties; for among a people with such a simple culture, food is the only economic commodity, and the duties with regard to it are treated by them as specific duties to individuals. The

[1] Spencer and Gillen, *Northern Tribes*, pp. 500-504; cf. also p. 334.

further duties of not quarrelling and avoiding adultery are obviously required for the harmonious functioning of the horde.

What is specially significant, however, is the way in which these rules are interpreted, and what we should call the exceptions to them which are not only permissible but obligatory; for these bring out clearly the importance of the institutions which constitute the cultural pattern of the Aborigines in determining their duties, as well as the way in which the good of the community serves to justify not only the rules which are regarded as right, but also the interpretation that is placed upon them, and the exceptions to them.

Take as an example the rule against adultery on which a great deal of emphasis is laid during initiation. Now by adultery the natives mean, not all intercourse between a married man and a woman who is not his wife, but such intercourse as is not permitted by tribal custom. There are, however, instances in which such intercourse is not only permitted but prescribed, and prescribed because it is believed to be for the good of the community.[1] For example, those who take part in a vendetta expedition always exchange wives just before the expedition starts, so as to unite them in friendly relations with one another. The same thing happens as part of the mechanism for settling disputes and for making peace between groups which have been at war. All these are situations which are fraught with great danger to the community; and the exchange of wives is part of the recognised and socially prescribed way of so dealing with them as to bring about the results which the natives desire — the success of the expedition or the establishment of lasting peace and harmony. Similarly, among the Aborigines, one of the marks of friendship and hospitality to a visitor is to lend him one's wife during his stay.[2]

Now none of these customs is regarded as a breach of the rule regarding adultery, which is taught during initiation; for each of them is a form of behaviour sanctioned by the institutions of the people. So that two acts which may appear to us the

[1] See Elkin, *op. cit.* pp. 121 ff.; Spencer and Gillen, *Northern Tribes*, pp. 137 ff., 570; *Arunta*, p. 444.

[2] Elkin, *op. cit.* p. 121; Spencer and Gillen, *Arunta*, p. 505.

same, and to which, therefore, we apply the same rule, may for the native be entirely different acts, the one right and the other wrong. Thus, to sleep with another man's wife is normally regarded by the natives as a most serious offence, punishable by death,[1] but when the first man is a visitor and the second his host, this act may be the expression of the highest regard and friendship. Thus it is not intercourse with another man's wife as such that is regarded as wrong. Sometimes it is right, sometimes it is wrong. And the rule against adultery does not enable us to tell on which occasions it is the one, and on which the other. It is the institutions which constitute the pattern of culture of the Aborigines which alone enable them to say when it is right and when wrong. It is for this reason that our authorities warn us against " the danger of drawing conclusions from general statements ",[2] and emphasise the need for getting detailed information regarding the beliefs and practices of the natives. Nothing less than such detailed knowledge of their institutions will enable us to understand the content of their moral rules ; for whether the rule against adultery does or does not apply to a particular situation is determined, not by one institution, such as marriage, alone, but by a whole complex of institutions concerned with war, vendetta, hospitality, etc.

The same considerations apply to other moral rules. For example, the initiated native believes it is his duty to deceive women and children by telling them that the sound of the bull-roarer is the voice of a supernatural agent ; and he does not seem to think of this as a breach of the rule of truth-telling. He does not seem in fact to think of this action in relation to that rule at all, nor does he think of the infanticide of twins, which is prescribed to him as a duty which he must perform for the good of the community, as murder, any more than he or we think of killing an enemy in war-time as murder. Within his cultural pattern or the requirements of his interrelated system of institutions, killing and deception are regarded as right in certain circumstances, wrong in others. Within ours also they are regarded as right in some circumstances and wrong in others. But the circumstances in which they are regarded as right in the two cultural patterns differ ; and as we have seen,

[1] Spencer and Gillen, *Northern Tribes*, p. 140.   [2] *Ibid.* p. 494.

in the case of the Aborigines at any rate, it is the system of institutions which they have built up which determines in which cases they are right and in which wrong.

I shall try to gather together the results of our discussion by considering, as we did in the case of the Trobrianders and the Bantu, what main classes of rules of conduct the Aborigines regard as right or obligatory, and why they so regard them. In dealing with this question, we may take as a guide the classification of Spencer and Gillen.[1] Their classification, which is based on the sanctions by which the different rules are enforced, is as follows : (1) There are rules or laws or customs which have a magico-religious sanction in the sense that breaches of them are believed to be followed inevitably and automatically by consequences which are distasteful and, it may be, disastrous to the individual and his group. Such, for example, are the rules in regard to incest or the killing of twins or totemic ritual. When asked for a justification of the conduct which these rules prescribe, the native may tell a story about a culture hero who acted in these ways, or he may merely say, ' Our fathers did so and we must do it too ', or again he may refer to the consequences which would follow their neglect. But whether his attitude to such rules is determined mainly by hope of good or fear of evil, he accepts them merely on authority and does not understand why the good for which he hopes or the evil which he fears should result from his performance or non-performance of the duties required.

(2) There are rules of conduct which are sanctioned by " public opinion or the fear of ridicule or opprobrium ".[2] These sanctions are not what makes the rules right. They are merely incentives to obey them, and deterrents against breaches of them. Spencer and Gillen lump together, under this heading, rules of manners and of morals ; but on the bases of the evidence available, it seems possible to distinguish between the attitude of the natives to the two. Yet while we can see evidence of such a distinction it is by no means easy to see precisely how it is drawn, and no doubt some natives draw it more clearly than others, and perhaps some do not draw it at all. There seems,

[1] *Ibid.* p. 25. [2] *Ibid.*

however, to be at least one important difference. In the case of etiquette, manners and conventions, of which we are told [1] the natives have quite a strict code, there is really no sanction required. The individual obeys this code because everybody else does so. It is not merely that he would be ridiculed if he were in this respect different from the others, but that he in fact wants to be like them. Therefore no question of duty or obligation arises in connection with them. In the case of morals the situation is different. The moral conduct required of him under tribal law by the institutions of his people often conflicts with his inclinations and his immediate interests. That is why the question of duty arises. When the native performs these duties, it may be from motives of self-interest, because he sees that the working of the principle of reciprocity will make him suffer if he does not, or it may be from a sense of loyalty to the group, or from respect for the rights of others, or from respect for tradition, or it may be from a combination of these or other motives. But these motives are not what makes the actions in question his duties. No doubt many of the Aborigines, like many people in more advanced societies, just accept their duties as binding because they are regarded as obligatory by their society, and without raising any further question about the grounds of the rightness of the rules. But there are others who, as we have seen and will see further, appreciate the way in which the effective functioning of their institutions requires the performance by them as well as by others of certain duties, and how other forms of conduct such as quarrelling, black magic, murder and so on, disturb the equilibrium of their life and prevent themselves and other people from achieving their ends.

(3) The other class of rules mentioned by Spencer and Gillen consists of those enforced by the informal council of elders of the horde. As regards the grounds of their rightness, if they are in fact right, these legal rules, as we may call them, do not differ in principle from the moral rules we have just been considering. The only difference is that breaches of some rules are so disturbing to the life of the group, and it may be to the relations between groups, that the elders, as representatives

---

[1] Spencer and Gillen, *Northern Tribes*, p. 569 ; cf. *Arunta*, p. 505.

of the group, take steps to prevent their happening and, if they happen, try to restore the disturbed equilibrium of the group by punishing them.   This they do in the case of the more serious crimes like black magic, murder or breaches of the laws of marriage, by sending an avenging party to punish the offender.   But such actions are not considered wrong merely because they are punished ; rather they are punished because they are considered wrong ; and they are considered wrong because they interfere with the welfare of the group, and the smooth working of its way of life.

We see, then, that the Aborigines distinguish what is morally right both from what is supernaturally sanctioned and from what is enforced by the elders.   It is much more difficult to be sure how far they distinguish between what is socially approved or prescribed by the pattern of their culture and what is morally right.   Their detailed duties at a given moment are determined by what is socially approved and prescribed ; that is the operative ideal in the light of which they judge their own and other people's conduct.   This operative ideal, however, is not so precise and definite as our language about it may suggest, for it exists in the minds of individuals ; and individuals, even among primitives, vary in ability and understanding, and, therefore, enter in different degrees into the spirit of their institutions.   It is, therefore, difficult to distinguish between what individuals think their institutions are and what they think they should be.   For all institutions, as we have seen, are part fact and part idea.[1]   How far, then, do the natives have any conception, however vague, of an ultimate moral ideal, whether the good of the group or their own good, which does not completely find expression in their way of life ; and in the light of which they sometimes modify their institutions ?

I shall mention three considerations which suggest that they distinguish what is morally right, not only from what is supernaturally sanctioned and what is legally binding, but also in some sense from what is prescribed by custom or required by existing institutions.

(1) Our authorities tell us that medicine men are allowed a freedom in their relations to other men's wives which is denied

---

[1] Cf. Goldenweiser, *Anthropology*, pp. 51-2.

to ordinary citizens. If they take advantage of this freedom, which we are told they seldom do, they cannot be punished. Nevertheless, " such conduct . . . is regarded as decidedly reprehensible ".[1] Here then we have conduct which is not punished, which is permitted by established custom, and which is no doubt regarded in this way because of the magico-religious standing of the medicine men ; yet it is regarded as morally wrong.

(2) There is the way already mentioned in which the Aborigines deal with problems that arise from contact between tribes with different practices or institutions. In this connection, Elkin writes : [2] " This point should not be lightly passed over. The Aborigines have, in the past, adopted changes in their social, religious and economic life. They have successfully solved problems arising from culture contact and they are doing so today. But when they are successful in this, the changes are not being pushed on them in an overwhelming manner, but are discussed, understood and adopted." If this judgement is well grounded, and it is supported by Spencer and Gillen,[3] then the native elders deliberately introduce modifications in their institutions and customs, and they do so after discussion and a reasonably clear understanding of what they are doing.

(3) But the clearest evidence that, in their dealing with moral and social situations and the duties arising in connection with them, the Aborigines do not just passively accept a social pattern handed on by tradition but think about the situation for themselves, appreciate social facts and show regard for the good of the group or the tribe, is to be found in the way in which they deal with some of the problems to which death gives rise. No doubt the limits within which their moral thinking takes place are narrowly prescribed by magico-religious and other traditional beliefs ; but this should not blind us to its existence.

According to their view, a view which they share with many other primitive people, the cause of most, if not of all, ill-health and death is magic. As Elkin puts it,[4] " it is seldom a case of

[1] Spencer and Gillen, *Northern Tribes*, pp. 486-7.
[2] Elkin, *op. cit.* p. 30.   [3] *Arunta*, pp. 11-12 and 224.   [4] *Op. cit.* p. 238.

something causing a death, but of *someone* doing so ". Accordingly, for them a death gives rise to two problems : (*a*) to discover the ' murderer ' and (*b*) to take vengeance on him. For according to the strict letter of their magico-religious beliefs not only must the proper burial ritual be performed, but the ' murderer ' must be found and punished before the spirit of the deceased is finally laid to rest and the outraged feelings of his kinsmen assuaged. Accordingly, an inquest has to be carried out on the corpse. Speaking generally and without going into refinements, we may say that the work of carrying out the inquest and interpreting the evidence discovered is done by the medicine men and the elders. And within the limits of their beliefs, their treatment of the problem shows both intelligence and wisdom and some moral insight, although they are mixed up with much that is crude and cruel and, to us, revolting.

(1) Sometimes no inquest is held. This happens in cases when the value which the group places on the deceased individual is not great, and therefore the emotional disturbance caused by his death is not serious ; as, for example, in the case of the death of an infant or young child [1] who, they believe, may soon be reincarnated again.

(2) When an inquest is held, the result is not nearly so fortuitous as appearances might suggest. For in interpreting the results of the inquest, the medicine man's " thoughts are guided by his knowledge of social happenings — of the jealousies, quarrels, enmities in existence — and of the social value or worthlessness of likely ' murderers ' ".[2] The evidence, for example, may be regarded as inconclusive ; the suggestion being that the deceased broke some taboo, and thus, as it were, brought about his own death. Or the evidence may be interpreted to mean that the ' murderer ' belonged to a tribe living so far away that it is not possible to send an avenging party. Or again, the evidence may only determine the direction from which the ' murderer ' came or the tribe to which he belongs ; and it is left to the medicine man or to the elders or sometimes to the tribe concerned to name the individual — a practice which is sometimes used to dispose of a person of whom they

---

[1] Elkin, *op. cit.* p. 239.   [2] *Ibid.* p. 220.

wish to get rid on other grounds. Still more significant is the case in which the ' murderer ' is found in a group which had an old grievance against the group of the deceased. When this happens, we are told, " a meeting is arranged in which matters are discussed and the two grievances and charges are balanced one against the other ",[1] and reconciliation brought about without bloodshed. Thus the sad occasion is turned into an opportunity for restoring amicable relations between estranged groups.

(3) Supposing the inquest duly completed and the ' murderer ' or his tribe discovered, what then ? Again it depends on the emotional disturbance of the group and what is required to satisfy it. In some cases, such as that of a woman or an old man, no action may be taken. Or again, a magical act may be performed against the ' murderer ' or his tribe but no expedition sent. Or yet again, negotiations may be opened with the group believed to be responsible for the death ; and, where the disturbance caused by a death is not very great, a gift may be accepted in compensation, and so on.

We must not, however, interpret the above facts as evidence that the medicine men and elders do not themselves believe that magic is the cause of death. They do believe it most sincerely. But what is most significant from our point of view is that, despite their belief in magic, they are guided by the conviction that the death of certain people does not justify much punishment, and that the directions in which they seek for satisfaction for their outraged feelings are largely determined by their sense of the interests of the group and the desirability of maintaining and promoting social harmony between groups. What we seem to find operating in these cases is not a passively accepted traditional doctrine, but that doctrine as modified by an appreciation of social facts and forces.[2]

Elkin sums up his account of the matter thus : The consideration of inquest and revenge " suggests that endless vendetta is not a general principle of Aboriginal life. Nor is the principle ' an eye for an eye and a tooth for a tooth ' always literally interpreted. . . . Generally speaking, the Aborigines have no desire to exterminate each others' groups. . . . When

---

[1] Elkin, *op. cit.* p. 239.   [2] *Ibid.* p. 246.

confronted with the problem of the magical causation of death, the necessity for dealing with the personal agent, and at the same time appreciating tribal and social facts, and the task of maintaining the coherence of the tribe, (the native) is able to find a solution even if it means some inconsistency " with the traditional beliefs of his ancestors.[1]

[1] *Ibid.* pp. 247-8.

THE CROW INDIANS [1]

IN the culture of the Crow Indians of Montana we have a way of life embodying a scale of values very different from any of those which we have so far considered. Nevertheless, many of their institutions and beliefs and practices are similar to those of other primitive peoples. But the significance even of these is different because of the way in which they enter into a way of life pervaded by certain distinctive principles; for it is not the detailed elements that enter into it which determine the nature of a culture so much as the way they are integrated and the value that is attached to each. [2]

The most characteristic principles of the Crow way of life are that social standing depends on individual merit, that merit is earned primarily through military exploits, that martial prowess is the result of supernatural blessing and protection, and that these are obtained by an individual in a vision following a lonely vigil in which he meets his supernatural patron face to face. The supreme value which they attach to the military virtues and the importance of the supernatural visions, which are so intimately connected with them, pervade and colour every aspect of Crow life, and modify the working of all their institutions.

Only the briefest outline can be given here of the institutions which they share with the tribes which we have hitherto considered, and most of my space will be devoted to describing those principles which are peculiar to the Crow, and to showing how these interlock with one another and with their other institutions to form their distinctive way of life, and to determine their duties and obligations.

There are, however, two other important points worth noting about the Crow culture. (1) In it we find not only social

---

[1] The main authority for the Crow is Lowie, *The Crow Indians* ; *Primitive Religion* ; and *Primitive Society*.
[2] Cf. Lowie, *Primitive Religion*, pp. 53, 75.

groupings for ritualistic, religious and economic purposes but also clubs and societies which are purely secular and whose functions are social and military. (2) The Crow have been in contact with Western civilisation for well over a century, though at first their contacts were mainly indirect. As a result we have a good deal of knowledge of what happened to their institutions during that period, through their borrowing of elements not so much from Western civilisation as from the other Indian tribes. From this information we can draw certain conclusions as to the way in which such borrowings take place ; and they are probably of general application. Unfortunately, an example of such borrowings with the detail necessary to bring out its significance would be too long to give here. All that can be noted, therefore, is that they seem to make three things clear. (1) An institution or element of another culture seems to be borrowed only when it meets a felt need which is either unsatisfied or less well satisfied in the special circumstances in which the borrowers find themselves. (2) Institutions are more likely to be taken over if the beliefs and practices embodied in them are capable of being fitted easily into the traditional way of life of the people concerned. (3) Such borrowing is not the mere passive reception of alien elements. The new institutions are modified so that they harmonise with the spirit and principles of the culture into which they are introduced, and, in the process, they are so transformed that they differ from what they would have been in any other culture. Thus, as Lowie points out [1] in his account of the borrowings of the Plains Indians, when the buffalo disappeared and their warlike activities were restricted by the U.S. Government, both psychological and historical considerations are required to explain them. Neither alone will suffice.

Till near the end of the nineteenth century, the Crow were a semi-nomadic people depending for their livelihood on hunting and gathering natural products such as fruits and berries. It was only when the buffalo, which was their staple food, disappeared that they reluctantly turned to cultivate the soil. We shall be concerned mainly with their way of life as it was before this change came about.

[1] *Primitive Religion*, ch. ix.

The Crow are divided into thirteen clans. The clans are linked into five pairs and one trio, the members of which have special obligations to one another. The clans are matrilineal, that is, the child belongs to his or her mother's clan. They are also exogamous and so serve to regulate marriage. They are the social units for entertainment and the vendetta, and they are the basis of many types of mutual helpfulness between individuals. But though the tie of blood through the mother, the basis of clan unity, gives rise to the most stringent obligations of mutual assistance and exchange of gifts, the Crow by no means ignore the tie of blood through the father. It, too, is the basis of sentimental and moral ties. Not only is it a person's duty to treat his paternal kinsmen with the utmost respect, he is also expected to make feasts for them and give them presents, while they are in duty bound to pray for him when he is on the warpath, to sing his praises on certain ceremonial and other occasions, and so on.

Moreover, it is kinship through the father that is at the base of one of the most remarkable Crow institutions, that of joking relatives. This relationship has two sides, a comic and a serious one. Persons who are related in this way have a right to play practical jokes on one another, and what is more important each has a right, and perhaps even a duty, to expose the other to public ridicule if he is guilty of a breach of tribal custom. And he can and does exercise this right with impunity when similar actions on the part of anyone else would be deeply resented. Thus the joking relatives act as guardians of one another's morals. The weapon of public ridicule, socially sanctioned in the institution of joking relatives, is one of the strongest safeguards of Crow morality. How effective it is we can see from their attitude to exogamy. Among them exogamy has only a social, not a supernatural, sanction. No disastrous consequences, either for the individuals concerned or for the community as a whole, are believed to follow a breach of the rule; but anyone who broke the rule would be exposed to public ridicule by his joking relative. So effective is this sanction that breaches of exogamy are no more common among the Crow than is usual among people who believe that such breaches are penalised by supernatural means.

The Crow is also under a strong obligation to respect his parents-in-law, especially his mother-in-law, and he and his parents-in-law have mutual duties to one another. In fact, we find among the Crow the same sort of classification of kin, including kinship by blood and marriage and tribal fiction, as we found among the Australian Aborigines, but it differs from the latter in details. It is not nearly so extensive as the all-embracing system of the Australians, and its operation is modified in more important ways by other principles of social organisation. Nevertheless, it is a very important determinant of social conduct. Into the details of the Crow system of mutual obligations and privileges based on kinship we need not enter. The system of exchange of gifts and services and the principle of reciprocity on which it rests are common to practically all small co-operative groups of people related to one another by personal contact and ties of kinship. They are, indeed, the foundations of their systems of social justice. It is, however, necessary to note, as I pointed out before, that all that the principle of reciprocity implies is that there are duties and privileges and that they are mutual. What precisely these duties and privileges are is mainly determined by the other institutions of the particular community, and the values which find expression in them. What these are in the case of the Crow, and how they determine their rights and duties, we shall see presently.

In the conditions in which the Crow lived, it was a very great advantage to have many kinsmen, for they could be relied on to help one another materially and morally, whenever such assistance was necessary, whether in peace or war, at work or at play. But however important such relatives might be, they were not sufficient to ensure social standing or success in life. To achieve these, certain personal qualities, especially prowess in war, had to be possessed by an individual himself. Indeed, these personal qualities alone were sufficient to ensure the highest standing in life, which was, therefore, open to everyone whatever his initial disadvantages. The Crow respected many other qualities, such as " liberality, aptness for story-telling or success as a doctor " ; [1] but they were mere " decorative frills "

[1] Lowie, *The Crow Indians*, p. 215.

compared with success on the warpath, which was the real substance of true greatness. With them " war was not the concern of a class nor even of the male sex, but of the whole population from cradle to grave ".[1] Children played at war, girls danced war dances, women showed special favours to the brave, and the glory of death in battle was the burden of the instruction given to youth. Is it surprising, then, that while the motives by which the Crow were actuated were many and complex, the desire for military fame should be their ruling passion ? To be a brave warrior was to have succeeded in life, and to have gained entry into the council of chiefs.

The game of war was conducted according to strict rules ; and while all prowess was given due credit, a man had to reach a certain standard of bravery and to exhibit it in certain specific ways before he could attain the status of a chief. " There were four normal types of creditable exploit, leadership of a successful raid, capturing a horse picketed within a hostile camp, being the first to touch an enemy, and snatching a foeman's bow or gun." [2] In order to rank as a chief, a man had to score at least once on each of these counts. The council of chiefs did not exercise much direct political authority. They did not issue decrees or even administer the tribal laws, but one of their number acted as head of the camp. He decided when the camp should move, and each year he appointed one of the military clubs to act as police. The main functions of the police were to regulate the buffalo hunts and war parties, to direct the movements of the camp, to settle any dispute within the camp, and generally to maintain order and punish offenders.

The membership of these military clubs cut across clan and other kinship loyalties. The members treated one another as brothers, while blood-brothers and other near kin might be members of different and rival clubs. This prevented an over-development of clan unity, and made for greater cohesion in the camp as a whole. Unlike religious societies, these clubs, whose functions were entirely secular, had neither entrance fees nor formal initiation of members, but each had " its distinctive regalia, decoration, dances and peculiarities of behaviour ".[3] Their affairs were controlled by their senior members, but

[1] Lowie, *The Crow Indians*, p. 215.   [2] *Ibid.* p. 5.   [3] *Ibid.* p. 172.

specially selected individuals, whom Lowie calls " officers ",
were appointed each year. The function of the officers, however, was not to lead or direct, but to show outstanding bravery,
and to occupy the most dangerous positions in the face of the
enemy. If, for example, a raiding party were being pushed
back by the enemy, the officers were expected to stand fast and
hold up the enemy to enable their comrades to get away.
Indeed everything connected with the clubs, such as the standing of the members, the nature of the ceremonies, the rivalry
between clubs, and so on, was pervaded by and subordinated
to military considerations. They served in fact the purpose of
keeping the military spirit alive in their members, and stimu-
lating it in one another, during the periods when they were not
engaged in raids against the enemy.

We can see the importance of these clubs and the strength
of their claims on the loyalty of their members in the influence
they exercised on family life, and the way in which their rules
overrode even the bonds between husbands and wives. This
comes to light most clearly in the custom of mutual wife-
kidnapping by rival clubs immediately before they went on the
warpath in the spring. It is difficult to say how far the original
motive of this practice was the same as that of the practice of
exchanging wives among the Australian Aborigines in similar
circumstances. Certainly the procedure in the two cases was
quite different ; and among the Crow the result was not always
harmony and cohesion. It is true that, in their case, sex morals
were lax and divorce easy and frequent. Even promiscuous
women, though disapproved, were treated with good-natured
tolerance. Nevertheless, chastity was highly honoured. Only
women against whom no reproach could be brought could
perform the most important parts in their religious ceremonies,
and it was only for virgins that bride wealth was paid. Similarly, although divorce was common, a stable union was regarded
as the ideal, and in such unions we find " loyal attachment and
even deep affection ".[1] Nevertheless, whatever the motive,
for two or three weeks in the spring, the two principal clubs
were engaged in kidnapping one another's wives. In theory, at
least, no woman could be kidnapped who had not previously

[1] Lowie, *Primitive Society*, p. 66.

shown favours to a man in the opposite club ; and in some cases the kidnapped woman took the initiative by inviting a member of the opposite club to call for her. Moreover, women who might have encouraged the hopes of particular braves in the past, but were now happy with their husbands, might, if they appealed to the chivalry of their former lovers, be left unmolested ; while others who did not want to be kidnapped took steps, such as hiding or running away to the mountains, to avoid it, and could count on the assistance of their women friends in their efforts. But what is specially significant from our present point of view is that, however happy a man might be with his wife, and however bitterly he might resent her loss, tribal custom decreed that he should not interfere or even show resentment against the kidnappers. It should, however, be added that there are cases on record where conjugal loyalty proved stronger than the sense of duty to tribal custom ; but the demand of tribal custom was that the husband should not interfere, and that he should assume an air of indifference even if he did not feel it. The subordination of conjugal loyalty to military glory appears in another way also. Exceptionally brave men enjoyed special privileges with other men's wives.[1] In these cases the women took the initiative. Sometimes their husbands resented it, sometimes they did not.

Why, then, do the military virtues occupy so high a place in the Crow scale of values ? Is it because they have a stronger or more uncontrollable instinct of pugnacity than other tribes ? Lowie, who knows them well, contends that there is nothing to suggest that their innate endowment is different in this respect from that of other people. In support of this contention he points out that among them fighting inside the tribe was regarded as a disgrace. Every effort was made to prevent internal brawls ; and if they broke out, the club on police duty tried to bring about a reconciliation. So that it does not seem to have been love of fighting as such that made the Crow regard the warpath as pre-eminently the path of glory. There are two other facts which tend to support this conclusion. The first is the recorded unwillingness of young men to accept office in the military clubs.[2] If mere love of fighting were their

[1] Lowie, *The Crow Indians*, pp. 48-9. [2] *Ibid.* pp. 177-8.

predominant motive, such offices should be specially sought after. The other is that they did not attach high merit to killing an enemy; merely to touch him or to take his bow or gun was regarded as evidence of much greater bravery. Similarly, to bring home a scalp was evidence of a kill, but it was not treated as on a par with the forms of bravery required to become a chief. It is true, as we have seen, that their instinct of pugnacity found expression not only on the warpath but in almost all their institutions; but this seems to have been the result rather than the cause of their scale of values and pattern of culture.

They had, of course, motives for warfare other than a love of military glory. Lowie mentions two in particular, desire for loot and for revenge. Loot consisted mainly of horses, and as most warriors had more horses than they could use, this motive was a social rather than an economic one. What they desired was the kudos that came from ownership of a large number of horses, or from giving them as gifts to their kin or their relatives-in-law. The motive of revenge entered, especially, when the enemy had killed a member of their clan, but in addition there were scores of long standing to be settled with the enemy. It should be added that, like most primitive people, the Crow did not fight for territory. We may conclude, therefore, that there is nothing to show that the position which they gave to war and military glory was the result of a different innate endowment or a stronger instinct of pugnacity in the Crow than in more peaceful tribes. It was the scale of values which was embodied in their way of life that caused the over-development of this side of their nature. In this we have another example of the plasticity of man's natural endowment and of the importance of cultural conditioning.

This interpretation of the facts is further confirmed by a consideration of the relation between the Crow views of war and of religion on the one hand, and between their religion and their cultural pattern or scale of values on the other. In both cases we have a relation of mutual dependence, so that it is impossible to say that the one is a cause and the other an effect. I want briefly to consider these two relations. On the one hand, every Crow military operation was inspired by a religious revelation;[1] and on the other hand, the contents of their supernatural visions were socially or culturally determined, that is, they were largely the result of their way of life.[2]

What, then, was the nature of the supernatural revelations that sanctioned the warlike enterprises of the Crow and enabled their raiding parties to go out in the assured confidence of divine protection and blessing ? The Crow had no ceremonies for initiating their young men into the status of full membership of the tribe. Instead, the youth who wanted to make a success of life went into the mountains alone to get a vision. There were variations in the procedure but the general pattern was as follows. The would-be visionary sought to arouse the compassion of the supernatural powers by fasting and self-torture. He refrained from all food and drink. He opened a vein; he cut off a finger or made a wound in some other part of his body. He prayed for success on the warpath, ability to cure diseases, long life, horses, or whatever else he specially desired. After days and nights spent in prayer and fasting and self-torture, he swooned, exhausted it might well be from lack of food or loss of blood; and, in this condition, there appeared to him, sometimes in human form but more often in the form of bird or beast, a being who adopted him as his son, blessed him, and usually in symbolic form promised him invulnerability in battle, fleetness of foot, capacity for leadership, success as a doctor, long life, horses, and so on. He also gave him instructions, mainly about ritual and diet, which he had to observe as a condition of continuing to receive the blessing.

While this was the normal way of obtaining a vision, some visions came unsought, for example in ordinary dreams; and sometimes beings in the form of birds or beasts appeared unsolicited, to succour those who were in dire distress or peril. Moreover, it was not youths only who might go in quest of a vision. Anyone at any age might do so, and might do it more than once; and women might do so as well as men. In fact, among the Crow, anyone in distress or difficulty, the bereaved father, the forsaken lover, a man seeking revenge, even a gambler who had staked and lost his all, might seek supernatural aid

[1] Lowie, *The Crow Indians*, p. 215.   [2] *Ibid.* p. 254.

through a vision; and the result of his quest might make or mar his whole career; for not all who tried succeeded in getting a vision. In some cases, night after night passed and no patron spirit appeared, and the unfortunate suppliant concluded that high achievement was not for him. On the other hand, the suppliant, who had seen his supernatural patron face to face and made his covenant with him, returned satisfied that if he carried out the instructions he had received, his guardian spirit would not fail him.

Perhaps the most remarkable thing about these visions is that, though the details might vary from vision to vision, the general pattern was strangely similar. The vision normally came, if it came at all, on the fourth night — four being the sacred number of the Crow. The words in which the supernatural being adopted the suppliant as his child were much the same in all cases. The suppliant was usually also taught a song. There was a similar resemblance in the blessings promised and in the instructions given to different individuals. In short, what appeared was mainly determined by what was expected, and what was expected was determined, partly no doubt by the special circumstances and personality of the suppliant, but still more by the cultural pattern and scale of values of his people. As Lowie puts it, " the individual Crow seems absolutely free in his religious life. He may believe what he will as to creation, cosmology or the hereafter. He is not coerced to worship this or that deity. He is apparently only guided by his own specific vision . . . [but he] does not receive an individual vision. The way he gets his revelation, and its very content as well, are determined by the ideas current in Crow society, though of course remodelled by his individual fancy or the needs of the moment." [1] But the relation between cultural pattern and vision is one of mutual, not one-sided dependence. The content of the vision is culturally determined, but the supernatural vision confirms and sanctions the way of life and scale of values of the suppliant. When the individual follows the socially prescribed pattern of his people, and finds what the pattern has led him to expect, he confirms, in his own personal experience, the truth of what his fathers have taught

[1] *Ibid.*

him.   Thus for him and for his fellows the way of life acquires a deeper meaning and a greater authority.

Nevertheless, the Crow do not believe that every vision is a valid supernatural revelation.   Before it is accepted as genuine, the vision has to be tested by its practical results.   Suppose the suppliant has been promised success as a leader of a raiding party.   However convinced he may be of the genuineness of the revelation and the reality of the blessing, he has still to inspire some of his kinsmen or friends with sufficient confidence to go with him on a raid.   He has also to get the sanction of the council of chiefs or the military club on police duty to undertake a raid; and it is only when he returns as victor from a raid in which some of the enemy have been killed, some of their horses captured, or some other deed of daring done, that the genuineness of the vision is finally confirmed.   Similarly, if a suppliant claims that his guardian spirit has granted him power to cure either all diseases or some specific kind of disease, he must submit his claim to the test of experience.   If he succeeds in practice in curing such diseases, then, but only then, is his claim accepted as valid.   The explanations which the natives offer of visions which are not confirmed by experience are that the supernatural patron may not have been powerful enough, or that the suppliant may not have faithfully carried out his instructions, or that he may have been deceived by a malicious spirit.[1]

Though some visions are thus proved to be illusory, a vision is still regarded as the one avenue to high achievement; and no Crow would think of embarking on an important undertaking without such a sanction.   But the vision need not necessarily be his own.   A man who has not had a vision of his own may resort to one who had, and thus get the necessary guidance and power.   But while visions are the ultimate source of power, objects which appear in visions, a feather, an arrow, a rock, etc., are sometimes regarded not only as symbols of such power, and of the supernatural being who gave it, but also as having such powers in their own right.   To such sacred objects, ' medicines ' or ' medicine bundles ' as they are called, the Crow prays.   He treats them with the utmost reverence.   He takes them into

[1] Lowie, *The Crow Indians*, p. 238.

battle or on other expeditions ; and, in connection with them, he performs various magical rites which were revealed in the original vision. Besides, these sacred objects can be transferred either by inheritance or by purchase ; and provided the proper ritual rules, which differ from object to object, are observed in connection with them, they still retain their supernatural efficacy. In this way, persons who have not themselves had direct supernatural experiences may enjoy the blessings which result from them. In short the Crow, like many other primitive peoples, do not draw a clear distinction between magic and religion. This becomes even more obvious when we consider the beliefs and practices and ceremonial ritual connected with their religious societies. To take one or two examples. We find as the core of the ceremonies of one society, the practice of growing sacred tobacco with appropriate magical rites, and the belief that this practice is essential to the welfare of the community as a whole. In another, the central place is taken by an individual who is publicly, and with the aid of a man with a powerful ' medicine ', seeking a vision to enable him to take vengeance on an enemy. He is, as it were, dedicating himself in the presence of the whole tribe to getting such vengeance at all costs. Round these central themes have gathered much subsidiary vision-seeking by individuals, and much ceremonial feasting and dancing and exchanging of gifts in which the whole tribe takes part. In fact, almost every aspect of tribal life enters into these ceremonies and no doubt thereby gains an added sanction. For example, as part of one ceremony, those related by kinship ties must exchange gifts according to the principles which we already described. The principle of family unity is strengthened by the fact that husband and wife have to act as a unit in connection with many of the ceremonies. Many of the songs and dances and much of the symbolism glorify war, and so support the Crow scale of values, and so on.

This enables us to see some of the social consequences of these magico-religious beliefs and practices, and some of the functions they fulfil in the Crow way of life. Some of the ritual and ceremonial practices make for the strengthening of social bonds and give an added authority to tribal customs. The visions and the belief in the efficacy of ' medicine bundles ' inspire confidence in the face of difficulties and trials. As a result, the ideals embodied in their way of life are pursued with greater vigour and ardour, and the duties which their realisation imposes on them are fulfilled with greater zest and hope. In this way, the different aspects of their life interlock to form a harmonious whole. In the resultant pattern, activities personal and social, peaceable and warlike, economic, political and religious, are so intertwined that the benefits and privileges of one provide an incentive to perform the duties required by another. Thus supernatural visions give courage in war; bravery in war determines social standing; and social standing determines political organisation. On the other hand, while the one avenue to success in war is a supernatural vision, the content of that vision is determined by the very social order which requires for its effective functioning the military activities dictated by the vision.

Though the magico-religious beliefs and practices of the Crow dovetail into the other aspects of their way of life, they neither prescribe nor justify the contents of their moral and social ideals. For, as Lowie points out, the direct connections between Crow religion and morality are very tenuous.[1] " The really vital social canons, such as incest taboos, the laws of chivalry and the ideals of chastity, have no supernatural sanctions. . . . When a prospective visionary calls upon the supernatural to favour him, he hardly ever stresses his moral worth but his pitiable plight. What he begs for is not moral elevation but some material benefit, and it is compassion which animates his patron in granting it. Often, to be sure, the visitant lays down rules of conduct but they have no bearing on social considerations. They are capricious taboos of a dietary or ritualistic character "[2] about such things as eating birds' eggs, throwing ashes from his hut, cooking fat, knocking the snow off his hut, turning a shield, and so on. These ritual rules are precise and definite; blessings are promised for their observance and dire consequences are threatened for disobeying them; but they provide little or no guidance as to how the individual should behave towards his fellow-men, what rights

---

[1] *Primitive Religion*, p. 29.   [2] *The Crow Indians*, p. 253.

he should respect, what duties he should fulfil; and they contain
no promise of reward or threat of punishment for such conduct.
Moreover, the supernatural patrons will support their suppliants
irrespective of the merits of their cause. They sometimes even
fight one another in defence of their followers.

In the light of these considerations, we may agree with
Lowie [1] that the conduct prescribed by Crow religion is
" purely personal ", " potentially anti-social " and " manifestly
unconnected with anything normally included under the heading of ethics ". While " the Crow did have a clear code of
social conduct ", he concludes, it " may be said to be almost
wholly dissociated from religious sanctions ".[2] And yet, as
Lowie clearly recognised, this is only one side of the truth; for,
as we have seen, once the individual has his moral and social
duties, once he knows what his duties to his fellow-men are, at
least some of his magico-religious beliefs and practices help him
to make the effort necessary to realise his ideals and fulfil his
duties.

From whence, then, if not from religion, does the Crow
derive the detailed content of his moral and social ideals?
Why does he regard as obligatory the duties which they impose?
He derives them in the first instance from the way of life of his
people, the way of life which has largely made him the sort of
individual that he is, and which exists not only around him
but in him, in the way of habits of thinking and feeling and
judging. The fact that they are the traditional customs of his
people seems to be accepted as a sufficient reason for regarding
some forms of conduct as right. This is true of manners and
conventions. It seems to be true also of the basic principles
of their social structure, such as matrilineal, exogamous clans,
and of the high standing of the military virtues. The rightness
of these principles is seldom or never doubted, and so no
question of justifying them arises.

We are on less sure ground when we consider why the Crow
regards as right the detailed requirements of the moral and
social institutions which function within the general framework
of their social structure. No doubt there are many among
them who just accept the socially prescribed duties as binding

[1] *Primitive Religion*, p. 30.   [2] *Ibid.*

and ask for no further reasons. The extent to which this is so varies in the case of different individuals and probably also in the case of different forms of conduct. But from many of the details of their institutions, and the conduct they prescribe, and especially from the statements of the more intelligent and reflective members of the community, it is clear that the final authority for the conduct which is regarded as obligatory is the good of the tribe or clan with which the good of the individual is intimately bound up. In other words, they regard as right that which they believe to be necessary to maintain and promote the smooth working of their way of life, a way of life which, as tested by experience, they find on the whole good. The Crow, we are told, are not given to systematic thinking, and no doubt few if any of them have a clear conception of the way of life of their people as a whole, or of the way in which the duties required of them in particular circumstances fit into the total pattern. But they at least see that the performance of certain duties is required for the efficient functioning of particular institutions ; and as they desire the benefits which the working of these institutions brings them, they regard the duties which they impose as binding, however irksome and contrary to their immediate inclinations they may be. When, for example, a number of them are engaged in a co-operative enterprise like a raiding party or buffalo hunt, they all desire the success of the undertaking, and they recognise that the condition of success is that each should play his part and treat the others in certain ways. They therefore regard it as obligatory that he should do so.

The same considerations apply to the working of other institutions such as mutual helpfulness between the members of a clan, exchange of gifts and services between patrilineal kin, or reciprocal obligations of the members of a military club. The smooth working of these institutions is seen to be good for all concerned, and the conduct necessary to effect this is therefore regarded as right. This does not, however, mean that such conduct is not often exacting and unpleasant. So long as the group is small, the relations personal, the privileges and obligations mutual and the purpose of the institutions clear — and this is true of most of their institutions — it is easy even for the least imaginative to see what the working of their institutions requires, and to recognise that their working is for the good of the group including his own. How fundamental the principle of reciprocity, on which most of their institutions is based, is in their ideas of justice and their system of morality can be seen from the ways in which they extend it even to regions where it seems to us least appropriate, such as the relation between supernatural patron and suppliant, the relation between moral censors in the institution of joking relatives, or the relations involved in the transfer of spiritual power. Even if the transfer is from father to child, an equivalent return has to be made.[1]

Now, as we have seen, the particular institutions interlock to form the whole way of life of the people, and in the resulting pattern the different institutions mutually modify as well as support one another. Accordingly the pattern of the culture helps to determine the precise nature and requirements of the institutions, and the maintenance of the way of life requires that the institutions should function effectively. So that the good of the whole community, as expressed in the pattern of their way of life, is the final justification of the rightness of the duties required by particular institutions. Of course, this may not be always clearly grasped by the person who is called on to perform a duty. He may not see beyond the requirements of the particular institution; but it follows from the nature of the way of life as a whole.

As additional evidence for this interpretation of the facts, we may note a few further considerations which support the view that for the Crow the final authority as to what is right is the good of the tribe. (1) We already saw that a supernatural vision has to be tested before it is accepted as a genuine revelation. What test, then, do they apply to it? In the first place, unless it is in conformity with the interests of the tribe as interpreted by the council of chiefs or the police on military duty, nothing further can be done to test it. In the second place, if the visionary is allowed to test it further, the test requires that it should be in the interests of the tribe; for, to be successful, not only must the raiding party, led by the visionary, do damage

[1] Lowie, *Primitive Religion*, pp. 16-17.

to the enemy, but it must do so without the loss of any of his own men. (2) This brings to light a second way in which the interests of the group modify the conduct which their professed ideal would seem to prescribe. From the instruction given to their youth who are told that old age is an evil and death in battle the greatest good,[1] as well as from their passion for military fame and the high importance which they attach to the military virtues, we might expect that the Crow would encourage reckless daring on the warpath. But that was certainly not the case. Their ideal of the successful military leader is the man who succeeds in inflicting casualties on the enemy or getting loot from them without any loss among his own men.[2] If he could at all help it, he should not run the risk of losing even one of his men, even in the hope of inflicting very much more serious losses on the enemy. And the reason is not far to seek. The loss of even one man was recognised as a serious loss for the tribe, and the interests of the tribe dictated the tactics of warfare.[3] (3) The paramount importance of the good of the tribe as a determinant of right conduct is also seen in the way they behaved when a member of the tribe was killed. The conduct which they regarded as right was quite different when the murderer was a fellow tribesman from what it was when he was an outsider. We should think that, if anything, the former was the more heinous crime, and therefore deserved the severer punishment. Not so the Crow. They certainly regarded the murder of a fellow tribesman as a serious crime, so serious that they were unwilling to associate with a pardoned murderer.[4] But in determining his punishment, the interests of the tribe seemed more important than considerations of justice to individuals. For even if the murderer belonged to a different clan, as long as he was a fellow tribesman, his death was not insisted

---

[1] Lowie, *The Crow Indians*, p. 218.   [2] *Ibid.* p. 227.

[3] It should be noted that the Crow have a strange institution which is more consistent with their professed ideal. Sometimes a man who is disappointed or disillusioned says that he will become a " crazy dog wishing to die ". He then turns his back on life and seeks death with extraordinary recklessness in the face of the enemy. ' Crazy dogs ' are treated with the highest respect, and their ideal is regarded as the loftiest that a Crow can entertain. See *The Crow Indians*, p. 331.

[4] *Ibid.* p. 12.

on. Indeed every effort was made to induce the kinsmen of the murdered man to accept compensation and not to insist on the death of the murderer. But if the murderer happened to belong to another tribe, nothing but his death, or that of one of his kinsmen, would satisfy the outraged feelings of the murdered man's relatives.

No doubt it was the interests of a tribe which lived precariously in the midst of enemies which also dictated the high value placed on military prowess, the special sexual favours shown to outstanding warriors, and many other features of their way of life. And the interests of the tribe often presented them with alternatives which were grim enough. For example, would the interests of the tribe be best served by abandoning their sick or wounded comrades on a raiding party or in battle, or by staying with them, or by trying to carry them away to nurse them back to health? There are many instances on record [1] of the heroism of wounded men who pleaded with their comrades to leave them and save the tribe, and also of self-sacrificing refusal by the latter to abandon their fellows.

The view that the good of the tribe was the main determinant of right conduct is further confirmed by the fact that, where the interests of the tribe were not believed to be at stake, the individual Crow, faced with conflicting loyalties, was given a very considerable measure of freedom to do as he liked. We find such conflicts, for example, between family loyalty and clan solidarity,[2] or between the claims of personal friendship with a member of another clan and the requirements of clan unity.[3] But in such cases no blame seems to have been attached to an individual whichever of the alternative lines of conduct he pursued.

We may sum up our conclusion about the moral ideas of the Crow as follows: However close may be the connection and even the interpenetration of different aspects of their way of life, and however much their institutions may help to support and sustain one another, it is legitimate to distinguish, within the behaviour which they regard as obligatory, between different kinds of conduct which they regard as right for different reasons.

---

[1] See, e.g., *The Crow Indians*, pp. 327 ff.   [2] *Ibid.* p. 43.   [3] *Ibid.* p. 10.

(1) There are forms of conduct, ritual and ceremonial, which have a supernatural sanction and are regarded as obligatory for that reason. Some of these, such as the ceremonial in connection with the magico-religious societies, are common to all members of the tribe. Others are peculiar to particular individuals, being the price they have to pay for the blessing and protection of their supernatural patrons. The former at least are social as well as sacred duties. Breaches of them are social offences as well as sacrilege. But whether public or private, these duties are all concerned with objects or institutions which evoke what Lowie and Goldenweiser call the religious thrill. (2) There are rules of etiquette and manners and the basic principles of their social organisation. These are regarded as right out of respect for tradition, or because they are the customs of their ancestors and they have no inducement to depart from them. (3) There are the detailed rules of secular and social morality. These are for the most part expressions of the principle of reciprocity of gifts and services, and of the conditions of effective co-operation; and their precise requirements are determined by the particular institutions which in their interrelation constitute the cultural pattern of the people. They are regarded as right because they are believed to be in the interests of the tribe and required to maintain the way of life which the Crow find good, a way of life which the individual regards as his own good as well as that of his people.

THE CONSTITUTION OF THE PRIMITIVE MIND

W E have now seen the ways of life which have been developed by four primitive peoples in their efforts to conceive and live the good life, a life which would satisfy their nature and its needs. We have seen the states of affairs which they regard as good and the rules which they regard as right, and the judgements which they pass on their own and other people's conduct. We have seen their ideals of personal development, of social welfare and of intergroup relations, and the conditions which they think must be satisfied by individuals and groups if these ideals are to be realised. We have seen the institutions in which they have embodied their rules and ideals, and the way in which the institutions of each are related to form a more or less unified way of life, in which they mutually support one another. It is their conception of this way of life in which their ideals are concretely embodied which calls forth their supreme loyalty. It is to them the ultimate source of moral obligation. What it seems to require they regard as a duty. What seems to be inconsistent with it, however strong its appeal, they regard as wrong. All their judgements of rightness and goodness are passed in the light of it.

Now I have been assuming that the moral judgements of these people are deliverances of the moral consciousness and that they are therefore part of the data of ethics, part of what has to be taken into account in formulating and testing ethical theories. In other words, I have been assuming that the primitive moral consciousness is the same as, and proceeds on the same principle or principles as, our own. But is this assumption really justified? Even if it is agreed that the ways of life in the light of which these people pass their moral judgements embody their conception of what is required to satisfy their nature and its needs, is that nature and are those needs the same as ours? Are these peoples, in fact, trying to do the same thing or to realise the same ideal as we are? Are the constitution and powers of the minds of those who developed these forms of life and find them good the same as our own? Only if this is the case are we justified in claiming that the moral judgements which they pass in the light of them are expressions of the moral consciousness as we understand the term, and therefore relevant to our ethical enquiries. And this is the case unless either the needs, desires and interests which constitute the contents of the self, or the ways of integrating them demanded by the nature of the self, or the self's powers to conceive and meet these demands, are different in the case of the primitives and ourselves. So far as I am aware, no one has suggested that the desiring nature of the self, which has its roots in the instincts which man shares with the lower animals, differs from one people to another. It is in the control, direction and integration of this material that the differences between different peoples are to be found, and it is the demand for this integration which makes man a moral being. Are, then, the ways in which the demand for this integration operates, the factors from which it arises and the powers required to meet it, thought and imagination, reason and self-consciousness, in principle the same among all peoples? And if they are the same, are they sufficiently developed among primitives to enable them to form the concepts and to grasp the relations and rules and principles which we use in our moral judgements?

When we compare with one another and with our own the ways of life of the peoples whom we have been considering, the moral judgements which they pass, the states of affairs which they regard as good, the rules which they consider right, the ideals which they try to realise, and so on, we find striking resemblances between them; but the differences between them are no less significant; and they seem to apply not merely to details but to ideals and rules and scales of value. It is easy to explain the resemblances, if we accept the assumption that the nature and needs of the peoples who developed the ways of life and pass the moral judgements are the same. But how, on this assumption, can we account for the differences not only in the actual conduct of the different peoples but in their judgements on conduct, in the things they regard as right and the ideals they regard as good? Can these differences be explained without denying the identity either of the constitution or of the powers of the minds of the peoples concerned with our own, i.e. without denying the assumption on which my argument in these lectures is based? This is the question which we have now to consider.

Three possible explanations have been offered for the differences between the ways of life of different peoples. The first tries to account for them by reference to differences in the natural environment of the peoples concerned. I think we may reject it as totally inadequate. Not that the natural environment, through the opportunities it affords and the limits it imposes, is unimportant in its influence on certain aspects of a way of life; but people in similar physical conditions are found with quite different beliefs and values, and people in quite different natural environments are found with the same institutions and ideals. The other two explanations which have been suggested are (1) differences in the mental make-up or in the powers of different peoples, and (2) differences in their history and experience, leading to differences in the social heritages which are passed on and modified from generation to generation.

These explanations, of course, are not mutually exclusive. The differences in the ways of life of different peoples might be due to differences partly in their nature and partly in their nurture, or differences in social heritages might themselves be traceable to differences in the natural endowment of the peoples concerned. I want, therefore, to examine the view that there are inborn differences of constitutions or powers between the minds of different peoples, and especially between the primitive and the civilised mind. If this view proves untenable, we shall be driven to look for the main cause of the differences in their moral judgements and rules and ideals to differences in their social heritage, the results of their history and experience.

Of those who hold that there are differences of innate endowment between primitive and civilised peoples, some take the view that the differences relate to the constitution of their minds or the principles according to which their minds work, others that they relate only to the scope and range of their mental powers. Differences of scope and range of mental powers are to be found among members of the same people or civilisation, but the principles according to which their minds work are the same. For example, all the members of a group of people may be able to solve simple problems in the same way, while only some of them can solve more advanced problems, which require the individual to hold before his mind at once and as an integrated whole a wide range of facts; and some may be able not only to solve very advanced problems, but to discover new principles; while others may be able to understand and apply such principles but could not discover them for themselves. The differences between such minds are usually regarded as differences of degree, but it is important to note that this term covers both the difference between those who can make original contributions to a subject and those who can assimilate these contributions, though they could not themselves have made them, and also the difference between those who can and those who cannot recognise the higher contribution, when it is pointed out to them. The distinction between these two sorts of differences of degree is important for an understanding of the view that the primitive mind is inferior to or less developed than the civilised mind, but as those who advocate this view do not draw the distinction it is often difficult to discover what precisely they mean to assert. In any civilisation, the number of people who can make original contributions is very small. The majority of the inhabitants of any country take over and use a social heritage which they themselves could not have discovered or invented. If, therefore, the view we are considering merely asserts that primitives could not discover the higher civilisation for themselves, the difference between their powers and those of the average member of civilised societies which it presupposes may not be very significant. The difference is much greater if the view is interpreted to mean that primitive minds are so inferior that they could not take over and use the higher civilisation which others have developed.

As distinct from those who hold that there are greater or less differences of degree between the primitive and the civilised mind, others take the view that there is a difference of kind or principle between them, that there are fundamental differences in the laws according to which they operate. By this is meant the sort of difference we would get if the minds of different persons operated in such a way that one combined without any sense of incongruity things which appeared to the other to be incompatible or that one could not distinguish between things which appeared different to the other. Such minds would not, except by accident, arrive at the same conclusions, and one would not understand the processes of the other. Each might act according to principles, but the principles being different, the results would be different. Such minds would be just different and one would not be better or worse, or more or less developed than the other. They could not be put at different stages on the same scale.

Thus we have three possible views of the nature of the primitive mind and its relation to the civilised mind, all of which have been advocated during the present century and perhaps still have their advocates : (1) that the fundamental constitution or structure of the two is different, that they operate according to different laws or principles; (2) that the two are fundamentally of the same kind and obey the same laws, but that they differ in their degree of development, the primitive mind being more immature and still at a stage through which the civilised mind passed centuries or millennia ago, and incapable in the lifetime of any individual of reaching the level of the civilised mind; and (3) that the innate endowment of the two minds is the same, or at any rate that there is no significant difference discoverable between them, and that the differences which we find in their contents and products are due to differences in the social heritage into which they entered, that is, to differences of opportunity and training and social environment.

The third view, or something like it, is held by practically all social anthropologists who have had first-hand and lengthy experience of primitive peoples. I might, therefore, be content to quote their testimony and pass on, fortifying myself with the declaration recently (10th December 1948) adopted unanimously by the representatives of more than fifty nations and now embodied in the Declaration of Human Rights, that " all men [1] are endowed with reason and conscience ". But the issue is so fundamental for my argument in these lectures that I propose to deal with it in some detail. For if the primitive and the civilised mind operate according to different principles or if there is such a difference of degree between them that the primitive mind cannot grasp our moral ideas and conceptions, the consideration of their ways of life will throw no light on the nature of morality as we understand the term. It is, as we have seen, on the basis of such an alleged deficiency in mental powers that one prominent school of contemporary ethical theorists explains the failure of certain peoples to recognise what these theorists describe as self-evident moral intuitions. Such people, they contend, have not " reached sufficient mental maturity ".[2]

Moreover, though the inferiority of the primitive mind has been rejected by the experts, the belief still persists in many quarters that it is, that in fact it must be, inferior to ours. This belief seems at times to be an article of faith rather than a reasoned conclusion. We see it in the attitude of the South African to the Bantu, of the American to the Negro, and generally in the attitude of the whites to the simpler peoples. The belief not only in the superiority of Western civilisation, but in the minds or mental powers of those who are its present carriers, is so pleasing to the vanity and arrogance of white men that many of the reasons given for it are put forward, not so much as evidence in support of it to be critically examined, but as explanations of an undoubted fact.[3] Even if the racial theories of the interwar years about the innate superiority of

[1] When the Declaration of Human Rights says " all men " it means *all* men, " without distinction of any kind, such as race, colour, sex, language, religion, political or other opinion, national or social origin, property, birth or other status " (Article 2).

[2] Ross, *The Right and the Good*, p. 29.

[3] As a corrective to this attitude it would be well to consider how much of what is basic in Western civilisation has been borrowed from Egypt and Babylonia, Persia and Palestine, Greece and Rome, China and India, and to remember that in recent years we have witnessed among the leaders of Western culture forms of savagery compared with which anything known among primitives pales into insignificance.

certain peoples have now found their way to the place where they rightly belong, the lay mind is still far from discarding the myth of the white man's superiority; and much of what has been written and spoken during and since the war makes it plain that men's ideas are still confused about the relative contributions of biological and social heredity to the ways of life of particular peoples.

A consideration of the nature of the primitive mind and its relation to our own should also help us to appreciate the difficulty of entering into the mind of the primitive and the effort of sympathy and imagination required to see his world as he sees it. In this connection it is essential to distinguish between the mental powers and processes of the individual mind and the social heritage to which he has been heir, and which profoundly influences the contents and products of the adult mind; for even if the mental processes of primitive minds are the same as ours, the social heritage which supplies their premises certainly is not. It is now generally recognised by sociologists that it requires patience and caution and sympathetic insight to put oneself in the position, and to appreciate the point of view, of a member of another class or nation, even if they share the common background of the same civilisation; and the sorry state of our industrial and international affairs bears striking testimony to the fact. The effort required is naturally much greater when no such common background exists. If the consideration of the different views about primitive mentality will help us to appreciate the difficulty of understanding and interpreting the beliefs and practices of primitives and enable us to guard against the many pitfalls to be avoided in trying to enter into their point of view, it will have been worth while.

Nor is the nature of primitive mentality merely a matter of theoretical interest; in recent years, as the result of the increasing contacts between peoples and the efforts of advanced nations to administer native territories and educate their inhabitants, it has become a matter of urgent practical importance. Consequently, there has been a good deal of research into the subject and there is now a considerable literature on it. Nevertheless, it is by no means easy to discover the constitution and powers of the primitive mind and to decide between the different views about its relation to the civilised mind which I stated above. The main reason for this is that we cannot isolate the innate endowment of a mind and consider it by itself. Many of the elements of the human mind are neither fully present nor finally fixed at birth, and therefore to discover their nature we have to consider how they develop. But during their development the individual is exposed to the influences of his social environment. His group never for a moment leaves him alone. Accordingly the developed mind is the joint-product of the innate endowment of the individual and of the social influences to which he has been subjected; and in this joint-product it is difficult to distinguish the contributions of the different factors. These joint-products — the concrete contents of the adult mind — do undoubtedly differ from primitive to primitive, from primitive to civilised, and from civilisation to civilisation. But we must distinguish between these joint-products and the institutions, customs, beliefs and values in which they find expression on the one hand, and, on the other, the constitution, capacities and processes of the individual mind. The difficulty is that we do not find the latter except as they function and express themselves through the former; and the differences in the ways in which they do so may be due either to differences in the make-up or capacities of the minds or to the influences of the social medium in which they have developed and by which they have been moulded.

Accordingly, in trying to decide between the different views about the nature of the primitive mind and its relation to the civilised, we have to proceed indirectly through examining their characteristic products. In doing this two lines are open to us. The one is to produce positive evidence that the constitution and powers of primitive minds are much the same as our own. The positive evidence available consists mainly of (a) the practically unanimous testimony of field workers (too numerous to mention) that this is so, and their achievements in understanding and explaining the customs and institutions and beliefs of primitive peoples on these assumptions; (b) the oft-reported ability of the field worker who immerses himself in the culture of a primitive people not only to understand but to forecast how the natives will react to particular situations ; and (c) the capacities shown by natives, and especially by native children, when they are educated and trained by white men. There are also certain general considerations which render it highly improbable that there are fundamental innate differences between the different branches of the human family or that, even if such differences existed, they would provide an explanation of the differences which we find in their ways of life. To mention just one such consideration. Radical changes in the ideals and values, beliefs and institutions of particular peoples have taken place in a much shorter time than would be necessary for changes in their hereditary endowment to establish themselves. The impressive and rapid progress and decline of the civilisations of particular peoples do not leave sufficient time for innate factors to operate. The other method of procedure open to us is to examine the evidence put forward in support of the view that the primitive mind is different from our own. If we can show that this evidence is not sufficient to warrant the conclusion, we seem justified in accepting the other and more natural view for which there is positive support. I propose to begin with the second method and let the positive evidence on which the first method relies emerge in the course of the argument.

Let us begin with the more extreme view, that held by Lévy-Bruhl [1] and his school, that the primitive mind works according to different principles or laws from the civilised. According to this view, the primitive mind is neither inferior nor superior to the civilised, but just different. It may help us to understand Lévy-Bruhl's position and to appreciate the very considerable contributions which he made to our understanding of primitive mentality, if we recall the sort of explanation generally offered at the end of last century of primitive beliefs and customs. These explanations were given in terms

---

[1] The classical statement of this view is to be found in Lévy-Bruhl's *Les Fonctions mentales dans les sociétés inférieures*, which has been translated into English under the title *How Natives Think*, and in *La Mentalité primitive*, also translated into English. The page references given below all refer to the English translations.

of the highly rationalistic psychology still current in many quarters at that time. Anthropologists, therefore, tended to account for the beliefs of primitives in terms of the rational and conscious processes of individual minds, and to ignore the importance of the social factor in determining them, that is the importance of the social heritage which had not been deliberately planned but had grown up piecemeal as the result of the contributions of many individuals, each of whom understood only a small part of the whole social structure and perhaps even less of the effects of his contribution on the whole. The individualistic and intellectualistic bias of the early English School of Anthropology, against which Lévy-Bruhl was mainly arguing, is, I believe, sometimes exaggerated, but in general it did tend to represent animism and totemism and other primitive beliefs as not only reasonable under the conditions of primitive life and knowledge, but also as arrived at by conscious reasoning.[1] It regarded them as in fact the simplest explanation which a mind, moved by intellectual curiosity, could give of the experiences and facts at the disposal of the primitive.

Now Lévy-Bruhl rightly rejects this over-rationalistic interpretation of the characteristic beliefs of primitive man. He points to the complexity of primitive language, and he might have added of primitive social organisation, as evidence that rational simplicity is not a characteristic of the primitive mind or indeed of the untrained mind anywhere. The structure of their languages, their systems of numeration, their elementary powers of analysis and abstraction, and their distaste of reasoning, show that even if they had the powers of reflection and reasoning necessary to formulate schemes of philosophy of the kind which Tylor and Frazer, for example, attributed to them, they certainly had not exercised them. But while rejecting this highly intellectualistic psychology as a description of the

[1] E.g. Tylor speaks of primitive beliefs as " schemes of primitive philosophy " (*Primitive Culture*, i. 68) and of animism as " the obvious inference " from the facts (*ibid.* i. 428) ; while Frazer writes of certain aspects of the social organisation of the Australian Aborigines as bearing the " impress of deliberate thought and purpose " plainly stamped on them (*Totemism and Exogamy*, iv. 121) and as " the reasonable inference that effects are due to causes " (*ibid.* ii. 108-9), and so on. Cf. Spencer, *Principles of Sociology*, i. 100, " Given the data as known to him, primitive man's inference is a reasonable inference ".

mental processes of primitive man, Lévy-Bruhl seems to accept it as a satisfactory account of those of the civilised. As a result, he seems to be contrasting the average primitive mind with that of the civilised scientist and philosopher in their most critical and rational moments. It is not surprising, therefore, that he distinguishes sharply between the two types, and contends that the processes of the one cannot be understood or expressed in terms of those of the other. There is between them, he thinks, a difference not of degree but of kind. The mental operations of the primitive, he holds,[1] are not an inferior variety of our own. The differences between the characteristic products of their minds and ours are due not to defects of understanding, to incapacity or inaptitude for reasoning on their part,[2] but to their methods of thinking.

The most significant differences between their methods of thinking and ours are that they ignore the teaching of experience and disregard the laws of contradiction and causality, the laws which are the basis of the thinking of civilised adults. It is not that the primitive mind deliberately violates these laws; but that it completely ignores them, and that it is equally satisfied with processes of thinking which do, and with processes which do not, comply with their requirements. In Lévy-Bruhl's own terminology, the primitive mind is not anti-logical or alogical, but pre-logical.[3] The principle according to which it works Lévy-Bruhl calls " the law of participation ", a law whose functioning is determined by " collective representations " or conceptions, which are of social origin, common to all members of the social group, transmitted from generation to generation, and so impressed on the individual by his group that they arouse intense emotional and volitional activity and determine his thinking and feeling in relation to the objects to which they refer.[4] These collective representations are not, strictly speaking, representations at all, that is, they are not ideas or concepts which result from the observation or the merely cognitive or intellectual processes of the individual.[5] They are the reactions of the total personality in its emotional and volitional as well as

---

[1] *How Natives Think*, p. 76 ; *Primitive Mentality*, p. 33.
[2] *Ibid.*, pp. 21-2, 29-30. [3] *How Natives Think*, p. 78.
[4] *Ibid.* pp. 13 ff. [5] *Ibid.* pp. 36-7.

its cognitive aspects, and the former rather than the latter are the more prominent and decisive factors ; nor is there any clear distinction drawn between the different aspects. When, e.g., the Australian native believes that he is identical with his totem and says that he is an emu or a witchetty grub, or that the symbols which represent the totem in his religious ritual or the individuals who personify it in his ceremonies are identical with the totem or with himself, he does not arrive at this conclusion as the result of observation and experience, nor by rational and intellectual processes. He lives and feels his identity with them and their identity with one another. For him all of them give rise to the same emoti_ns, and these emotions are social in origin, communicated to the individual from his social environment. The things which arouse the same emotion are regarded as identical. They ' participate ' in one another through ' an invisible mystic bond '. All the things which are united in this way form parts of the same collective representation. Therefore for the primitive any one of them can take the place of any other, and so, in complete disregard of the law of contradiction, he says that the one is the other. Similarly, when the primitive says that crow is thunder, that the child who is born but not ceremonially named is alive and not alive, that the man who has died but has not received his second burial is dead and not yet dead, that a particular rock was a woman and had children, and so on, his mind is operating according to the law of participation and disregards the law of contradiction which dominates our thinking.

Lévy-Bruhl examines almost every aspect of primitive life and thought, their beliefs about life and death, nature and the supernatural, their languages, their systems of numeration, their magical rites in connection with hunting and fishing, illness and war, to show the essentially mystic character of their mentality, the fact that they think of things not as they appear to sense, but as the vehicles of mystic properties. Nothing, he contends, is perceived by the primitive as it is by us ; for though he perceives with the same senses as we do, he perceives with a different mind.[1] Now it is the mind which

[1] *How Natives Think*, p. 43.

determines the interpretation which we put upon what we observe, and as the primitive mind is determined by collective representations, according to which the operative forces are mystic and invisible, it pays little regard to objective or causal connections, and experience cannot undeceive it.[1] In short, the primitive mind is lacking in analysis, insensible to contradiction, impervious to experience, and prevented from functioning freely by intense emotions aroused by objects interpreted through collective representations.[2] And, therefore, Lévy-Bruhl concludes : " It is useless to try and explain the institutions and customs and beliefs of undeveloped peoples by starting from the psychological and intellectual analysis of ' the human mind ' as *we* know it. No interpretation will be satisfactory unless it has for its starting point the pre-logical and mystic mentality underlying the various forms of activity in primitives." [3]

Now the mass of evidence in support of his thesis which Lévy-Bruhl collected from all parts of the primitive world is very impressive, and it throws an important light on the nature of the primitive mind. It conclusively demonstrates the importance of the social factor in determining many primitive beliefs and practices ; and it shows that the mental processes of primitives are not so intellectual as some earlier anthropologists thought. It is true, as he himself points out,[4] that the evidence on which he relied was mainly collected by untrained observers ; and the more accurate observation of trained field workers has since shown that the pressure of the social group on the individual is not nearly so overwhelming as Lévy-Bruhl suggests.[5] Instances of individuals outstanding as thinkers, or men of affairs who left their mark on the culture of their people, are given even by some of the authorities quoted by Lévy-Bruhl himself, and many more have been brought to light by the more recent researches of Radin and Malinowski, Mead and Hogbin and many others. All these show that the role of the individual in primitive societies is much greater, and that in many of them the individual has much more freedom

---

[1] *Ibid.* p. 75.   [2] *Ibid.* pp. 107-9.
[3] *Ibid.* p. 361 (italics in text). [4] *Ibid.* p. 30.
[5] See Lecture V, p. 149, note 1, and references there given.

than Lévy-Bruhl suggests, and that in none of them is he merely the automatic vehicle of social forces. Indeed Radin [1] produces impressive evidence in support of the view that the proportion of thinkers and philosophers, poets and prophets is probably not much less among primitives than among civilised.

Despite the modifications which recent researches have made in the evidence available to Lévy-Bruhl when he formulated his theory, the main facts regarding primitive beliefs and institutions from which he drew his conclusion remain unquestioned. What we have to ask, therefore, is whether these facts warrant his conclusion that the primitives disregard the laws of contradiction and causality, and the teaching of experience, or that their minds act according to principles different from our own.

Before directly attacking this question, I want to note two facts which serve to make the contrast between the primitive and civilised mind less sharp than the above account would suggest. These facts are admitted, somewhat grudgingly no doubt, by Lévy-Bruhl himself, but it is doubtful if he recognises all their implications.

(1) There are spheres of life in which the primitive mind is not dominated by collective representations and in which his mental processes do not obey the law of participation. In these spheres he observes as accurately, appreciates objective connections as clearly and learns by experience as certainly as we do. In the construction of his tools, the cultivation of the soil and the growth of crops, in the processes involved in fishing and hunting, in building a house or making a canoe, the primitive is as objective as anyone could desire. Here he is guided by the teaching of experience and his thought and his actions do not ignore the laws of contradiction or causality, and he builds up empirical concepts in the same way as we do.[2] " In such activities ", Lévy-Bruhl admits, " the primitive . . . will usually feel, argue and act as we should expect him to do." [3] In short, in dealing with such matters, the primitive mind is as

---

[1] *Primitive Man as Philosopher.*
[2] *How Natives Think*, pp. 121-2.   [3] *Ibid.* pp. 78-9.

logical and as rational as our own. It is true, however, that he sees the objects and situations with which he is concerned even in such activities against a background of invisible forces of which he also takes account. It is in relation to the latter that Lévy-Bruhl regards his mental processes as pre-logical. Nevertheless, even according to Lévy-Bruhl, we find in the primitive mind logical as well as pre-logical activities.

(2) Lévy-Bruhl also admits that there are pre-logical elements in the minds of most civilised adults. He finds some of these in folk-lore [1] and in superstitious beliefs in relation to such matters as hunting, fishing and fighting,[2] but especially in moral and religious beliefs and customs,[3] and he might have added, in political convictions. In these spheres we find beliefs which have not been arrived at by the intellectual processes of the individual who holds them, beliefs which the individual has accepted from his society, and which he has not subjected to the critical scrutiny of reason. They are in fact what Lévy-Bruhl calls collective representations and man's thinking in relation to them obeys the law of participation.

Now if there are logical and pre-logical elements in both the primitive and the civilised mind, the difference between logical and pre-logical can scarcely be regarded as a criterion for distinguishing the two types of mentality. This is a line of argument used by Durkheim and other members of the French School of Sociology, who are as emphatic as Lévy-Bruhl about the importance of collective representations but hold that they help to determine the beliefs and attitudes of all men, primitive and civilised alike. But Lévy-Bruhl tends to minimise and underestimate the logical element in primitive mentality and the part played by collective representations in the workings of the normal civilised mind. He admits that complete rationality is a desideratum rather than a fact in the working of the civilised mind;[4] but he still thinks of it in terms of the intellectualistic psychology which he rejects as a description of the primitive mind. If, as is now almost universally agreed, this rationalistic psychology is inapplicable even to the civilised mind, the fact that the mental processes of primitives do not comply with it

---

[1] *Ibid.* pp. 67-8.   [2] *Ibid.* pp. 245-6.
[3] *Ibid.* pp. 383-6.   [4] *Ibid.* p. 386.

does not prove that they are pre-logical or, in principle, different from those of more advanced peoples.

Moreover, Lévy-Bruhl tends to identify the rational with the consciously reasoned and to regard as pre-logical, if not irrational, all beliefs and conclusions which are not arrived at by the individual who entertains them as the result of such reasoning.[1] But beliefs, whether entertained by the primitive or the civilised, may be rational in the sense of complying with logical principles, though they may not have been arrived at by conscious reasoning. It is perfectly true, as Lévy-Bruhl contends, that the primitive does not arrive at his animism and totemism by consciously reasoned processes. He does not first have a clear idea of himself or his mental processes and of his bodily activities as due to the operation of these processes on the one hand, and of natural events and processes as inanimate on the other, and then proceed consciously to interpret the latter, on the analogy of the former, as due to the activities of minds or spirits. But neither is this the way in which the civilised man arrives at such beliefs as, e.g., that other men have minds like his own. He recognises them as like himself and attributes to them experiences like his own before he reflects on, or introspectively observes, the nature of his own mental activities or the relation between them and the bodily behaviour in which they find expression. Similarly the primitive, with his less reflective and more undifferentiated experience, in his interactions, not only with men and animals but also with natural objects and events, especially those which profoundly affect his welfare, interprets them in the light of his own experience and regards many of their processes as being the results of wishes and desires, thoughts and purposes, such as he finds in himself. He does not first recognise natural events as inanimate or dead, and then by a conscious process of reasoning attribute to them the sort of processes which he discovers in his own mind. Rather, he has not yet drawn so clear a distinction as we do between men and animals and natural events, nor between the outward and visible behaviour, whether of his own body or natural happenings, and the invisible mental processes which he experiences in his own case and attributes to others. Even

[1] See, e.g., *How Natives Think*, p. 386.

for the civilised adult, the process of divesting nature and natural events of all traces of such animism and regarding it merely as matter in motion, or whatever the present scientific equivalent of matter in motion is, is the result of a long discipline which requires a considerable effort of thought. Much of what we call the common-sense attitude to nature has many activist and personalistic elements in it.

If Lévy-Bruhl had merely contended that primitive mentality is pre-scientific, as Hoernlé [1] suggests that he should have done, we could certainly accept his view, but we should have to add that some of the thinking of all, and perhaps all of the thinking of many, civilised adults is pre-scientific, that scientific thinking is of quite recent origin, that there is no evidence that its appearance is due to a change in the constitution or powers of the mind, and that it differs from pre-scientific thinking, not in the principles on which it proceeds, but in the greater care, exactness and systematic thoroughness with which it is carried out.

It is necessary also to distinguish between the magico-religious beliefs of the primitive regarding man and nature, such as totemism and animism, and the conclusions which he draws from them — in other words, between his premises and his processes of reasoning. The premises no doubt contain much ignorance and superstition, accepted on authority from his social environment, but the evidence suggests that the processes are logical and rational and differ in no way from our own. This is shown by the fact that anthropologists who steep themselves in the native atmosphere and way of life will not only understand but also anticipate the conclusion at which the primitive will arrive in any given case.[2]

Moreover, it is not the primitive alone who responds to objects and situations with all the powers of his mind, and not merely with the intellectual and cognitive side of it. As we have already noted the civilised mind does so too, much more frequently than Lévy-Bruhl admits. He sees objects, not as

[1] " Prolegomena to the Study of the Black Man's Mind ", *Journal of Philosophical Studies* (January 1927), p. 60.

[2] See, e.g., Linton, *The Cultural Background of Personality*, pp. 101-2; do. *The Study of Man*, pp. 43-7 ; Driberg, *At Home with the Savage*, p. 41 ; Fox, *The Threshold of the Pacific*, pp. 250-51.

they are to bare cognition but as having a significance which his own emotional and volitional reactions to them have led him to read into them. Much of this emotionally charged significance is of social origin, and the individual responds emotionally to it before he thinks rationally about it, if he ever does so at all. This is specially true of situations where his life and livelihood or those of his group are, or are believed to be, at stake. A flag, a certain colour of shirt, a form of greeting, or a few bars of a song, may become as deeply charged with significance and may arouse as profound an emotional and volitional reaction as any of the symbolic objects of primitive ritual. The colossal scale on which such ' collective representations ' flourished in the interwar years, even among people who were regarded by themselves and others as cultured and civilised, is only an outstanding example of a phenomenon which is always with us, and which shows the extent to which collective representations are apt to dominate our minds. It is true that in our critical moments we distinguish between connections which are based on causal and logical principles and those which are based on emotional reactions. But in the ordinary life and thought of the average man, whether primitive or civilised, the distinction between them is often blurred.

We conclude, therefore, that logical thinking, recognition of objective connections and respect for the teaching of experience are to be found in the primitive as well as the civilised mind, that collective representations and connections based on emotional association are common among civilised as well as primitives, and that beliefs, whether arrived at by the individual for himself or accepted by him from his society, may be rational, that is, based on logical principles and objective or causal connections, though the individual who entertains them has not arrived at them for himself by consciously reasoned processes. What we have to consider, then, is whether the actual beliefs of primitives which are quoted in such rich profusion by Lévy-Bruhl, show that they in fact ignore the laws of causality and contradiction and the teaching of experience.

Take first the law of causality. We have already seen that in relation to the mundane affairs of life the primitive observes objective causal connections and acts upon them. Moreover, Lévy-Bruhl himself admits,[1] and many other observers have noted, that for the primitive there is no such thing as an accident or uncaused event. In view of this, it is difficult to assert that they ignore or contradict the law of causality. What is true is that they do not regard what we call the natural or apparent causes of events as their real causes. It is not so much that they ignore natural causes as that they seldom seem to them a sufficient explanation. They find the real causes in the invisible powers which they believe reside in or operate through the visible happenings, just as they and we find the causes of our own bodily activities in the volitions and desires which operate through them. Thus they do not deny or ignore the principle of causality but they find the real causes in factors which do not appear to sense. On this state of affairs it is worth while making two observations. (1) Emphasis on natural causation is quite modern. In earlier times it was largely neglected by many whose mental powers were undoubtedly the same as our own. (2) Our experience is not confined to sense and the real operative causes which we first and most directly experience are invisible, namely the operation of our own minds.

Do primitives, then, ignore or deny the law of contradiction? Some of the evidence which Lévy-Bruhl gives in support of this conclusion seems to rest on a confusion between the different or the contrary, and the contradictory. When, for example, the primitive regards the unnamed infant as born and not yet born, or the man who has died and not yet had his second burial as dead and not dead, the apparent contradiction is due to neglect of the difference between physical and ceremonial birth and death. When this distinction is borne in mind, we realise that the view of the primitive is no more a denial of the law of contradiction than the assertion of the man who says on different occasions that man is mortal and that man is immortal, mortal as regards his physical organism, immortal as regards his soul. The primitive does not state

[1] *How Natives Think*, p. 73.

explicitly the conditions under which he makes his statements, but neither does the civilised man always do so. They both make them in the light of the conditions which seem to them important at the time. When the primitive asserts that the man who has not had his second burial is not yet dead, it is the ceremonial death that seems to him important; while to us in the same circumstances physical death may seem the only relevant consideration. Given his beliefs about life and death, however, his mind does not operate on a different principle from ours.

Take again the primitive's identification of things which seem to us radically different, like a man and his totem. This does not mean that for him a man and an emu, for example, are in all respects identical, for he never confuses the two. It means only that the respect in which they are identical seems to him an important one. In no proposition does the copula assert the complete identity of the subject and predicate, otherwise the mere mention of the subject would be sufficient and the predicate would add nothing to it. In considering the totemism of the Australian Aborigines,[1] we saw that there are different kinds of totemic groups and that, therefore, the bond of identity between the members of the group and between them and their totem is not always the same. This fact was not recognised by Lévy-Bruhl nor by the observers on whose work he relied.

To give an adequate explanation of such statements as are quoted by Lévy-Bruhl in this connection it would be necessary to consider each separately, but we can say in general that the ordinary primitive (as distinct from the occasional thinker among them) is not much interested in the abstract qualities of the objects or individuals concerned. He is interested rather in the way they behave, and especially in their effects on himself and his group. If, therefore, two things act in the same way or produce the same emotional reaction in himself and his fellows, he tends to regard them as so far identical. Indeed Aldrich[2] suggests that " acts the same " would be a better rendering than " is " or " is identical with " of what the

---

[1] See p. 205 above.
[2] *The Primitive Mind and Modern Civilisation*, p. 140.

aborigines mean when they say that a man is an emu or that a churinga is an ancestor ; [1] and Sommerfelt,[2] who does not seem to have been aware of Aldrich's suggestion, arrives at the same conclusion on linguistic grounds. Sommerfelt points out that many primitive languages are constructed on the basis of forms of classification different from ours. In one group of languages, which includes that spoken by the Central Australian natives, there are no words for qualities. The people who speak these languages, being interested in how things behave rather than in their formal qualities, do not classify entities into substances and attributes or things and qualities. Their verbs convey what we call the qualities of things ; that is, the qualities a thing has are the ways in which it behaves. " A language constructed on such lines ", he points out, " is quite sufficient for all the needs of the people concerned." [3] Accordingly, when they say what we translate as " an emu is, or acts in the same way as, a man or a churinga ", they are not in any way contradicting the laws of our thinking ; they are merely putting things in a different way or in terms of a different principle of classification from that used by us. But while the two ways of putting the matter are different, the one does not contradict the other, nor does the difference show that the minds of those who use the different forms act according to different laws of thought.

Or take the primitive's continued belief in the efficacy of magic despite the mass of empirical evidence that the desired results do not follow its application, which is quoted as evidence that the primitive ignores the teaching of experience. Does it, in fact, prove that he is impervious to experience or that his mind works differently from ours ? Apart from the fact that such beliefs were common among our recent ancestors and that vestiges of them are still to be found among us, it is not difficult to see why they are not easily disproved by experience. The

---

[1] Compare the view of Radcliffe-Brown : When the Australian native says " Kangaroo is my elder brother ", he does " not mean that individuals of Kangaroo species are his brothers. He means that to the Kangaroo species . . . he stands in a social relation analogous to that in which a man stands to his older brother in the kinship system ". (" Religion and Society " in the *Journal of the Royal Anthropological Institute*, vol. lxxv. (1945), p. 40.)

[2] *Is there a Fundamental Mental Difference between Primitive Man and the Civilised European?* (Earl Grey Memorial Lecture, 1944), pp. 7 ff.

[3] *Ibid.*

fact is that most experiences seem to confirm them, and those which are inconsistent with them can be plausibly explained away. For consider : good harvests, a safe return to port, and good health are the normal conditions of affairs. Bad harvests, shipwrecks, epidemics and fatal accidents are the exceptions. Every year the magic of the crops is performed, and in most years the harvest is good. On every canoe that goes to sea appropriate rites are performed, and almost all of them return safe to port. Persons who fall ill are magically treated, and most of them are restored to health.

But what about the exceptions ? It is true, as has often been pointed out,[1] that untrained observers tend to note favourable rather than unfavourable instances. As Bacon says, " Men mark when they hit, not when they miss ". And for the exceptions which are observed there are various quite plausible explanations. There may have been some flaw in reciting the spell or performing the ceremony. The magician or other persons concerned may not have complied strictly with the food or other taboos which are essential to the success of the magical rites ; or an enemy may have used a more powerful magic to counteract the results which would otherwise have surely followed.[2] For there are different kinds of magic and they vary in strength. And as the exercise of black magic is always secret, it provides an easy explanation for occurrences which are not understood.

When a belief can explain anything which happens equally well, it cannot be disproved by experience, for no experience is inconsistent with it. Such is the case with the belief in magic. Most experiences seem to confirm it, and no experience can disprove it. That is, at any rate, part of the explanation for its continuance, and it does not suggest any difference of principle between the primitive and the civilised mind. The other part of the explanation is to be found in the important functions which, as we have seen,[3] the belief in magic performs in the lives of primitives, especially the function of inspiring them with hope and confidence in the face of dangers and difficulties.

---

[1] See, e.g., Jevons, *Principles of Science*, p. 402.

[2] Cf. p. 236 for the way in which the Crow test the genuineness of their visions and explain the exceptions.   [3] See, e.g., pp. 117-21.

Most of the other beliefs and practices quoted by Lévy-Bruhl can, I think, be explained along somewhat similar lines. It is true that there are many of them whose origins we do not know : they are shrouded in the mists of antiquity. The key to them has been lost, and attempts to explain them are speculative and uncertain. But we can understand the functions which they fulfil in the lives of those who entertain them and the reasons why they continue to accept them. It is also true that the accounts given by primitives often contradict the accounts which we should give of the same facts or events. In that sense, their beliefs contradict the facts or the teaching of experience ; but, so far as this is true, it means that their beliefs are false, not that the minds of those who entertain them are differently constituted from ours. It may also be admitted that, though they are not devoid of intellectual curiosity and although they demand an explanation of every phenomenon and a cause for every event, the curiosity of primitives is usually easily satisfied. They do not carry the process of explanation far, or work out its implications in relation to the rest of their experience. In this respect, however, they are not greatly different from many civilised adults. Neither type of mind will rest content in the presence of a recognised contradiction, but both often entertain mutually contradictory beliefs. But there is nothing in these circumstances, or in the facts relied on by Lévy-Bruhl, which proves that the primitive disregards the law of contradiction or causality or the teaching of experience, or that his mental processes follow different laws from our own.[1]

No social anthropologist with whose writing I am acquainted and who had first-hand experience of primitives accepts Lévy-Bruhl's main conclusions without reservation. It is true that a few of them quote his views with approval, but they do so to emphasise the great gulf between the beliefs entertained by the adult primitive and the adult civilised mind. Such approval as they give seems based on a confusion between the beliefs or conclusions of the primitive mind and its mental processes. For they all explicitly deny that it works according to different laws from our own.

[1] For more positive refutations of Lévy-Bruhl's view based on intelligence tests, see next lecture, pp. 273-4.

In this lecture I have been concerned only with Lévy-Bruhl's conclusion that the primitive mind is pre-logical; but while rejecting this conclusion I do not wish to belittle his considerable contributions to our understanding of the primitive mind. He demonstrated clearly, though perhaps with pardonable exaggeration, the need, for the understanding of the primitive mind, of taking account of the social factor which had been largely neglected by earlier anthropologists. He proved conclusively that rational simplicity is not specially characteristic of the primitive mind, and that its processes are less intellectual and reflective than most of his predecessors assumed. He emphasised that the differences between the primitive mind and our own are not due to lack of capacity or aptitude, and that it cannot be regarded as a more rudimentary or childish form of our own mind. And his account brings clearly to light the need for great care and caution and imaginative sympathy, if we are to understand its beliefs and practices. These are significant contributions to the study of the primitive mind, but they are all quite consistent with its constitution being the same as that of our own.[1]

[1] After this lecture was delivered I discovered that Lévy-Bruhl's now partially published note-books show that in his later years he was constantly re-examining the view that the primitive mind is pre-logical; and that as a result he reduced considerably the difference which he earlier believed to exist between their methods of thinking and our own.

THE POWERS OF THE PRIMITIVE MIND

W E have next to consider the view which is more commonly held that the primitive mind is inferior to the civilised in degree of development, that it is more rudimentary, still at a lower stage of evolution. Even if it obeys the same laws and acts according to the same principles as our own, its powers may be more limited, its range narrower, so that it may be incapable of reaching the level of our achievements, perhaps even incapable of assimilating the higher results of our civilisation, let alone of making original contributions to its progress. If we find no evidence of such inferiority, we shall be justified in assuming the identity of the primitive's moral consciousness with our own, and all that we shall have to show will be, not that the primitive has the necessary powers, but that he does in fact exercise them. Moreover, even if there were evidence to show that the primitive mind is inferior, perhaps markedly inferior, to our own in intellectual powers, it might still have the very modest equipment necessary to grasp the simple concepts involved in our ordinary moral ideas and rules, such as truth-telling and promise-keeping, gratitude for services rendered, reparation for injuries and the sorts of acts in which they find expression.

Now about the same time as Lévy-Bruhl first put forward his view of the pre-logical nature of primitive mentality, Boas,[1] in the light of his own field work and of the available evidence from other sources, came to the conclusion that the constitution and powers of the primitive mind do not differ in any important respect, either in kind or even in degree, from those of the civilised mind. Boas is as much in revolt as Lévy-Bruhl against the rationalistic psychology and the rigid determinism of what we might call the later nineteenth-century view of the development of culture as unilinear, gradual and progressive, and of the

[1] *The Mind of Primitive Man* (1911); Revised Edition (1938).

minds of contemporary primitive peoples as a less developed form of our own. He finds the explanation of the differences in the ways of life of different peoples, their beliefs and customs and institutions, not in the structure or the constitution of their minds, but in the cumulative social heritages of which they are heirs; not in their innate powers or mental processes but in the premises from which they start. He is even more emphatic than Lévy-Bruhl that the elements of a culture are intimately interconnected, and that beliefs and practices and institutions can only be understood in their context as parts of a way of life. But he contends that this intimate interconnection does not imply any law of participation or any mystic union which ignores or defies the law of contradiction or causality or differentiates the primitive from more advanced minds. What it does imply, he says, is that in order to understand man we must consider him in his environment, and his judgements and beliefs, ideals and values in their cultural context. When we so consider the characteristic products of the primitive mind, he contends,[1] we shall find its constitution and powers and processes differing in no significant way from our own.[2]

These general conclusions were accepted, developed and defended, though with some differences of detail, by Lowie and Goldenweiser, Radin and Malinowski, and others too numerous to mention, and they have been amply confirmed by the concentrated research and the intensive surveys of primitive peoples by many trained field workers during the past forty years. Despite this, however, the belief that the powers of the primitive mind are inferior still persists in many quarters, and there have

[1] *Op. cit.* pp. 29, 122-3 *et passim.*

[2] Boas did not put these views forward as an alternative or a reaction to the views of Lévy-Bruhl which we considered in the last lecture. He developed them quite independently and published them about the same time as the first statement of Lévy-Bruhl's views appeared. His reaction to Lévy-Bruhl's views is stated in a passage which he wrote sixteen years later. " Anyone who has lived with primitive tribes, who has shared their joys and sorrows, their privations and their luxuries, who sees in them not solely subjects of study to be examined like cells under a microscope, but feeling and thinking human beings, will agree that there is no such thing as a ' primitive mind ', a ' magical ' or ' pre-logical ' way of thinking, but that each individual in ' primitive ' society is a man, a woman or a child of the same kind, of the same way of thinking, feeling and acting as man, woman or child in our own society " (*Primitive Art*, 1927).

been a few anthropologists who continued in some degree to share it. What grounds, then, have been advanced for this belief, and what considerations are relevant for enabling us to arrive at a conclusion regarding it ?

The argument has been conducted on three levels : (a) physical, especially anatomical and physiological considerations ; (b) psychological, mainly concerned with intelligence tests; and (c) sociological, concerned with the general performance of different types of mind, as revealed in their characteristic products. Let us briefly consider the evidence at each of these levels in turn.

We need not delay long over the evidence at the physical level, for by general consent it is entirely inconclusive. Nevertheless, people will from time to time revert to it. There are, of course, physical differences between different sections of mankind, such as extent of hairiness and kind of lips. Some of these features are believed to be more, and others less distinctively human, and it has been held that those who possess the more distinctively human characteristics are further removed from the animals. If they are so in body, it is natural to suppose that they are mentally more developed too. But the evidence shows that those races, primitive or civilised, who are most distinctively human by one criterion, such as extent of hairiness, are nearest the animal by another, such as kind of lips ; so that all attempts to grade existing peoples on the basis of their physical characteristics as being more or less developed have entirely failed.

The evidence from the development of the brain is equally inconclusive. It is true that the greater size and complexity of his brain is perhaps the chief anatomical difference between man and the higher animals, and that it is very closely connected with his higher mental powers ; but the evidence for a comparison between the brains of primitives and civilised is meagre, and experts are not in agreement as to how it should be interpreted. The evidence available suggests (we cannot put it any higher) that, among civilised peoples, the brains of persons of outstanding ability are, on the average, rather larger and heavier than those of persons of normal ability. But the differences so far observed may be due to the better nourishment of the members of the former group who have been examined; and, in any case, some men of the highest ability have been found with very small brains. The evidence also suggests that the brains of primitive people are, on the average, rather lighter and smaller than those of advanced peoples, but the evidence is too limited to enable us to generalise, for size of brain tends to vary with size of body. Moreover, there are great variations in size of brain in any group; and therefore, while the average in the civilised group may be higher, the highest in the primitive group is much above the average in the civilised.

More important, however, than mere size of brain is the development of the cortex; but here the evidence is even more meagre, and its interpretation more doubtful. For example, the analysis of the brains of a number of Australian Aborigines showed qualitative differences in the cell development of the cerebral cortex as compared with that of some civilised peoples. These differences were interpreted by Seligman,[1] who saw the results before they were published, as evidence of lower mental development on the part of the Aborigines, but Shellshear,[2] who carried out the investigation, suggests that they might equally well indicate greater possibilities of future development, possibilities which no man can measure. In addition, we have to remember that inferences from brain to mind are highly speculative and uncertain, and that we in fact know much more about the powers of mind of different peoples than about the characteristics of their brains. We may therefore agree with the verdict of the experts that the evidence at the physical level leaves our question where it was.

When we turn to the psychological evidence, the direct observation of mental powers, we find it almost equally inconclusive. Intelligence tests in particular have proved singularly unhelpful. No test has yet been devised which can be applied to primitive and civilised peoples with any confidence that the results will enable us to compare their degrees of intelligence, and some psychologists [3] are doubtful if a suitable test for this

[1] *Psychology and Modern World Problems* (ed. Hadfield), pp. 60 ff.
[2] Quoted by Firth, *Human Types*, pp. 31-2.
[3] E.g. Nadel, *The Study of Society* (ed. Bartlett, Ginsberg, Lindgren and Thouless), p. 186; Bartlett, "Psychological Methods and Anthropological Problems", *Africa*, x. 412-14; Boas, *Anthropology and Modern Life*, p. 55.

purpose ever can be constructed, that is, one which will completely eliminate the influence of cultural factors. When intelligence tests, which had been devised to test civilised peoples, were first applied to primitives, the results were simply fantastic. They showed the intelligence of the primitive so low that no one with any knowledge of them could accept the results. It soon became obvious, however, that the reason for these results was that the tests did not eliminate differences of education and cultural background and manner of living. It has in fact been suggested [1] that, if tests really suitable for bringing to light the degree of intelligence of members of a primitive society were applied to civilised people, the latter would be at a similar disadvantage and would show correspondingly poor results. All that the psychologists have succeeded in doing so far has been to construct tests which enable them to compare the mental powers of people with more or less the same background and training. This is specially true of verbal tests, but it seems to apply to the performance tests as well. It is true that some progress has been made in trying to devise more general tests and more particularly in trying to find primitives and civilised with the same educational background, such as the whites and negroes in North America. So far, those who have interpreted the results of such tests seem to think that they do not show any difference of intelligence between the two groups. Garth, who devoted most of his life to constructing and applying such tests and who admits that he began his work with the conviction that he would find such differences, came at the end of his work to the conclusion that " differences so far found in the intelligence of races can be easily explained by the influences of nurture and of the selection ".[2]

But even if intelligence tests do not enable us to reach a final judgement on the relative degrees of intelligence of primitive and civilised, they have not been entirely without a bearing on our problem. Firth [3] claims that the results of simple performance tests have shown that the mind of the primitive

[1] E.g. by Lowie, *An Introduction to Cultural Anthropology*, p. 8 ; and Linton, *The Study of Man*, p. 53.

[2] *Race Psychology : A Study of Mental Differences*, Preface, p. vii.

[3] *Human Types*, p. 38.

functions " in the same logical way as our own minds ". Now
if this is true, it disproves Lévy-Bruhl's theory of the pre-
logical mentality of the primitive. Other and more general
psychological tests also have led to important conclusions.
Nadel constructed and applied tests to West African natives
with results which he claims " finally refute the theories of
Lévy-Bruhl and his school about the pre-logical nature of the
primitive mind ".[1] Nadel also devised tests [2] intended, not to
provide a comparison between white and primitive mentality,
but rather to compare natives with one another, and, in particular, to discover whether there are any significant psychological
differences between the members of neighbouring tribes who
are of the same racial stock, and roughly at the same stage of
civilisation, but whose ways of life are markedly different. The
results " reveal a close correspondence between the cultural
differentiation and the psychological differences of the two
peoples ".[3] This strongly suggests that the differences in
habits of thinking and lines of mental development are due rather
to differences in social heritage than to differences in innate
intellectual powers.

Tests of sensory acuteness such as sight, hearing and reaction
times show no difference between primitives and civilised.[4]
This has a twofold significance. First, the results of these
tests are less likely to be affected by education and social background. It is significant, therefore, that when cultural influences are thus excluded, no differences in powers appear.
Secondly, they show that conclusions which have sometimes
been drawn from the alleged greater sensory acuteness of the
primitive are without foundation. Observers have often been
impressed with the extraordinary grasp of concrete detail shown
by many primitives, as well as by their powers of hearing light
sounds, and noting footprints of men and animals, and so on.
This was usually attributed to the greater sharpness of their
senses. Now it has sometimes been suggested that marked

[1] *Study of Society* (ed. Bartlett, Ginsberg, Lindgren and Thouless), p.
194, note 1.
[2] *British Journal of Psychology*, General Section (October 1937), pp.
196 ff.
[3] *Ibid.* p. 211.
[4] See, e.g., Linton, *The Study of Man*, p. 52 ; Firth, *Human Types*, p. 33.

superiority in sensory powers shows an affinity with the higher animals rather than with civilised man, and that it is incompatible with abstract thinking and high intellectual powers generally, that is, with some of the distinctive characteristics of the civilised mind.

As the experimental evidence shows that the sensory powers of the primitive are no more acute than those of the civilised, his greater powers of accurate observation can no longer be used as evidence that he is at a lower stage of mental development. The undoubted difference between the powers of observation of many primitive and most civilised men must, therefore, be attributed to differences in training and experience, not to inborn differences. When primitive man's livelihood, and often his life, depends on his noting the slightest movements, or his recognising the footprints of man or beast, and when he has been trained from his earliest years in such work, it is not surprising that he should notice differences which civilised man will miss. There is, however, ample evidence that in similar conditions some civilised men will develop similar powers. Canadian trappers, for example, have been cited as an instance ; [1] but we need not go so far afield to look for examples. I have known at least one shepherd and one deerstalker in the Highlands of Scotland whose powers of observation would well-nigh rival those of any primitive of whom I have read. And there have been plenty of examples during two world wars of even town-bred civilians turned soldiers, who in the Burma jungle or on the plains of Mesopotamia or the fields of Flanders, when their own lives and those of their comrades often depended on their observation, after a time developed powers scarcely inferior to those reported from primitive people.

These examples also prove that such powers are not incompatible with high intelligence and capacity for abstract thinking. It is true that few people have the opportunity to develop both equally, but the civilian soldiers who developed such powers of observation included, among others, students and teachers of high intellectual gifts, and the shepherd and deerstalker to whom I referred gave indications of the same combination of qualities. Reckoned by our usual standards

[1] Goldenweiser, *Early Civilisation*, p. 7.

they might not be regarded as men of high intellectual attainments, but they could discuss the metaphysical basis and implications of Calvinistic theology, if not with the analytical skill of logical positivists, at least with a concentration and consistency which showed considerable intellectual ability and powers of abstract thought.

I think we may therefore conclude that no psychological test yet discovered has revealed any marked difference of mental powers among the different sections of mankind.[1] There are, of course, great differences between individuals within any section, but there is no evidence of such differences between one section and another.

The main evidence which has been advanced in support of the view that the mind of primitive man is inferior has been derived from the observation of its characteristic products, as revealed in his simple material culture, his fantastic beliefs and crude customs, and, in general, his lowly achievements. " By their fruits shall ye know them ", we are told; the real test of powers is performance; and judged by its achievements, the primitive mind must be regarded as inferior. This is the stock argument of the layman, and we also find it used by at least two anthropologists, Pitt-Rivers [2] and Seligman.[3]

In reply to this contention, two considerations may be urged. (1) What is our criterion of achievement? What test are we to apply to civilisations to discover which of them are more advanced, unless, as is often done, we just accept our own as the highest, and grade others according as they approximate to it? If we accept as our criterion science and technology, the extent and accuracy of scientific knowledge, and the control over nature and the material comforts which such knowledge has made available, there is no doubt that ours is far in advance of any other civilisation. But science and technology are very recent discoveries and their effects are cumulative at a very rapid rate. The result is that our material civilisation differs more from that of our ancestors of two centuries ago than the

[1] Cf. Linton, *op. cit.* p. 68.
[2] *The Clash of Culture and the Contact of Races*, p. 161.
[3] *Psychology and Modern World Problems* (ed. Hadfield), p. 73.

latter differs from that of the most primitive peoples known to history or anthropology. But no one suggests that this difference indicates on our part a different kind of mentality from, or greater intellectual powers than, our forefathers of the eighteenth century.

If, on the other hand, we take art or social organisation or religion as our criterion, it is not at all so clear that we represent the acme of achievement. Indeed, as regards such features, it is difficult, perhaps impossible, to get any standard by which we can grade civilisations as higher or lower. Until we have a standard of comparison other than extent and complexity of material culture, it is unwise to speak so dogmatically of higher and lower civilisations, and greater or less achievements.

(2) Possible achievement depends on starting-point as well as aptitude and powers. Where a man can get depends on where he starts, as much as on his powers. I have already mentioned Newton's generous acknowledgement that his own achievements would not have been possible but for the labours of his predecessors. He had the advantage, as he put it, of standing on the shoulders of giants. If Newton had been born among a primitive people, he might well have left his mark on their thought and their way of life, but he certainly would not have composed the *Principia*. Outstanding mental powers are a condition, but not by themselves a guarantee of high achievement. Other conditions are also necessary, and these other conditions are cumulative, and after a certain point proceed at a progressively more rapid rate ; so that, while we can argue from achievement to aptitude for achievement, we cannot argue from absence of achievement to absence of aptitude for achievement.[1]

In addition to the general argument from the absence of a high civilisation to the absence of powers of developing such a civilisation, certain specific characteristics of primitive life and conduct have been pointed to as evidence that their minds are inferior to ours. They are alleged to be lacking in foresight and volitional control, in powers of concentration and ability to endure pain, in capacity for sustained labour, and in powers

[1] Boas, *The Mind of Primitive Man*, pp. 2 ff. ; Cf. Hoernlé, " Prolegomena to the Study of the Black Man's Mind ", *Journal of Philosophical Studies* (January 1927), p. 56.

of abstraction and classification. They are said to be lazy and shiftless, irresponsible and unreliable, easily discouraged, and lacking in initiative and originality. Now such judgements are not without foundation. They are not merely biased reports of prejudiced white men. Detailed evidence can be, and has been, produced to support them. Nevertheless, trained observers, who have watched primitive peoples in their daily life, and have understood their interests and points of view, hold that none of these judgements are justified, and that the natives do not, in fact, fall below our standards in most of the qualities which these judgements deny them.

The explanation of the discrepancies between these accounts of the behaviour and mentality of primitives is not far to seek. It is to be found in the point of view from which, and the interests in the light of which, the judgements are passed. The adverse judgements come mainly from such people as travellers, traders and plantation managers, and they are based on the point of view and the interests and values of the white man. They are due to considering practices and beliefs apart from their cultural context and looking at them against the background of the ideas and values of Western civilisation. The opposite judgements by field workers are made from the point of view of the natives and in the light of their interests and scales of value, i.e. in the light of their cultural context. Judged from such different points of view, the same piece of behaviour may be regarded as evidence of opposite qualities. For example, when, as we have seen,[1] the Trobriand Islander discontinues his pearl-diving because he hears that his inland partners want fish for a ceremonial feast, his action may be regarded by the white trader as evidence of unreliability and irresponsibility. But to the Trobriander it is evidence of a sense of duty and responsibility. Or again, when the Australian native employed as a guide by a white man refuses to continue far beyond the boundary of his tribe,[2] his action may seem to the white man evidence of laziness and unreliability. To the native, it may be evidence of devout religious feeling and loyalty to the claims of his tribe.[3]

[1] See p. 125 above.   [2] Elkin, *The Australian Aborigines*, p. 34.
[3] See p. 202 above.

No man will work strenuously, endure hardship and carry on in the face of obstacles unless he has an incentive to do so, that is, something that arouses his interest and appeals to his sense of value. To the Trobriander pearls have no value and the reward which the trader gives him in return for them does not provide a real incentive. Beyond a very limited amount, he has no use for it. Therefore, he will not work hard nor continuously at pearl-diving. But we must not conclude from this that he is incapable of working hard or with sustained purpose. He will work hard for spondylus shells which are as valueless in the eyes of the white man as pearls are in the eyes of the native. He will work hard in his gardens, not only to grow crops, but to make the gardens beautiful, because that seems to him important. Look at him as he prepares for months in advance for a Kula expedition, and what better evidence of sustained purpose could you wish ? Look at him as he braves the perils of an overseas expedition in a frail craft, and you will find him facing danger and enduring hardship. It is all a question of values and incentives, and the values of the native are not the values of Western civilisation. Give the native an incentive that appeals to him, and he will work hard and with sustained purpose as he often does in fishing and hunting, and on the warpath ; and we have seen that many of the incentives that appeal to him are of a non-utilitarian kind.

Similar considerations apply to the native powers of volitional control and concentrated attention. Watch the funeral rites of the Australian Aborigines and you may well conclude that they have no control of their emotions. But watch their youth as they submit without murmur or complaint to the painful rites of initiation, and the verdict will be very different. They have the same capacity for volitional control as we have, but we and they exercise it on different occasions and in different connections. Again, in order to promote concentrated attention, you must arouse interest. We should not conclude, therefore, that the native has no powers of concentration, merely because some of the things which interest us do not call such powers into play. They may seem to him the merest foolishness. Boas makes the following comment on the conclusion, drawn by a traveller, that the natives of a particular Indian tribe, with whom Boas was well acquainted, had no powers of concentration because they showed evident signs of weariness after a short conversation in which the traveller asked them questions which required an effort of thought and memory. " The questions put by the traveller seem mostly trifling to the Indian and he naturally soon tires of a conversation carried on in a foreign language, and one in which he finds nothing to interest him. As a matter of fact, the interest of these natives can easily be raised to a high pitch, and I have often been the one who was wearied out first." [1]   Other field workers have had the same experience in this respect as Boas.   Rouse the interest of the native and you will get sustained effort and concentrated attention.   It is, however, true that the most primitive peoples live mainly in the present.   The conditions under which they live do not normally call for long-term projects and comprehensive plans, but this does not prove that they are incapable of sustained effort in the pursuit of distant ends ; and, before we pass final judgement on their attitude in this respect, we should remember that it has been commended by the greatest moral teachers as the highest wisdom.

What, then, of the capacity of the primitive for abstraction and classification ?   An analysis of primitive languages shows that different people classify according to different principles.[2] Therefore the fact that primitive people do not always classify according to the same principles as we do does not prove that they do not classify at all.   Nevertheless it is true that, on the whole, primitive people are more concrete and specific than we are, both in their thought and in its expression.   Yet there are some primitive languages in which abstract terms are quite common,[3] and experiments conducted by Boas with people whose language is lacking in abstract terms showed that they could easily construct and use them.[4]   But, in the main, the modes of life of these people make little call for abstract thinking.   This, and not any absence of capacity for it, is the reason why it is less common among them.   Radin may be guilty of

[1] Boas, op. cit. p. 111.

[2] Boas, op. cit. pp. 144 ff. ;   Sommerfelt, Is there a Fundamental Mental Difference between Primitive Man and the Civilised European? p. 7.

[3] Boas, op. cit. pp. 150-51. Cf. Radin, Primitive Man as Philosopher, p. 384.

[4] Boas, op. cit. pp. 150-51.

exaggeration when he claims that the proportion of abstract thinkers among primitives is probably no less than among more advanced peoples, but the impressive evidence which he has quoted [1] about such thinkers goes far to justify the description by Goldenweiser [2] of the belief that primitives are lacking in capacity for abstract thought as " an obsolete dogma ". Similar considerations apply in reference to the other qualities in which the primitives are said to be lacking.[3]

There is one other important piece of evidence regarding the mental powers of primitive man, namely, the performance of natives, and especially of native children,[4] when educated and trained by whites. I propose to consider this evidence along with the views of the three recent field workers who, against, or it may be in ignorance of, the considered opinion of the overwhelming majority of their colleagues, suggest that the mental powers of primitives are markedly inferior to our own. I want to consider their views not so much because they bring out any points of importance which we have not already considered, but partly to show the grounds on which such views are based, partly because the main evidence for them relates to two of the peoples whom I have chosen as representative primitives,[5] and partly because one of them may be cited as a hostile witness in support of the contention of this lecture; for while he draws the conclusion that there are important differences between the powers of the native and the white mind, his admissions and much of his evidence seem to point in the opposite direction. The three writers in question are Pitt-Rivers,[6] Seligman [7] and Bryant.[8]

[1] *Primitive Man as Philosopher.*

[2] *History, Psychology and Culture*, p. 100. Cf. Lowie, *Primitive Religion*, p. 247, which describes it as " a hoary fallacy ".

[3] For a detailed discussion of them see Boas, *op. cit.* pp. 105 ff. ; Goldenweiser, *Early Civilisation*, pp. 6 ff.

[4] If we want to discover innate powers, it is to children that we should go rather than to adults whose habits of thinking and feeling have been already formed under the influence of their social environment.

[5] The Australian Aborigines and the Bantu.

[6] *The Clash of Culture and the Contact of Races.*

[7] In *Psychology and Modern World Problems* (ed. Hadfield), pp. 55 ff.

[8] In *Eugenics Review* (April 1917), pp. 42 ff.

Pitt-Rivers is concerned with the problem of why primitive peoples tend to die out when they come in contact with Western civilisation. The explanation seems to him to be psychological, a weakening or failure of the will to live, due to innate mental disabilities which render the primitives incapable of adjusting themselves to changed environmental conditions. This lack of " culture potential ", he thinks, cannot be modified without an infusion of new blood which would change the innate constitution of their minds.[1] We are not concerned with his general thesis,[2] but only with the difference which he alleges to exist between the primitive and civilised mind, and the evidence which he submits in support of this difference. Using Jung's distinction between psychological types, and especially his distinction between introvert and extrovert, Pitt-Rivers suggests that the difference between the primitive and the civilised mind can most simply be explained on the hypothesis that the extrovert type predominates among the primitive and the introvert among the civilised.[3] The extrovert type he considers the less developed, the more infantile ; it is less analytic, draws fewer distinctions ; it relies more on concrete imagery, memory and imagination, and less on abstract reasoning ; it has a narrower range of imagination, and shows less originality. The more mature introvert type has the opposite characteristics. Now Pitt-Rivers admits that we find both types of mind in every society and at every level of development, but he thinks that the introvert type predominates at the civilised level and that it is responsible for its higher achievements.[4] His other line of argument we have already considered, the argument from absence of high achievement to the absence of aptitude

[1] *Op. cit.* p. 240.

[2] For a criticism of this thesis see Hogbin, *Experiments in Civilisation,* pp. 132 ff.

[3] *Op. cit.* pp. 153-4.

[4] It is interesting to note, in passing, that Aldrich, one of Jung's pupils, writing at a later date than Pitt-Rivers, and applying the principles of his master's psychology to the evidence about primitives, arrives at the conclusion that there are no fundamental differences between primitive and civilised mentality [a], and that Jung himself, in a foreword to his work, endorses this conclusion [b].

[a] *The Primitive Mind and Modern Civilisation,* pp. 62, 224.

[b] *Ibid.* p. xvi.

for such achievement. The only test which he will admit of the nature and powers of a mind is the height to which it can rise,[1] and he seems to assume that this is shown by the height to which it has in fact risen. In other words, he assumes that mental powers are not only a necessary but a sufficient condition of high achievement. Apart from general considerations of this kind, the only empirical evidence which Pitt-Rivers gives for his contention is taken from an article, the materials for which were supplied by Bryant, and put into form for publication by Seligman. The contents of this article will be considered below.

I can find no evidence that Seligman himself accepted the conclusions which Bryant drew from the experiences recorded in his article.[2] He does not refer to it by way of support for the conclusion which he derived from his own examination of the mentality of the Australian Aborigines. That conclusion is, and he states it without any sign of dogmatism, that the " available evidence furnishes indications of intellectual differences between the less and the more advanced races, which may fairly be regarded as correlated with differences in brain structure, and hence as racial ".[3] The evidence on which he bases this conclusion is threefold : (1) the evidence regarding the relatively undeveloped character of the Australian brain to which I have already referred ; [4] (2) the rudimentary nature of the culture of the Aborigines ; [5] and (3) observations which he made on natives engaged in domestic service and farmwork in connection with a mission. These observations were supplemented by the reports of the whites who supervised the native workers. The results of these observations suggest that the native men were competent in any activity which depended mainly on memory, but not in any activities which involved the solution of problems, and that, when unwatched, they showed no tendency to persevere till the job was finished ; and that the women showed little ability to plan ahead. In games, on the other hand, the natives showed themselves

---

[1] *Op. cit.* p. 161.

[2] I mention this because the way in which Pitt-Rivers refers to it might lead the reader to believe that Seligman shares the responsibility both for its content and its conclusions.

[3] Seligman, *op. cit.* pp. 98-9.   [4] *Ibid.* pp. 60 ff.   [5] *Ibid.* pp. 66 ff.

capable of good teamwork. The ' general impression ' left by these observations is summed up thus : " The Australian is perhaps less capable of being trained to lead even a simple form of European life than a high-grade defective ".[1]

On this evidence, two comments may be made. (1) The observations were made on natives, not engaged on their traditional activities in their natural environment, but working under the direction of whites on a mission settlement, and on tasks which were quite alien to the native way of life. (2) The natives observed were adults who began this work after they had become habituated to the ways of their own people. In fact they worked on the settlement for only part of the year, and returned to the bush for the rest of the time. It is, therefore, difficult to say which, if any, of the characteristics displayed by them were due to their innate endowment rather than to their early training and cultural background. In view of these considerations it is doubtful if Seligman would have drawn even the tentative conclusion that he did, if he had not been so impressed with the anatomical evidence regarding the structure of their brains. Be this as it may, a considerable body of evidence has since come to light which shows that his conclusion is untenable. This evidence consists partly of the observations of trained field workers like Elkin [2] who learned the language of the natives and lived with them in their normal environment, and partly of the performance of the natives after they had more experience of European contacts. In this connection, the record of the native schools is particularly impressive. Let me quote the summary statement of Ashley Montagu which is duly documented, and also confirmed by all recent field workers among the aborigines. He writes : " The Australian Aboriginal native endowment is quite as good as any European, if not better. In support of this statement their exists a certain amount of evidence of the weightiest kind, such, for example, as the opinion of observers who have lived among them for many years, and who are not by any means inclined to be prejudiced in their favour. Then there is the more direct evidence of the effects of schooling. The

[1] Seligman, *op. cit.* p. 73.
[2] *The Australian Aborigines*, pp. 20, 30, 188.

rapidity with which the native learns, and, what is more important, the consistency with which he generally maintains that learning, is abundantly borne out by such a fact as the recent achievement of a school whose scholars were comprised entirely of Aborigines and which, for three successive years, was ranked as the highest ranking school from the point of view of scholarship in Australia. The ease with which the natives acquire good English when it is spoken to them, as compared with the difficulty with which the white man acquires the native language, has often been remarked upon by white observers. Such a fact as that a pure-blooded Australian Aborigine, who had learned to play the game of draughts by watching over the shoulder of players playing the game, recently (1926) decisively beat the ex-draughts champion of Australia in a series of matches, is also worth mentioning. Instances of this kind can be greatly multiplied." [1]

Finally I want to consider the arguments of Bryant's article to which I have already referred, not only because it deals with the Bantu mentality, but also because of the use Pitt-Rivers makes of it, and because of the writer's long and intimate knowledge of the Bantu. He lived among them for thirty-three years, during several of which he taught " at the same time and in the same classroom "[2] European and native children and adolescents.

His main conclusions, which refer " solely to Africans in the untutored state ", are: (1) " that *some* innate difference does at present exist between the minds of the *average adult male* of the European race and that of the average adult male of the African "; (2) that the mental powers of the African (male) " develop more rapidly than those of the European up to about 12 ". This is followed " first by a gradual arrest of normal growth, and then by an actual decline of mental powers " ; and (3) that " no appreciable difference is discernible either in the development of their mental faculties or in their powers between the *female* sections of the two races ".[3]

It is impossible to discuss here all the interesting questions raised by this article. I must content myself with calling

[1] Ashley Montagu, *Coming to be Among the Australian Aborigines*, pp. 10-12 ; cf. also the authorities there quoted.
[2] Bryant, *op. cit.* p. 42.   [3] *Op. cit.* p. 43 (italics in text).

attention to three of the most important points. (1) Bryant reports that the retardation in the rate of mental development after puberty is much more marked in the case of those boys who began their education after puberty than in those who entered school at the age of 6. But this difference cannot be due to differences in innate endowment. No conclusion about innate mental powers can be drawn from the performance of one class unless it applies to the other class also. (2) The writer assumes that there is an important difference between the mental powers of European boys and girls. Even if we grant this very questionable assumption, the difference between the mental powers of the Bantu and the white is not very significant if it is only of the order of the difference between the powers of European boys and girls. (3) Bryant reports three facts which throw much greater doubt on his conclusion than he seems to realise. (a) He tells us that he can find no significant difference in mental powers between the Bantu native who has grown up under native conditions and has received no formal education and the back-veldt Boers who live under similar conditions. " Developing under like conditions," he writes,[1] " the two types of mind tend to approximate and ultimately attain an equal level." (b) Native boys attending the native colleges in Natal generally prove themselves able to tackle work of the highest standard as successfully as white boys.[2] (c) South African native students who have had the opportunity of getting a university education in Europe and America have shown themselves able to hold their own against their white rivals.[3]

The first of these facts, which seems about as damaging as any fact can be to his thesis, the writer records without comment. The second, which as he admits might be supposed to disprove his conclusion, he tries to explain away on the ground that those " powers of reasoning and understanding " in which he maintains the whites have the advantage are not adequately tested by anything in the college curriculum.[4] The third fact he regards as a " difficulty " which he must " honestly note ", but of which he cannot offer any satisfactory explanation. But he thinks that " the number of such natives is at present so

Bryant, *op. cit.* p. 45. [2] *Ibid.* p. 48. [3] *Ibid.* p. 49.
[4] *Ibid.* pp. 48-9.

exceedingly small as hardly to justify any modification of [his] general position ".[1] But the fact that, in the only instances in which natives have been tested on relatively [2] equal terms against whites, the natives have not been found wanting in intellectual capacity is rather more than a difficulty for a theory which holds that they are so inferior in such powers; and the numbers which were so small in 1917 have since increased considerably but there is no indication that the intellectual powers of the enlarged numbers are significantly different.[3]

It is in view of these damaging admissions that I have claimed Bryant as a hostile witness for the conclusion that there are no fundamental innate differences between the primitive and the civilised mind. In addition, other field workers among the African natives deny some of the facts on which Bryant bases his conclusion, especially the alleged decline in native mental powers after puberty. Nadel,[4] who carried out intelligence tests on natives between 12 and 18, found not a decline but an increase corresponding to age. Junod,[5] who had as long an experience in teaching natives as Bryant, and who is regarded by those competent to judge as a keener and more critical observer, states that, while he met examples of such a decline, they were by no means the rule; and he reports that his opinion, in this respect, is shared by other white teachers of the Bantu.[6] To this testimony has to be added a considerable and growing body of evidence of the intellectual powers and achievements of educated natives despite all the disadvantages of the colour bar which, as Hoernlé[7] shrewdly suggests, was erected because the Bantu showed, not too little, but too great a capacity for assimilating Western civilisation.

We have now before us the views of the only recent field workers, with whose writings I am acquainted, who maintain

[1] *Ibid.* p. 49.

[2] Relatively because they have to study in a foreign country and often in a foreign language.

[3] As further evidence of confusion in the author's mind we may note his statement that the differences between the native and the European to which he attaches so much importance " though innate are not fundamental and permanent but transient and accidental " (p. 43).

[4] *British Journal of Psychology* (October 1937), p. 197.

[5] *Life of a South African Tribe*, i. 99.   [6] *Ibid.*   [7] *Op. cit.* p. 57.

that there is a marked difference between the innate powers of the native mind and of our own. I have perhaps considered them at greater length than their intrinsic merits or their place among anthropological writings deserve. But I have done so deliberately. The belief that the primitive mind is inferior to our own is so pleasing to our vanity, and is still so widespread that it is important to consider the only kind of evidence which has been advanced in favour of it. That evidence is not impressive and will not stand critical examination. I think we may therefore accept the conclusion of the overwhelming majority of trained field workers and anthropologists that there are no good grounds for believing in the existence of such differences. This conclusion is all that the evidence warrants, and all that the more cautious anthropologists draw.[1] It is quite compatible with the belief that there may be a larger proportion of outstanding individuals among one people, and that the talents of their most outstanding individuals may reach a rather higher level. But it does mean that there is no difference of principle between the primitive and the civilised mind and that the innate endowment of the great majority of individuals in different cultures is much the same. For our purpose this is more than sufficient. If it is true, it means that the moral consciousness of man is everywhere the same, and that such differences as we find in the moral judgements of different peoples, in the ideals they regard as good and the rules they regard as right, cannot be attributed to differences in the innate constitution or powers of their minds. Their moral judgements must, therefore, be regarded as expressions of the same moral consciousness as our own, and ethical theories which claim to explain the deliverances of the moral consciousness must account for them.

It might, however, be contended that, even if primitive people have the innate capacity which would enable them to grasp our moral ideas and concepts, they may not have exercised it or attended sufficiently to these concepts or to their relations. But as far, at any rate, as the concepts and relations involved in our ordinary moral rules are concerned, there is overwhelming evidence that the facts are otherwise. As we

[1] See, e.g., Boas, *op. cit.* pp. 122-3 ; Goldenweiser, *History, Psychology and Culture*, p. 394.

have already seen and shall see further, the moral codes of all primitive peoples include some, and some of them include all, of the rules which we find in ordinary lists of moral rules among ourselves, such, for example, as rules about truth-telling, promise-keeping, reparations for injuries, respect for person and property, and so on. General compliance with these rules is so obvious a condition of mutual confidence and effective co-operation between individuals that it is well-nigh universally recognised as essential to the well-being of any group. Indeed this is taken so much for granted by workers among primitives that they seldom call attention to the many cases in which such rules are accepted as obligatory. They dwell rather on the many and seemingly strange exceptions to them which the natives regard as right, the many circumstances in which they do not seem to think of applying them, and the narrow circle of people within which alone they regard them as binding. We shall therefore have to consider not only what rules primitives recognise as right, but also and more particularly what interpretation they put on those which they do recognise, to whom they regard them as applicable, why they regard them as right, what exceptions to them they recognise, and what they consider the justification for these exceptions.

Before we consider the light which the ways of life which we have described and other evidence about primitive peoples throws on these and allied subjects, there is another question to which we must devote some attention. It is often held that primitives obey the moral rules and customs of their people, mainly if not merely, for fear that failure to do so will arouse the anger of supernatural agents and bring misfortune or disaster on themselves or their people. According to this view, the moral customs of primitives are largely magico-religious taboos, not understood to be obligatory in their own right, but accepted on authority and obeyed because of their magico-religious sanctions. If this view of primitive conduct were true, we could scarcely call it moral at all, and a consideration of its nature would throw little light on the nature of morality as we understand it. We shall therefore have to examine the evidence for this view and consider the extent to which primitive moral rules have magico-religious sanctions, and the influence which their magico-religious beliefs exercise on their moral ideas. A consideration of some aspects of the relation between primitive morality and religion is also necessary to justify my attempt to treat primitive morality by itself, and not as a part of religion. This task will occupy us in the next two lectures.

PRIMITIVE MORALITY AND RELIGION

MORALITY and religion are both complex subjects and the relationship between them, even among primitives, is neither single nor simple. Generalisations about it are therefore apt to be ambiguous and misleading, the results of abstraction and over-simplification. Indeed there is no other aspect of our subject about which there seems to be so much confusion and about which many of our authorities are so unhelpful and such unsafe guides ; and, as I said in an earlier lecture, I believe this confusion to be largely responsible for the neglect of primitive morality by both social anthropologists and ethical theorists. This confusion is, no doubt, partly due to the complexity and difficulty of the subject [1] and to differences of opinion as to the nature of morality and religion ; but it is also partly due to the lack of clear definition of the sense in which the terms are being used, and especially to failure to distinguish carefully between the different aspects of morality and religion, and between the different questions which may be raised about their interrelations. This is specially true of morality, which even careful writers like Radcliffe-Brown and Malinowski, who are at pains to analyse and define most of their other terms, seem to use uncritically without distinguishing its different aspects or elements. As a result, they seem to use the term with different senses in different connections, meaning by it sometimes moral sentiments and motives, at other times moral rules and principles. This is not only apt to confuse their readers, who often find it difficult to discover in what

---

[1] Some anthropologists are well aware of these difficulties. See, e.g., *Cambridge Expedition to the Torres Straits*, v. 272 : " There is perhaps no subject on which it is more difficult to obtain satisfactory information than on that of morality ". Cf. Linton, *The Study of Man*, p. 437 : " The current neglect of this field seems to be due less to an underestimation of its importance than to the extreme difficulty of approaching it through any of the usual anthropological techniques ".

sense the term is being used in a particular context, but, what is more important, it is apt, as I shall try to show, to confuse the writers themselves. They are apt to assume that, when they have shown that religion is related to morality in a particular way in one sense of the term ' morality ', they have proved that it is so related in a different sense of the term ' morality '.

The position is further complicated by the fact that few anthropologists have devoted any separate consideration to the relationship between morality and religion, and that their views about it have to be gathered from incidental references to it which are scattered throughout their treatment of other subjects. Accordingly, each such statement has to be considered in the light of its context and of the evidence submitted in support of it; and, when so considered, many of them do not mean what they appear to say. We may find, for example, that for the purpose of a particular writer in a certain connection one aspect of the complex interrelation of morality and religion may be more important, and that therefore it is the only one which is mentioned; but the other aspects may also be there, and though the writer does not mention them, he may not wish to deny their existence or their importance. But, however we interpret them, some of the statements about our subject made in different connections even by the same authority are not only ambiguous and misleading but actually inconsistent.

My procedure throughout these lectures has been based on the assumption that morality is autonomous in the sense that it is possible to discover the grounds of the goodness of moral ideals and of the rightness of moral rules by an analysis of the moral consciousness, without introducing the idea of the supernatural or the religious view of life, as the source of the authority of moral rules or the justification of moral ideals; and that it is therefore permissible to treat morality by itself without taking account of its relation to, or any support it gains from or gives to, religion. There are, however, several reasons which make it necessary to examine and defend this assumption.

(1) The belief is still widely held that the rules of conduct of primitive peoples are magico-religious taboos, not understood to be obligatory in their own right but accepted on authority

and obeyed because of their magico-religious sanctions ; that, in short, primitives obey their moral rules and customs, mainly if not merely, because they believe that failure to do so will bring misfortune or disaster on themselves or their people, either through the displeasure of personal supernatural agents or through the automatic working of impersonal supernatural forces. Now, as we have seen in part already in considering the beliefs of the representative primitive peoples whose ways of life I tried to describe, this view is not in accordance with the facts, and it is not shared by field workers among primitives ; but it is still so common that it will be necessary to consider it further.[1]

(2) Many anthropologists who explicitly reject this view use language which suggests, and sometimes explicitly states, that morality is dependent on, or even a part of, religion, and that moral ideals and rules are prescribed and sanctioned by it and derive their authority from it. This seems to me the result of a confusion due to a loose use of terms and a failure to distinguish between different questions. The confusion seems to have come about in the following way. Whatever differences there may be among anthropologists as to the nature of religion, they are all agreed on two points : (a) that primitive peoples have a religion, that is, that they believe that they are surrounded by supersensible or supernatural powers ; and (b) that the beliefs, the emotional attitudes and the ritual practices, which constitute their reaction to these powers, profoundly affect their characters, their attitude to their fellows and the cohesion of their society. It is from these psychological and social effects of religion that many anthropologists conclude that primitive morality is dependent on, or sanctioned by, or a part of religion. But the inference seems to me hasty, the result of a confusion between functional interdependence, or mutual influence and support, and one-sided or causal dependence of morality on

[1] To give just one or two examples of the prevalence of this view among recent scholars : " Everywhere the moral law is based ultimately on religious sanctions . . . the rules by which the life of a primitive community is governed are all sacred rules enforced by religious sanctions " (Dawson, *Religion and Culture* (1947), p. 155). " Historically, all ethics undoubtedly begins with religion " (Popper, *The Open Society and its Enemies* (1945), i. p. 55). See also Gore, *The Philosophy of the Good Life* (Everyman ed.), p. 183 ; Aldrich, *The Primitive Mind and Modern Civilisation*, pp. 143-4 ; Driberg, *At Home with the Savage*, p. 42.

religion, or of a confusion between religion producing moral effects and religion prescribing moral rules or ideals.

(3) There is yet another sense in which morality is sometimes held to be dependent on religion. It is contended that man, whether primitive or civilised, has not in himself the wisdom to recognise what is good and right nor the strength to do it; and that for both he is dependent on religion.

Now any views which assert, on whatever grounds, that religion is the source of moral authority, or that the relation of morality to religion is a relation of one-sided dependence, deny the autonomy which I claim for morality, and imply that we cannot treat the nature and foundation of morality satisfactorily without taking account of the religious view of life. And, owing to the confusion to which I have referred, such views can appeal for support to many statements by anthropologists of eminence. I shall therefore have to examine carefully the evidence on which such statements are based in order to discover whether it warrants the conclusions which have been drawn from it.

I am concerned with only some of the questions which may be asked about the relation between morality and religion; and it will be necessary to distinguish these questions from others with which they sometimes seem to me to be confused. All I want to establish is that primitive morality is independent of religion in the sense that the moral ideals of primitive peoples do not derive their goodness, or their moral rules their rightness, from a religious source; and that, even among primitives, fear of supernatural punishments or hope of supernatural rewards, here or hereafter, is not the only or even the main incentive to pursuing the one or obeying the other.

This conclusion is quite consistent with a very intimate connection in the way of mutual influence and support between morality and religion. I do not wish to belittle, much less to deny, the undoubtedly profound influence which religion exerts on the character and conduct of its devotees or the support which it has given to individual and social morality; but I want to suggest that the influence is mutual and not one-sided and that it is not inconsistent with the autonomy which I claim for morality. Such mutual influence is what we should expect on the functional theory regarding primitive culture, for which I have already quoted so much evidence. Nor do I wish to deny that morality has theological implications or that we may legitimately argue from morality to religion. Even if we can discover our moral duties without any reference to religion, even if we can see their binding character by considering the nature of persons and the relations between them, it may still be that, when we consider the view of reality which the existence and nature of morality presuppose, we may find ourselves driven to a religious view of the world as the most reasonable interpretation of the facts. In that case, though morality would still be autonomous in the sense that our knowledge of moral rules and ideals would be independent of religion, the religious view of the world would be the ontological condition of morality. So that morality would be first in order of knowledge or learning, but religion would be first in order of reality. All I contend is that, whatever be the conditions of the possibility of morality and whatever inferences we may draw from it, in the order of knowledge it comes first; and that we are more certain of the value of moral goodness than we are of any inferences, religious or other, that we may draw from it. Nor do I suggest that the view which a man takes about the supernatural makes no difference to what he believes to be right or good. In order to understand a man's judgements of value, his views as to what ends he ought to pursue and what acts he ought to do, we must take account of his beliefs about his supernatural as well as his natural and social environment. But I suggest that a man's ideas about what is right and good may exercise as much influence on his conception of the supernatural as his ideas about the supernatural exercise on his moral conceptions. My contention is simply that, whatever its presuppositions and implications and whatever support it may receive from or give to religion, morality is autonomous, containing its authority, the grounds of its goodness and rightness, within itself. I am concerned with the relation between morality and religion only so far as is necessary to establish this conclusion. There are therefore many interesting and important and highly controversial questions about their relation which are not germane to my purpose and with which I do not propose to deal. And I want to make it plain that I am not attempting to answer these questions, nor prejudging what the answer to them should be.

In view of the complexity of the subject and the confusion regarding it which I seem to find in the utterances of even distinguished anthropologists, it seems desirable that we should try to disentangle the issues in order to expose and, if we can, to remove the confusion, before we try to draw the conclusions as to the relation between primitive morality and religion which the available evidence suggests. This seems to me all the more necessary because, if I am not mistaken, such confusion is not confined to anthropologists dealing with primitive people. It seems to be no less evident in the writings of publicists and theologians, and perhaps even of philosophers, concerned with our contemporary situation; and it is today a source of bewilderment to many men and women of goodwill in our midst. For one of the most significant and perplexing features of our time is a growing divorce between morality and religion, combined with frequent statements that morality needs the support of religion if it is to survive and flourish.

As evidence of this divorce I need mention only two facts. On the one hand, there is the decay of religious beliefs and practices and the increasing secularisation of morality which is today admitted by both those who deplore the fact and those who rejoice at the prospect. Nor is the decay confined to the careless and irresponsible. Many sincere and thoughtful people in all walks of life, people with a high standard of personal conduct and a keen sense of social justice, people who devote themselves in the spirit of unselfish service to the well-being of their fellows, find themselves unable to accept any creed and have given up the separate practice of religion. On the other hand, a considerable and apparently growing body of theologians, in revolt against the rationalistic idealism and the liberal theology of the early part of the century, preach a form of theology which not only rejects any support from the moral consciousness, but seems to be inconsistent with its main assumptions, and to regard any suggestion that upright and honest living has any religious value as evidence of an irreligious spirit, if not even of being " in the bondage of sin ".[1] I have no time to develop this point ; nor would it be relevant to my subject to do so ; but I am profoundly convinced that the absence of mutual understanding and support between the saint and the moral and social reformer is a misfortune for both. Unless the vision of the saint is transformed into moral energy to sustain and strengthen the drive, not only to change the individual, but to transform society, not elsewhere and hereafter but here and now, it will be apt to grow dim and religion to become a private luxury or an emotional thrill. And unless the ethical and re-forming spirit is reinforced and strengthened and sustained by the vision of the saint, and the life of moral goodness put in a cosmic setting and regarded as the service of God, the moral agent will be apt to lose heart in the struggle and perhaps also to lose his direction. The ethical religions at their best suc-ceeded in combining the inner peace which religion gives with the moral dynamic of the reformer in such a way that each supported the other : they called on men to do justly as well as to walk humbly ; while the moral consciousness has always claimed the right to criticise the teaching of religion in the light of its own insight. Today it seems to me they are in danger of parting company and ceasing to understand or support one another ; organised religion being content to look backwards rather than forwards, to sit at the feet of ancient teachers rather than stand on their shoulders ; while many in whom the moral spirit is strong find neither spiritual refreshment nor moral stimulus in the services of the church and are tending to give up the separate practice of religion. When side by side with this growing rift between morality and religion in both theory and practice he finds grave concern expressed in many quarters, that the decay of religious faith and practice is in danger of undermining the moral fibre of our people and the very foundations of our way of life, is it surprising that the ordinary man should be perplexed and bewildered ? [2]

Whether or not a consideration of the relation between morality and religion among primitives will help to throw light on our contemporary situation, the present widespread

[1] See Lewis, *Morals and the New Theology*, pp. 30 ff.
[2] For the extent to which he is so, see *Puzzled People*, by Mass Observation.

bewilderment and uncertainty about the question, as well as the confusion which I seem to find in the writings of anthropologists, makes it desirable to try to analyse and define our terms, to distinguish the different aspects of or elements in morality and religion and to disentangle the different questions which may be raised about their interrelation, so that we may discover which of them are relevant to our enquiry. To this preparatory work of clarifying the issues and clearing the ground I propose to devote the remainder of the present lecture. In the next I shall consider the answers, which the facts seem to warrant, to those questions about the relation of primitive morality and religion which specially concern our subject.

Following the general practice of anthropologists, and in order to avoid difficult and controversial issues, such as the distinction between magic and religion, I am going to use the term ' religion ' in a very wide sense, to include all experiences and beliefs, practices and emotional attitudes in relation to the supernatural, i.e. to cover what might be more accurately described as magico-religious beliefs, attitudes and practices. Religion so defined includes (1) an element of belief — beliefs regarding the existence and nature of the supernatural, whether it be thought of in personal or impersonal terms; (2) an emotional element, the sense of the sacred or the uncanny and the emotional response which it evokes, what some anthropologists call the religious thrill; and (3) practices in which the beliefs and emotions find expressions, actions and abstentions, rites and ceremonies, dances and sacrifices and prayers. Closely connected with these are the legends and myths, the sacred traditions, which contain what we might call the theology and cosmology of the primitives. These tend to confirm by precedent, i.e. by reference to events which are believed to have happened in the past, the present beliefs and practices. They provide the reasons why certain things should be believed and done. For so far as ritual practices at any rate are concerned, the primitive does not usually draw a very clear distinction between reasons which explain and reasons which justify. As Robertson Smith [1] puts it, " the precedent once

----

[1] *The Religion of the Semites*, p. 20.

established is authoritative and does not appear to require any proof ".

In morality also, as we have already seen, we may distinguish three aspects or elements : (1) the ends or ideals which are regarded as good or worthy of pursuit ; (2) the moral rules or principles according to which actions are judged as right or wrong ; (3) the motives or sentiments or attitudes of mind which find expression in the pursuit of ends and the obedience to rules. The term moral is commonly applied to all three, that is, to motives, ends and rules. But it is important to distinguish them because what is true of one need not be true of another.

The reference to good and bad or right and wrong conduct, however, does not enable us to distinguish between morality and religion, for these terms may be used either in a moral or a religious sense. It is necessary, therefore, to try to distinguish specifically moral from specifically religious conduct. I shall call specifically moral, conduct in relation to one's fellow-men, individually and collectively. It is true that a man may have duties to himself and to supernatural beings, and such duties, if they exist, are in a quite legitimate sense moral duties. But if we are to distinguish at all between morality and religion or between moral and religious duties, it must be on the basis of a distinction between, on the one hand, duties to himself and his fellows which can be described and understood without introducing any reference to the supernatural and, on the other, those duties which involve a direct reference to the supernatural. It is true that duties to one's fellow-men, duties of truth-telling and promise-keeping, acting justly and respecting life and property, may be, in whole or in part, regarded by a particular people from a religious point of view as duties to God who is believed to require from them that they treat their fellow-men in certain ways. But they can be understood without any such reference. In other words, they are moral duties whether or not they are also religious duties. And even if they are also religious duties, these moral duties are to be distinguished from strictly religious duties which cannot be understood without introducing the idea of the supernatural. The latter are of two kinds : (1) duties to personal supernatural agents in the way of ritual or worship, actions and abstentions, such as sacrifices or refraining from certain foods, which are believed to be prescribed by such agents; and (2) duties, I should not say to, but in respect of impersonal supernatural powers or forces which are believed to affect the welfare of an individual or his people, and which can be influenced by magico-religious means. It is true that both of these classes of strictly religious duties may be, and the latter must be, also, either prudential duties to oneself or social duties to one's fellow-men, or both, because a breach of them is believed to bring misfortune on the individual or his group. Nevertheless, they are primarily religious duties, because they cannot be understood without introducing the idea of the supernatural.

When the terms morality and religion are used in this sense, there is no people of whom we have any record, whether contemporary primitives or the early ancestors of people who are now advanced, who have not both morality and religion. A complete account of the relation between the morality and the religion of any of these peoples would have to consider how the different elements in their religion, the beliefs, the emotional attitudes and the ritual practices, are related to one another, and how, if at all, each of them is related to each of the three elements in morality, the rules, the ends and the motives. My purpose, as I have explained, is much more limited, but one or two further remarks on the wider issues may not be irrelevant to it.

On the relation between, and the relative priority of, the different elements in religion there is considerable difference of opinion among anthropologists as well as among other students of religion. The earlier anthropologists, like Tylor and Frazer, regarded the element of belief as fundamental and the other elements as secondary. Similarly, they emphasised the cognitive element in morality, rules and codes rather than motives and sentiments. Recently the tendency has been to regard the emotional and ceremonial elements in religion as basic and to treat religious beliefs as rationalisations to explain and justify the other elements. Thus, Marett, Goldenweiser and Lowie tend to regard the emotional element — the religious thrill as they call it — as the distinguishing characteristic of religion;

while Radcliffe-Brown, following the line taken earlier by Robertson Smith and Durkheim, treats the ritual or ceremonial element as fundamental. According to this view, the performance of the ceremonies gives rise to the emotional aspect, and the beliefs about the supernatural are rationalisations to justify the ritual behaviour. Those who take these views tend also to emphasise the emotional element in morality, motives and sentiments rather than codes and rules, ends and ideals.

I cannot enter into the merits of these views, but so far as they bear on our problem they seem to me to call for two comments : (1) Wherever we find religion, while one of the elements may be more explicit or prominent, all of them are present in some degree or at least they are liable to emerge at any moment.[1] They seem to develop together and in their development they interact and mutually modify one another. (2) No doubt the earlier views were over-intellectual, but the later views seem in danger of erring in the opposite direction. They tend to regard the supernatural as unknowable if not non-existent and all beliefs about it as irrational; and so they treat one set of myths, or one form of wishful thinking about the supernatural, as being as good as any other as long as it produces desirable effects on the lives of those who believe it. They therefore find it difficult to explain why changes in religious beliefs come about.[2] Nor can they account for the fact that religion is never content to regard itself as merely a matter of feeling or ritual practices. The element of ideas and beliefs about the supernatural seems to be an essential part of it, a part without which it could not fulfil the functions in the

[1] For example, the emotional element may at times be very slight or even disappear altogether as in some of the ritual without reverence of the Bantu, just as among ourselves religious practices may become habitual and lifeless. But if such practices never gave rise to the sense of the uncanny and the emotions appropriate to it, they could not be regarded as religious at all. Without the beliefs and emotions associated with the supernatural, ritual practices would not differ from other purely secular ceremonies which are to be found among primitives. In the same way, a belief in the continued existence of the dead has in itself no religious significance. To make it religious, the dead must be regarded as interested in and capable of affecting human affairs, and liable to be influenced by human actions, and the thought of them must give rise to the religious thrill.

[2] Cf. Firth, *Religious Belief and Personal Adjustment* (Henry Myers Lecture, 1948), p. 17.

lives of individuals and societies to which the anthropologists attach so much importance. And so we have the paradoxical situation of professed sceptics and agnostics stressing the necessity of religion, including religious beliefs, if morality and civilisation are to survive. Let me give just one example. Malinowski begins his Riddell Lectures on *The Foundations of Faith and Morals* by declaring himself a rationalist and an agnostic, who cannot accept the dogmas of any religion and has no faith except a faith in humanity and its powers of improvement; [1] but he confesses himself so alarmed by certain tendencies of our age and by the failure of science to provide a basis for ethics that he goes on not only to profess his belief in the value of religion, but to call on his readers to defend its " eternal truths " against all attack; [2] and he concludes with words which remind us of Voltaire's dictum that, if God did not exist, men would have to invent him. " The rationalist and the agnostic ", he writes, " must admit that even if he himself cannot accept these truths, he must at least recognise them as indispensable pragmatic figments without which civilisation cannot exist." [3]

I have quoted this personal confession of Malinowski's not just as an interesting item of biographical information, but partly because it will help us to understand some confusions in his thinking about the relation of morality and religion to which I want to call attention later, and partly because the idea of " pragmatic figments " which are to be defended as " eternal truths " seems to me a rather glaring example of an attitude, and a sort of confusion about our subject, which is not uncommon among our contemporaries.

Now the questions which I want specially to consider are : (1) How far and in what sense, if in any, do primitive people regard their moral duties to their fellow-men as also religious duties, in the sense that they are prescribed or sanctioned by their religion ? And (2) how far and in what ways, if at all, do their beliefs about the supernatural, the emotions which it evokes and the performance of their ritual or strictly religious duties, directly or indirectly influence their attitude and behaviour to their fellows, that is, the nature and performance of

---

[1] P. ix.   [2] *Ibid.* p. 62.   [3] *Ibid.*

their strictly moral duties ? As I have said, these are not the only, or even the only important, questions about the relation between morality and religion, even among primitives. But I want to concentrate attention on them partly because they are specially relevant to my subject, and partly because it seems to me essential that we should distinguish clearly between them. I believe that some anthropologists have confused them, and that when they submitted evidence in support of an answer to the one they assumed that they had answered the other also. I want, therefore, to bring out the distinction between them and between the evidence which is relevant to an answer to them, in more detail, and then to illustrate the way in which they have been confused and the consequences of such confusion.

When we say that a moral rule is prescribed by religion or has a religious sanction, this normally means one or more of three things. (1) That the rule was promulgated or revealed as the will of a supernatural power. This may take the form of a direct revelation to the individual, as we saw among the Crow Indians, or of a pronouncement by an accredited representative of the supernatural power such as priest or shaman or medium, or of a revelation to some wise man of bygone days, handed down by tradition in myth or legend. Moreover, this promulgation of the rule may be interpreted either as what makes the rule right or as a reason for believing it to be right. (2) That a breach of the rule will be followed by disastrous consequences to the individual or his group, either automatically through the operation of some impersonal supernatural power or as the result of the intervention of a superhuman agent who disapproves of the breach. Or (3) that a man's destiny in an after life will be affected according as he observes or breaks the rule.[1]

Now some or all of the moral rules of a particular society may have supernatural sanctions in one of these senses and not in another ; and the same rule may have a supernatural sanction in one sense in one society and in another sense or not at all in another society. Moreover, a rule which has a supernatural

---

[1] If we think of morality not from the point of view of rules but from that of motives, we get a corresponding number of supernatural sanctions regarded as incentives to action and the same rule may have any or all of these sanctions, and obedience to it may result from any one or any combination of these motives.

sanction in any or all of these senses may have moral and social and legal sanctions as well — just as among ourselves a particular sort of act such as murder may be regarded as morally wrong, legally a crime against society, and, from the religious point of view, a sin against God. Thus the rules which have, and the senses in which they have, supernatural sanctions vary from one primitive people to another. For what we find are not primitive morality and primitive religion but primitive moralities and primitive religions; and the rules which are regarded as right and the sanctions, supernatural and other, which are attached to them, vary from people to people.

I shall return to the question which of the moral rules of primitive peoples have supernatural sanctions and in what senses they have them. At present I am concerned not with the answer to this question but with the distinction between it and my second question, namely: Does primitive man's religion influence his attitude to his neighbours, either in the way of determining or helping to determine what he takes his duties to them to be, or in the likelihood that he will perform those duties to them which he independently regards as binding? For even if we find, either generally or in the case of a particular people, that few or none of their moral rules have supernatural sanctions in the senses I have indicated, it by no means follows that their religion does not exercise an important influence on their individual and social morality.

To understand the ways in which this may happen it would be necessary to go in greater detail than is here possible into primitive man's conception of the supernatural — a conception which varies within wide limits from one primitive people to another.[1] One or two illustrations must therefore suffice. If, for example, a man believes, however mistakenly, that his neighbour is a wizard or a magician endowed with deadly supernatural powers, this is likely to influence his attitude to him and what he believes his duty towards him to be. Again, the beliefs which a man entertains regarding the situations to

[1] For a good summary of the primitive's conception of the supernatural, the forms which it takes and the way in which it attaches itself to different features of man's life and environment in different places, see the section on " Religion " by Ruth Benedict in *General Anthropology* by Boas and others ; especially pp. 633 ff.

which he has to respond, and the consequences of the actions open to him, will make a difference to what he thinks he ought to do. If, for example, he believes that human heads are necessary for the fertility of the soil, or that to allow twins to live will cause drought and bring disaster and possible starvation on himself and his people, this will make a difference to what he regards as his duty. In this way what we should call beliefs about non-ethical matters of fact, whether about the situations in which he has to act, the consequences of actions, or the persons towards whom he has to act, may help to determine what he regards as his moral duty; and such beliefs may be, and often are influenced by his views about the supernatural.

But whether or not the religious beliefs of the primitive in this way help to determine what he takes to be his moral duties, there is another and more important way in which his religion influences both his character and his attitude to his neighbours. These influences are mainly due to the ritual and ceremonial aspects of religion and to the emotional attitudes to which either they or the conception of the supernatural gives rise. Some of these ritual duties are difficult and arduous and their performance teaches endurance and self-restraint. Some are undertaken in the belief that the community as a whole would suffer if they were neglected, and their performance teaches unselfishness and devotion to the common good. Others, like religious dances and other ceremonial performances in which many or all the members of the community take part together, produce an intensified tribal consciousness which makes for social harmony and cohesion. Nothing binds men more closely together than the common sharing of deeply moving experiences; and the more deeply moving the experiences the stronger the tie they produce between those who share them. Now many of the situations which are matters of religious concern to the primitive are themselves such as to arouse deep emotion; for they concern his most vital interests and the crises of his fate — his means of livelihood, illness and death and war and so on; and the sense of the supernatural in these situations further intensifies the emotions to which they naturally give rise. For nothing moves a man so profoundly or to the depth of his being as the consciousness of the presence of the supernatural.

Consequently the religious ceremonies in which they take part together unite a people to one another and separate them off from others. In this way they foster strong social sentiments, and a spirit of goodwill and mutual trust and help-fulness, among the members of the group. Moreover, the sense of the presence of the supernatural drives a man back upon himself, at once humbling and exalting him. It tends to restrain the cruder and more selfish passions and to produce an attitude of seriousness and a sense of responsibility which make it more likely that he will do what he believes to be his duty to his neighbours.

Now it is these psychological and social consequences of religion which have specially impressed field workers among primitive peoples, and it is on them that they dwell when they discuss the moral value of religion. But however important these effects of religion may be, it seems to me essential for our understanding of the relation between morality and religion that we should not confuse them with the ethical content of religion nor regard them as evidence that morality is a part of or dependent on religion, in the sense that it prescribes the duties to be fulfilled, the rights to be respected or the ideals to be pursued, or that it provides a sanction for moral rules either by way of supplying grounds for believing them to be right or direct incentives to comply with their requirements. Many people, anthropologists and others, seem to me to be guilty of this confusion. They, therefore, assume that by producing evidence to show that religion has desirable effects on the character of individuals and the cohesion of society — effects which may in one sense of the term be called moral — they prove that religion is the foundation and justification of morality.

In trying to expose this confusion and to show the way in which evidence in support of the one conclusion is treated as a proof of the other to which it is irrelevant, I think it is more profitable to examine the statements of one writer in some detail than to deal in a sketchy way with those of several. The writer whose views I am going to consider is Malinowski, but I should add that I regard his views, in this respect, as an example of a confusion which seems to be widespread. My reasons for choosing him as my illustration are : his writings illustrate the point I want to make very clearly; he is one of the few recent anthropologists who have devoted some attention to the relation between primitive morality and religion; I have already given some of his views about their relation and it is only just that I should also give the rest; the evidence which he submits in support of his view is taken mainly from two of the peoples whose ways of life I have described in detail; his deservedly high reputation as a field worker and as interpreter of primitive life and thought gives his utterances great weight; and, finally, he states the facts which he discovered in his field work so clearly and he distinguishes so carefully between the facts and the conclusions which he draws from them, that we can check his theories by facts which he has himself provided. This, he tells us,[1] was the ideal which he set before himself in his descriptive work, and he has succeeded to an unusual degree in realising it.

Malinowski is so impressed with the undoubtedly important influence of primitive religion in promoting the mental integrity of the individual and the social harmony of the group that he often writes as if their morality were merely a part of their religion and as if their religion were the source and justification of all their moral rules and ideals and provided their incentive for obeying the one and pursuing the other.

This is what I now want to illustrate. I shall first quote statements from his writings which seem to show (1) that he thinks of morality as a part of, or at least as dependent on religion, and (2) that in doing so he is referring not only to the motives of moral actions or to the influence of religion on character, but also to moral rules and principles, to what is regarded as right. I shall then examine the evidence which he gives in support of these statements in order to show what it proves and what it does not, and in particular to show that evidence in support of a conclusion regarding the inner or subjective aspect of morality is treated as a proof of a conclusion regarding the outer or objective aspect, to which it is irrelevant. Having done this, we shall be in a better position to consider the empirical

[1] See, e.g., *Crime and Custom*, p. 31, note; *Argonauts of the Western Pacific*, p. 3; Introduction to Fortune, *Sorcerers of Dobu*, p. xxvi.

evidence which Malinowski and others have provided regarding the relationship between primitive morality and religion, and in particular, to see whether, and if so how far, their religion prescribes or sanctions their moral rules.

Let me begin then with some quotations from Malinowski. In his Riddell Lectures, which he describes as " an anthropological analysis of primitive beliefs and conduct with special reference to the fundamental problems of religion and ethics ", and which he claims " is documented with the most relevant and most telling facts ",[1] he tells us that in all religions there are three elements which are inseparably connected, dogma, ritual and ethics.[2] The first element, the dogma, consists of legends and myths about the nature and activities of supernatural beings. It constitutes the sacred tradition of the people concerned. Its function is to provide reasons for the other two elements. These reasons take the form of precedents and, according to Malinowski, they are reasons which justify rather than reasons which explain. He speaks of them as " validating ", " sanctioning ", " justifying ", " being the charter of " both ritual and moral rules. The second element, the ritual, consists of rites and ceremonies, whether magical or religious, the ways in which individuals should behave towards supernatural powers. The nature of the third element, the ethical or moral element, is far from clear. At times it seems to be an emotional attitude, an attitude of friendliness and loyalty and goodwill between the fellow-worshippers which is produced by belief in the dogma and, more especially, by the performance of the ritual. At other times, in his references to it, Malinowski explicitly includes moral rules and principles and codes of conduct, the kind of actions which are regarded as right or morally obligatory. For example, he writes : " Every religion, however humble, carries instructions for a good life ; it invariably provides its followers with an ethical system ".[3] In every religion " there must be an ethical code of rules which binds the faithful and determines their behaviour to one another ".[4] And again : " Every religion carries its own morals ",[5] " it implies some reward of virtue and punishment of sin " ;[6] and yet again : into the ritual

---

[1] *The Foundations of Faith and Morals*, Preface, p. x.   [2] *Ibid.* pp. 2 ff., 25.
[3] *Ibid.* p. 2.   [4] *Ibid.* p. 58.   [5] *Ibid.* p. 6.   [6] *Ibid.* p. viii.

practices of ancestor worship " ethics comes in because the spirits and their reactions are determined by moral principles . . . they expect . . . good behaviour ".[1] In another work, he writes of " the place of morals in early, primitive, religion ", and of " the problem of morals as an early religious function ".[2] " Religious ritual, in the ceremonies of initiation, . . ." he tells us, " establishes the existence of some power or personality from which tribal law is derived and which is responsible for the moral rules imparted to the novice." [3] Again, " all the morality of primitives is derived from religious belief " ; [4] and even the public performance of religion is necessary for " the maintenance of morals ".[5] Of the function of myths and their relation to conduct he writes : sacred myth " safeguards and enforces morality . . . and contains practical rules for the guidance of man ".[6] We " find sacred stories wherever there is . . . some fundamental ethical process at stake ".[7] " The sacred tradition, the myth . . . controls moral and social behaviour." [8] " Myth supplies a . . . pattern of moral values." [9] Again, he describes religion as " moral in its very essence ",[10] " always the mainspring of moral values ",[11] " the permanent source of moral control ".[12] Finally, he writes of " the ethical element intrinsically inherent in all religious activities ", and he describes " taboos, vigils and religious exercises " as " essentially moral ".[13]

I admit that, torn from their context, these statements convey a very inadequate impression of Malinowski's position taken as a whole, but I submit that, in any context, the natural interpretation to put upon them is a one-sided dependence of morality on religion, and that this dependence applies to moral rules as well as to the motives of moral actions. Partly to confirm that this is the natural interpretation of such statements,

[1] *Ibid.* p. 25.   [2] *Science, Religion and Reality,* p. 25.
[3] *Ibid.* p. 60.   [4] *Ibid.* p. 64.   [5] *Ibid.* p. 63.
[6] *Frazer Lectures* (1922–32), p. 73.
[7] *Foundations of Faith and Morals,* p. 21.   [8] *Ibid.* p. 68.
[9] *Encyclopaedia of the Social Sciences,* iv. 640 ; cf. *Frazer Lectures* (1922–32), p. 116.
[10] *Foundations of Faith and Morals,* p. 7.
[11] *A Scientific Theory of Culture,* p. 201.
[12] *Science, Religion and Reality,* p. 41.
[13] *Foundations of Faith and Morals,* p. 7.

X

and partly to show the difficulties and confusion to which, as so interpreted, they give rise, I want to refer to an article in which Godfrey Wilson, one of Malinowski's most distinguished pupils, so interprets them. Wilson tried to apply what he took to be his master's principles to the morality of an African tribe. He gives the result in an article [1] which he tells us was inspired throughout not only by the writings, but also by the oral teaching of Malinowski. Wilson begins his account by defining morality as " those forms of right conduct which have a supernatural sanction ".[2] He soon finds, however, that some of the rules and forms of conduct which are usually regarded as moral have no supernatural sanction in any ordinary sense of the term among the tribe with which he is concerned. And what does he do ? He just points out that he is precluded by his definition from calling such rules and conduct moral. Instead he calls them rules of good manners.[3] It does not seem to have occurred to him that the facts called rather for a rejection of his original definition — so strong and persistent is the assumption that morality must have a religious sanction.

Now, as far as I am aware, Malinowski has not anywhere in his writings committed himself to Wilson's definition of morality, but it is significant that his views should be so interpreted by one of his ablest pupils ; and this interpretation is the natural one to put on many of the statements I have quoted from him. So interpreted, however, they are not warranted by Malinowski's evidence and, as we have already seen in considering his account of the Trobrianders and shall see further, there is much in his writings that is inconsistent with them.

What, then, is the evidence which he submits in support of these statements ? I shall confine myself mainly to that which is given in the *Foundations of Faith and Morals*. The examples which he there gives of duties which have a supernatural sanction, in the sense that breaches of them are punished by supernatural means, are of the nature of ritual obligations and do not directly concern man's relation to his fellows — such, for example, as carrying out fishing magic and the observance of mortuary ritual.[4] This is true of all his examples from the

[1] *Africa*, ix. (1937), pp. 75 ff.   [2] *Ibid.* pp. 75, 78.
[3] *Ibid.* p. 80.   [4] P. 15.

Trobrianders and the Australian Aborigines from whom most of his illustrative material is taken. It is equally true of his examples from the Bemba and the Toda. The only possible exception is from the Pueblo Indians. Among them, we are told, " virtue and morality in the ordinary conduct of life are enjoined under supernatural sanctions ".[1] Even this, however, is supported by a quotation (from Coolidge, *The Rainmakers*, p. 204) which leaves something to be desired in the way of clearness. It is : " These virtues (i.e. goodness, unselfishness, truth-telling, respect for property, etc.) are [among the Pueblo] closely connected with religious belief and conduct, but not their principal object ".[2]

Similarly, the examples which he gives of forms of conduct, which are prescribed or justified by the sacred tradition, the legends and myths of these people, are of the same ritual and ceremonial nature.[3] They concern strictly religious duties, not moral duties to their fellow-men. And none of the peoples to whom he refers believe that they will be called to account hereafter for the way in which they behave to their fellow-men ; nor that their happiness in another world will in any way depend on such behaviour. Thus, Malinowski gives very few, if any, examples of moral rules or ideals being prescribed or sanctioned by primitive religion in any of the three senses which these terms normally bear.

The rest of the evidence in support of his thesis — and it contains the greater part of the argument of the Lectures — consists in pointing out the psychological and social consequences of religion, the effects produced on the character and attitude of mind of individuals, and on the cohesion and solidarity of society, by the performance of the ritual and ceremonial duties which their religion obliges them to undertake. Many of these duties, he points out, are irksome and exacting. Their performance, therefore, makes for self-control and discipline and submission to leadership. Some of them are believed to be necessary for the welfare of the community. Their performance, therefore, fosters the spirit of unselfish service, the subordination of one's own inclination to the good of others ; and, as Malinowski points out, though the belief is

[1] Pp. 56-7.   [2] P. 56, note 2.   [3] Pp. 21 ff.

mistaken and the benefit to others illusory, the unselfishness is real and valuable.[1] Similarly, the joint participation by the members of a community in ritual ceremonies makes for social unity and harmony, and produces a sense of common responsibility and a spirit and attitude of mind in which they are more likely to perform their duties to one another. For, as Malinowski says in support of the contention that " ethics is an essential element in religion ", " men cannot worship in common without a common bond of mutual trust and assistance, that is, of charity and love ".[2] In the same way, the conclusion that " taboos, vigils and religious exercises are essentially moral " is derived from the fact that they require the sacrifice of a man's personal comfort for what he believes to be for the common weal.

Malinowski's argument, therefore, seems to be : Religion prescribes and sanctions ritual and ceremonial duties. The performance of these duties produces in the individual certain qualities of character and a spirit of goodwill to his neighbours. These in turn stimulate him to do his duties to his neighbours. Therefore, religion prescribes and sanctions these duties ; it tells a man what his duties are and provides the justification for doing them ; it is, in fact, the foundation and justification of morality.

Now we may accept all Malinowski's premises ; his evidence in support of them is conclusive.[3] But they do not warrant the conclusion which he draws from them. All that they entitle us to conclude is that religion produces or promotes goodwill and moral motives. They do not entitle us even to conclude that religion alone produces or promotes them or that they would be impossible without it ; much less that it prescribes or sanctions them. For it is one thing to influence a character for good or to produce moral motives or a spirit of goodwill ; it is quite another to prescribe or sanction these things. And even if we were to admit that religion prescribes and sanctions — and not merely produces and promotes —

---

[1] P. 43.   [2] P. 3.

[3] This statement is subject to one reservation. The evidence shows that religion tends not so much to produce or create social sentiments and bonds between individuals, as to intensify existing sentiments and to strengthen existing bonds. See below, p. 344, note 1.

goodwill and moral motives, it does not follow that it tells a man what his duties are, that it prescribes moral rules or attaches sanctions to them.

Moreover, despite the ambiguous and misleading language which Malinowski's enthusiasm for the important function which religion fulfils in the life of primitive people leads him to use, I do not believe that he really wants us to draw such a conclusion. For it is inconsistent with positions which he takes in other parts of his writings, and which constitute some of his most significant contributions to social anthropology. Indeed, no one has done more than Malinowski to show that most of the rules of conduct of primitive peoples have no supernatural sanction, and that they do not obey them, merely or even mainly, from fear of supernatural powers. But he did not work out the implications of these facts for morality or its relation to religion ; and I believe he was prevented from doing so largely by the presupposition, which he never seems to have questioned, that morality must in some sense have a religious sanction. Far from belittling the importance of the contributions which he has made to the subject, I am merely trying to work out the implications of the facts to which he himself called attention in a field to which he did not devote much attention ; and to reconcile these implications with the important function which, as he and other field workers realise, religion performs among primitives ; I want also to point out the modification which a recognition of these implications requires in some of his statements, which, as they stand, seem to be misleading.

What, then, are some of the facts which he has himself recorded which are inconsistent with the above conclusion ? There is, so far as I have been able to discover, only one rule governing the relations between individuals which he reports as having a direct supernatural sanction among the Trobrianders. It is the rule against incest, breaches of which are believed by them to be followed automatically by eruptions and boils and, it may be, by death.[1] Respect for the chieftainship and rank is also believed by them to have at least a semi-supernatural sanction, due to the powerful magic which the

[1] *Crime and Custom*, p. 79.

chief is supposed to possess. He also mentions a vague feeling which is sometimes found among them that their ancestors will be angry at breaches of custom, and that disasters may follow as a result ;[1] but whether this applies to secular as well as to ritual customs is not clear. The examples which he gives are of ritual duties only.[2] As regards all other rules governing the relations between persons as members of a society, i.e. the ordinary rules of individual and social morality, not only their principles of justice, distributive and corrective, but their moral code about respect for person and property, about truth-telling and promise-keeping — all these, he tells us explicitly and repeatedly in his detailed discussion of them in *Crime and Custom in Savage Society*, have neither a religious origin nor a supernatural sanction. " They have in no way the character of religious commandments ", he writes ;[3] " they are not endowed with any mystical character . . . not set forth in the name of God, not enforced by any supernatural sanction, but provided with a purely social binding force ".[4]

As we have seen, in that work Malinowski is concerned primarily with the incentives which the natives have to obey the rules which they regard as right and the sanctions or social machinery which encourage compliance with their requirements. They are sanctioned, he tells us, by the working of the principle of reciprocity, the mutuality of services, which underlies all their institutions ; and among the motives which the natives have for obeying them, he mentions " sense of duty and recognition of the need for co-operation ",[5] " regard for the rights of others ",[6] and loyalty to the group, as well as self-interest and fear or hope of consequences, economic or other. In that work, he calls these rules of right conduct rules of primitive law. In a later work, in response to the criticism that it is misleading to speak of rules of law among people who have no *ad hoc* machinery for enforcing them, he calls them sanctioned customs, but he again emphasises that the sanctions for them are not supernatural rewards or punishments but the working of the principle of reciprocity and moral and social approval

---

[1] *Coral Gardens*, i. 468.   [2] *Foundations of Faith and Morals*, p. 15.
[3] *Crime and Custom*, p. 31.   [4] *Ibid.* p. 58.   [5] *Ibid.* p. 20.
[6] *Ibid.* p. 28.

and disapproval.[1] But, by whatever name they are called, they include practically the whole of what we normally call the rules of secular morality; and I suspect that nothing but the pre-conceived idea that morality is either a part of, or intimately connected with, religion prevents Malinowski from regarding them as moral as well as legal rules or sanctioned customs.

This interpretation of the situation is supported by another fact. Malinowski does sometimes speak of these rules and principles as moral or ethical. He does so when he considers them in relation to religion and thinks of ritual and ceremonial practices as strengthening the bonds between members of the community and promoting a spirit of goodwill among them which acts as a motive for carrying out their duties to one another. In other words, when he regards them as moral rules and principles, he tends to think of them as a part of religion or, at least, as having a supernatural sanction. Thus, for example, he writes of " the moral principle of give and take ", " the ethical principle of co-operative services " as applying not only to the relations between the living members of the community but also to those between the living and the dead, and so having a supernatural sanction.[2] Again, he speaks of " the principle of mutuality of services on which the possibility of co-operation depends " as requiring for its maintenance the sanction of " the public performance of ritual " and even of religious or sacred myths.[3]

Thus we find the same rules and principles described some-times as rules of primitive law or sanctioned customs, without any religious or supernatural sanction but enforced by the automatic working of the principle of reciprocity, and at other times as moral rules having a religious sanction and maintained only by the public performance of religious ritual. And the facts which these apparently inconsistent statements, when considered in the light of their contexts and the evidence offered in support of them, describe seem to be : (1) that the rules in question are moral rules which are recognised as right,

---

[1] Introduction to Hogbin, *Law and Order in Polynesia*, especially pp. xxiv-xxx.

[2] *Foundations of Faith and Morals*, p. 28 ; cf. p. 43.

[3] *Science, Religion and Reality*, pp. 63-4.

because they are the conditions of effective co-operation on which individual and social well-being and the smooth working of institutions depend; (2) that the need for complying with their requirements is brought home to the individual through the working of the principle of reciprocity; and (3) that the performance of magico-religious duties and ceremonies promotes social sentiments and a spirit of goodwill, as a result of which individuals are more likely to comply with the rules which they regard as right.

There are certain considerations — such as failure to distinguish clearly between different aspects of morality, the relative importance of these aspects for the work on which anthropologists are engaged, and the somewhat unusual terminology which they use — which may help us to understand how anthropologists come to make statements such as I have quoted from Malinowski. I want to explain how these considerations seem to me to have led the anthropologists to make these statements; but however they came to make them, nothing will enable us to reconcile some of them with one another or with the facts, except on the assumption that some of them do not mean what on the surface they appear to say.

To every piece of conduct there is an inner or subjective side, the motives or attitudes of mind from which it is done; and an outer or objective side, the external actions performed. In passing moral judgement on an act we have to take account of both aspects. For no action is, in the full sense, morally good unless it is both done from a good motive and aims at producing what is believed to be objectively right. Now, anthropologists tend to think of the objective aspect, what is right or obligatory, as determined by the social structure; and, therefore, they deal with it under the heading of social organisation. For example, A. W. Hoernlé writes: " by ' social organisation ' or ' social structure ' . . . is meant the more or less permanent framework of relationships between members of the community which manifests itself in an ordered group-life, with reciprocal rights and duties, privileges and obligations, of members, determining behaviour-patterns for each individual member towards other members, and moulding the feelings, thoughts, and conduct of members according to these patterns, so that it is only in and through them that the individual can achieve his personal self-realisation and participate in the satisfactions offered by the life of his community ".[1]   In the same way, Radcliffe-Brown describes his chapter on ' social organisation ' as concerned with " the customs and institutions by which the natives regulate the conduct of persons to one another " ; [2] and we find a similar view expressed by Malinowski in his article on culture in the *Encyclopaedia of the Social Sciences*.[3]

Now if the outer aspect of morality, the rules of right conduct, as determined by a person's station and its duties, are regarded as part of social organisation and thus taken for granted as fixed and known, it is natural, in considering moral conduct, to think mainly or even merely of the inner aspect, the motives and attitudes of mind of the actors.   This is the variable aspect. The appropriate attitude of mind, the right sentiments, the spirit of goodwill may or may not be present ; and even if it is present, it may be of varying degrees of intensity.   But while this inner aspect is morally very important, motives and sentiments and goodwill are not the whole of morality.   They may provide the drive and dynamic, but moral conduct also needs direction ; and for this right rules and good ideals are necessary. Indeed, as Radcliffe-Brown points out in connection with religious feeling, feelings and sentiments tend to be vague and indefinite until they are crystallised into definite modes of behaviour.

One effect of their exclusive emphasis on the inner aspect of conduct as being alone moral is that anthropologists tend to think of the same rule of conduct as moral, when people comply with it from one motive, as legal, when they comply with it for another, and as economic, when they comply with it for a third, and so on.   In addition, some of them write at times as if all rules of conduct, at least among primitives, required a non-moral or extra-moral sanction.   It is significant in this connection that in classifications of rules of conduct, which are based

[1] *The Bantu-speaking Tribes of South Africa* (ed. Schapera), p. 67.
[2] *The Andaman Islanders*, pp. 22 ff. Cf. *Journal of the Royal Anthropological Institute* (1940), p. 3 : " I regard as part of the social structure all social relations of person to person ".   [3] iv. 622.

on the sanctions attached to the rules, moral rules as such are seldom included.[1]   It is, however, difficult to reconcile such a position with frequent statements that natives sometimes comply with rules from a sense of duty or from regard for the rights of others.   In any case, a rule does not derive its moral rightness from the motives from which people comply with its require- ments ; and if a rule is morally right and recognised as such, it does not lose this character when legal or economic or other sanctions are attached to it, or even when people comply with it from such non-moral motives as fear of punishment by society or hope of economic reward.   Only when this happens the actions of those who obey it from such motives are not morally good.

Now once the nature of a rule is supposed to be determined by the motives from which people comply with it, it is not a long step to the view that rules have a religious sanction, if religion produces the motives which make people comply with them.   This, at any rate, is the view which some anthropologists seem to take, and such is the only evidence which they give in support of it.   But does the evidence justify the conclusion that all or most primitive moral rules have a religious sanction, even in this sense of the term ?   In other words, are we justified in concluding that, even if primitive religion does not generally prescribe moral duties and does not attach supernatural rewards or punishments to their performance or neglect, primitive morality is still dependent on religion in the sense that religion produces the motives without which moral duties would not be performed ?   That is what some of Malinowski's statements suggest.   But such statements give us only one side of the picture ; and there are others which give the other side, and show that, even in respect of its inner side, the side of moral and social sentiments, the relation between morality and religion is not one-sided dependence but mutual influence and support. In the latter passages he represents moral and social sentiments as spontaneous developments of the nature of men who live in close contact with one another ; and he traces the origin of certain religious beliefs and ritual ceremonies to these inde- pendently existing sentiments.   " Human relations ", he writes

[1] See above, pp. 150-51.

in one such passage, " do not rest merely or even mainly on constraint coming from without. Men can only work with and for one another by the moral force which grows out of personal attachments and loyalties. . . . Lifelong bonds of co-operation and mutual interest create sentiments, and sentiments rebel against death and dissolution." [1] Hence arise mortuary ritual, and the belief in immortality and ancestor worship; and once these come into existence, they strengthen and support the social sentiments in which they had their source. These moral and social sentiments he here regards as the source of the inner constraint which finds expression in moral motivation and which he describes variously as sense of duty or loyalty to the group, conscience or sense of responsibility; and the sentiments themselves he describes as products partly of " lifelong bonds of co-operation and mutual interests ", and partly of " gradual training . . . within a definite set of cultural conditions ".[2]

Elsewhere, he tells us that, especially among ancestor-worshipping peoples, certain forms of religious ritual and the beliefs connected with them are " the religious extension of the ethical rules of conduct as between the members of the family ".[3] This extension in turn tends to give the rules a supernatural flavour and thus to strengthen and intensify the motives to obey them; but it is neither the source of the motives nor the justification of the rules. So that however important religion may be in promoting goodwill and intensifying moral motives, it is not the sole source of such motivation.

Thus, when we take Malinowski's different statements into consideration, we find that, from whatever point of view we look at the relation between primitive morality and religion, what we have is not one-sided dependence but a complex system of interactions in which each influences and supports and strengthens the other. This is what his detailed account of the way of life of the Trobrianders shows to be true in their case. But whatever support their morality gains from or gives to their religious beliefs and practices, none of their rules of

---

[1] *Encyclopaedia of the Social Sciences*, iv. 641-2.
[2] *Ibid.* p. 623.   [3] *Foundations of Faith and Morals*, p. 26.

conduct governing the relations of individuals to one another, except the rules about incest, is either prescribed by their religion or has a direct supernatural sanction.

Moreover, as I have pointed out already, Malinowski's account makes it clear that there is a significant difference between the attitude of the natives to the rules of their secular morality which have not, and their magical and ritual rules which have, supernatural sanctions. They do not understand why the ritual and magical rules should be as they are. They accept them merely on authority. They obey them partly out of respect for custom, partly because the custom is sacred and partly because of fear of the consequences to themselves and their people which they believe would follow any breach of them. To their rules of individual and social morality their attitude is quite different. While they accept them in the first instance because they are the customs of their people, they understand why they should be as they are. They see that they are necessary for the smooth working of their institutions which they understand and find good. They regard them as right and reasonable because they recognise that they are the conditions of effective co-operation on which their own well-being and that of their people depend.

Among the Trobrianders, then, we find a relatively clear distinction between strictly religious duties with a supernatural sanction and duties to their fellow-men with a merely moral and social sanction. We find a similar state of affairs among the Aborigines of Central Australia — the other primitive people to whom Malinowski specially refers in his *Foundations of Faith and Morals*. I have already quoted the statement of Spencer and Gillen on whom Malinowski mainly relies for his information about these tribes. They write: " The Central Australian natives . . . have not the vaguest idea of a personal individual other than an actual living member of the tribe, who approves or disapproves of their conduct, as far as anything like what we call morality is concerned ". " But ", they continue, " it must not, however, be imagined that the Central Australian native has nothing in the nature of a moral code. As a matter of fact, he has a very strict one . . . but he quite understands that any punishment for [its] infringement . . .

will come from the older men." [1]   On the other hand, as we have already seen, their totemic and other magico-religious beliefs and practices exercise a profound effect on their character and their attitude to their neighbours.   While they do not tell them how to behave towards one another or prescribe or sanction moral rules, they strengthen the social bonds between individuals and promote goodwill and a spirit of co-operation. Some of them even provide incentives, direct and indirect, for the performance of moral duties.[2]   So that among the Australian aborigines, too, we find religion producing important effects on the character of individuals and the social harmony of groups, while the main content of their moral rules and ideals is of non-religious origin and has no direct supernatural sanction, personal or impersonal.

[1] *Northern Tribes of Central Australia*, pp. 491-2.
[2] See p. 212 above.

PRIMITIVE MORALITY AND RELIGION
(continued)

IN my last lecture I examined the grounds on which it is sometimes held that among primitives religion is the source of moral authority, the ground of the rightness of moral rules. I pointed out that, while the evidence shows that the magico-religious beliefs and practices of primitive peoples exercise a profound influence on the character of individuals and promote among them strong social sentiments and a spirit of co-operation and goodwill, this does not warrant the conclusion that their religion prescribes or sanctions or justifies their moral rules. I also called attention to an important difference between the attitude of the natives themselves to their magico-religious and their moral rules. The former they accept on authority without understanding the reasons for them. The latter they understand to be the conditions of individual and social well-being. And this difference holds even when moral rules are believed to have supernatural as well as social sanctions. Their obligatoriness can be understood without any reference to the supernatural. To comply with their requirements is a moral duty whether or not it is also a religious duty.

We can bring out the nature of this distinction between the attitude of the native to magico-religious or ritual rules on the one hand, and to moral and social rules on the other, if we compare it with a parallel distinction which we find in his attitude to his natural environment. In considering primitive man's dealings with nature, Malinowski distinguishes carefully between the way in which the native uses knowledge and experience on the one hand, and magico-religious practices on the other ; but he does not seem to have recognised the parallel distinction in the native's attitude to his social environment nor the implications of this distinction for morality.

In his efforts to extract a living from his natural environment, and in constructing and using the primitive tools which help him in his task, in hunting, fishing and tilling the soil, in constructing his bow or his canoe, primitive man, as we have seen, shows powers of accurate observation, exact knowledge and sound reasoning. He is guided by experience and uses strictly rational methods. " In all matters in which knowledge is sufficient ", Malinowski writes, " the native relies on it exclusively." [1]   It is only when he reaches the limits of his knowledge and skill and comes up against situations which he does not understand and cannot control, situations which nevertheless he cannot ignore because they are fraught with important consequences for his own welfare and that of his people, that he resorts to magico-religious practices. These practices are a supplement to, not a substitute for, skill and energy and honest toil; and we are assured that the native never confuses the two.[2]   The native has recourse to supernatural aid only to guard against unseen evils due to causes which are beyond his comprehension and control. As Malinowski himself puts it, " magic and religion and ritual step in only where knowledge fails "; or again, " sacred tradition is concerned only with things where experience and reason are of no avail ".[3]   And while his magic and ritual practices do not produce the effects which the native expects from them, they strengthen his morale and give him courage and confidence which enable him to persevere in the face of dangers and difficulties. Thus, in regard to primitive man's dealings with nature, we have by common consent both a secular and a sacred tradition, the former concerned with technical skill and knowledge, the latter with the magico-religious practices by which he supplements the limitations of the former. But while both are handed down by tradition, the native understands the reasons for the former : their " practical utility is recognised by reason and testified by experience ".[4]   The latter he has to accept on authority. However inextricably the two are mixed up in primitive life, the field worker never experiences any difficulty

[1] *Foundations of Faith and Morals*, p. 33.
[2] *Ibid.* pp. 20 ff.   [3] *Ibid.* p. 34.
[4] Malinowski, *Crime and Custom*, p. 52.

in knowing when the native is engaged in secular and when in
magico-religious practices.[1]

Now what I have been suggesting is that, according to the
evidence which Malinowski himself provides, we get a similar
distinction between a secular and a sacred tradition concerning
the way in which primitive man should deal with situations
presented by his social environment. The former gives him
rules as to how he should behave towards his fellows in the
ordinary affairs of life. The latter prescribes what he should
do in the crises of life, where he meets forces which he can
neither understand nor control, as in the presence of such events
as illness and war, and above all death. Here, too, he understands the reasons for the ways he is expected to behave in the
former, in a way in which he does not those required of him in
the latter. Here, also, even if the practices enjoined by his
religion do not have the effects which he expects from them,
they have, as we have seen, other important psychological and
social effects.

What we find, then, is that among every people, however
primitive their culture and however simple their way of life,
there are technical rules governing the way they master their
natural environment and extract from it the means of livelihood.
There are, also, rules dealing with the relations between individuals, rules necessary for the smooth working of their institutions and the maintenance of an ordered social life. These two
together constitute their secular tradition. They are the results
of experience and experiment, the products of the accumulated
skill and wisdom of their ancestors. In dealing with them the
native feels at home ; he understands what he is doing and why
he is doing it. He believes himself master of the situation.
But both in their dealings with nature and in their relations
with their fellow-men, situations arise where the issues are
important and the outcome uncertain, situations with which
their primitive skill and knowledge and powers of understanding do not enable them to deal. It is in such situations that
they turn to religion ; and the ways which it prescribes for
dealing with such situations constitute the sacred tradition of
magico-religious beliefs and practices. In dealing with these

---

[1] Boas and others, *General Anthropology*, p. 628.

situations, the native senses the presence of something which makes him uneasy, the presence of the sacred or the uncanny, that which arouses the religious thrill.

I am going to give one more quotation to show how near Malinowski comes, even in the *Foundations of Faith and Morals*, to adopting this conclusion, and yet how in the end he fails to draw it. Referring to the Australian Aborigines he writes: " There is a body of rules, handed from one generation to another, which refers to the manner in which people live in their little shelters, make their fire by friction, collect their food and cook it, make love to each other and quarrel. This secular tradition consists partly of customary or legal rules determining the manner in which social life is conducted. But it also embodies rules of technique and behaviour in regard to the environment. . . . The rules which we find here are completely independent of magic, of supernatural sanctions, and they are never accompanied by any ceremonial or ritual elements." Here the individual " relies on reason " and the resulting tradition is " plastic, selective and intelligent ".[1]

Here we have a clear distinction drawn between a secular tradition based on reason and experience and a sacred tradition relating to the supernatural which transcends knowledge and experience ; and the rules of right conduct governing the relations of the members of the community to one another are included in the secular tradition. But when Malinowski so includes them he calls them customary or legal rules, in the same way as he does in his account of the Trobrianders where, as we saw, he refers to them as rules of primitive law or principles of social justice. On the other hand, whenever he refers to them as moral rules he associates them with religion and with the attitudes and feelings which religious beliefs and the performance of ritual ceremonies arouse ; and, because of this association, he tends to include them in the sacred tradition. But whether they are called legal or moral, they are the same rules of right conduct — the ordinary rules of individual and social morality.

It should, however, be added that the parallelism between man's secular attitude to nature and his moral attitude to his

[1] *Foundations of Faith and Morals*, pp. 32-3.

fellows is not quite complete. For in every personality there is a supersensible or spiritual element, an element which is in the strict sense supernatural; and the emotional attitude which the recognition or the consciousness of this element tends to produce, the sense of restraint and embarrassment and intensified self-consciousness which we tend to experience in the presence of another person, especially in the presence of the very young and the very great, is akin to the feeling aroused by the supernatural.[1] This feeling is at least an element in the respect or reverence for personality which arises from our recognition of others as persons or expressions of the moral consciousness, a recognition without some degree of which morality is impossible. But the point which I wish to make at present is that, given this recognition, the most primitive men of whom we have any knowledge understand the rules, which are the conditions of effective co-operation with their fellows, and, therefore, the requirements of social well-being, as clearly as they understand the rules for building a canoe or growing crops. The moral rules involved in the former are as much the results of experience and experiment and, therefore, as rational as the technical rules involved in the latter.

The purpose of my argument is not to belittle, much less to deny, the part which religion plays in the life of primitive peoples or the influences which it exerts on their individual and social conduct; but rather to reconcile the evidence of the anthropologists that it does fulfil such undoubtedly important functions with the fact that primitives have a secular morality which is relatively autonomous. But so far, though I have used language which has a general reference, I have relied mainly on the evidence regarding the two primitive peoples dealt with by Malinowski — the Trobrianders and the natives of Central Australia. The same state of affairs prevails in the two other tribes whose ways of life I described earlier, the Batonga tribes of South-East Africa and the Crow Indians of Montana. In both, magico-religious beliefs and practices exercise a profound influence on their character and conduct, but in neither does religion prescribe their moral code, nor does it hold out to them hope of reward or fear of punishment, here or hereafter, for the

[1] Cf. Bowman, *A Sacramental Universe*, pp. 399-400.

performance or neglect of most of their moral and social duties. I want now to consider the evidence from other primitive tribes to see how far it confirms my argument, and what further conclusions can be drawn from it.

Let me first state, tentatively and provisionally, the general conclusions which this wider evidence seems to support. They are : (1) that in the course of the continuous interaction between moral and religious beliefs and practices, in which they mutually modify and support one another, there is a tendency both for the concept of the supernatural to become moralised and for morality to acquire a religious sanction ; but the latter tendency, at least, is by no means universal ; (2) that, whether or not it acquires a religious sanction in whole or in part, morality is of independent origin and authority, springing from the nature of man as a being who is rational and social as well as a creature of impulses and desires ; and (3) that primitive religion, while in the main non-moral and perhaps in origin entirely so, exercises an important influence on the formation of the character of the individual and on the social solidarity of his group. It should be added that, however they conceive the relations between them, we find both morality and religion among all men of whom we have any record. They all believe that some actions are right and others wrong. The differences between them concern which actions have which character. Similarly they all believe in the existence or reality of the supernatural but they entertain very different views about its character. It is the second of the above conclusions which specially concerns my argument ; but in order not to leave a one-sided impression, I shall touch on the evidence for the others as well. As we have seen, it is the third which has been specially emphasised by field workers among primitive peoples.

I cannot give more than a few examples of the evidence on which I base these conclusions. So far as I am aware no one has made a survey of all, or even of a representative selection of, primitive peoples to discover either which of their moral rules have supernatural sanctions, and in which of the senses I have mentioned they have such sanctions, or what influence their religion exercises directly and indirectly on their character and conduct, and in what ways it exercises the influence which it does. But nothing short of such a survey would enable us to make generalisations about the relations between their morality and religion with any confidence. For the number of primitive peoples is so large [1] and the relations between the different aspects of their religion and morality so various that by a judicious selection of examples one could prove almost any conclusion about them. What I have done is this.[2] I have examined the reports of trained observers about some thirty or forty primitive peoples who are at different stages of development in the level of their material culture and the complexity of their social organisations, and widely scattered over different continents. I have selected the particular peoples concerned partly because we have a good deal of information about their ways of life, and partly because the information about them has been collected by experienced observers. I trust they are a representative selection.

Before trying to sum up the results of this examination, I want very briefly to give a few further illustrations, i.e. in addition to the four peoples whose ways of life I described earlier. I am, however, well aware that these illustrations can only give a very imperfect picture. For, as I have repeatedly pointed out, the moral codes and the magico-religious beliefs and practices of different primitive peoples are so diverse and the relations between them and the other aspects of their cultures so complex, that we cannot hope to understand them properly without considering the whole way of life of each of the peoples

---

[1] Hobhouse, Wheeler and Ginsberg give a list of more than 650 (*Social Institutions and Material Culture of the Simpler Peoples*, pp. 30 ff.).

[2] I have, of course, also examined the general statements of anthropologists on the subject, and many of them directly confirm some of my conclusions — especially the conclusion that few of the moral rules of primitives have supernatural sanctions (see e.g. Firth, *Human Types*, p. 133 ; Westermarck, *Early Beliefs and their Social Significance*, pp. 24 ff. ; Lowie, *Primitive Religion*, pp. 29 ff. *et passim* ; Fortune, *Manus Religion*, p. 375 ; Benedict in Boas and Others, *General Anthropology*, pp. 627-65 ; Hopkins, *Origin and Evolution of Religion*, pp. 247-8 ; Karsten, *The Origins of Religion*, pp. 201-2, 239). But as few anthropologists have interested themselves in most of the questions with which I am concerned, I have preferred to go directly to the empirical evidence regarding particular peoples.

concerned and bringing out the parts which their morality and their religion play in it. Nevertheless, the illustrations may be of some value. I have chosen them to bring out the great contrast between different peoples as regards the extent to which, and the ways in which, their moral rules are prescribed or sanctioned by religion.

We have seen that the moral code of the natives of Central Australia has little or no supernatural sanction. But among their fellow tribesmen of New South Wales, whose principles of social organisation and material culture are very similar to theirs, what is much the same moral code is believed to have been established by their chief god, and is taught to their youth at initiation in his name and with his authority.[1]

In the exhaustive account which Radcliffe-Brown gives us of the natives of the Andaman Islands, I can discover only one moral rule which has a supernatural sanction, that against homicide,[2] a breach of which exposes the guilty person to illness, unless he takes certain ritual precautions. The chief god of these islanders, we are told, is not disturbed by moral faults.[3] All the actions which arouse her anger and cause her to show her displeasure, which she does by sending storms, are non-moral, such as burning or melting bees-wax, or eating certain foods.[4] We find a somewhat similar state of affairs among the Murray Islanders, a very primitive but enterprising and intelligent people whose code of conduct is said to " exhibit a delicacy of feeling which is quite comparable with our own code of social morality ".[5] Among the injunctions which they give to their youth during initiation are " reticence, thoughtfulness, respectful behaviour, prompt obedience, generosity, diligence, kindness to parents and other relatives in deed and word, truthfulness, helpfulness, manliness, discretion in dealing with women, quiet temper. . . . The prohibitions are against theft, borrowing without leave, shirking duty, talkativeness, abusive language, talking scandal, marriage with certain individuals." [6]

---

[1] Radcliffe-Brown, *Religion and Society*, p. 9.
[2] Radcliffe-Brown, *Andaman Islanders*, p. 133.
[3] *Ibid.* p. 160.   [4] *Ibid.* p. 152.
[5] Haddon, *Frazer Lectures* (1922–32), p. 217 ; cf. *Cambridge Expedition to the Torres Straits*, v. 272 and vi. 250.
[6] *Ibid.*

This code, Haddon tells us, is " a purely secular affair ". The natives believe that a dead ancestor might be angry if his children were wronged or his lands and chattels taken by people who had no claim to them. But " with this exception ", he writes, " there is no evidence that their code of morality gained either sanction or support from religion ".[1] No punishment for its infringement was anticipated from a supernatural source either here or hereafter.

On the other hand, Hogbin reports that the natives of Ontong Java in Polynesia believe that their dead ancestors " are able to observe all human conduct and are aware of all hidden motives ".[2] They punish with illness and misfortune and even death not all breaches of their moral code but only some,[3] the commonest of which are " acts of violence within the joint family, for example, murder, adultery and displacement of the true heir ; [and] incest or sexual relations between two persons who are within the forbidden degrees of kinship ".[4]

In the same way, according to Mead [5] and Fortune,[6] the Manus people of the Admiralty Islands, another ancestor-worshipping people, have two main ideals in life, to maintain a high standard of sexual morality and of commercial integrity ; and the spirits of their ancestors, whom they regard not as omniscient or omnipotent, but as more knowledgeable and powerful than mortals, are believed to punish breaches of their code of conduct in relation to sex and business. " Sex offences which interfere with the Manus social order . . . light words, chance physical contacts . . . careless jests, non-observance of the proper avoidance reactions towards relatives-in-law, all these ", we are told, " may bring down the spirits' righteous wrath, either upon the sinner or upon some one of his relatives." [7] The spirits also " abhor economic laxity of any sort : failure to pay debts, careless manipulation of family properties, economic procrastination, and unfair allotment of funds among the needs of several relatives ".[8] Any of these is liable to bring

---

[1] Haddon, *Frazer Lectures* (1922–32), p. 216.
[2] Hogbin, *Law and Order in Polynesia*, p. 144.   [3] *Ibid.* p. 79.
[4] *Ibid.* p. 152.   [5] Mead, *Growing Up in New Guinea.*
[6] Fortune, *Manus Religion.*
[7] Mead, *op. cit.* pp. 61-2.   [8] *Ibid.* p. 62.

illness, misfortune or death on the guilty person or on one of his relatives.

In order not to create a false impression, it should be added that these guardians of the morality of the natives of Ontong Java and Manus are believed to be in many respects as capricious, spiteful and even unjust as any mortal. For example, the spirits of the Manus will vent on their descendants their resentment for events which happen to themselves beyond the grave, events for which mortals are in no way responsible ; [1] while those of Ontong Java are sometimes believed to be guilty of such mean and spiteful acts that their descendants relieve their feelings by digging up the graves and burning the remains of those who are believed to be responsible, not necessarily to influence their conduct but merely to show that they no longer have any respect for them.[2] But, as Fortune reminds us,[3] these spirits, in punishing breaches of tribal morality at all, are the exception and not the rule among primitive supernatural beings.

When we turn from Australasia and Polynesia to Africa and America, we find the same contrasts between the views of different peoples about the relation between morality and religion. We have already seen that the Bantu tribes of South-East Africa have a keen sense of right and wrong and have developed a very remarkable system for the administration of justice. Yet Junod writes that " their religion is non-moral and their morality non-religious ".[4] The only moral faults of which their ancestor gods take notice are dissolute sexual conduct, which they punish with death, and displacement of the true heir, which results in no children being born. Their other demands on their worshippers — and they are numerous and exacting — are all of a ritual and ceremonial character. On the other hand, according to Wilson,[5] many, if not most, of the moral rules of the Nyakyusa tribes have a supernatural sanction. Gross breaches of their moral code are punished, if they occur in the relations between members of the group, mainly by

[1] *Ibid.* [2] Hogbin, *op. cit.* pp. 159-60.
[3] Fortune, *op. cit.* p. 375.
[4] Junod, *Life of a South African Tribe,* ii. 427-8, 582-3.
[5] Wilson, " An African Morality ", *Africa,* ix. 75 ff.

their ancestor gods; and, if in the interrelation between groups, by sorcery and magic, some forms of which are believed to be effective only when those who exercise them are satisfied of the justice of the cause in which they are being used. And Culwick reports that among the Wabena, a Bantu tribe of Tanganyika, all moral rules have supernatural sanctions.[1]

Similar contrasts are found among the American Indian tribes. We have already seen that, according to Lowie, the conduct prescribed by the religion of the Crow Indians is " manifestly unconnected with anything normally included under the heading of ethics ". Their " really vital social canons . . . have no supernatural sanction ".[2] On the other hand, Cooper tells us that in their initiation ceremonies the Yahgans, a South American tribe, give their young people " elaborate moral instructions with very concrete counsels on the obligations of altruistic behaviour, respect for the aged, peaceableness, industry, not spreading scandal or carrying tales, and so on ". These instructions are presented to them as the will of their supreme being who sees everything and will punish delinquents with shortened life and the death of their children.[3] Similarly the Luisino, a tribe of Californian Indians, instruct their youth to respect their elders, to refrain from anger, to be polite and cordial to their relatives-in-law and so on; and tell them that prosperity here and hereafter will follow the observance of these rules, while breaches of them will give rise to many misfortunes. They believe, however, that both rewards and punishments will come about automatically. There is no suggestion that they are the result of the personal intervention of supernatural agents, though the rules themselves are believed to be the will of such agents.[4]

Some of the statements which I have made in the course of these illustrations would require further elaboration and refinement, in the light of the ways of life of the peoples to whom they refer, before they could be regarded as quite exact. But they are sufficiently precise for our present purpose.

[1] See below, pp. 342-4.   [2] Lowie, *Primitive Religion*, p. 30.
[3] *Handbook of South American Indians*, i. 99-103 (*Bureau of American Ethnology Bulletin*, No. 143).
[4] *Handbook of Indians of California*, pp. 683-5 (*Bureau of American Ethnology Bulletin*, No. 78).

I want to give one more illustration with a little more detail, partly because one of our most cautious and competent anthropologists has recently made an intensive survey of the way of life of the people concerned, partly because they are still relatively untouched by Western influences, and partly because they provide an excellent example of the intricate interrelationships between morality and religion among primitives.[1] These people inhabit the island of Tikopia in Polynesia. This island is less than three miles in circumference and capable of maintaining rather more than 1200 persons. It is seventy miles from the nearest island, and that is smaller than itself. The Tikopians have a complex social structure based on an intricate system of kinship together with a principle of rank determined partly by birth and partly by religious considerations. They are divided into three clans, each with its chief who is the intermediary between the people and one of their principal gods. They have a protracted system of seasonal ritual in which all the chiefs and the whole of the people play some part. This ritual is mixed up with their economic and social and political arrangements and so confers on them an added authority. In addition to their principal gods, who are non-human, they also invoke the blessing of their ancestors, whom they believe to have the power and will to do them good or harm. The moral ideas which they attribute to their gods, whether human or non-human, are mainly the ideas about right and wrong entertained by the present inhabitants. They have also ritual performances of a more magical character connected with canoe building and repairing, fishing and agriculture and other activities.

The moral and social obligations of the Tikopians are largely determined by considerations of kinship and neighbourhood, and they are sanctioned by the principle of reciprocity, rather loosely interpreted.[2] Some of these rules, such as those requiring respect for parents and chiefs, have a direct supernatural sanction, in the sense that breaches of them are believed to bring disasters on the offenders; but they have also a moral

[1] For the way of life of this people see — Firth, *We, The Tikopia*; do. *Primitive Polynesian Economy*; do. *The Work of the Gods in Tikopia*.
[2] Firth, *Primitive Polynesian Economy*, p. 348.

and social sanction. On the other hand the rule against incest has a supernatural but no social sanction. The fact that breaches of the rule are believed to be punished by supernatural means seems in this case to be regarded as a reason or, it may be, an excuse why men should not interfere with the culprits.[1]

Most of their other rules seem to have no direct super- natural sanction and yet some at least of them derive a direct support from religion. For, as part of their principal religious ceremonies, all the people meet together once a year in a sacred glade ; and, while the others sit with bowed heads, one of the chiefs recites a remarkable proclamation which, among other things, " cautions against theft, against disturbance and brawl- ing . . . advises economic forethought . . . and enjoins re- straint in the matter of procreation in the interests of communal welfare ".[2] This proclamation contains no threat of punish- ment to wrongdoers, nor does it directly refer to any of their gods. But it is made as part of a sacred ceremony by a chief who is the accredited mouthpiece of the gods ;[3] and this gives the injunctions contained in it the support and sanction of religion. The proclamation, however, does not contain all their moral rules ; and those which are, as well as those which are not, contained in it have also a moral and social sanction, and the people approve them and understand the reasons for them in a way in which they do not those for their ritual duties.

We may take as an illustration of their attitude to their moral rules, and their conscious understanding of their social value, the way they deal with their most pressing problem, the problem of population. The Tikopians are a virile and fertile race and would increase rapidly if they did not take steps to keep the population down. As they have no way of dealing with a surplus population, and as they have had for many years as large a population as the island can support, they have deliberately taken steps to prevent an increase. This they do in a variety of ways. We saw that the proclamation which I

[1] Firth, *We, The Tikopia*, pp. 335-6. For a similar state of affairs in Ontong Java see Hogbin, *Law and Order*, pp. 153-6. When an attempt to punish some of those who break some of their rules would be liable to dis- rupt the group, these people soothe their consciences with the belief that such breaches will be supernaturally punished.

[2] Firth, *Work of the Gods*, ii. 201.   [3] *Ibid.* ii. 189.

have already mentioned calls attention to the need to keep
families small; and it delicately refers to a contraceptive
method which is one of the ways of doing this. Another way
of limiting the population is the voluntary celibacy of the
younger members of families, and a third is the infanticide of
children who arrive after the family is as large as its means
of livelihood will support.[1] These methods of limiting the
population have no supernatural sanction, except that the first
gets an indirect religious authority through its inclusion in the
proclamation made during a religious ceremony. And they
cannot be strictly enforced; nor is there any attempt so to
enforce them. Nevertheless, they are not merely the customs
of their people, passively and unreflectively accepted on the
authority of tradition. The natives understand the reason for
them and practise them consciously and deliberately.[2] Indeed,
some of them pleaded with Firth when he lived among them to
try to persuade the authorities under whose jurisdiction the
island now comes not to interfere, as they understood they
wanted to do, with the practice of voluntary infanticide — this
being in their opinion necessary to keep the population within
the limits which the island can support.

Given the framework of their social structure and their
magico-religious beliefs, the attitude of the more thoughtful,
at least, among the Tikopians to most of their other moral rules
and ends seems to be equally conscious and rational. Not that
they do not break their rules and evade their obligations, but
they recognise the conditions of effective co-operation and social
well-being, even when they do not comply with them. We are
told that their rules of distributive justice are based on rational
principles,[3] that they regard their institutions as good,[4] and that
they understand the conditions on which their smooth working
depends. Just as they understand and can explain the technical
rules with which they should comply in constructing a canoe
or tilling the soil, so they understand that regard for the person

---

[1] Firth, *We, The Tikopia*, pp. 414 ff. ; do. *Primitive Polynesian Economy*,
pp. 43 ff.
[2] Firth, *We, The Tikopia*, pp. 417, 491 ; do. *Primitive Polynesian Economy*,
pp. 5, 44.
[3] *Ibid.* pp. 282-3.   [4] *We, The Tikopia*, pp. 49, 417.

and property of others, respect for truth and fair dealing and mutual helpfulness, a certain measure of self-restraint between husbands and wives, of respect by children for parents and by kin for one another, are necessary for the effective functioning of their institutions and the welfare of their society.

This reflective attitude to many of their institutions and customs may be further illustrated by another consideration. Firth tells us that they sometimes complain about some of their customs.[1] They feel they ought to comply with them out of regard for the rights which they confer on others, rights which they think they ought to respect; and yet they do not regard the customs as good; just as we may comply with a law of which we do not approve and which we would like to see changed. In none of these ways are the Tikopians, who are described as " perhaps the most primitive people in Polynesia ",[2] unique among native peoples; but Firth gives us more information about their inner attitudes than we usually get from field workers among primitives; and among the conclusions which he draws from this information is that " custom and tradition are not such rigid monitors in primitive life as they are often represented ".[3]

The state of affairs which the accounts from which I have selected these illustrations reveal is this. (1) There are primitive peoples no part of whose moral code has a supernatural sanction. (2) There are others many or most of whose moral rules have such sanctions in one form or another. (3) Perhaps the most common state of affairs is that in which some moral rules have such sanctions, while others, usually much more numerous, have not. (4) There is no important difference that I can discover between the nature of the moral rules which have and those which have not supernatural sanctions; nor between the content of the moral codes as a whole of peoples some or all of whose rules have such sanctions and of those whose rules have a merely moral or social sanction. The one kind cannot be regarded as higher or lower than the other. Nor is the presence of such sanctions confined to, or more common at any particular

---

[1] *Primitive Polynesian Economy*, p. 321.
[2] *We, The Tikopia*, p. 31.   [3] *Ibid.* pp. 564-5.

level of cultural development. What is much the same rule may be regarded in one community as sanctioned by the intervention of a personal supernatural agent, in another by the working of impersonal supernatural forces, and in yet another merely by moral or social approval and disapproval. It may even be that some rules which have a merely customary or social sanction for the ordinary man may be regarded as having a supernatural sanction by a specially gifted individual — a thinker, a prophet, a myth maker — of whom we are assured some are to be found from time to time among all primitive peoples. (5) Whether or not some of their moral rules have supernatural sanctions, all primitive societies recognise purely religious or ritual duties, the sanction for which is purely supernatural ; and, as we have seen, these indirectly play an important part in their moral and social life. (6) When morality acquires a supernatural sanction an additional incentive to well-doing and deterrent to vice is provided ; but whether or not, and if at all to what extent, this incentive and deterrent are to be regarded as moral depends on the way in which the supernatural is conceived.

In this connection it is necessary to remember that there is no such thing as a primitive conception of the supernatural, in the sense of one all whose details are common to different primitive peoples, any more than there is a primitive morality or a primitive religion. Some people think of the supernatural in more personal, others in more impersonal terms, according as they conceive it after the analogy of one or the other of the two entities which they know best, things and persons.

When the supernatural is thought of on the analogy of things, we get such conceptions as mana, wakan, orenda, etc., conceptions which in one form or another and with great variation in detail are to be found among most primitive peoples. The supernatural in this sense is thought of as a supersensible quality of, or power in, certain objects or events. It is like other qualities, such as colour or hardness, except that it is unseen. It has often been compared to an electric charge which is released on contact. Its operation is less discriminating and more automatic than that of personal agents. It is liable to affect anything or anybody who touches the object or brings

about the event, whether by accident or design makes no difference. Its results are usually disastrous, such as disease or
drought or death. When the supernatural is conceived after
the analogy of persons, we get such conceptions as spirits or
ghosts or gods, whether or not they are thought of as persons
who once existed in human form.

Among most primitive peoples we find the supernatural
conceived in both these ways, though one form is usually more
prominent than the other. Both forms may provide supernatural sanctions for moral conduct, but only the personal form
can take account of intentions and motives and, therefore, be a
genuine moral sanction. It therefore provides the line of
development to the ethical religions. No doubt the impersonal
form is less arbitrary and more impartial than most of the
personal supernatural powers of the primitive; but its impartiality is the impartiality of nature rather than the expression of
justice. While it may at times punish breaches of moral rules,
it takes account only of the external act and not of strictly
moral considerations. For example, we find among many
primitive people a belief that a homicide is defiled or impure,
and that this pollution will produce disastrous consequences
unless steps are taken to avert them. Now this pollution is
regarded as the same, and as liable to have the same effects, in
the case of the morally praiseworthy action of the warrior who
kills an enemy in battle, the morally neutral action of the man
who accidentally kills his friend and the morally reprehensible
action of the man who murders his neighbour. There are
other cases, such as the misfortune which is believed to result
automatically from incest, where the operation of such forces
seems more like a form of cosmic justice; but similar effects
are believed to follow from events or occurrences, like the birth
of twins, which have no moral or immoral character.

Not only do many primitives conceive the supernatural in
both personal and impersonal terms, but they do not usually
draw so sharp a distinction between the personal and the impersonal as we do. Indeed throughout the whole of this argument, though I have followed my authorities quite closely, I
am conscious that I have been using abstract terms and drawing
sharp distinctions which are apt to leave the impression that

primitives are more analytic and reflective than in fact they are. If it is true that men generally are only partially and intermittently rational, it is even more true of primitives, though there are among them, as Radin and others have demonstrated, thinkers as well as prophets, and sceptics and agnostics as well as rebels against the established order. As we saw in considering the nature of primitive mentality, it is difficult to convey in a language like ours, which has been developed to express abstract and analytic thinking, the ideas of those who think mainly in concrete terms, and draw fewer distinctions and draw them less clearly than we do. Even though their attitude and behaviour show that they recognise distinctions between the natural and the supernatural, the mental and the material, the animate and the inanimate, the distinctions are usually operative in their experience rather than consciously reflected on.   And even when they thus distinguish, or behave as if they distinguished, they do not sharply separate the distinguished elements. For example, few, if any, of them have the idea of a purely disembodied or immaterial spirit. It is therefore much easier for them to think of what we call natural happenings as being the results of the activities of conscious agencies.

The way they conceive the supernatural also helps to explain why more primitive peoples do not have supernatural sanctions for their moral codes. It seems to us natural that morality and religion should be intimately associated, that morality should be a matter of cosmic concern and that no man should be regarded as religious unless he is at least morally good ; and we can offer good reasons for this association. Morality and religion use the same terms, good and bad, right and wrong. They both call forth a strong emotional reaction and command man's supreme loyalty. There is a strong resemblance between the emotional reaction aroused by the consciousness of the presence of another person, especially a person whom we regard as morally better or purer than ourselves, and by the sense of the presence of the supernatural. Moreover, when a course of conduct calls forth the most profound reaction of which a man's nature is capable, the judgement of approval or disapproval which he passes on it is apt to seem to him as much cosmic or supernatural as individual and social. It is natural, therefore, that he should expect some cosmic reaction to it, some reaction by the powers that rule his universe, whether he conceives these as personal or impersonal. It may therefore seem surprising that the tendency to give their moral rules and ideals a more than human significance is not more marked among primitives. No doubt there would be a greater tendency for them to do this if they derived their ideas of the character of the supernatural merely from their own ideas of right and wrong. But they do not. They derive them in part also from what we would call the natural happenings which profoundly affect their life and welfare, drought and disease and death, and all the other hazards and hardships and tragedies to which man, especially primitive man, is heir. When we take this into consideration, need we be surprised that the ritual performances of most primitive peoples should be designed rather to prevent their supernatural powers from harming them than as an expression of gratitude or worship, or that they should not consider these powers as much better or more moral than themselves, or that when they conceive them in personal terms they should some-times criticise them on moral grounds ? [1]

It is also worth noting — for it has implications for our understanding of morality to which we shall have to return — that we sometimes find supernatural sanctions, both of the personal and the impersonal kind, for breaking moral rules, the general observance of which is socially approved by the community concerned. For example, a people like the Australian Aborigines, who in general disapprove of lying, may consider it a duty to lie on certain occasions as part of the requirements of their religion ; and there is a supernatural sanction for their so doing ; or a people who punish with death the killing of a fellow tribesman may regard the killing of twins as a duty supernaturally prescribed.

What we seem to find, then, in the relation between the morality and religion of different peoples is an exceedingly complex process of mutual interaction and modification. In

[1] These considerations also explain why those who conceive the super-natural in personal terms and regard their gods as good believe also in evil spirits. To account for life as they see it there must be devils as well as gods.

the course of this process there is a tendency, among many peoples at least, for the supernatural to be conceived more and more in personal and moral terms and for morality to be put under supernatural guardianship. And when this happens, the moral qualities which are attributed to the supernatural beings tend to be those which the people who attribute them believe they ought to have, that is those which they themselves or their prophets and teachers think good ; and when they, slowly and imperceptibly, but none the less surely, modify their ideas of what is right and good, whether as the result of changing conditions, or contact with other people, or because individuals arise among them with a deeper insight into the conditions of moral and social well-being, they tend to attribute the altered views of what seems to them right and good to the same supernatural authorities, thus reinterpreting their character and requirements.

Moreover, when a primitive man, some or all of whose moral rules have a supernatural sanction, is asked why a particular line of conduct is right and he replies, as anthropologists tell us that he does, that it is the will of his gods or that his gods would be angry or that certain misfortunes would befall him if he did not act in that way, we are not to suppose that he draws any clear distinction between being right and being the will of his gods or being supernaturally sanctioned. He does not raise the question whether forms of conduct are right because they are the will of his gods (in the sense that they might equally well have been otherwise and still right, if his gods had willed otherwise) or his gods will them because they are right. In other words, he does not distinguish between his reasons for believing that a course of conduct is right and the grounds of its rightness ; nor indeed do most civilised people draw such a distinction. If we may draw the distinction for them, I think we may say that, as regards moral rules, being the will of their gods is the guarantee rather than the ground of their rightness, their reason for believing them to be right rather than what constitutes their rightness. But however natural may be the twofold tendency to moralise the supernatural and to give moral rules a supernatural sanction, and however little primitives or others distinguish, in the case of those rules which have a supernatural sanction, between their being so sanctioned and the grounds of their rightness, it is not the supernatural sanction which makes them right; and even when moral rules have a supernatural sanction, the primitive is capable of understanding the reasons for his moral and social duties in a way in which he does not understand the reasons for his ritual duties; just as he understands the reasons for the way in which he has to construct a canoe to make it seaworthy in a way in which he does not understand the reasons for the ritual of canoe magic.

This is confirmed by the testimony of some field workers among peoples whose rules of conduct have a supernatural sanction. While they emphasise most strongly the indispensable function which religion plays in the lives of these peoples, they point out that in the case of the more important moral rules supernatural sanctions are not the really operative or effective sanctions. Like the sanction of mere custom, the belief that they have supernatural sanctions may be sufficient to make the natives accept rules which are not irksome or troublesome, rules which do not make demands on the individual which are opposed to his inclinations or immediate interests. But for rules which do make such demands nearer, more tangible and more positive sanctions are required. Such rules are accepted as binding only when they are found by experience to be for the good of the group and the welfare of its individual members. When this is not the case, despite the supernatural sanctions, not only do the natives find means of evading them and discovering supernatural sanctions for so doing, but the rules themselves soon cease to be regarded as binding.

To quote just one authority. Culwick, whose main field work has been done among the Wabena tribe in Tanganyika, a people all whose rules of conduct are sincerely believed to have a supernatural sanction, emphasises the very important part which their religion plays in their lives, a part the value of which he says " it would be difficult to over-estimate "; [1] but he points out that we must distinguish " between religious beliefs in and about supernatural beings or powers as a source of courage

[1] Culwick, *Good Out of Africa*, p. 15.

and hope and good morale, and rules of mundane behaviour introduced in the name of religion. The latter are given the support of religious authority and appear to be part and parcel of men's religion, but they are in fact extraneous and their . . . value must be assessed separately from that of primary religious beliefs." [1] The rules of mundane behaviour, that is the moral and social rules governing the relations of individuals to one another, owe most of their binding force to " their essentially practical nature ", the fact that " in men's experience they have been found to work ".[2] The supernatural sanctions " have their part to play in enforcing them, but they are only effective because they are compelling people to conform not to a dead ' cake of custom ' but to a living system . . . of mutual obligations with corresponding rights, binding each member of the tribe to his fellows. The whole is a network of duties and privileges, and dislocation of the system in one part upsets others not immediately or obviously connected with it." [3]

Culwick warns us not to think of the native " as that mythical spineless creature who follows the dictates of custom blindly, intuitively, spontaneously, in all his dealings with fellow-members of the group. . . . Custom unbacked by potent practical sanctions ", he continues, " fares badly when it comes into conflict with human nature ; and a man's observance of its rules so far from being automatic and unconstrained or induced by purely supernatural sanctions is clearly forced on him . . . by sanctions inherent in the system of mutual rights and obligations in his group." [4] After giving detailed illustrations of the operation of supernatural and social sanctions, Culwick concludes : " It is plain that the effect of his religious beliefs on the actual everyday behaviour of the Bantu African is secondary to that of his social organisation and is very much smaller than either he believes or many students of his society imagine ".[5]

As regards its bearing on our present argument Culwick's contention may be summed up thus : Unless in addition to

<hr />

[1] Culwick, *op. cit.* p. 15.
[2] Culwick, " Religious and Economic Sanctions in a Bantu Tribe ", *British Journal of Psychology* (1935–36), p. 185.
[3] *Ibid.*   [4] *Ibid.* p. 189.   [5] *Good Out of Africa*, p. 18.

having supernatural sanctions, being the customs of his ancestors or the will of his gods, moral and social rules are also proved by the experience of the native to be good, in the sense that they contribute to the welfare of the group and therefore to his own good, they cease not only to be effective but to be regarded as binding; but if, in addition to being recognised as in this sense right, they also have supernatural sanctions, this gives them a higher prestige and provides an additional incentive for complying with them.[1] Such sanctions and incentives, however, do not make them right unless they are found by experience to be so.

But whatever be thought of this interpretation of the complex interaction of morality and religion among peoples whose moral rules have a supernatural sanction, many, if not most, primitive peoples have developed and still practise a complex system of individual and social morality without any or with very little religious or supernatural sanction, and this seems to show that morality is in origin and authority independent of religion.[2]

This conclusion, drawn from the study of contemporary primitive people, receives some support from an examination of the relation between morality and religion, both among the early ancestors of men who are now advanced and in the systems of the great moral teachers and reformers of mankind. I can only touch briefly and dogmatically on this large subject.

It is true that many of the teachers and prophets who arose during the great moral and religious awakening which took place about the second quarter of the first millennium B.C. (i.e. about 700–400 B.C.) and which extended from Greece to China and from Egypt to Persia, put forward their moral and

---

[1] For the view that the function which religion fulfils among primitives is to " re-affirm " moral rules and to " strengthen and intensify " the sense of moral obligation, and not to create social obligations or to justify moral rules, see Radcliffe-Brown, *Religion and Society*, p. 8; Hogbin, *Law and Order*, pp. 143, 165, 200; Kardiner, *The Individual and His Society*, p. 234; Hobhouse, *Morals in Evolution*, p. 43; Richards, *Hunger and Work in a Savage Tribe*, pp. 189–90; Firth, *Primitive Polynesian Economy*, p. 223; Hocking, *Meaning of God in Human Experience*, p. 14.

[2] Cf. Bowman, *Studies in the Philosophy of Religion*, ii. 37, 72.

social doctrines in the name and with the authority of their gods. This is true of Zoroaster, whose enlightened moral teaching was enunciated in the name of Ahura Mazda. It is true of the remarkable succession of Hebrew prophets, whose revolutionary moral and social doctrines were put forward as the will of Yahweh. It is true of Iknaton, the moralist king of Egypt, who propounded the requirements of justice, truth and love in the name of Aton. But it is only very partially, if at all, true of Buddha, and not at all true of Confucius. The latter regarded the religion and ritual of his people with good-natured tolerance, but he did not seek from it any sanction for his moral doctrines which he propounded as the conditions of a way of life which is right and reasonable in itself. And yet the central principle of these doctrines, according to which a people with a high civilisation have ordered their lives for some 2500 years, is much the same as the golden rule of the Christian gospel. Nor is the connection of morality with religion and supernatural sanctions any more evident in the reflective moral awakening in Greece as we find it, for example, in the teaching of Socrates with his gospel of goodness as the end of life, knowledge as the means to goodness and critical enquiry, which will accept nothing that cannot justify itself before the bar of reason, as the method of attaining knowledge. It may also be added that those teachers and prophets who propounded their ethical doctrines in the name and with the authority of their gods, made it clear that, whatever other demands religion may make on man, no man can be regarded as really religious unless he is at any rate morally good. They demanded of their followers that they should love mercy and do justly as well as walk humbly with their God. And many, if not most, of them criticised the requirements of the established religion of their day in the light of their own moral insight.

What we find, then, is that neither in the case of contemporary primitive peoples, nor in the thought of the great moral teachers who developed it to its highest level, has morality always been connected with religion or supported by supernatural sanctions, and that the nature of the morality does not seem to differ greatly in the cases where it is and in those where it is not regarded as so sanctioned. The conclusion which I draw from these facts is that, both as regards its historical origin and the grounds of its rightness, morality is autonomous, carrying its authority within itself, whatever additional sanctions may from time to time be attached to it.

I am well aware that this conclusion still leaves unanswered many important questions about the relation between morality and religion, even among primitives. But it is the conclusion which specially concerns my argument. For if it is well-grounded we are justified in considering primitive morality by itself, without trying to answer many difficult and controversial questions about the nature of primitive religion. I want, however, in conclusion to sum up very briefly the influences which primitive man's magico-religious beliefs and ritual practices have exerted on, and the support they have given to, his individual and social morality. I need say little about some of them because I have described them already.

(1) When rules are given a religious and not merely a moral and social sanction, there is an additional incentive to comply with them. How far it is a moral incentive depends on the way in which the supernatural is conceived. It may merely lead to the right thing being done from the wrong motives; but there may be occasions when this is better than that the right thing should not be done at all.

(2) His magico-religious beliefs give primitive man the hope and confidence which enable him to face the difficulties and overcome the dangers with which his life is beset. The beliefs may be mistaken, but their psychological and social effects are very real. The practices in which they lead him to engage may not control the forces which he has not succeeded in understanding, but they put him in a condition in which he can face them with hope of success. Whether his attitude to the supernatural forces to which he appeals in his difficulties be that of humble prayer — the attitude of religion strictly so-called — or that of aggressive command like the magician, or, as more often happens, a mixture of or a compromise between the two (varying with his conception of the powers with which he is dealing), there is one respect in which the effect on him is the same. It provides him with an ally which he believes to be

stronger than the forces arrayed against him, an ally with whose assistance he will confidently proceed to face and conquer them.[1] This is an effect of religion specially emphasised by Malinowski. But as Radcliffe-Brown has pointed out,[2] there are occasions when religion produces not so much hope and confidence as a sense of seriousness and responsibility, even anxiety; and this attitude is very appropriate in situations where important matters of common concern are at stake.

(3) The ritual and ceremonial practices which religion requires, initiation rites, ceremonial dances, mortuary ritual, etc., produce important psychological and social effects. They refresh and reinvigorate the individual; they strengthen the bonds which bind the members of the group together; they promote goodwill and mutual trust. In these and other ways which we have already seen they promote the mental integrity of the individual and the social solidarity of the group.

(4) Some of the duties required of the individual by his religion are arduous and exacting and many of them are believed to be for the well-being of the community. Compliance with them therefore strengthens the self-discipline of the individual and his loyalty and devotion to the common good.

(5) The person who reproves wrongdoing or neglect of duty, or calls on men to undertake difficult and unpleasant tasks, in the name or with the authority of religion is in a very much stronger position than he who speaks merely in his own name or even as the representative of the community. He is less likely to be regarded by his neighbours as an impertinent meddler in their affairs. His adverse judgement is less likely to be resented, and his call for service is more likely to meet with a favourable response.

(6) There is still another way in which religion may influence morality. It may do so more directly and immediately than through the relatively external prescription of rules or the attaching of rewards and penalties to them, and it may affect character more profoundly than through the indirect effects of ritual and ceremonial practices. This happens when it

---

[1] Cf. Wallace, *Lectures and Essays on Natural Theology and Ethics*, pp. 192-3.

[2] *Taboo* (Frazer Lecture, 1939).

presents men with the conception of a supersensible reality which, whatever its other characteristics, is regarded as the embodiment of moral perfection and purity. The thought of such a being, especially when it is conceived in the form of a person, produces in the believer a profounder sense of the moral evil of wrongdoing and evokes in him a desire to reform and purify his own life so that it may approximate more closely to the perfection which he contemplates; and this desire tends to find expression both in worship and in a life of moral goodness. The consciousness of the abiding presence of such a being who evokes respect and loyalty, and to whom moral evil is regarded as disloyalty, provides a stimulus to moral steadfastness and an incentive to rightdoing, the importance of which cannot be over-estimated. Moreover, the belief that the ultimate power in the universe is on the side of goodness gives the believer an assurance that in his moral struggles he is not alone and that, despite appearances to the contrary, the good will prevail; and this assurance not only brings him an inner sense of peace and tranquillity, when powerful forces of evil are arrayed against him, but it also strengthens and sustains him in doing what he believes to be right when appearances might suggest that all effort is vain or that in being moral he is simply playing the fool.

Now we find such conceptions in one form or another in all the developed ethical religions, but if they exist among primitives our authorities have little to say about them. It is true that even if they were to be found among them, they would not be the most obvious or easily observable aspect of their religion; and therefore it may be unwise to deny entirely their presence and power in the lives of some individuals among them. Indeed there seems to be some evidence that among some ancestor-worshipping peoples respect for, and a sense of loyalty to, their dead ancestors, whom they regard as the ideal exemplars of the sort of persons they ought to be, mingles with and is often as strong an incentive to the observance of tribal custom as fear of any consequences to themselves which might result from the displeasure of their ancestors, or any sense of awe due to their supernatural status. So far as this is so, the experience of the wrongdoer is more akin to what we call the sense of alienation from God than to fear of punishment, here or hereafter. No doubt there are considerable differences in this respect between individuals and between peoples. But, as I have said, our authorities make little reference to such conceptions among primitives, and when they discuss the moral value of religion among them it is the other influences which I have mentioned that they specially emphasise.

But these undoubtedly great benefits which his magico-religious beliefs and practices confer on the primitive are sometimes bought at a heavy price. For while they make for social stability and solidarity, they tend to retard moral and social progress; while they give him hope and courage with which to face the problems and crises of life, they tend to prevent him from trying to understand his environment and to control it by his skill and energy. For magico-religious ritual is apt to be more rigid and less modifiable than secular rules, because its neglect or infringement is believed to be fraught with more desperate consequences. Accordingly, when moral and social duties are given a religious sanction, change and progress tend to be regarded as sins, liable to bring down on the individual or the community the wrath of supernatural powers. The reformer who wants to change existing customs tends to be classed with the sinner who rebels against them, and both are apt to be treated in the same way. Thus the action of the reformer comes to be regarded not merely as a crime against society, but as sacrilege — sin against its gods. Hence the proverbial fate of prophets and reformers, a fate usually meted out to them in the name of the established religion of their day.

It is true that the most difficult problem which any society or civilisation has to face is how to reconcile the requirements of individual initiative and personal development with those of the common good, how to combine the tolerance and openness to new ideas which is necessary for progress with the respect for established institutions and customs which is a condition of the stability of the moral and social order. In the precarious conditions of many primitive societies, where unity has to be maintained at the cost of life and survival, and where unity is apt to mean uniformity, there are many factors making for intolerance to would-be reformers. And though many of the greatest reformers have claimed to speak in its name, religion has always tended to be on the side of stability rather than progress; so that intimate association with it has not always been an unmixed blessing for morality.

In the same way, the belief in magic, however valuable it may be in promoting hope and confidence in the face of dangers and difficulties, tends to prevent men from trying to understand their environment and taking steps to control it. For example, the belief in rain magic has prevented men from undertaking schemes of irrigation, and the belief in curative magic has retarded the development of medicine.

What concerns us, however, is that, profound as may be the influences which the magico-religious beliefs and practices of primitives exercise on their individual and social life, the content of their moral codes and the principles governing their social institutions were not derived from, and are not dependent on, their religion. Religion may support them; they may be given supernatural sanctions; but they are of independent origin and authority, and therefore we are justified in considering them without further direct reference to religion.

MORAL RULES

W E have now considered a number of primitive ways of life. Each of them we regarded as being, in ultimate analysis, the result of the attempts of a particular people to give concrete embodiment to their idea of the good life. I have tried to show that the peoples who developed these ways of life and on the whole find them good are people like ourselves, with the same endowment of reason and passions, the same nature and needs, so that any differences between their ways of life, or between them and our own, cannot be explained as due to differences between the natures or the minds of the peoples who entertain them. We have also seen that each of them has a secular morality, that their moral ideas and ideals, the virtues they approve and the vices they condemn, do not derive their authority from religion, and that most of their moral rules are not regarded as obligatory merely or even mainly because of fear of supernatural powers.

We may assume, therefore, that the primitive moral consciousness proceeds on the same principle or principles as our own, and that its judgements are as much entitled to be regarded as deliverances of the moral consciousness as ours. What light, then, do they throw on the nature of morality, the principle or principles of moral judgement, the nature of the moral ideal, the authority of moral rules, the conditions of moral progress? How far are they consistent with, or capable of being explained by, or give support to recent and contemporary ethical theories which are based mainly on the study of the ways of life of white men and the moral ideas and ideals of Western civilisation? How far do they confirm or disprove the provisional theory of the structure of the moral life which I outlined in an earlier lecture? If the primitive moral consciousness proceeds on the same principle as our own, how are we to account for the great difference between many of its

351

moral judgements and ours ? These are some of the questions to which the consideration of primitive morality gives rise. I have time to consider only a few of the most central of them.

It might be thought more appropriate that I should devote all my time to the task of making explicit and illustrating the ethical theory which primitive moralities seem to suggest and support, rather than to showing that they are inconsistent with certain other ethical theories — always a thankless task. There are, however, certain advantages in following the latter, more indirect, course. For we are concerned not merely with primitive moral judgements but with the moral judgements of all men everywhere. We have, therefore, to consider how far any theory suggested by an analysis of primitive morality can account for civilised moral judgements ; just as we have to examine whether theories suggested by civilised morality can account for primitive moral judgements. And in considering civilised moral judgements, it would be unwise to dispense with the help of the careful and critical analyses of them given by recent ethical writers.

Moreover, the attempt to compare the anthropological evidence regarding primitive morality with some widely held contemporary ethical theories will help to bring into clearer relief than I have hitherto done certain aspects of primitive morality itself. It will also help to bring to light the differences between the presuppositions of the anthropologists, and of the methods which they have developed in their attempts to understand primitive ways of life, and some of the assumptions which not only underlie the methods of many contemporary ethical writers, but are also widespread in our ways of thinking about moral phenomena. It is desirable, therefore, that we should see the full range of the facts for which a satisfactory ethical theory must account — the moral judgements of all men everywhere — and that we should consider the presuppositions and methods of procedure of different ethical writers in the light of them. Moreover, if it is found that the anthropological evidence regarding primitive moral judgements is, in important respects, inconsistent with certain widely held contemporary theories, and with some common assumptions about moral facts which they presuppose, this may dispose the reader to consider more favourably the claims of the alternative theory which I am suggesting, a theory which, though not entirely without adherents among contemporary philosophers, is certainly very much out of fashion at present.

I think the most fundamental difference between the views of anthropologists dealing with primitives and most recent and contemporary ethical theorists is to be found in the difference between the answers which they respectively give to the question : What is the simplest unit of conduct which has to be taken into consideration in passing a considered moral judgement, or in trying to understand the moral judgement of another ? As I pointed out earlier, a moral judgement is a final or ultimate judgement, one from which there is no appeal to a higher court or a wider context. What, then, is the simplest entity, which is sufficiently self-contained to warrant a final judgement of rightness or goodness — a judgement which is not liable to require alteration or modification in the light of any further facts or factors ?

Recent ethical theorists tend to regard the units in question as relatively simple. They tend to use what I have called the method of isolation. They regard isolated, or at least isolable, elements in the moral life or moral ideal as capable of sustaining such a judgement. Thus it is held that the obligatoriness of certain moral rules can be recognised as self-evident, when the rules are considered by themselves apart from any context. The judgement that certain sorts of acts are right is regarded as final or ultimate, in the sense that it does not need any reason or justification beyond itself. It is true that the obligatoriness of such acts is no longer regarded as absolute but as prima facie, i.e. they are actually obligatory unless they conflict with more urgent obligations ; but the judgement that they have this obligatoriness is infallible or self-justifying without reference to any context. Again, certain ends or states of affairs or experiences are regarded as intrinsically good, by which is meant that they would be good even if they existed quite alone, even if there were nothing else in the universe. We find this view in a variety of forms — not only in the Ideal Utilitarianism of Moore, or combined with Intuitionism as by Ross, but also in some theories of the self-realisation type. Urban,[1] e.g., gives a list of values which, when considered by themselves, can, he thinks, be arranged on a scale which has universal validity.

We are not here concerned with the details of these views but only with the method of isolation by which they try to get rules, ends or values which have by themselves an absolute or self-evident claim that they should be obeyed, pursued or realised. It is worth pointing out, however, that, even if we could get such atomic absolutes the task of the moral agent would not be so easy as it might at first sight appear. For an act is not normally just an instance of one rule or just the pursuit of one end or just the realisation of one value. It may also be the violation of another rule, the neglect of another end or the denial of another value. And the real problem of the moral agent, in trying to discover what he ought to do, is to discover which rule is the more urgent, which intrinsic good or sum of intrinsic goods is the greater, which act will realise the higher value. The theories in question suggest no principle by which the moral agent can make his choice. They counsel him merely to do his best and trust his fallible judgement. But until some principle is forthcoming on which he can make this, his most crucial choice, the principles ' obey the most urgent rule ', ' produce the greatest amount of intrinsic good ' or ' realise the higher value ' are of little practical use to the moral agent.

What concerns us, however, is whether such atomic absolutes, which contain the grounds of their rightness or goodness within themselves, can in fact be found. The unanimous and oft-repeated view of recent and contemporary social anthropologists is that, among primitives, at least, they cannot. They hold in effect that the results of any attempt to apply the method of isolation to the moral judgements of primitives are not only valueless but misleading. Indeed, as we have seen, their main criticism of the earlier anthropologists is just that they used the method of isolation, and tried to understand primitive actions and customs and value-judgements without taking account of the cultural context which alone renders them

[1] *Fundamentals of Ethics*, ch. viii.

intelligible. According to their view, what we find among primitives is not rules whose obligatoriness is self-evident when they are considered in isolation, but rules which are the conditions of the working of certain interrelated institutions ; not acts which have intrinsic goods as consequences, but acts which are good in their context ; not a scale of values whose relative order can be decided in abstraction, but a system of values embodied in a way of life which determines their order of preference at any given moment.

I have already repeatedly quoted the views of anthropologists that we cannot understand any item in a primitive culture without taking account of its concrete setting in the context of the way of life of which it forms part ; and, in my description of the ways of life of particular primitive peoples, I illustrated in some detail the intimate interconnections between the elements of their ways of life. We see it in the items on their scales of value, in the provision which they make for different human needs, in the ends they pursue as good and in the duties which they consider binding. None of these can be understood by itself.

This of course does not mean that it is not legitimate, and even necessary, to distinguish the different elements in a way of life and to consider them separately. What it does mean is that we cannot appreciate the way in which they appear to the person who lives the life and passes judgements of value on them, unless we look at them in their context. Nor does it mean that the ways of life of most, or indeed perhaps of any, peoples are the consistent expression of one principle. Their degree of coherence varies from people to people, and the unity of the resulting patterns generally takes the form of functional interdependence between the parts, rather than the expression of a rationally coherent plan of life. Similar variations are to be found in the extent to which different individuals, even in the same community, enter into the spirit of their way of life and appreciate its pattern as a whole. But whatever be the degree of integration of the pattern and to whatever extent individuals appreciate it as a whole, the anthropological evidence suggests that their conception of it provides the operative ideal which determines their duties and obligations, that what appears to them right and good is conditioned by it, and that, therefore, however immediate and intuitive their judgements may seem, they are not unconditional or self-justifying, but at least partly dependent on, and conditioned by, the background of the way of life of the people concerned. In the discussion of moral questions this background is normally taken for granted ; and as long as it is common to all the individuals concerned in the discussion, the neglect of it, and of the way in which it conditions their judgements, need occasion no difficulty. But when we consider the differences between the value-judgements of different peoples, and especially of primitives and ourselves, the relevance of the different ways of life which they presuppose becomes clear. We find that they are all conditioned by the context in relation to which they are made. The only judgement which is strictly unconditional and self-justifying is that passed on a way of life as a whole.[1]

Now if this view is sound and if it applies to civilised as well as to primitive morality, however useful the analyses of the contemporary ethical theorists to whom I referred may be for certain purposes, their prima facie obligations, their intrinsic goods, and their scales of value are the results of undue simplification and abstraction, and the judgements on acts and ends to which their method of isolation leads must be reconsidered, and it may be corrected, when the acts and ends are looked at in the context of the way of life in which they actually occur. For what the view of the anthropologists really amounts to is that the simplest self-contained unit of conduct, which can justify or render intelligible a final moral judgement, is a way of life as a whole, or at least a very substantial part of such a way of life. I want, therefore, to consider in some detail how far theories which proceed by the method of isolation are consistent with the facts of primitive morality ; and how far the views of the anthropologists about primitive morality apply also to civilised morality ; and, if they do, what implications this has for ethical theory. In this lecture I propose to discuss

---

[1] This still leaves open the question of the criterion by which the relative value of different ways of life themselves is to be tested — the question of the relation of the operative ideals, with which we are here concerned, to the formal or ultimate ideal of which they are all more or less imperfect embodiments. This question I shall consider in my last lecture.

these questions with special reference to moral rules. In the next I shall consider them with reference to goods and scales of value.

Those who proceed by the method of isolation contend that certain moral rules are self-evident, unmediated, containing the grounds of their rightness within themselves. Now rules which have this character should be recognised as such by all who have the capacity to grasp the concepts involved in them and have sufficiently attended to them. And if such rules are recognised at all, they should be recognised as being strictly universal. For their rightness is independent of any context and, therefore, holds in every context. Their rightness is independent of, and additional to, the goodness of any state of affairs to which their observance leads, or of which it may be a condition. That certain moral rules have this self-evidence and strict universality and independent rightness is the claim of the intuitionists. What we have to consider is how far this claim is consistent with the facts about primitive morality.

In considering this question we have to ask : (1) How far do primitives recognise as binding the same rules as we do, in particular those which intuitionists claim to be self-evident? And (2) so far as they do recognise them, how far do they regard them as self-evident or self-authenticating? There is a way of interpreting these rules according to which it may be said that all primitives recognise some, and some primitives recognise all of them, but only within definitely prescribed limits. And this seems to me to be sufficient to show that they understand the concepts used in them and have sufficiently attended to them to recognise them as self-evident, if they are in fact self-evident. They have satisfied the two conditions usually regarded as necessary and sufficient for such recognition.

What, then, is the reservation subject to which they recognise them? Primitives do not recognise the rules which they regard as right as universal in the sense that they apply to their relations with all men. There is always, or almost always, a group of men beyond which they do not regard themselves as having any duty to the outsider. This in-group may be the family, the clan, the tribe, the group of tribes, the inhabitants of a certain locality, and so on; but there is always an in-group and an out-group; and the members of the latter are not regarded as subjects of rights or objects of duties.

Is this state of affairs consistent with the view that the rightness of the rules in question is self-evident, and that the rules are therefore strictly universal and applicable to the relations between all moral beings? It seems to me that there are two, and only two, possible ways in which the intuitionist might try to show that it is; but I do not think either of them will account for the known facts.

One way is to hold that, in so far as the primitive recognises the outsider as a fellow-man, he does recognise prima facie obligations to him; but that fear of the outsider gives rise to a stronger obligation to promote his own welfare and that of his group, and that this overrides the obligations which he recognises towards the outsider as a man. Now it is quite true that many primitive people entertain very strange ideas about outsiders, even about those who live beyond a mountain range, an arm of the sea or a belt of forest, let alone about those who live in more remote parts. They are unknown and the unknown is apt to be a source of danger and dread. It is also true that many primitives have good reasons to fear the hostility of outsiders. But there is no evidence whatsoever that they do recognise obligations to the outsider, and that they are just overborne by stronger obligations to the in-group. All the evidence points to the opposite conclusion, that they recognise no obligations to the genuine outsider and that they feel no compunction in treating him in ways which involve breaking every rule in the moral code of the in-group.

The other possible way of trying to reconcile the facts with the intuitionist theory is to contend that primitives do not recognise outsiders as human or at least as moral beings like themselves. It is, however, difficult to accept this contention. For as Goldenweiser has pointed out,[1] it is difficult to believe that one dog will recognise another as his fellow whatever the difference in size or shape or colour or breed, and that a man will not do the same. But even if we accept this contention, while it might explain the failure of primitives to recognise any

[1] *Anthropology*, p. 27.

obligations towards persons from remote parts of the earth whose language and habits they do not understand, and about whose purposes and powers they are ignorant and often entertain very strange notions, it would not explain their failure to recognise such obligations — if they are really self-evident — to members of neighbouring peoples with whom their relations are relatively intimate and often not unfriendly. It is not true that all primitives regard their neighbours as dangerous enemies. Some of them are quite friendly and unwarlike, and yet most of them do not recognise any obligations to those outside the group.

Moreover, if this contention were true, members of one group would recognise either all or none of the moral rules of the in-group as binding in their relations to members of another group. But this is not what we in fact seem to find. The line of demarcation between the in-group and the out-group is not so clearly defined as it is often represented. There are sometimes intermediate groups to whom, or to some of whom, either all or some of the members of a particular community recognise some obligations and not others. For example, the Trobrianders recognise the inhabitants of neighbouring islands such as the Amphletts and Dobu as human beings like themselves, and they engage in some forms of exchange with them as in the institution of the Kula. The partners in these exchanges recognise duties to one another, duties of promise-keeping, protection, hospitality, friendship and so on, but outside such partnerships there seems to be no recognition of any moral rules as applicable to the relations between the members of the communities concerned. They will cheat and deceive and, until the white man prohibited it, they would kill one another without any sort of compunction. Thus a Trobriander will recognise moral rules as applicable to his relations to a native of Dobu who is his partner in the institution of the Kula, but not in his relations to him simply as a man or a Dobuan. In other words, he finds some forms of co-operation with the members of another group good and he recognises as obligatory, in his relations to them, the rules required to make such co-operation possible ; and the close association with them which such co-operation involves creates a situation in which man's natural interest in his fellow-men and their welfare has an opportunity to assert itself; and as a result other moral rules than those which are involved in the particular form of co-operation are extended to his relations with them. Again, many primitive people recognise a duty of hospitality to the stranger and of respect for the person of messengers and heralds, while they may recognise no other duties either to the individuals concerned or to the other members of the groups from which they come. We find a similar state of affairs in the relations of some natives to the white men who live among them and with whom they are on friendly terms. They seem to regard some but not others of their moral rules as applicable to their relations with them. Thus the Trobrianders feel gratitude for benefit received from white men and an obligation to make a return for them; but while they condemn stealing among themselves, Malinowski tells us that they do not regard stealing from the white man as " a breach of law, morality, or gentlemanly manners ".[1]

I could quote many other examples, both from the peoples whose ways of life I have already described and from other primitive peoples, to show that all the moral rules which they regard as right they do not regard as applicable to their relations with all whom they recognise as human beings like themselves. But I must be content with one further illustration. I take it from one of the very few peoples whose attitude to breaches of their moral and social rules, both among the members of a group and between the members of different groups, has been the subject of a special investigation.[2] They are the inhabitants of Wogeo, a small island off the coast of New Guinea. The island is about fifteen miles in circumference and has about 900 inhabitants; and all, or almost all, the adults among them know one another. They are relatively untouched by Western civilisa-tion. When Hogbin went to carry out his investigation in 1934, he was the first white man who had ever lived on the island. The island is divided into five districts, each of which consists of several villages, and in each village there are two and in

[1] *Crime and Custom*, p. 118.
[2] The results of the investigation are reported in the *Journal of the Royal Anthropological Institute* (1938), pp. 223-62.

some cases three clans. For some purposes the clan is the unit, and the relations between clansmen are very close and intimate; but for many other purposes the unit is the village, and the natives recognise the implications of their common citizenship and the conditions necessary for co-operation. Members of different districts, while recognising one another as human beings, tend to regard each other as strangers if not foreigners; but the same culture and customs prevail throughout the island.

Hogbin illustrates the state of affairs which he found by the attitude of the natives to theft and adultery, which he tells us is typical of their attitude to breaches of moral rules in general. In the abstract all the natives regard theft and adultery as wrong. They have been so taught from their youth up. They strongly disapprove of them between the members of a clan or village, whether their own or another makes no difference. Their disapproval is less marked when they are committed against a member of another village within the same district; and when they are committed against someone from another district they are not considered wrong at all. For example, they will openly boast of adultery with the wife of a man from another district; but they feel embarrassed and ashamed in the presence of a member of their own district, and especially of their own clan, whom they have wronged in this way; even though he is not aware, and they know he is not aware, that they have done so.

The same principle applies to their attitude to theft. For instance, some of them killed and ate a pig belonging to a man from another district which had strayed into their village. In discussing this incident with Hogbin the natives did not try to find extenuating circumstances for their action; they just denied that it was theft, though they would have regarded it as theft if the pig belonged to a man from their own district. Hogbin succeeded in getting the more thoughtful of them to admit that it really was theft, and in recognising the inconsistency of saying that theft is wrong and yet that killing and eating a pig belonging to a man from another district is not. He says the natives found it difficult to explain away this inconsistency; but no doubt they regarded the act as theft in the sense of taking another man's property, but not as theft in the sense of the wrongful taking of another man's property, i.e. not as theft in the sense in which theft is morally wrong. Be this as it may, we are told that they still continued to denounce action of this kind within the village (any village and not just their own), but failed to recognise it as equally or indeed at all wrong when committed against a member of another district. And they were prepared to give reasons for their view. They pointed out that theft was inconsistent with the relations between members of a clan or village, that it would involve a disturbance of the life of the group, and that if it became general the group would disintegrate; whereas the relations between members of different districts were less intimate and involved an element of suspicion, if not even of hostility.

Whether we regard this attitude as due to a lack of imaginative capacity to put themselves in the owner's place, or, as seems to me more likely, to the lack of any form of co-operation between the different districts and, therefore, to the absence of any need to comply with the conditions necessary to make co-operation effective, and the absence of social sentiments which result from co-operation, what is significant from our present point of view is that they do not regard the moral rules, which they recognise as right in the relations between the members of the smaller group, as applicable in their relations to all the inhabitants of the island, though they undoubtedly regard them all as human like themselves, and though their relations with them are on the whole not unfriendly. This clearly shows that they do not recognise their moral rules as rules of prima facie obligation, whose claims are overborne by more urgent claims. In other words, it is not the sort of act or forbearance as such or in its own right which they regard as obligatory. For the same sort of act is regarded as right in one context and wrong in another.

Hogbin produces evidence that the judgements of these natives are genuinely moral judgements, that they are not deterred from wrongdoing merely by fear of punishment, that they have their ideals of conduct and that these relate to the inner as well as the outer aspect of conduct, that they are no strangers to moral conflict and successful resistance to temptation, and that they not only experience but value the satisfaction of having a good conscience. One native, e.g., is reported as saying that when an " opportunity to do evil presented itself and he declined to take it, ' his inside felt good ' " ; [1] and he seemed to regard that as a sufficient reward for following the path of duty.

The evidence regarding the attitude of primitives towards the rules which they recognise as binding between the members of the in-group, the group which is always regarded as fully human and moral beings, seems to confirm the conclusion that such rules are not regarded as self-authenticating or carrying the grounds of their rightness within themselves. It is true, as I have said, that there is a way of interpreting moral rules according to which we may say that, as between the members of the in-group, many primitives recognise most, and some recognise all, the rules which we recognise as binding. And this way of interpreting moral rules seems to me to have misled many people into minimising the differences between primitive moral rules and ours. But according to this interpretation moral rules are mere tautologies, not significant or synthetic statements. Moreover, the terms used in them have different meanings in different communities; and so the rules do not really tell us what conduct is considered right in different communities. If, e.g., by a lie is meant not all deliberate telling of what is known to be untrue, but only such forms of untruth as are disapproved by the community to which the individual making the judgement belongs, if by homicide or adultery is meant only such killing of another human being or such inter- course between a married man and a woman not his wife as is disapproved by the particular society, then the propositions, that lies, homicide and adultery are wrong, are universal and self-evident among all peoples. But in that case the terms ' lie ', ' homicide ', and ' adultery ' have different meanings in different communities, and in each community the propositions are merely verbal, indicating how the terms are being used. If, on the other hand, by a lie is meant any deliberate mis-statement of fact with intent to deceive, by homicide the killing of any man, by adultery any intercourse between a married man and a

[1] *Journal of the Royal Anthropological Institute* (1938), p. 262.

woman not his wife, the proposition that all lies, homicide and adultery are wrong, does not accurately describe the beliefs of many, or perhaps of most, primitive peoples.

Similar considerations apply to all other rules. Among all primitives some, and among most primitives all, moral rules admit of exceptions which are not only permissible but obligatory. It is true that most of these exceptions are not recognised as exceptions, because, as we illustrated in the case of the Australians [1] and the Trobrianders,[2] they are not thought of in relation to the rules in question but as the requirements of other institutions. Instead, therefore, of being thought of as e.g. lies, homicide or adultery, they are thought of as e.g. loyalty to a friend, regard for the welfare of the group, taking vengeance on an enemy, consecrating a new village or generosity to a friend.

It is, of course, true that we too admit exceptions to many of our moral rules, and that this is admitted by, and quite consistent with the contention of those who hold that the prima facie rightness of some of them is apprehended as self-evident. The point I want to make is rather that the interpretations which different peoples put on the terms used, even in the rules which they seem to have in common, are so different, and the exceptions which they admit to the rules vary so widely that it is difficult to say that the rules which they recognise are the same rules in any precise sense. These differences tend to be concealed by the use of general terms, and especially general terms like lies and murder, which not only describe facts but also convey moral judgements. For example, to say that a statement is a mis-statement of fact is merely to describe it, but to say that it is a lie is not merely to describe it but to pass a moral judgement on it. Now the factual part of the meaning of a term may vary, while the moral judgement involved in its use may remain the same, and vice versa. It is failure to recognise this which is responsible for the confusion to which I am calling attention, the confusion, that is, between the sense in which moral rules are universal but only verbal tautologies and the sense in which they are significant or synthetic, but generalisations true in the main and yet having many exceptions.

[1] Above, pp. 217-19.　　　[2] Above, pp. 159-60.

Even so acute an observer as Boas seems to be guilty of this confusion ; and as a result he regards the moral rules of primitives as more akin to our own than the evidence warrants. " There is no evolution of moral ideas ", he writes. " All the vices that we know, lying, theft, murder, rape, are discountenanced in the life of equals in the closed society. There is progress in ethical conduct, based on the recognition of larger groups who participate in the rights enjoyed by the members of the closed society." [1] By the closed society Boas means what I have called the in-group ; and his contention seems to be that the only difference in moral ideas between the most primitive and the most advanced peoples is the greater extent of the group to whom moral considerations apply. In the relations between the members of the in-group, those who are regarded as moral beings, all peoples recognise the same moral rules and the same virtues and vices. Now if this only meant that the fundamental nature of the moral consciousness is the same everywhere, I should entirely agree. But in saying that the same moral rules, the same virtues and vices, are recognised by the primitives and ourselves, Boas seems to have been misled by the ambiguity of such words as lying, murder, theft and so on — terms which not only describe forms of conduct but convey moral judgements.

It is true that among all peoples there are forms of conduct regarded as right and others regarded as wrong ; and these relate, among other things, to life, property, sex relations and intercommunication between individuals. Now if by murder, theft, adultery and lying, we mean the forms of conduct disapproved by particular peoples in relation to life, property, sex relations and intercommunication, we can say that they all discountenance them. But this does not mean that they all discountenance the same acts or sorts of acts. For the forms of conduct in relation to life, property, etc. of which different peoples disapprove and which they, therefore, describe by the terms, murder, theft, etc., vary from people to people. Take, e.g., murder. When, as Boas himself tells us,[2] a Chuckchee son kills his father before he loses his vigour and vitality, because he believes that a man will continue for ever in the

[1] Boas, *Anthropology and Modern Life*, p. 219.   [2] *Ibid.* p. 186.

state in which he is at the time of his death, the Chuckchee do not regard this as murder, but as a filial act, the discharge of a difficult and painful duty.   Or when a Bantu parent kills one of his twin offspring to prevent, as he believes, disaster to himself and his people, his act is not regarded as murder.   Indeed Boas himself provides the corrective to the passage which I have quoted above, when he tells us in an earlier work : [1] " The person who slays an enemy in revenge for wrongs done, a youth who kills his father before he gets decrepit in order to enable him to continue a vigorous life in the world to come, a father who kills his child as a sacrifice for the welfare of his people, act from such entirely different motives, that psychologically a comparison of their activities does not seem permissible.   It would seem much more proper to compare the murder of an enemy in revenge with destruction of his property for the same purpose, or to compare the sacrifice of a child on behalf of the tribe with any other action performed on account of strong altruistic motives, than to base our comparison on the common concept of murder."

Whether we call such acts murder because we consider them wrong, or refuse to call them murder because the people concerned consider them right, it is clear that they are forms of killing which they approve and we disapprove.   Similarly, both we and the Australian Aborigines may be said to condemn adultery, but, as we have seen,[2] there are acts such as wifelending which we consider adultery and they do not, but regard as obligatory.   It is, therefore, misleading to say that the primitives and ourselves disapprove of the same vices ; and nothing but confusion can result from a failure to distinguish the forms of killing and intercourse of which they disapprove from those of which we disapprove, despite the use of the common terms murder and adultery, in the sense of wrongful killing and intercourse, applied to both.

Now these considerations have a direct bearing on the intuitionist view that the rightness of certain moral rules is self-evident and apprehended by an act of direct insight.   Ross seems to recognise that this is so ; and while he does not, so far as I know, discuss the evidence in detail, he assumes that

---

[1] Boas, *The Mind of Primitive Man*, pp. 57-8.   [2] Above, p. 217.

the differences between the moral rules of different peoples are less than the facts which we have been considering suggest. He does not go as far as Boas and hold that all men recognise the same moral rules; nor is it necessary for him to do so in order to reconcile the facts with his theory. But in several places he implies, and at least once he explicitly states, that the differences between the rules accepted by different peoples apply only to the more specific " rules such as those which prescribe monogamous marriage and forbid unchastity ", and not to " the very general rules " [1] such as truth-telling and promise-keeping, which he claims to be self-evident. The former he regards as empirical generalisations, " the crystallised product of the experience and reflection of many generations " ; [2] the latter he regards as necessary truths, apprehended by direct insight.[3] But if we have correctly interpreted the anthropological evidence, it would seem to show that the differences apply to all rules, the more general as well as the more specific. For if a proposition is to be apprehended as self-evident, the concepts involved in it must be conceived and stated in a precise and unambiguous way as is the case with mathematical propositions to which the intuitionists often compare moral rules. And in view of the variations of the meanings of the terms used in moral rules from people to people, it is impossible to state even the more general rules with the necessary precision and yet claim universal recognition for them.

It has often been pointed out that even among ourselves, where acts and sorts of acts are interpreted against the background of a common way of life, few, if any, of the terms which we use in moral rules have the precision and freedom from ambiguity which would entitle us to claim self-evidence for the propositions in which they occur. When, e.g., we say that the obligatoriness of promise-keeping is self-evident, what precisely are we to understand by a promise ? Is a ' promise ' extracted under physical torture or threat of blackmail a promise in the required sense ? And even if we say that the promise must be

---

[1] Ross, *Foundations of Ethics*, p. 312.   [2] *Ibid.* p. 174.
[3] Failure to apprehend them is, therefore, attributed by the intuitionists to mental immaturity, a view which I examined in Lecture X.

freely given, is a promise, however freely given, to assist in a burglary, or to show favouritism to a candidate for an appointment, or to give financial assistance to another man, when the promise was made as the result of misrepresentation by him as to his means, a promise within the meaning of the rule? Again, in considering whether an act of promise-making comes within the scope of the rule, is any account to be taken, and if so how much, of unforeseen changes in the situation contemplated when the promise was made? When we ask what promises ought to be made, and if made ought to be kept, it is by no means easy to get an answer that will command universal assent even among ourselves, let alone among all peoples. Similar considerations apply to other rules, most of which are even less precise. We should tell the truth, but how much, to whom and on what occasions? We should not steal, but what taking of property is theft? We should make a return for services rendered, but what and how much should be given in return for a particular service, and indeed what is a ' service ' in the required sense? If we reply : ' What is considered right by our own society ' the rule becomes a tautology, and in addition it is not precise; if we give any other answer the rule fails to command anything like universal assent.[1]

Thus while the normal application of many of the terms used in moral rules is clear enough, there is a considerable margin where this is not so, and we have to consider the context of acts in order to discover how they should be characterised. Intuitionists themselves seem to me at times to admit this, implicitly if not explicitly. For example, in answering criticisms of the view that the obligatoriness of promise-keeping is self-evident, Ross [2] insists, and it seems to me rightly insists, on the need to take account of the ' spirit ' of a promise; and he calls attention to the fact that there are " implicit conditions and qualifications ", " underlying assumptions " and " tacit conditions " subject to which the promise has to be interpreted.

[1] For other examples of ambiguities in the terms used in so-called self-evident rules, see Campbell, *Moral Intuition and the Principle of Self-realisation* (British Academy Lecture, 1948), pp. 5-6 ; Russell, " Ideals and Practice " in *Philosophy* (April 1942) ; Macbeath, *Proceedings of the Aristotelian Society*, Supplementary Vol. xx. (1946), pp. 103-4.

[2] *Op. cit.* pp. 94 ff.

Similar considerations apply to other prima facie obligations, most obviously to reparation for injuries and return for services rendered. The implication of this seems to me to be that we must think of such obligations subject to the conditions of a way of life, as interpreted in the spirit of that way of life by those who actually live it. And if this is so, we are far from considering promises or other sorts of acts which are regarded as obligatory in isolation, apart from any context or conditions.

Thus, even among one people we find a degree of ambiguity and lack of precision in the terms used in moral rules, which seems to be incompatible with the claim that their rightness is self-evident. And when we compare the meaning of such terms as used by different peoples, and especially by primitives and ourselves, the ambiguity is much greater and the precision much less. Until these rules are made precise, it is difficult to see how their claim to self-evidence can be granted; and in the degree to which they are made even relatively precise, it is impossible to claim that they are universally recognised as right, let alone as self-evidently right, even in their application to the in-group among primitives or to all men among ourselves.

It is, of course, true that any tolerable form of social life requires that there should be rules governing the relations between persons in regard to such matters as intercommunication, return for services rendered, sex relations, respect for life and property, etc., and that they should be generally obeyed. And the rules contained in lists of prima facie obligations are in a general way such obvious conditions of individual and social well-being that most of them are included in the moral codes of most peoples. Their value, and indeed their fundamental importance, in this sense is not in question here. What is in question is the ground of their rightness — whether they contain it within themselves and are therefore self-evident, or whether they derive it from the form of life whose conditions they are. My contention is that the ambiguity of the terms used, the great variety of the ways in which the rules are construed by different peoples and of the exceptions which they admit to the rules which they recognise, show that the rules lack the definiteness and precision necessary to self-evident intuitions; and that the rightness of the rules themselves, in those cases in which they are recognised as right, the ways in which they are construed, the exceptions to them which are regarded as justified, and the relative order of urgency which is assigned to them, are explicable by, and derive their authority from, the way of life of the people concerned. In other words, they have not a rightness which is independent of the goodness of the state of affairs whose conditions they are.

This conclusion is further supported by the fact that some primitive people do not recognise some of the so-called self-evident rules as in any way binding, unless conformity to them is regarded as being for the good either of particular individuals or of the group as a whole. It is not just that they regard exceptions to them as right when their requirements clash with those of other rules: they recognise no obligation at all to obey them as such, i.e. unless obedience to them promotes a state of affairs which they independently recognise as good. Take, e.g., the rule of truth-telling. Junod, as we have seen, reports that the Tonga do not regard a breach of this rule as wrong unless it harms someone. This is not because they do not understand what lying is. For they condemn and punish both perjury in court and defamation of character. They do so, however, not because they regard lying as such as wrong but because such lies harm others, either in their reputation or through interfering with the administration of justice.

The Tonga are by no means unique in this respect. According to Smith and Dale, a similar state of affairs exists among the Ba-Ila, another Bantu tribe. This highly intelligent people have a detailed code of morals, and they teach it to their youths during initiation. " Their ideas about family duties and privileges ", we are told,[1] " scarcely differ in any way from our own "; and they have a system of justice and judicial administration not unlike that of the Tonga. Yet they neither regard truth as a virtue nor lying as a vice. " Among themselves ", Smith and Dale write,[2] " they lie in the most barefaced and strenuous manner . . . without the least shame. They lie often when it is to their advantage to tell the truth."

[1] Smith and Dale, *The Ila-speaking Peoples of Northern Rhodesia*, i. 284.
[2] *Ibid.* i. 379.

And in case we should conclude from this that they are amoral, our authorities state explicitly that this is not so. " Immoral they may be," they write, " they are not unmoral ".[1] " The principles of conduct are there and they are well known ", they continue, but they do not include truth-telling. Other rules they sometimes break ; the rule to tell the truth they do not recognise. It is not among the virtues taught to their youths during initiation ; and in their folk-lore, which, we are told, faithfully reflects the character of the people, success comes " by lying and cheating ", " by downright chicane ", " by treachery ", " by promises made and not fulfilled ", and so on.[2]

Smith and Dale offer a possible explanation of this attitude to lying. " Much lying ", they say,[3] " may be attributed to their sense of politeness ; they do not wish to hurt one's feelings." But they recognise that such an explanation can at best be only partial. Nor can we attribute this attitude to incapacity to understand what lying is or to not having attended to it. Like the Tonga, they condemn lying by a witness in court ; and Smith and Dale called their attention to what they regarded as the nature and evils of lying, but the Ba-Ila still held that they saw nothing wrong with lying as such.

Contrast with this the attitude of the Manus people of the Admiralty Islands, a people with a much less keen sense of social justice and, in other ways, less advanced morally than the Bantu. The Manus moral code, as we have seen, includes strict rules of truth-telling and promise-keeping ; and they regard these rules as having a powerful supernatural sanction. For them one of the two supreme virtues is a high level of commercial morality, and this requires honesty and mutual trust. In case we should imagine that the supernatural sanction will explain the difference between the Manus and the Bantu attitude to truth-telling, we may note that the Murray Islanders of the Torres Straits, a still more primitive people whose morality is entirely secular, have an equally strict rule of truth-telling.[4]

What, then, is the explanation of this difference of attitude to truth-telling ? It might be suggested that differences in the

[1] Ibid. i. 343.   [2] Ibid. ii. 438 ff.   [3] Ibid. i. 379.
[4] Haddon in Frazer Lectures (1922–32), p. 217.

economic conditions and the natural environments of the peoples concerned provide an explanation. The Tonga and the Ba-Ila are agriculturists who till the soil and rear cattle; and the land which they occupy is relatively infertile and sparsely populated. Their kraals or small villages are often separated by considerable distances. Each is relatively self-sufficient. There is little trade with or dependence on the members of other kraals. Mutual trust and confidence between the members of different kraals is, therefore, relatively unimportant for them. In the Manus way of life, on the other hand, commercial transactions — some of them based on a credit system — play a very important part. Such a form of life could not succeed without a considerable measure of mutual confidence and the virtues which make confidence possible. Therefore, truth-telling and promise-keeping rank high in the Manus code. But I do not think that this can be accepted as a satisfactory explanation. For one thing it is difficult to say whether the Manus attitude to truth-telling and promise-keeping is the cause or the effect of their particular form of economic life; and no doubt the one tends to support and strengthen the other. In any case, this explanation could not account for the attitude of the Murray Islanders, among whom commerce, though not unknown, plays a relatively unimportant part. In addition, the Bantu kraals are only relatively independent. Members of one kraal have to get their wives from another; and the members of different neighbouring kraals all owe allegiance to the same headman or chief, who administers justice between them in cases of dispute. Moreover, the Bantu attitude to lying applies not merely to relations between members of different kraals but also between members of one kraal.

The real explanation of the difference of attitude to truth-telling is, I think, to be found in the important part which the belief in black magic or sorcery plays in the life of the Bantu and its relative insignificance in the lives of the Manus and the Murray Islanders. If a man believes, as the Bantu does, that any of his neighbours may be, and that some of them in fact are, endowed with supernatural powers which may be used to do him or his neighbours harm; and if he further believes that giving them information provides them with the means of using these powers, we have a state of affairs in which not mutual trust and confidence but mutual suspicion and fear are likely to flourish. In such circumstances, truth-telling is not likely to be regarded as a virtue except in situations like giving evidence in court, where truth-telling is likely to result in good to others and lying in harm to them.

When *we* think of truth-telling and promise-keeping as right, we think of them in relation to conditions in which the possession of accurate knowledge and the performance of what is promised are on the whole good, independently of any rightness of telling the truth and keeping promises as such. Under such conditions it is obvious that truth-telling and promise-keeping have a value, whether or not they have, in addition to that value, an independent rightness. But in a way of life riddled with the belief in black magic, the free interchange of information is likely to do more harm than good. This is the state of affairs among both the Tonga and the Ba-Ila, whereas among the Manus and the Murray Islanders black magic plays a very insignificant role. What we find, then, is that wherever the possession or interchange of information is not regarded as good, truth-telling is not regarded as obligatory; and this suggests that its rightness, where it is regarded as obligatory, does not belong to it as such, but is dependent on the goodness of the state of affairs of which it is a condition.

In further confirmation of this interpretation of the facts, and in case it might be thought that the difference of attitude to truth-telling is a geographical difference between the Bantu and the natives of the Pacific islands, we may note that there are many Pacific islands in which the belief in black magic is rife, and that wherever this is the case the rule of truth-telling is not to be found. If, e.g., we consider the moral code of the natives of Dobu — the home of sorcery *par excellence* — we find no rule of truth-telling.[1] Even perjury in court (since courts have been established by the white man) is not regarded by the natives as wrong. In the atmosphere of fear and suspicion and hatred which exists in Dobu, there are even fewer than among the Bantu of the conditions which would make the free

[1] The facts about the natives of Dobu are taken from Fortune, *Sorcerers of Dobu*.

interchange of information contribute to individual and social well-being. The traveller from one part of the island to another has to go round the villages on the way in case he should use magic against person or property, or gather the information which would enable him to do so. Children are used to spy on their parents; and the surviving partner to a marriage is liable to be accused of having killed his or her spouse by magic. In such circumstances it is natural that truth-telling should not be regarded as a virtue nor lying as a vice. Nevertheless, even in Dobu, a certain minimum of co-operation and of the mutual trust required to make it possible is essential to any form of social life. But the amount of it is very strictly limited, and it is significant that it tends to be confined to circumstances in which, and to occur between persons between whom, the powers of black magic are believed to be either non-existent or less effective.

Now all this suggests that the rule of truth-telling is regarded as obligatory only in the societies and within the limits in which it is believed, in the light of the beliefs which are entertained about human beings and their natural and supernatural environment, that a free interchange of information is a condition of or contributes towards individual and social well-being. I believe the differing attitudes of different peoples to other rules could be explained on the same principle. I find no evidence of any primitive people who recognise any rule as right unless general compliance with it in the spirit of their way of life seems to them, in the light of their view of the human situation, likely to result in a state of affairs or to contribute to a form of life which they regard as on the whole good.

This conclusion is also supported by the testimony of field workers about the attitude which natives take to the rules which they do recognise as right. Junod, as we have seen, tells us again and again that the Tonga regard their rules of conduct as right not, as he puts it, because breaches of them are regarded as immoral,[1] but because such breaches would be disruptive of their way of life, or detrimental to the good either of the

---

[1] By immoral, Junod, I think, means recognised as opposed to the will of God.

group as a whole or of some of its members. We get similar testimony from Haddon about the Murray Islanders, and from many others.

Apart from the evidence which I submitted to show that the primitive mind is not markedly inferior in powers to the civilised, the examples of their moral rules which I have quoted should by now have made it clear that, if primitives do not recognise particular rules as binding or do not regard those which they do recognise as self-evident, it is neither because they lack the capacity to grasp the concepts used in them nor because they have failed to attend to them. It may well be that there are some primitive people who do not formulate such rules in abstract terms, though there are others who do. We find such formulation of them, e.g., in the instruction given to the youth of some tribes during initiation and in the discussions which take place in the courts of justice of the Bantu. But even those who do not explicitly formulate their rules in abstract terms should still be able to appreciate their rightness and their self-evidence, if they are in fact self-evident. For, as the intuitionists themselves admit,[1] the way in which people come to recognise the self-evidence of such propositions as are really self-evident is by seeing their truth in particular cases, and, in so doing, seeing the universal in the particular. And, of course, all peoples have seen plenty of concrete examples of the sorts of act whose prima facie rightness is claimed by intuitionists to be self-evident. If, then, as the evidence suggests, primitives do not recognise their self-evidence, and if the moral judgements of primitives are genuine pronouncements of the moral consciousness, it is difficult to accept the view that the rules in question are really self-evident in the required sense, i.e. evident to all who have the capacity to grasp them and have had the opportunity of attending to them.

Moreover, many primitive people regard as obviously right rules which we do not recognise, and which even seem to us abhorrent, e.g. rules about wife-lending, scalp-hunting, infanticide of twins or the punishment of one man for the sins of another. I believe a detailed examination of these rules, in the

[1] Ross, *Foundations of Ethics*, p. 320.

context of the ways of life of the peoples who think them right, would show that they, too, are regarded as obligatory, because, in view of the beliefs these people entertain, the rules seem to them to be conditions of a way of life which they regard as good.

But, even if the moral rules recognised by primitives as right thus appear to be relative to the ways of life of the peoples who recognise them, there is an important sense in which they are not relative. They are not relative to the individual moral agent or to his inclinations or desires or likings. As far as the members of the in-group to whom moral considerations are regarded as applicable are concerned, moral rules are universal in the sense that if it is right for one individual to act in a particular way in certain circumstances, it would be right for anyone else similarly situated to behave in the same way. In that sense primitive people claim objective validity for their moral rules. They do not admit that there is anything arbitrary or capricious or strictly individual about them.

Let me try to sum up the results of this lengthy survey of the attitude of primitive peoples to their moral rules : (1) Few, if any, primitive people regard their moral rules as universal in the sense that they apply to all men. Some of them do not regard all their moral rules as applicable to all even of those to whom some of them are applicable. (2) While many moral rules abstractly stated may appear to be common to the codes of many peoples, the interpretations which different peoples put on the terms used in them, and the exceptions to them which they regard as right, are so different that the rules in question, in any sense in which they can be said to be common to most peoples, lack the precision and freedom from ambiguity necessary to any rules which are to be apprehended as self-evident. (3) Many people fail to recognise as right at all some of the rules regarded by contemporary intuitionists as prima facie obligations. (4) The rules which primitives do recognise as binding they do not regard as self-authenticating or unmediated, but as deriving their authority from the form of life whose conditions they are. And (5) some primitives regard as obviously right some rules which we do not recognise as right at all and which are indeed inconsistent with some of those which we do regard as binding obligations.

If these conclusions are well founded, they seem to show that most of the moral rules, for which self-evidence has been claimed, are not really self-evident in the sense that they are recognised as such by all who understand them and have attended to them. And if we accept the view, as I think we must, that a satisfactory ethical theory must be consistent with the moral judgements of all men everywhere, this means that intuitionism cannot in any of its forms be regarded as a satisfactory ethical theory. This, however, does not mean that moral rules are less important or obedience to them less obligatory than if they were self-evident intuitions. It means only that the grounds of their obligatoriness have to be sought elsewhere than in themselves. It is to be found in their being the conditions of a way of life which is an attempt by the people concerned to embody what they take to be the good for man. It is their relation to such embodied or operative ideals which justifies both the rules and the exceptions to them which are regarded as right, and which also determines the relative urgency of different rules when their requirements clash.

This is not to say that, when even the more thoughtful, let alone the ordinary unreflective, member of a primitive community regards an act or a rule as right, he always consciously thinks of it as a condition of a way of life which he recognises as on the whole good. To the suggestion that the interpretation of the facts which I have given need involve such conscious reference to the good of the society as a whole, Ross has, in another connection, given what he himself calls " a perfectly proper answer ". I cannot put this answer more clearly than Ross has done; but in quoting it I substitute the present theory for Ideal Utilitarianism which he was discussing when he used it. " Certain types of acts have in practice been found [to fit into a way of life, or to be conditions of its smooth working], and have in consequence been judged to be right; and so, for plain men, the character of rightness has come to seem to belong to such acts directly, in virtue of their being, e.g. fulfilments of promises, and the middle term which established their rightness has come to be forgotten. *Media axiomata* such as ' men should keep their promises ' have come to be accepted as if they were self-evidently true, and people habitually judge acts to be right on the strength of the *media axiomata*, forgetting the method by which the *media axiomata* have themselves been established." [1] This is, I think, as Ross says, " a fair answer ". But I should add that in a small, closely knit primitive community it is much easier to see that the observance of a rule is necessary for the good of the group as a whole than it is in a large-scale modern society; though even in primitive societies the rule is more often thought of as the requirement of a particular institution than in reference to the way of life of the people as a whole.

There are, however, two rules which are often included in lists of prima facie obligations which seem to be in a different position from the others. They are the rule to produce as much good as we can and the rule of justice or equity. These are not so much particular rules among others as general statements of what every way of life is trying to do, and, for that reason, whatever other rules are or are not recognised by particular peoples, these rules are in some sense recognised by all. There could not be any way of life without them. But these rules, or, as I should prefer to call them, principles, remain theoretically vague and practically valueless till they are embodied in a way of life whose structure determines the particular rights and duties in which their requirements find expression; and within that structure the one cannot be understood except in relation to the other.

The rule to produce as much good as possible is just a rule to realise the moral ideal regarded as the pursuit of ends or the realisation of interests. And it remains vague and indefinite till the ends and interests are systematised into a structural pattern, which embodies the conception of the people concerned of what is required to satisfy their nature as a whole. When this is done, the principle of justice or equity is found to be the structural principle of the pattern — the principle which determines the interrelation of ends and interests, and especially those of different persons, to one another. This principle takes a large variety of forms, but in one form or another we find it

[1] *Op. cit.* p. 69.

expressed, sometimes more and sometimes less adequately, in the way of life of every people. It is a kind of moral symmetry which underlies every system of rights and duties. Its ultimate basis is the recognition, however dimly, by individuals of other people as moral persons and, therefore, entitled, in virtue of their common humanity, to a certain respect and consideration of their interests. But it, too, remains vague and general until it is embodied in a system of interrelated institutions constituting a way of life in which the ends and interests of individuals are dovetailed into a relatively coherent pattern.

With what is involved in the rule to produce as much good as we can I shall deal in my next lecture, and I shall try to explain the nature of justice in the last lecture. Meantime I want to state in general terms what I take to be the relations of the different prima facie rules to one another in the moral ideal, and in the ways of life which are attempts to embody it. The rule to produce as much good as possible expresses the requirement to realise the moral ideal from the point of view of ends or goods. The principle of justice is the principle of inter-relation between ends, and between the individuals whose they are, which is necessary to enable the individuals to realise their ends in such a way that they will be on the whole satisfied; while the more specific and detailed rules are the conditions of the co-operation and mutual trust and respect between persons on which the realisation of their ends, in accordance with the principle of justice, depends; and the concrete systems of rights and duties of particular peoples, and the institutions in which they are embodied, are the flesh and blood of the body of which the more abstract rules, and especially the principle of justice, is the skeleton.

There are other questions about moral rules which would have to be answered, and objections which would have to be considered, before the view of their nature and authority for which I am contending could be regarded as established. The answers to most of them seem to me to be contained in what I have said already. But even at the risk of some repetition, I want to consider one or two of them further. Others will be dealt with in later lectures.

If moral rules are not binding in their own right but have only a borrowed authority, why, it may be asked, do they occupy so important a place in the life and thought of every people, primitive and civilised ? Why do we, as we often seem to do, recognise the rightness of moral rules, and react to breaches of them more directly and immediately and spontaneously than we recognise the goodness of a way of life, or react to what hinders or promotes it as such ? Why do we feel compunction, as we undoubtedly do, when we feel obliged to break a moral rule, such as that of truth-telling or promise-keeping, even when we believe that it is our duty to do so, and that more good is likely to follow from the action in which we do so than from any alternative action open to us ? Why do we feel compunction about breaking the rule of truth-telling and the Tonga do not, or about certain forms of adultery and the Australian Aborigines do not ?

There is no doubt that, in the ordinary business of living, morality presents itself to most people most of the time, and perhaps to some people all the time, not so much as the promotion of a way of life or the production of good, but rather as obedience to rules which are accepted as right. I do not want to deny or even to minimise the importance of rules in the moral life. As I have repeatedly pointed out, any form of ordered social life requires that there should be rules and that they should be generally obeyed. These rules, as Ross reminds us in the passages which I have already quoted, embody the accumulated wisdom of our ancestors and their value is attested by each generation in its own experience. Some of them are such obvious conditions of individual and social welfare that even the least imaginative can recognise the fact. Accordingly, to break one of them is to run a grave moral risk. The moral agent is usually much more certain of the value of their general observance than he is of the problematic good which he expects to follow an exception to one of them.

Moreover, to break a rule which is generally recognised as right is to be guilty of discourtesy or disrespect towards the person or persons in relation to whom we do it, and who have a right to expect us to observe it ; without the general observance of such rules people would not know what to expect of one another. In this, and in other ways, breaches of rules tend to undermine mutual confidence. For example, other people may see the breach and may not be aware of the good motive for it. And such breaches are in danger of producing in the individual who is guilty of them a habit of ignoring the rules concerned in other connections, and this may also affect his attitude to other rules — as we have seen in the recent great increase in disrespect for both laws and moral rules which was the result, in large part at least, of people living in war-time under conditions in which it was often regarded as a merit to break them, or at least to make exceptions to them. Again, the individual may quite rightly hesitate to trust his own moral insight as to the good which he expects to follow from the breach of a rule against the deeper insight and the greater wisdom of those whose experience is embodied in the rule. The fact that rules are generally recognised as right and embodied in a moral code is not what makes them right; but it may be a good ground for believing them to be right. It suggests that they have been tested by experience and found good.

For the greater part of the time, the moral thinking of most people is imitative or repetitive, not original, and there is therefore no need for them to go behind or beyond the accepted moral rules. They sufficiently indicate their duties; if they obey them they will have done their duty. And if there is any situation in which it is more unwise than another to question the authority, or to ask for the credentials of a moral rule, it is when an individual is faced with a practical decision in which it would be to his interest or convenience to make an exception to it. Rules act as a warning against making exceptions in favour of oneself.

And there is another reason why rules are much in evidence in our ordinary moral thinking, and occupy more than their fair share of our attention. They are often in conflict with our natural inclinations and desires. This is so not only in childhood, when they are presented to us mainly in negative form as restraints on what we want to do, but throughout life; and the highest moral conduct, action done from a sense of duty, always involves such conflict with our immediate desires. Now anything which conflicts with our desires attracts our attention and is apt to occupy the focus of consciousness. Just as the citizen does not notice the laws of the land except when they prevent him from doing something which he would like to do, or compel him to do something which he does not very much want to do, so the moral agent is naturally more conscious of the rules which conflict with his desires than he is of the purposes for which the rules are imposed or of the ends which their observance promotes. Moral rules are, therefore, apt to occupy the foreground of consciousness, while the form of life whose conditions they are tends to occupy the background. But in our more reflective moments when we engage in original moral thinking, the form of life comes into the foreground. This is specially apt to happen when an accepted rule is challenged and requires justification or modification. When we say, e.g., that a particular rule is not right, or that the institution or form of life of which it forms part should be changed, we tend to give as our reason that those who live under it have no chance of living a reasonable human life or of developing their powers or personalities. This is the sort of argument which we find used, and it seems to me rightly used, in recent discussions on such matters as divorce laws, education, the conditions in slum areas revealed by the air raids, the conditions in certain industries, and so on.[1] In the last resort the appeal is to a way of life as the ultimate criterion by which rules are to be tested.

It is also worth noting that in the smaller and more intimate societies, like the family, the team, the college, in which relations are personal and friendly, and in which the individual feels at home and at ease in co-operating with others to carry out the common plan — in such groups, while there are rules and patterns, they are not much in evidence, and they are not usually felt as irksome restraints. It is in the larger groupings, where relations are more impersonal and less intimate, that rules are

---

[1] This contention is supported by the results of one of the few attempts with which I am acquainted to make an empirical survey of the moral reactions of different groups of people to certain situations and of the reasons which they give for the ways in which they think people ought to act in such situations. The majority, we are told, sought to justify their reactions by an appeal not to general rules but to the ways in which the individuals involved in the situations would be affected. (Sharp, *The Influence of Custom on Moral Judgement*, pp. 84 ff.)

more in evidence; and even there they are, at most, the framework and not the whole of the moral life.[1] Indeed as I said earlier, if many or even most men in most societies were not better than the rules required of them, if they were not at times prepared to do more and exact less than the strict letter of the rules lays down, it is doubtful if any form of social life would really prosper.

At present, however, we are concerned not with the limitations of a life based on rules alone, but to reconcile the prominent place which rules occupy in the moral life with the theory of the nature and authority of moral rules which the anthropological evidence, as I have interpreted it, suggests. And the considerations which we have been discussing seem sufficient to explain the importance which we attach to moral rules, the necessity for general compliance with their requirements, and the compunction which we feel when we consider ourselves obliged to break one of them, even if they have not an independent rightness in addition to the goodness of the form of life whose conditions they are. Breaches of them require justification; to comply with them does not. And this is all that we seem to get on the intuitionist theory; for intuitionists admit that particular moral rules ought to be broken, both when the requirements of different rules clash and when much greater good would result from breaking them than from complying with them. On any theory the practical problem of deciding whether in particular circumstances it is right to break a moral rule presents considerable difficulties. The only advantage of the present theory is that it claims to bring to light the principle which guides the reflective moral agent in his attempts to solve this problem, however difficult it may be to apply the principle in detail; whereas the intuitionist theory leaves the moral agent without any principle to guide his efforts.

But why, it may be asked, do we feel compunction when we break certain moral rules and the primitive does not? The answer, I think, varies from people to people and from rule to

[1] Cf. Aristotle, *Nicomachean Ethics*, 1155a: " If citizens be friends they have no need of justice, but though they be just they need friendship also; indeed the completest realisation of justice seems to be the realisation of friendship also ".

rule. We may distinguish three sets of circumstances in which primitives break, without compunction, rules which we recognise as binding: (1) when they do not recognise the rule in question as right at all; (2) when a rule which is recognised in the relations between members of the in-group is not regarded as applicable in their relations to outsiders; and (3) when a rule which is accepted as right in some relations between the members of the in-group is broken without compunction in others. The explanation of cases of the first kind is to be found, I think, in the principle which we discovered in our analysis of the attitude of certain tribes to the rule of truthtelling. In their circumstances, as they conceive them, general compliance with the rule in question would not promote their welfare; indeed, it would do more harm than good. Therefore, they do not recognise the rule as binding. The same principle, I think, supplies at least part of the explanation of cases of the second kind. The way in which the principle operates in these cases and the other considerations which enter will be discussed in my last lecture. Many factors seem to contribute to produce cases of the third kind. For example, the individuals towards whom the exceptions show disrespect may not be recognised as persons in the full sense, as seems to be true of women and children among the Australian Aborigines. But the main explanation seems to be that the exceptions are not thought of in relation to the rule but as the requirements of particular institutions and, therefore, not as exceptions. What the anthropological evidence suggests is that most or even all rules are first recognised as the requirements of particular institutions and in the relations between small groups, where the forms of conduct of which the sorts of act in question form parts are found to be good. Once a rule is thus recognised as right in one connection, there is a tendency for it to be carried over to other institutions and relations, till it comes to be regarded as right in all relations between those who constitute the group of those who are recognised as persons in the full sense. The same principle seems to apply among ourselves, as Russell has illustrated in detail in his treatment of professional ethics.[1] The smaller and more intimate the group, the

[1] *Philosophy*, July 1942; especially pp. 205-6.

higher the ideal and the more exacting the standard demanded in the relations between its members ; and progress in ideas of rightness or righteousness largely consists in extending these standards, and the rules which they imply, to the relations between individuals in larger groups.

THE MORAL IDEAL

IN dealing with the nature and authority of moral rules in my last lecture, I tried to show, on the negative side, that the method of isolation used by many contemporary ethical theorists will not account for the moral rules which are regarded as right by primitives; and, on the positive side, that these rules derive their authority from the fact that they are recognised as being involved in, or conditions of, the realisation of the conception of the good life entertained by the people who regard them as right; and I argued that in these respects what is true of primitives is true generally, of all men and all moral rules. In the present lecture, I propose to follow the same line of treatment in dealing with the moral ideal, considered as the system of goods or states of affairs which we try to realise in the moral life, and to develop my theory by contrasting certain widely held contemporary conceptions with those suggested by the anthropological evidence regarding primitives. The main questions which we have to consider are : How is the conception of the moral ideal built up ? How are its elements related to one another ? How do men come to know that these elements, and the whole which in their interrelation they constitute, are good; and what sort of knowledge have they of their goodness ? In dealing with these questions I shall first outline the answers given by the contemporary writers who rely on the method of isolation. Secondly, I shall compare their answers with those suggested by our consideration of primitive morality, partly in order to bring out by contrast the nature of the latter, and partly to show that the method of isolation will not account for our knowledge of the good any more than for our knowledge of the right, that it will not yield any better results when applied to the moral ideal, considered as the pursuit of ends or the realisation of values, than it does as an account of moral rules. Thirdly, I shall try to show that the conception of the moral ideal to which the method of isolation leads has grave defects even as an account of civilised morality; and, finally, I shall explain in more detail the conception of the moral ideal suggested by the anthropological evidence, and try to show that it applies to all morality, primitive and civilised alike.

Those who use the method of isolation in dealing with the nature and knowledge of the good hold that there are certain sorts of things, experiences or states of affairs which, when considered in isolation, are directly apprehended as intrinsically good, and that we build up our conception of the moral ideal or the sort of life that is worth while by adding such goods together. They contend that the moral ideal can be analysed into units which, when considered without reference to any consequences they may have or any context in which they occur, are apprehended as good — good being regarded as a simple, indefinable quality which belongs to such units in their own right, a quality which belongs to the things which have it independently of any context, and which, therefore, they retain in every context. The test which they apply to discover whether anything has intrinsic goodness is to consider whether it would still be regarded as good if it existed quite alone, or if there were nothing else in the universe but itself. They, of course, admit that such things never do in fact exist quite alone, but they hold that to treat them as if they did, in isolation from their context and causes and conditions and consequences, is the only way to discover their intrinsic goodness, if they have any. And if anything has intrinsic goodness it retains it in every context or whole of which it forms part. Other things or states of affairs or experiences, which have no intrinsic goodness, may have instrumental goodness because they are the means to such intrinsic goods. Intrinsic goods themselves may also be instrumentally good, because they have results which are intrinsically good; but their intrinsic value is independent of any such results, however good the latter may be.

But intrinsic goodness as the opposite of instrumental goodness, and so as meaning good as an end or good for its own sake or good independent of consequences, is not necessarily identical with intrinsic goodness in the sense of good if it existed quite alone. For in the latter sense intrinsic goodness is independent of context as well as consequences; and some writers [1] who use the term in the former sense, i.e. to describe goodness independently of consequences, do not hold that all things which are intrinsically good in their sense would be good if they existed quite alone, or if there were nothing else in the universe. They find it difficult to be sure that under such circumstances they would have any goodness. The goodness which they attribute to intrinsic goods is independent of consequences only, and not of context also; and therefore the things which have it may not retain it in every context. But the stricter sense of the term, good independently of both context and consequences or good if it existed quite alone, is the logical implication of the method of isolation, and it is with this sense of the term that we are therefore concerned.

According to those who use the term intrinsic good in this sense, there are elements or units in the good life which are not only distinguishable, but so far isolable that final or incorrigible judgements of value can be passed on them in their isolation. The goodness of these intrinsic goods can be measured and compared and added; and the goods can be arranged on a scale of value. The whole value of life consists in the amount of such good which it contains. The conception of the moral ideal is arrived at by combining such goods; and the principle which guides the moral agent in deciding what he ought to do is : ' produce as much intrinsic good as possible ', or ' of all the acts open to you, do the one which would produce (or which you believe would produce) the greatest sum of intrinsic good '.

Now this conception of the moral ideal or the good life is diametrically opposed to that which, according to the anthropologists, is entertained by primitive peoples. For, as we have seen again and again, the anthropologists are never tired of emphasising the intimate interrelation and interlocking of the different goods which a particular primitive people are trying to realise. Their conception of the moral ideal or the good life does not consist of a series of independent goods, each of which can be considered in isolation and have a final judgement of value passed on it by itself. The states of affairs, the activities, the experiences which they regard as good form an

[1] E.g. Ewing, *The Definition of Good*, p. 114.

interconnected whole, the parts of which are valued not as independent items on a scale but as elements in a context, with the rest of which they do or do not harmonise. They are integrated into patterns or systems of compossible or functionally interdependent goods. The different goods which they try to realise are not just added to one another. We cannot alter one or take it away or add another and leave the rest as they were, however desirable the results of so doing might seem when separate items are considered in isolation. For these items are considered by the person who lives the life and passes judgements of value on them, not in isolation but in the context of a way of life. The judgements of value which he passes on the different items, and the extent to which, and the ways in which, they should be realised, are determined, and can only be understood, when they are considered in their context.

No doubt there are things which, when described in quite general terms, all peoples may be said to regard as good. And these include not only what we usually call the higher goods such as personal affection, enjoyment of beauty, health, freedom and religious peace of mind which tend to be regarded as intrinsic, but also very humble goods such as food and shelter and a mate. This is so because human nature and its needs are everywhere the same; and what satisfies a need, when considered simply in relation to the need, is regarded as good. But none of these goods is to be pursued always and to be realised in every context. When we ask, then, to what extent and in what ways they should be promoted or produced, we find the answers varying from people to people; and the answer which a particular people give with regard to a particular item cannot be understood by considering it alone, but only by considering it in relation to the system of goods of which they approve. The detailed evidence for this I gave in my account of the functional interdependence of the different states of affairs which the primitive peoples, whose ways of life I selected for detailed description, regard as good; and it is not necessary to repeat it here. It can be found in abundance on almost every page of any recent work on social anthropology. If this evidence is accepted, and it seems to me very difficult not to accept it, it means that the application of the method of isolation to the value-judgements of primitives distorts the facts, rather than helps us to understand them; and this suggests that any theory of the nature of the moral ideal arrived at by means of this method can at best have only a limited and conditional validity.

Here, then, we have two diametrically opposed views about the nature of the moral ideal and the principle or principles of moral judgement, the one arrived at by contemporary ethical writers who use the method of isolation, the other suggested by the anthropological evidence about primitive morality. The two views differ also in their accounts of the way in which we get knowledge of the moral characteristics of things, and of the sort of knowledge and the degree of certainty which we can hope to get in our moral judgements; and this difference applies to judgements both of goodness and of rightness, i.e. whether we are concerned with states of affairs or sorts of acts, with the kinds of things which are good or the sorts of rules which are right. Before considering which of them is the more adequate, I want to make some aspects of the contrast between them clearer by comparing the differences between them with those between mathematics and natural science, where we get the same contrast in a more familiar form. This comparison seems to be specially appropriate, because those who claim that in morality we can get direct apprehension or insight, the results of which can be expressed in incorrigible judgements, rely explicitly on the analogy of mathematics. According to the view of the anthropologists, on the other hand, the procedure of the moral agent in arriving at his moral judgements seems to resemble the empirical method, and the degree of certainty at which he arrives the fallible conclusions of the natural scientist.

Those who rely on the method of isolation point out that in mathematics we have more certainty about the truth of isolated propositions than we have of the way in which the propositions are connected together in the system of mathematical knowledge as a whole. The truth of the isolated propositions is apprehended in ' crystal-clear intuitions '. However these propositions are combined, each retains its initial character of self-evident certainty. Similarly, they contend, in our ethical knowledge we find intrinsic goods and rules of prima facie right which have such definiteness and precision in their isolation that we can apprehend their characters in self-evident intuitions. The moral ideal or the conception of the good life is arrived at by combining such units, whether intrinsic goods or rules of right or a combination of both; but, however they are combined, each retains its character of goodness or rightness. If we are to have truth and certainty at all in our value-judgements, we must get it in the isolated units. If we do not have it from the outset we shall not get it at all. Ross states the position and the analogy on which it is based quite explicitly. " Both in mathematics and in ethics ", he writes, " we have crystal-clear intuitions from which we build up all that we can know about the nature of numbers and the nature of duty. . . . We do not read off our knowledge of particular branches of duty from an ideal of the good life, but build up our ideal of the good life from intuitions into particular branches of duty." [1] And again, " we do not start with a general notion of the ideal life of a community, and read off, as consequences that can be deduced from this, that promises should be kept, and the like. Rather, because we see that promises ought to be kept, that people should make restitution for the ills they have done, and render good for the good they have received, as well as promoting the general welfare, we build up from these intuitive insights the conception of an ideal community in which people would do these things, and do them because they know them to be right." [2]

Similar considerations apply both to the apprehension of isolated intrinsic goods and to the way in which they are combined; but I need not labour the point: the analogy with mathematics is not only clear but often explicitly stated. So widespread, indeed, is the use of the mathematical analogy that even Joseph, who defends a view of the moral ideal much more akin to that which the anthropological evidence suggests, accepts it. The mathematician, he writes, " may come to know, independently of one another, many facts between which he may later discover necessary connection. Indeed, in this field it is hard to doubt that all facts are mutually involved,

[1] *Foundations of Ethics*, pp. 144-5.   [2] *Ibid.* pp. 142-3.

though we cannot see this. Some have urged that, if this is so, the apprehension of the facts in their isolation is not properly to be called knowledge of them ; we do not really know anything unless we know it in all its linkages. Perhaps there is a parallel here between Ethics and Mathematics. We think we know of certain actions separately that we ought to do or forbear them. But if the obligation is grounded in some goodness or badness which the action would have, and which is not independent of its being so linked with other actions as to make good or bad the form of life to which it and they would belong, it might be said that we could not really know our obligation till we viewed the action in these linkages." [1]   But the language which Joseph uses suggests that the parallel between ethics and mathematics is not so close as the argument assumes. In reference to mathematics, he writes, " a man may come to *know*, independently of one another, many facts " ; whereas of our moral knowledge he says " we *think we know* of certain actions (in isolation) that we ought to do or to forbear them ".[2]   Others make no such qualification of the finality of our isolated moral judgements. For them the parallel with mathematics is complete : we not only think we know, but in fact we do know that certain things are intrinsically good and certain rules prima facie right.

Now contrast the procedure of the natural scientist with that of the mathematician, and let us see the view of the process of building up the moral ideal and the degree of certainty which we can hope to get in our moral judgements, if we think that natural science provides a closer analogy to the procedure of the moral agent than mathematics does. The data of the natural sciences consist of observed phenomena. A phenomenon considered by itself may be capable of more than one interpretation, and the natural scientist is not satisfied that he has correctly interpreted it till he sees how it is connected with other phenomena according to a law. The more comprehensive the system into which a given phenomenon, as interpreted in a particular way, fits, the more certain he is that he has correctly interpreted it. In other words, no certainty attaches to the interpretation of the datum in isolation, but a high degree of certainty attaches to the judgement regarding it, when it is considered as an

[1] *Some Problems of Ethics*, p. 108.   [2] My italics.

element in a comprehensive and consistent system of data. Here we have a much higher degree of certainty at the end, when the data are considered in their interrelation, than we have at the outset, when they are considered in isolation. To use Joseph's language, the scientist may think that he has correctly interpreted the datum in isolation, but he cannot be sure till he has succeeded in connecting it with others in a coherent system; and he may find that, when he so considers it, he may have to reject his first interpretation.

Now if we interpret the thinking of the moral agent on the analogy of the procedure of the natural scientist, we would represent it somewhat as follows. When we consider experiences, states of affairs or sorts of acts by themselves in isolation, our estimate of their value is the result not of crystal-clear intuitions but of fallible judgements of varying degrees of probability. Our judgements of value may, therefore, have to be modified or even reversed when we consider the facts to which they relate in their context, as parts of a purpose, or a system of purposes, or a way of life. We cannot pass a final judgement of goodness or rightness on a state of affairs or an act, nor can we understand the judgement of value of another on it, unless we take account of the system of acts or states of affairs of which it forms part; and the more comprehensive the system in relation to which we consider it, the more certain our judgement on it is likely to be.

According to this view, we do not begin with either of the alternatives suggested by the analogy of mathematics and propounded by Ross as being apparently the only alternatives open to us. We begin neither with ' crystal-clear intuitions ', whether of the form of apprehension of simple qualities or of insight into necessary connections, nor with a clear conception of an ' ideal community from which we can read off as consequences which can be deduced from it ' particular judgements of value. Neither are the premises of our moral reasoning incorrigible judgements nor are its processes the tracing of logical implications. At no stage in it do we get demonstrative certainty or necessary judgements. Nevertheless our judgements of value are not irrational or arbitrary. For according to the analogy of natural science we may arrive at conclusions for which we can advance reasons, and some of which we can see to be more reasonable than others, even though none of them is infallible or incorrigible.[1]

Let me try to put the difference between the procedures of the mathematician and the moral agent, and the appropriateness of the method of isolation to the former and its inappropriateness to the latter, in another way. Consider the mathematician trying to solve a problem and the moral agent trying to discover his duty. Suppose each of them has arrived at what he believes to be the correct solution of his problem, and asks the opinion of a friend on the result. The mathematician will naturally consult another mathematician, and the latter will check each step in the argument by which the conclusion is arrived at separately, and, if he is not satisfied with the result, he will point out the specific step in which the error or non-sequitur occurs. But the wise man to whom the moral agent appeals for advice will proceed quite differently. He will try to look at the situation in which the moral agent finds himself as a whole, try to take account of all the relevant factors and hold them before his mind at once. If he wants to question the result at which the agent has arrived, he cannot put his finger on any one specific point at which he has made a mistake. All he can do is to ask whether he has taken certain factors into consideration, e.g. his relations to A, his previous commitments to B, the consequences and collateral effects of the proposed action on C and D, the strain to which it will subject E (who may be the agent himself), and so on. None of these considerations is by itself decisive, but all of them have to be taken into consideration.

Now the procedure of the morally wise man is as rational as that of the mathematician, but its rationality is of a different kind. They are both processes which only a rational being could perform; and just as in the former the conclusion follows

---

[1] In this connection it is worth noting that moral judgements differ from mathematical propositions in two important respects. Mathematical propositions do not conflict with one another, nor do those of one person conflict with those of another. If they are apprehended at all, they are recognised as necessary and therefore as strictly universal. But even the so-called self-evident moral rules of the intuitionists in practice conflict with one another; and the value-judgements of one people clash with those of another.

from the premises, so in the latter the discovery of what is right, which is also the determination of the agent's duty, emerges from the consideration of the whole situation, but it does not follow with the demonstrative certainty with which the mathematical conclusion does. The result never amounts to knowledge. Moral wisdom consists more in recognising what premises are relevant, seeing that they are all taken into consideration and each given its due weight than in seeing how a conclusion follows from a few premises. Thus, while the procedure of the moral agent is rational, the method of isolation does not apply to any part of it, and its result is never infallible.

What we begin with, according to this view, is human nature and its needs. Now human beings not only have desires rooted in their natural needs but they are also self-conscious and social beings. The objects or states of affairs which would satisfy a given desire, or the activities in which it would find expression, when considered by themselves in relation to that desire, may appear good; but they may be incompatible with the states of affairs or activities required to satisfy other desires of the same self-conscious individual. Accordingly, as the result of the interaction of desires in the experience of the self-conscious individual, he builds up the conception of a complex state of affairs or a system of activities which are necessary for the compossible satisfaction of systems of desires, and finally of the desiring self as a whole. The states of affairs or activities which enter into, or are required by, this system are regarded as really good; and those which conflict with it are regarded as really bad, however strong may be the desire for them. So far as the individual is self-conscious and judges reflectively, he does not pass judgement on states of affairs or activities in isolation, but in their interrelation.

Nor is this all. Man is not only self-conscious but social. He not only requires the co-operation of others for the satisfaction of most even of his non-social needs, but he desires the friendship and the welfare of others directly. And so in building up his idea of the state of affairs or system of activities which he regards as on the whole good he has to take account both of his social desires and of the desires of other people. The resulting conception, therefore, takes the form, at least in part, of patterns of co-operative behaviour between individuals embodied in a way of life in which the requirements of the desires of different individuals are adjusted to one another, and the ways in which these desires should be satisfied are determined accordingly. The only final justification of the value of a state of affairs or an experience or an act is to be found in its being an element in, or a condition of, the realisation of such a way of life. The judgement of value on the way of life itself is final but not infallible. It cannot be justified by considering its object in a wider context; but it may have to be modified because the way of life to which it relates may be an imperfect expression of the ideal for which it stands. It may be lacking in the comprehensiveness or the internal consistency required to satisfy the nature and needs of man. The only judgements of value which seem to be unmediated and self-justifying are (1) the judgement that what is required by the way of life which is on the whole good is obligatory, and (2) the judgement that the doing of what is obligatory because it is obligatory is morally good. These judgements express self-evident intuitions in the sense that a person who is confronted, whether in actual practice or in ideal experiment, with the situations to which they relate cannot help acknowledging them. Unless so much at least is taken as self-evident, it is difficult to see how there can be such a thing as morality or how moral considerations can arise at all.

I tried in earlier lectures to describe some aspects of the exceedingly complex process of integration and adjustment, which is involved in arriving at the conception of the way of life in the light of which final judgements of value are passed, as it is found (1) in the personality of the individual, where desires and systems of desire are mutually modified through their interaction as the experiences of one self-conscious agent; (2) in the individual's personal ideal, which is the objective counterpart of the unity of the self as self-conscious; and (3) in the interaction of the institutions which constitute the way of life of a people; and we have seen examples of the results of this adjustment and integration in the ways of life of the primitive peoples whom we considered in detail. Accordingly, all I need do here is to call attention to one or two points which emerge from our consideration of primitive morality.

(1) Even if, as I believe, this process of adjustment and integration plays as important a part in building up the personal ideals of individuals and the social ideals of communities among civilised peoples as it does among primitives, it is easier to see its operation in the smaller, more closely knit primitive societies, where the differences between the personal ideals of individuals and between the personal and social ideal are less marked than in large-scale modern societies.

(2) The individual finds the way of life of his people already in existence and embodied in institutions, whose forms represent the results of the experience of many generations of his ancestors; and it is in response to them and under their influence that he forms his personal ideal. The extent to which he enters into the spirit of this way of life and grasps its pattern as a whole varies from individual to individual. Many accept the forms of behaviour of their society more or less unconsciously. For some of them life is just one thing after another without much conscious unity of plan or purpose. They recognise their various duties through the promptings of their social environment; and they do not engage in much reflection, still less in much original moral thinking. Others reflect and deliberate and, in their deliberations, have before their minds considerable sections, if not the whole, of the pattern of their way of life. For some, again, the integration of the pattern is more on the emotional and conative side; for others it is more on the intellectual side; but the formal ideal, that which will finally satisfy, is a harmonious development of all three.

(3) The degree and the manner of integration of the way of life varies considerably from individual to individual and from people to people. It is seldom, if ever, a logically coherent whole. It is generally little more than the interlocking of patterns of behaviour or institutions through their interaction in the ideas and habits and feelings of the members of the society who entertain it. And even when the way of life has a high degree of integration, the principle on which it is unified, and the scale of values which it embodies, may be inadequate

to express the moral ideal which it is an attempt to express. For unity of pattern may be achieved by subordinating all other interests and values to one interest, or one system of interests, in a way which is inconsistent with the realisation of the good of the self or of the community as a whole, or which may be incapable of being extended beyond the bounds of the group or applied to the relations between all men without denying the humanity of some of them.

(4) Such integration as we get is seldom consciously planned. It is more the result of practical disappointments and partial successes in actual living than of conscious thinking, though many of the results could be, and some of them are, brought about with less trouble through pre-living in imagination or ideal experiment rather than by the wasteful process of trial and error. In the main, however, it is what has been in practice found good but incomplete that points the way of advance; and the formal ideal which people are trying to express in their embodied or operative ideals exists in many of their minds as a sense of frustration and dissatisfaction with things as they are, rather than before them as a consciously entertained ideal guiding their efforts.

But however incomplete and imperfect may be the integration of the ways of life of many peoples, and however partial and inadequate may be the grasp of many among them of its pattern as a whole, the fact that men are self-conscious and that the different elements and aspects of their way of life meet and interact in their experience, tends to produce a certain congruity or affinity between the parts of their operative ideals; and the ideal to which they all point and which they are trying, however imperfectly, to embody in a way of life, is one in which there would be complete mutual congruity between the spirit of which it is the outward manifestation, the type of character which it fosters, the system of activities in which it finds expression, the rules of conduct which it implies, and the ends or states of affairs to which it gives rise. And this natural affinity applies not only to the relation between the different ends and different motives and different rules, which are found in a way of life, among themselves, but also to the interrelation between its ends, motives and rules. Certain motives and types of character more naturally find expression in complying with certain rules and in the pursuit of certain ends or the production of certain states of affairs. But rules of conduct not only express, but also tend to form, a certain sort of character, as well as to lead to certain states of affairs. And while such states of affairs may arise more or less accidentally from other motives and complying with other rules, they are more likely to result from particular kinds of motives and obeying particular sorts of rules. For this reason ends, rules and motives tend to influence one another, and when they are in harmony to support and strengthen one another. Thus what is ultimately or morally good is not just certain states of affairs or activities or experiences considered by themselves; they are also those which naturally result from certain motives according to certain rules. And the rules which are morally right are not just particular sorts of rules considered in isolation; they are also the rules which are the natural expression of certain motives and help to form and to express a certain type of character and to produce certain states of affairs. So that intelligence, strength of will and goodness of motives are all necessary not only to live the good life but also to build up the conception of the ideal to be realised in it; and stupidity, weakness of will and badness of motives mar both. And as this way of life is lived in the spirit of which its different elements in their interrelation are the expression, the motives and types of character which are manifested in it, the rules of conduct which it involves and the states of affairs or experiences to which it leads are found to be on the whole good by the people who live it.

That, then, is the kind of conception of the moral ideal, of the way in which we get knowledge of what is good, and of the degree of certainty which we can hope to get in our judgements of value, which is suggested by the analogy of natural science; and, according to the anthropological evidence, it is the kind of conception which we find among primitive peoples. It is inconsistent with the presuppositions of the method of isolation used by those who rely on the analogy of mathematics. The theories which use that method, therefore, cannot account for the moral conceptions and judgements of primitives. Accordingly, we have to consider whether the theory supported by the anthropological accounts about primitive morality is consistent with, and capable of explaining, civilised morality. As a preliminary to doing so, I want to call attention to certain respects in which the account of the nature of the moral ideal and of the way in which we get knowledge of what is good given by those who rely on the method of isolation seems to be not only unhelpful but misleading, even as an account of civilised morality. I refer especially to their analysis of the moral life in terms of the concept of means and end, their quantitative conception of the good life in terms of a scale of values arrived at by considering goods in isolation, and their comparative neglect of the importance for morality of persons and co-operation between persons. Let us look at each of these briefly.

However convenient the distinction between instrumental and intrinsic good may be for certain purposes, the value of the category of means and end as a tool of ethical analysis seems to me very limited. It is true that some of the activities in which we engage may be quite conveniently divided into parts which may be described as means and ends to one another. Thus I may go to the library for the purpose of getting a book, and I may want the book to consult a passage which a colleague tells me is relevant to a lecture which I am preparing. If somebody else brought me the book or if the colleague himself showed me the passage, it would serve my purpose equally well, and I might prefer not to have to go to the library; so that going to the library is a means to the realisation of my purpose and done only for that reason. But many other series of activities which are the realisation of purposes cannot thus be divided into means and ends. Thus the activities involved in giving the lecture or the series of lectures cannot be divided into means and end. Their purpose is realised in and through the series of activities rather than as a result of it. Some of the activities are a preparation for, and necessarily precede, others but they are not a means to the others. The purpose is not something external to the activities, but something which is realised in them as a whole. It is not realised in one activity more than in another. The series of activities is the realisation of the purpose.

Thus there are many pieces of living which we describe as the realisation of purposes to which the category of means and end does not apply. But even in cases in which the category can be appropriately applied, the theories which rely on it as their tool of ethical analysis tend to cut off means and ends far too sharply from one another. They break up the continuous process or series of activities which are life as it is actually lived into a number of detached or detachable units, some of which are relatively static states of affairs or forms of enjoyment which have value, and others of which are transitions between them and have none, and may even have positive disvalue. The former, it would seem, would be just what they are and have all the value which they have, even if the latter were to disappear altogether ; indeed, life would be much better and have more value if this were to happen. But is this how we in fact think of the process, within which we distinguish means and end, when we make it the subject of a value-judgement ? Do we not rather think of the piece of living, which we call carrying out a purpose or realising a value, as a whole, if not also as part of a wider whole ? While it is true that what we call the means considered out of relation to the end has no value, the moral agent does not so consider it ; neither does he consider the end as the subject of a considered value-judgement out of relation to the means. Is that not implied in the accepted moral maxim that the end does not justify the means ? The value belongs to the piece of living, the activity or experience of producing the end by the means.

An act as something which takes place in time is forward-looking. It is the initiation or realisation of a state of affairs or an end. And the thought of the agent who is reflectively considering the desirability of bringing about the state of affairs moves backwards and forwards from end to means and from means to end ; and if the end or purpose is realised, it is being realised throughout the process rather than at a given point in it. If it is being realised more at one point than at another, that point may not be last in the series of activities, still less need it be something which remains after the series is completed. The means, in the sense of the price which is paid for realising the purpose, may come after rather than before, or may come partly after and partly before, that part of the process which would be specially described as the end or the realisation of the purpose. But even if the end, in the sense of the realisation of the purpose, is the last stage of the process, nonetheless before being realised it is present in the thought and intention of the agent, directing and giving value to the process ; and when it is realised, it is what it is and has the value which it has as a part of the process. When we think of triumphing over obstacles, striving for a goal, rest after toil, solving a difficult problem, would the end be what it is or have the value which it has if divorced from the process of which it forms part ? Indeed the process of trying to realise it may have a value, even a high value, even if the end is not in fact realised at all. And the whole process which is thus divided into means and end is itself part of a larger process, part of the life of a person who is, and is aware of himself as being, one in relation to all of it. From this wider context it can be distinguished but it cannot be separated, if we are so to understand it as to enable us to pass a considered value-judgement on it. In other words, the good life is not good just in spots or patches. It has a certain unity because it is the expression of a certain spirit or because it is the objective embodiment of the unity of the self ; and if it is good it is good as a whole.

Some of the theorists whose views I have been considering put forward a conception which seems more consistent with the view which I am advocating. I want to mention it not only because it helps to correct what seems to me the defects of an analysis of the moral life in terms of the category of means and end, but also because it provides some qualification of the quantitative conception of the moral ideal as a sum of independent goods. I am referring to Moore's doctrine of organic unities,[1] that is, unities or wholes whose intrinsic value is greater than the sum of the intrinsic values of their parts. It is true that as used by Moore this conception does not take us very far in overcoming the difficulties of a quantitative conception of the good life, but it brings to light a principle which may be capable of much further extension. The significance of this conception from our point of view is that, in recognising

[1] *Principia Ethica*, pp. 27-36.

that there are entities which when considered in isolation have little or no value but which in their interrelation constitute a whole which has a very great value, it introduces the idea of a kind of value which is neither intrinsic nor instrumental, namely, the value of an entity as a part of a particular kind of whole. This value is not intrinsic because, according to Moore's definition, intrinsic value belongs to the entity which has it out of relation to the other entities which together with it make up the whole; and it is not instrumental because the entity is a part of, and not a means to, the whole. Ross [1] suggests the name contributive value to describe it because it belongs to the part in virtue of the contribution which the part makes to the whole, and therefore to its value. Moore denies any value to the part as a part. " To have value merely as a part ", he writes, " is equivalent to having no value at all, but merely being a part of that which has." [2] But this is so only if by value we mean intrinsic value. Otherwise the means would not have instrumental value: to have value merely as a means would be equivalent to having no value at all, but merely being a means to that which has. If, therefore, we admit the conception of instrumental value, there is no good reason why we should deny the conception of contributive value.

It is true, as Ross [3] has pointed out, that some of the examples of organic unities given by Moore are neither happy nor convincing; and, on the basis of his analysis of these, Ross doubts whether there are any organic unities. Among his examples, however, Moore includes most if not all works of art, such as poems or pictures; and though Ross rejects these because he does not regard beauty as an intrinsic value, they are sufficient for our purposes; for we are not concerned with the conception of intrinsic value as the term is used by these writers. What concern us are rather the conception of a whole whose value, however we describe it, is different from and greater than the sum of the values of its parts in isolation and the conception of contributive value as the value of a part in virtue of its being an element in such a whole; and of these conceptions a work of art is a sufficiently good illustration. The contributive value

---

[1] *The Right and the Good*, p. 72. [2] *Op. cit.* p. 35.

[3] *Op. cit.* p. 70.

of the part of such a whole depends on its appropriateness or fittingness or suitability as a constituent element of such a whole.

Now if we regard a piece of living, and especially a way of life or the moral ideal, as an organic unity, we get something like the view which is suggested by the anthropological evidence and which I have been trying to defend by an analysis of civilised morality. For our understanding of the moral life, this seems to me a much more fruitful conception than the category of means and end. It is true that Moore applies the concept of organic unity only to relatively simple wholes, but he points out that there is no theoretical reason why even the universe as a whole should not be such a unity. There is, therefore, no reason why the series of acts which express a purpose or the system of purposes which constitute a way of life should not be such unities. Whether they are or not is just a question of fact. If they are, and the evidence seems to me to suggest that they are, each act or state of affairs has the value or disvalue, which makes it right or good or wrong or bad, as the result of its fittingness or unfittingness, its appropriateness or inappropriateness, to take its place in a way of life which is as a whole good. According to this view, the moral ideal is not a sum of goods, but a system ; and the rightness of acts depends not on their consequences but their context. It is true that on such a view the principle ' maximise good ' or ' produce as much good as possible ' can still be accepted as a general statement of the purpose of the moral agent, but it is quite unhelpful as a means of discovering what good he ought to realise at a given time, until the goods to be realised are adjusted into a system of compossible goods, and this system embodied in the conception of a detailed way of life. If the principle is interpreted as involving the consideration of separate acts as means to the production of isolated intrinsic goods, it seems to me not only unhelpful but misleading.

The view that, by considering goods in isolation from the context of any way of life, we can arrange them on a scale, and that, if one good is higher on the scale than another, it should in all circumstances be preferred to one which is lower, seems to be equally misleading. Indeed, however the scale of values is constructed, it seems to me that the principle ' in case of a clash always choose the higher value ' cannot be accepted as an adequate expression of the principle of moral judgement. But the view that it is an adequate guide to the moral agent, in trying to discover what his duty is, is by no means confined to ethical theorists who rely on the method of isolation. We find it in the writings of some who in general support a conception of the moral ideal more akin to that which is suggested by the anthropological evidence and which I have been trying to defend.

Consider, as an example, the view of Urban,[1] who adopts a self-realisation type of ethical theory. Urban does not accept a strictly quantitative conception of the moral ideal ; nor does he rely on the method of isolation in drawing up his scale of values. In deciding what place different goods should have on the scale, he takes account of the respective contributions which they make to the realisation of the good of the self as a whole. But having got his scale, he lays down the principle that wherever he has to choose between two goods the moral agent should always realise the higher.

Now there seem to me to be fatal objections to this principle as a guide to the moral agent trying to discover his duty ; and they seem to apply however the scale is constructed. I shall state them as they apply to Urban's formulation of the principle ; but they apply with even greater force to the formulations which rely on the method of isolation. Urban arranges goods in an ascending scale as bodily, social and spiritual.[2] According to his scale, therefore, the pursuit of knowledge is a higher good than the production of food, and aesthetic enjoyment has a higher value than good health. Now circumstances arise in which we may have to choose between the pursuit of knowledge and the production of food, or between the promotion of health and the production or the enjoyment of beauty. Is it feasible to suggest that in all such circumstances we ought to choose the so-called higher good ? All the goods on the scale, the lower as well as the higher, are necessary to the good or complete life. No good, however high on the scale, is by itself the complete

[1] *Fundamentals of Ethics*, ch. viii.   [2] *Ibid.* p. 169.

good. Fulness of life requires all of them in due proportion. Circumstances, therefore, arise in which the lower goods ought to be realised, and, in these circumstances, the duty to realise them is our moral duty, not just an economic or other kind of duty. In these circumstances no other good, however high on an abstract scale, can be substituted for them without a failure to do our duty. Therefore we cannot discover when we ought to realise them by reference to the scale of values alone. For the good which is higher on the scale may not be the one which is in place here and now.

To discover when and how far a particular good ought to be realised we must consider it, not in relation to an abstract scale, but in relation to the pattern of a way of life in which the different goods are so adjusted as to realise the good life as a whole. When, e.g., the procuring or production of food clashes with the pursuit of knowledge, as it sometimes does, it may very well be my moral duty not to pursue knowledge but to provide food. Urban himself admits that this may be so; but he thinks that " such exceptional circumstances do not alter the general principle " [1] — which suggests that the principle is rather academic and remote from the realities of the moral life. It is true that man cannot live by bread alone; but neither can he live without it; nor can he live by knowledge alone or by anything else alone. It is also true that the lower values on Urban's scale can be realised without the higher, and that men are in greater danger of neglecting the higher. They do not normally need any exhortation to pursue the lower, which are a condition of, though I should think not a means to, the realisation of the higher. But ethical theory is not concerned with practical exhortation, but with the principle according to which decisions between the different values and their requirements should be made.

In the conditions of human existence, many more duties arise in connection with the production and distribution of the lower goods than most of our ethical theorists seem to recognise. But though they are concerned with the lower goods they are not, therefore, lower or less urgent duties. The person who performs them is doing his moral duty and realising his moral

[1] *Fundamentals of Ethics*, p. 176.

personality. In the concrete business of actual living, circumstances arise in which the realisation of a lower good is inconsistent with the simultaneous realisation of a higher, and in which, therefore, a choice has to be made between them. In some of these circumstances it is the realisation of the lower good which is morally required. When this is so, the humbler duty of realising it is our moral duty; and to neglect it for anything else, even for the promotion of goods which are higher on the scale, is to fail in our moral duty. This seems to me so obvious that I can see no point in labouring what I should think nobody would deny. And if it is accepted, it follows that the principle ' in case of a clash realise the higher good ' is not only unhelpful to the moral agent trying to discover his duty; it is positively misleading.

I am not suggesting that we do not need a scale of values but only that a scale arrived at by considering goods in isolation is unhelpful; and that the principle ' realise the higher good ' on a fixed scale is not the principle used by the reflective moral agent in trying to discover his duty. The different goods which the good man tries to realise in his conduct seem to me to be related not as fixed points on a scale, nor as means and ends, but as elements in a system or way of life in which each has its place which no other can fill. Some goods and systems of goods are more permanent and more comprehensive. They represent major interests of the self, and its welfare is more deeply implicated in their realisation. In ways which I have already tried to describe, they help to integrate other goods in the sense that, if they are to be realised at all, other goods have to be realised at certain times and in certain ways. Now it is true that the goods which are higher on Urban's scale have in a general way more of these characteristics; and he himself takes account of these characteristics in drawing up his scale. Accordingly, his scale and the principle of moral judgement based on it are less abstract than those which are arrived at by the strict use of the method of isolation. Nevertheless, his scale is still too abstract, and the principle which appeals to it cannot be accepted as an adequate expression of the principle of moral judgement; and their defect is, in principle if not in degree, the defect of all scales and principles arrived at by the method of isolation. They make abstraction from some fundamental aspects of human life ; they neglect some of the conditions in which the moral life is lived and in which, therefore, the moral ideal, which is the good for man, has to be realised, if it is to be realised at all.

All theories which arrange goods on a scale, and formulate the principle of moral judgement as ' in case of a clash always choose the higher value on the scale ', neglect the temporal aspect of human life, and therefore of the good for man. But, in fact, there are very narrow limits to the goods which an individual can realise at once ; and so if the different goods which in their interrelationship constitute the good for man are to be realised at all, they must be arranged in a temporal sequence. And every duty is a particular duty, a duty to do a particular act at a given moment of time. Therefore, at any given moment a choice has to be made between different possible goods though all of them may be desirable. If a man's experience or the unity of his self were confined within the limits of the passing moment, his good or moral ideal would have only a vertical pattern, and at any moment it would be his duty to realise the highest value possible at that moment.[1] But man is aware of himself not only as the unitary subject of different simultaneous desires, but also as a unity persisting from moment to moment. Therefore his good has a temporal aspect ; the goods which he is to realise must be integrated into a temporal pattern ; and in deciding what he ought to do now he has to take account of this pattern. There is no good which he ought to be realising all the time, except moral goodness which, as we shall see, is realised in-directly as a by-product of realising, or of attempting to realise, other goods. Owing to the time-conditioned character of human life, the condition of realising a particular good com-patibly with realising the greatest good of the self as a whole may be the denial of it now, and the realising of something else instead. It is true that different goods are so inextricably inter-twined that, in realising one good, we may be realising others as well. But, owing to the limitations which constitute our finitude, conflicts between the requirements of realising different

---

[1] If in such circumstances we could legitimately speak of his having an ideal or a duty at all.

goods may arise at any moment, and we may have to make a choice between, say, pursuing knowledge, enjoying beauty, promoting friendship and procuring food. And any theory which makes abstraction from the fact that our existence is time-conditioned, that all duties are duties to do particular acts at a given time, and that there are limits to the number of goods that we can realise at once, leaves out of account the conditions which alone enable us to decide what good we ought to realise now.

As a result of the characteristics of human life which I have just mentioned clashes between goods arise in two different ways, and a choice between them has to be made for two different reasons. The one kind of clash is between goods, such as self-assertion and friendly co-operation or unlimited freedom and social order, which are in principle incompatible, because they are expressions of a different spirit or character. The realisation of one of these renders impossible the realisation of the other as part of a life which is a unitary and self-consistent whole. The other and more common kind of clash is between goods, such as the enjoyment of beauty, the possession of knowledge, the promotion of health, the provision of shelter, and so on, which are not only in principle compatible and, therefore, capable of being combined in a life which is self-consistent, but which are essential elements in every full life. They are all possible and desirable, but they may not be compossible; for conflicts between their requirements are liable to arise at any moment because of our finite limitations which prevent us from realising them all at once. It is true that a clash of this kind need not involve the final abandonment, but only the postponement, of the goods not chosen. Such postponement, and the realisation of another or other goods now, may be a condition of the fuller realisation of the postponed goods later; but at times it may mean real loss. What concerns us, however, is that at a given moment a choice has to be made and that the principle, that at any given moment we should realise the highest good which is possible at that moment, will not enable us to make the right choice. The good which ought to be realised now is not the one which when considered in isolation is highest but the one which is required here and now by the pattern of the good life as a whole; and, as that pattern has a temporal as well as a vertical aspect, no theory which leaves the temporal aspect out of account can supply a principle which will not mislead us in our choice.

Such a view as is here advocated does not mean that when the moral agent passes judgement on a state of affairs or an act he need have before his mind its relation to the whole way of life of which it forms part. For he has learned by experience, his own and that of other people, that certain states of affairs or sorts of acts are normally elements in, and expressions of the spirit of, a certain way of life. And for the rough-and-ready judgements of everyday life this is usually sufficient. But such judgements are not regarded by the moral agent as infallible. When they are challenged he does not say that he is sure of their truth but rather that certain acts and states of affairs require a great deal of explaining or justifying, if the judgements which he has passed on them are not to stand. This explanation and justification are to be found, if they are to be found at all, not in the acts or states of affairs themselves, but in their relation to the context of the way of life of which they are parts. The more considered and reflective the judgements, the wider the context which they take into account, the less likely they are to need revision. But at the best none of them is infallible or incorrigible.

Now this theory may seem to make the task of the moral agent in trying to discover his duty more difficult and more hazardous than the theories which hold that we get crystal-clear intuitions of rightness or goodness. As I shall point out below, I am not at all sure that, in the end, this will be found to be so. But be that as it may, is the theory not in this respect a more faithful account of the facts of the moral life and the process of moral deliberation? Is there not in the moral life an experimental element, an element of adventure or of faith, which involves taking risks on an insight which is short of absolute certainty? Does not moral insight grow and do not moral judgements become more certain in the process of pre-living in imagination and ideal experiment which we get in moral deliberation, and in the process of putting our insight to the test of actual living in practice?

It is true that both the Ideal Utilitarians and the Intuitionists admit the fallibility of the moral agent in deciding what in any given circumstances he ought to do. For their incorrigible judgements of goodness and rightness refer to abstract aspects of the moral life and not to particular states of affairs or acts. The rules of prima facie rightness have varying degrees of urgency; intrinsic goods have varying degrees of goodness; the consequences of acts can only be partially computed. Accordingly, in deciding what he ought to do in particular circumstances, the moral agent has to rely on his fallible judgement. But, as I have already pointed out, what is more important is that neither theory provides nor admits any principle on which the individual faced with this problem can base his decision. Accordingly, while at the outset they appear to give greater certainty than the view which I advocate, in the end they give less. And by leaving the moral agent without a principle on which to decide the really crucial issues of the moral life, they fail to account for the growing insight which seems to come with experience, and for the fact, for fact it seems to be, that the more we reflect and deliberate the more likely we are to arrive at a right decision as to what our duties are.

These considerations seem to be connected with the other defect which I mentioned in the theories which rely on the method of isolation. As the result of concentrating their attention on isolated aspects of the moral life, these theories tend to neglect the central place of selves or persons in morality and the implications of this for the nature of the moral ideal. It is true, and I think significant, that Ross holds,[1] and that Moore is inclined to hold,[2] that only experiences have intrinsic goodness. Now experiences are the experiences of persons or selves; and selves, at least moral selves, are self-conscious, which means that they are aware of their own identity amid the variety of their experiences. As a result of this unitary character of the self as self-conscious, the experiences of one self are not isolated and self-contained. They mutually interact and modify one another within the unity of the self. Accordingly, the system of activities or goods or the way of life which is the

---

[1] *The Right and the Good*, p. 86.   [2] *Principia Ethica*, pp. 188 ff.

good of the self must have a corresponding unitary character. But the theories which I have been considering seem to pay insufficient attention to this unitary character of the self and its implications for the interrelation of the goods which constitute the moral ideal. Ross has himself called attention to the fact that Ideal Utilitarianism, with its summation of independent goods, does not sufficiently recognise the fundamental significance of persons in morality; and it seems to me that the same is true, though to a less marked degree, of Intuitionism. Indeed, it would appear that no theory which begins with isolated units, which are given in incorrigible judgements of goodness or rightness, and which regards the moral ideal or the good life as a combination of such units, can do justice to the unity of selves or persons, or to the unitary character of the ideal which is the objective counterpart of the self's unity. But it is with persons, and relations between persons, that we are primarily concerned in morality; and therefore theories which neglect the distinguishing characteristics of persons are unlikely to be satisfactory. And the unity of persons is their most distinctive characteristic, that without which they would not be moral selves at all; and experiences, acts, goods and states of affairs have moral significance only in relation to such unities.

I have dwelt on the shortcomings of the theories which rely on the method of isolation, partly to bring out by contrast certain features of the moral life of which, as it seems to me, any satisfactory ethical theory must take account, partly because the assumptions which underlie these theories seem to be widespread not only among recent and contemporary ethical writers but also in much of our moral thinking, and partly in the hope that a recognition of their inadequacies may weaken the resistance which is aroused in many quarters by anyone who mentions the kind of theory which I outlined in earlier lectures. That theory, which regards the procedure of the moral agent as more akin to the procedure of the natural scientist than to that of the mathematician, is a reformulation or modification of the self-realisation type of theory in the light of the anthropological analysis of primitive ways of life. In this reformulation I have tried to supplement the self-realisation theory and give it greater concreteness, partly by reference to some of the facts brought to light by the anthropological analysis, and partly by a more explicit recognition of the importance, for our understanding of morality, of the temporal aspect of human life. I have also tried so to state the theory as to remove the ambiguities which have led to its being regarded as an egoistic theory. I want now to try to show (1) how the theory, as thus reformulated, accounts for those aspects of the moral life which we have just been considering and which have been largely neglected by the theories which we have been discussing; and (2) how it connects with the anthropological evidence: how it explains that evidence and draws support from it.

The self-realisation theory gives selves or persons their central place in morality; for it derives both the content and the structure of the moral ideal from the nature of the self — the former from its needs and desires, social and non-social, the latter from its unitary character as self-conscious. It thus makes morality a peculiarly human phenomenon. Now human needs and desires are plastic, capable of finding expression and satisfaction in many different ways; the unitary nature of the self requires that they should be so integrated as to find satisfaction compatibly with one another; and such success as is achieved in bringing this about is the result of experience and experiment. Recognition of these facts enables the theory to do justice to those aspects of the moral life for which theories which rely on the method of isolation find it difficult to account, such as the element of adventure and experiment, the developing insight which comes with reflection and practice, and the fact that the moral ideal is not a sum of goods but a system with a unitary character. The experimental and tentative character of all attempts to conceive the good for man and to articulate it in a detailed way of life also explains both the similarities and the differences between the particular moral judgements of different peoples — the similarities by references to the common human nature and needs, the differences by the partial and inadequate character of all efforts to conceive in detail how that nature and those needs are to find satisfaction. Thus it is consistent with the moral judgements of all men everywhere, primitive and civilised alike.

It is true that the conception of the moral ideal as self-realisation is purely formal, and that the principle ' realise the self ', taken abstractly, is as unhelpful as a guide to the moral agent trying to discover his duty as the principle ' maximise good ' or ' choose the higher value '.[1] But the classical exponents of the self-realisation theory have pointed out that in the course of history men have given concreteness to this formal principle by embodying its requirements in patterns of behaviour which have both an inner or psychological and an outer or institutional side. On their outer side these patterns of behaviour find expression in systems of institutions " from the family to the nation " which constitute " the body of the moral world ".[2] In this way the self-realisation theory emphasises the intimate connection between the moral and the social ideal, and between moral and social philosophy ; but it does so without making all morality, or even all the values which together constitute the moral ideal, social. For it not only insists that morality has an inner or personal side, the side to which moral goodness belongs, but it also recognises that, though man has social desires and requires the co-operation of his fellows for the satisfaction of many even of his non-social needs, some of the values which he seeks to realise and which form part of the good for man, like truth and beauty and, it may be, holiness, are non-social. But though it does not regard all moral values as social, this theory emphasises the importance for our understanding of morality of the social aspect of human nature ; and so it regards the moral ideal as a way of life in which different people co-operate to realise their ends, both social and non-social.

Now none of the ways of life which result from the efforts of different peoples to embody the moral ideal is entirely adequate. The different patterns of behaviour which constitute them are never entirely consistent and the provision which they make for the different needs of human nature are never entirely adequate. Therefore, the formal ideal, of which at

[1] The objection to all these principles is not so much that they are necessarily false as that it is impossible to know what they require till they are embodied in detailed ways of life.

[2] Bradley, *Ethical Studies* (2nd ed.), p. 177.

best they are only imperfect expressions, stands over against them as the critic of their imperfections and a challenge to further progress.

It is by its account of the intermediate links between human nature and its needs, on the one hand, and the formal ideal, on the other, that the work of the social anthropologists supplements and supports the classical expression of the self-realisation theory. This it does in two main ways : by its analysis of the nature of institutions and its emphasis on their importance as determinants of right conduct; and by its account of the functional interdependence of institutions as constituting operative ideals or ways of life. By interposing institutions and operative ideals between the formal ideal and the particular needs and desires of individuals, it makes it easier for us to see how the duties to realise particular values in given situations are determined; while its account of the functional interrelation of institutions within operative ideals shows us that these ideals are not completely coherent, and yet that each of them has a certain unity of spirit, that there is a certain congruity between its institutions.

Now the self-realisation theory reveals the source of this mutual adjustment or affinity between the institutions which, in their interrelation, constitute the way of life of a people. It is to be found in the unitary character of the self. The requirements of the different institutions of a people meet and mutually modify one another in the minds of its members. The same individual takes part in the working of many institutions, and when their requirements conflict he is frustrated and unhappy. Accordingly, adjustment is continually taking place. The forms which this adjustment takes we described earlier. What concerns us at present is that its source, and the stimulus to further integration, is the unity of the self as self-conscious. In this way, then, the anthropological analysis enables us to give greater concreteness to the self-realisation theory, and the theory gains support from the anthropological evidence.

The other way in which the self-realisation theory seems to me to need to be supplemented and made more concrete is by a more explicit recognition of the implications of the temporal aspect of human life for the determination of our particular duties. It is true that some of the values which men seek to realise are non-temporal or independent of time; but our duties to realise them are not. If they are to be realised at all, they must be realised in a life in which they cannot all be realised at once. Our duties to realise them are all particular duties, duties to do particular acts at given moments of time. Therefore, the duties to realise them must be arranged in a temporal pattern, which determines which value we should realise at a given moment.

The self-realisation theory is not only consistent with and supported by the anthropological evidence about primitive ways of life; it is also capable of accounting for certain parts of that evidence which have troubled the anthropologists themselves because they find it difficult to reconcile them with each other. Before discussing this further evidence and the support which it gives to the self-realisation theory, and as an introduction to doing so, I want to consider, and, if I can, to remove the ambiguities in the self-realisation theory which have led to its being regarded as egoistic. The criticism that it is an egoistic theory — a criticism which, if substantiated, would rightly be regarded as a fatal objection to it as a moral theory — seems to me to be due to a failure on the part of some of its chief exponents to recognise, or at least to make explicit, the peculiar relation of moral goodness to the moral ideal, and to their consequent tendency to speak of moral goodness or the perfection of the self as an end, if not the only end, to be consciously aimed at by the moral agent. This seems the natural interpretation to put on the view that the moral end is self-realisation, and that the principle which should guide the moral agent in trying to discover his duty is ' realise the self '. It is not necessary to discuss here whether or not this interpretation is the result of a misunderstanding of the theory,[1] though I should admit that, so far as it is, the exponents of the theory must bear their share of the responsibility for it. What I want to do is rather to try to state what I take to be the fundamental contention of the theory in such a way as to make it proof against the charge of egoism.

[1] For a discussion of this question see Campbell, *Moral Intuition and the Principle of Self-realisation* (British Academy Lecture, 1948), pp. 17-25.

The position as I see it is this. Moral goodness finds expression in doing what is believed to be right because it is believed to be right. This seems to me the only good which has intrinsic value in Moore's sense. It is good in every context and it would be good even if it existed quite alone. It is recognised as good everywhere and always, by every people whatever their stage of development. But, in fact, it could not exist alone, partly because it consists in doing what is right, and what is right is what is believed to be required in the particular situation by a way of life or an operative ideal as a whole ; and partly because it is realised or comes into existence in the pursuit of other goods. It is true that moral goodness or perfection of character is usually included among the list of goods which constitute the moral ideal, and which are, therefore, to be aimed at in trying to realise the ideal. But, as I said in an earlier lecture, this seems to me to be a mistaken way of regarding it. Moral goodness seems to me not to be a constituent element in the moral ideal and not an end to be consciously aimed at. Rather it is manifested or revealed or comes into existence in the pursuit of the ends which do constitute the ideal. Instead of being an end, it is a by-product of the pursuit of other ends, when these are regarded as best and, therefore, as obligatory in the circumstances, and pursued for that reason. In other words, the way to get this, the highest of all values and, as it seems to me, the only intrinsic good, is to forget about it, and do whatever particular duties are here and now required, or try to realise whatever particular goods, the welfare of others, beauty, friendship, knowledge, health, etc., are here and now required, as part of the system of goods which is the good for man.

Self-realisation or the attainment of moral goodness or perfection seems to be the description of the moral process as it appears to one who looks at it from the outside ; whereas the moral agent, who is engaged in the process and sees it from the inside, has before his mind, or consciously aims at, particular goods, not at self-realisation. The pursuit and realisation of the goods at which he aims are the conditions of self-realisation, but he does not aim at them as such. Nevertheless, self-realisation comes as the by-product of their pursuit and attainment.

As the goods at which he aims are objects of interest of one self and as that self is self-conscious, they are, or become, to a greater or lesser degree, mutually adjusted and integrated into a system. Otherwise the self would not find its realisation in them. In the process of realising them, it would seem, the self is forgotten but not lost : forgotten in the sense that it is not consciously before the mind, but not lost because it is operative and being realised. It is not by anxious thought about our own goodness or perfection that we improve our character, but by doing our particular duties in pursuing the things which are good. But these goods or interests must be integrated in a certain way, if the self whose they are is to be realised ; and it is the self which supplies the integrating force, the bond of interconnection between them.

Now the self-realisation theory rightly insists (1) that the moral ideal must have a unitary character, because it is the objective counterpart of the self which, as self-conscious, is a unity ; and (2) that the realisation of the goods, which in their interrelation constitute the moral ideal, involves the realisation of the self. But exponents of the theory are sometimes apt to leave the mistaken impression that the realisation of the self in its unitary character is consciously before the mind and deliberately aimed at, and that other goods or ends are means to self-realisation, and pursued for that reason. Interpreted in this way, the theory becomes an egoistic one ; and, however much its advocates emphasise the social and altruistic character of many of the self's interests and ends, as long as the realisation of the self is regarded as the end to be consciously pursued, it will be difficult to meet the criticism that the theory is egoistic. If, on the other hand, we recognise that the self as self-conscious is the unitary centre of many interests, that as such it introduces order and system among them, that in their being realised it finds expression and realisation, but that they are not pursued as a means to self-realisation but rather as parts of a system of ends which is as a whole good, because it is the objective counterpart of the unity of the self's interests, we can do justice to the facts of the moral life and to both aspects of the fundamental contention of the self-realisation theory without any appearance of egoism. Of course, other ends may be pursued as a means to self-realisation, and then we get selfishness and egoism; but they need not be, and, in the typical attitude of the moral agent, they are not so pursued.

Now this double character of the moral ideal as a unitary system which is centred in, and the counterpart of, the unity of the self, and yet not selfish or egoistic, because many of the self's interests are altruistic and social, seems to provide the explanation for the apparent inconsistency which I mentioned in the descriptions given by anthropologists of the ways of life and attitudes of mind of primitive peoples. When we take together the two aspects, which are alternately emphasised by the anthropologists and whose apparent inconsistency seems at times to trouble them, we shall find, I think, that they support the interpretation of the moral life which I have been advocating, and which constitutes the essential contention of the self-realisation theory, as I understand it. In describing the way of life of a primitive people, the anthropologist finds it necessary to emphasise both sides. When he gives an account of one side, he seems to feel that he must supplement it by stating the other side, in order to correct the impression which an account of the one side alone is in danger of leaving. Yet he has no theory of the way in which the two sides can be reconciled. These facts seem to me to give strong support to the theory which regards the two accounts, not as inconsistent but as referring to supplementary aspects of the moral ideal, and which tries to show how both aspects are essential to it.

I shall illustrate this point by reference to Malinowski's description of the Trobrianders, though the work of almost any other recent anthropologist, who has given a detailed account of a primitive people, would serve equally well. Malinowski, as we have seen, made a special study of the motives and incentives which primitives have for doing what they regard as right, especially when it is difficult and burdensome, and so opposed to their inclinations. The conclusion at which he arrives is that, in the main, they carry out such duties, neither from mere pressure of custom nor from fear of supernatural punishment, but because they recognise that only by so doing can their interests be realised and their deepest desires satisfied.

This is specially clear in his account of the principle of reciprocity as the basis of the native's sense of obligation to behave in certain ways. Unless the native believes that the results of the working of the principle are on the whole good, in the sense that its operation gives him what he really wants, his own welfare and that of his people, he does not feel under any obligation to comply with its requirements. Such is one of the main results at which Malinowski arrives from his detailed analysis of Trobriand morality; and he illustrates the social machinery which brings this home to the native, both from the working of separate institutions and from the relations between institutions.

Now such a description is apt to leave the impression that the native never does his duty except from motives of self-interest, and that he has no sense of obligation except one based on considerations of prudence. But Malinowski reminds us again and again, even in the middle of his account of sanctions and incentives, that such an impression would be entirely mistaken. The interests of the native, for the realisation of which he will work strenuously, endure hardship and deny himself many immediate advantages, are largely altruistic and social. They include a direct interest in the welfare of other people, a desire for the friendship and approval of his fellows, and so on. Among the motives which move the native, Malinowski repeatedly insists, are loyalty to the group, respect for the rights of others, sense of duty, recognition of the value of co-operation, etc. No primitive society, he contends, could continue to exist without the operation of such motives. But he is equally emphatic that no primitive community could continue to exist without the operation of the principle of reciprocity, and the recognition by the native, through the operation of the principle, that doing his duty is in his own interest, and on the whole gives him what he wants.

Now, according to the view which I have taken of the structure of the moral life and the nature of the moral ideal, the inconsistency between these two contentions is only apparent. For, when the anthropologists emphasise the aspect which seems to make the primitive egocentric and selfish, they are just insisting that, in order that anything may arouse in him a sense of obligation or move him to difficult and unpleasant action, it must be something which arouses his interest, something which appeals to him because he believes it to be necessary if his interests are to be fulfilled. When, on the other hand, they point out that the primitive's sense of obligation is not aroused, or that he is not moved to action, merely by a desire for his own personal comfort or selfish pleasure, they are explaining the nature of the primitive man's interests, that they include an interest in the welfare of others as well as his own pleasure, in friendship as well as in food, in the esteem and approval of his fellows even more than in his own personal comfort; and that he is interested in all of these directly, and not as means to personal satisfaction. In other words, the interests of the self are not necessarily selfish interests; the desires of the self are not necessarily desires for self-satisfaction. Nevertheless, the realisation of the interests and the fulfilment of the desires is the realisation and expression of the self.

But, as we have seen, the interests of the self are not all on the same level. They are interconnected and integrated into systems in which some are subordinated to others. We have therefore to distinguish between the short-term and the long-term interests, the relatively transitory and the more permanent interests, the narrower and the more comprehensive interests, the relatively isolated and the more integral interests. The latter are those in which his self is more deeply implicated, and, therefore, their claims are accepted as obligatory as against those of the former. For this reason also their fulfilment provides the fuller realisation of the self.

According to the anthropological evidence, then, the primitive does not regard anything as obligatory which is not a part of, or a contribution to, what he believes to be good. The only self-evident intuition which he seems to recognise is that of a necessary connection between value and obligation, between what is on the whole good and what he ought to do; and the only intrinsic good which he seems to recognise is that of doing what he believes to be right or obligatory. This suggests that the main structure of the moral life is the same among all peoples, and that the moral judgements of primitives are based on the same principle as our own; and that our account of that structure and that principle are essentially sound.

It may be objected that this line of argument assumes in the primitive a degree of reflection and conscious rationality which is rare among the members of any community and which is seldom practised even by those who are capable of it. Is it seriously suggested, I may be asked, that in the ordinary business of living the average citizen of a primitive community thinks of his interests as an integrated pattern or of the way of life of his people as a whole, and deliberately decides what value he should realise or what action he ought to do here and now by reference to it? Does he not leave to social anthropologists and moral philosophers the task of discovering the intricate interconnections between the different parts of the way of life of his people, and do they not find the task difficult enough? From what has been said above, the answer to this question should be clear. Neither the facts nor the theory here advocated suggests that the individual, whether primitive or civilised, who arrives, or is trying to arrive, at a decision on a moral issue, even under the simplest conditions and in the smallest society, has consciously before his mind the whole pattern of the way of life of his people. To show that this is so, all we need do is to gather together a number of considerations to which we have already called attention.

Even an intuitionist like Ross, who believes that some moral rules are self-evident, regards many, if not most, rules — the *media axiomata* of morality — as " the crystallised products of the experience and reflection of many generations " who have been engaged for longer " than we can tell exploring the consequences of certain types of acts and drawing conclusions accordingly about the rightness and wrongness of types of acts ".[1] According to the self-realisation theory, all moral rules are of this kind, and the crystallised products of experience are embodied not only in rules but in institutions. And the anthropological analysis further shows that these institutions are functionally interconnected to constitute ways of life. Now the main structure of the institutions and of the way of life of his people is there before the individual arrives. They are available to guide his faltering steps and his fallible judgement, and to act as constant reminders to him of his duties.

[1] *Foundations of Ethics*, p. 174.

It is true that the extent to which different individuals enter into the spirit of their way of life and see its pattern as a whole varies greatly. The integration of the personalities of all of them and the building up of their personal ideals takes place within the framework and under the influence of this pattern. In the case of some individuals neither their personalities nor their personal ideals have much integration beyond what the way of life of their people supply; and the integration both of them and of the way of life may be mainly at the conative-emotional level rather than at the reflective and rational level. For others the integration is more conscious, their grasp of the pattern firmer and more extensive, their moral thinking more reflective. But even if what is consciously before the mind of an individual when he makes a moral judgement or decision is only a particular situation, or the requirement of a particular institution, the institution is part of a system of interrelated institutions and the way of life forms the context of the situation. And though the pattern of the way of life may not be consciously before his mind, it is operative in it as habits of thinking and feeling and acting. For it has helped to mould the mind from which judgements and decisions emerge. Thus it exists in him as much as around him; and so it tends to influence even his more considered and reflective moral judgements. And most moral judgements are not original but imitative or repetitive. As far as they are concerned, it is easy for him to see what the rules and institutions which constitute the way of life which his people have developed, and which he has made his own, require of him. In familiar circumstances they seldom fail him, and therefore it is seldom necessary for him to consider an act or situation in the light of the pattern of his way of life as a whole. But whatever be the degree of reflection and conscious rationality which an individual brings to bear on the situation before him, and whether the way of life of his people is consciously before his mind, or operative in it, or the background against which he sees the situation, it is always there as a determining influence; and we must take account of it, if we would understand the judgements of value which he passes.

These ways of life are not static. None of them is a perfect embodiment of the ideal which they are all attempts to express.

There is, therefore, a duty not only to comply with their requirements but also so to alter them as to make them approach more
closely to the formal ideal.   There is, however, no difference
of principle between the two types of duty.   The work of the
average conscientious citizen merges into that of the moral
and social reformer.   Indeed the way of life of a people has not
the definiteness which some of my statements might suggest.
For it exists mainly in the minds of the individual members of
the society ;   and different individuals enter some more and
some less fully into its spirit and purpose.   Accordingly, its
requirements may appear different to the average man in his
average moments and to the best men in their best moments.
Those who enter more fully into its spirit and recognise more
clearly what that spirit requires for its expression may be
already on the way to modifying it.   The moral and social
reformer who wants to change it more or less radically is only
a stage further along the same road.[1]   With the nature of the
process of growing moral insight or enlightenment by which
men have arrived at increasingly adequate embodiments of the
ideal, the direction in which it points and the criterion by which
it is to be tested, I shall deal in the next lecture.   Meantime
there are two other considerations which I want to mention
briefly.

I have used the term ' way of life ' to describe the operative
moral ideal of a people, and this might leave the impression
that, among primitives at least, I regard morality as the whole
of life, all questions which arise in connection with a way of
life as moral questions, all right rules as moral rules, every
choice as a moral choice, and every good as an element in the
moral ideal.   This, however, is not so.   Morality seems to me
to be concerned with the whole of life, without being the whole
of it.   It is concerned with the whole of life in the sense that
moral considerations may arise in any sphere of life, that in all
spheres the moral judgement is the final judgement, and that
we cannot understand or justify a moral judgement without
taking the whole way of life into account.   But in trying to

[1] For a more detailed discussion and illustration of this point see *Proceedings of the Aristotelian Society*, Supplementary Vol. xx. (1946), pp. 108-11.

understand a way of life, we have to consider many questions which are not moral questions and with which ethics is not directly concerned, though the answers to them may be relevant to moral issues; there are goods which are not moral goods and which do not form part of the moral ideal; and some of the decisions which we have to make in the course of living are not moral decisions and are not based on moral principles. I want to illustrate each of these points briefly.

(1) Clarity of thinking and effectiveness in action demand that we should distinguish certain aspects of life, consider them by themselves, and discover the consequences and collateral effects of certain actions and lines of policy. Thus we may isolate the economic aspect of life, and consider whether one system of production or distribution or one financial system is more or less efficient than another, in the sense that it contributes to the provision of a greater quantity or better quality of goods; or we may consider different systems of legal administration from the point of view of their relative efficiency in securing the impartial administration of the law; and so on, with such things as different systems of education and different forms of social organisation. But though all these questions concern persons and the relations between persons, the answers to them cannot by themselves enable us to decide what we ought to do in any set of circumstances. The conclusions at which we arrive in such enquiries have to be considered in relation to a way of life as a whole before a final judgement of value can be passed on them; and, when this is done, it may well be that what seems best in isolation, as, e.g., the economically most efficient policy, may not be socially or morally the most desirable. But though such questions are not moral, the answers to them may be relevant to our moral decisions; and, so far as this is so, it is our duty to make and keep ourselves as enlightened as we can about them. Nevertheless, we have to consider the states of affairs which these enquiries disclose in the context of a way of life before we can discover whether they are morally right.

(2) There is another sense in which morality is less than the whole of life. Morality is concerned with conduct and the goods or values which are realisable through conduct — those

which can be striven for or result from striving. But there are goods, and some of them are among the most precious in life, which come unsought, and so are not the results of action or striving. They come unbidden, a sort of unearned increment, gifts of nature or of grace. Nevertheless, when they come, they are found good and gracious, like the song of birds, the beauty of the sunset, the smell of flowers, the touch of a friend's hand or the smiles of children. These are among the things that make life worth while, but they are not the results of moral effort. Their goodness is a natural goodness. No moral considerations arise in connection with them, except perhaps the way we respond to them and use them. There are other goods, such as an equable temper or a friendly disposition, which may be the results of moral effort, the fruits of the moral spirit; but they may equally well be natural goods, gifts of nature, for which their possessor can claim no moral credit. They always have a value; but in some cases it is a natural value, in others it is a moral value.

(3) Even when we are concerned with conduct and moral questions are involved, not all decisions which we are called on to take need be moral decisions. It is true that moral considerations are ultimately decisive, and that therefore it is never legitimate to take a moral holiday; but moral principles may themselves demand that within certain spheres decisions should be left to liking or convenience or aptitude and not be made a matter of moral principles. For example, it may be my moral duty to take exercise in the interests of my health but whether I take it in the form of walking or swimming or playing golf is not a moral question.

But while there are many questions about the way of life of a people which are not moral questions; while there are goods which are neither the results nor the objects of action, and therefore not moral values; and while not all decisions about what to do are moral decisions, no final judgement of rightness or goodness can be passed on an act or a rule or a state of affairs which results from action except in the context of a way of life as a whole.

The other point which I want to mention is this. I have been concerned with the work of conceiving the moral ideal and of embodying it in a way of life as this would take place, if all the individuals in a society had both the imagination and intelligence to grasp what the way of life of their people requires of them, and the goodwill to carry it out. But the most difficult and perplexing moral problems arise when some of those who co-operate in a way of life fail to carry out its requirements, or to pay regard to the feelings or the interests of their fellows. But though there are elements in human nature which militate against the recognition or the realisation of operative moral ideals and though the practical moral problems to which they give rise are very important, it is not necessary to discuss them here. For they do not seem to raise any questions of principle which we have not already considered.

MORAL PROGRESS

As a way of approach to the subject of this lecture I want to sum up briefly the line of argument which I have followed and the main conclusions at which I have arrived.

I have been concerned with the nature and knowledge of our duties and obligations, the principle according to which they are determined and the way in which we discover them — whether they are regarded as duties to obey rules or to realise ends. Accordingly, I have been dealing mainly with the outward and visible side of morality, the sorts of acts which are right and the kinds of ends which are good, and the patterns of behaviour, the institutions and ways of life in which they find expression. But morality has also a personal or inner and spiritual side, a side of motives and attitudes of mind, of sentiments and goodwill; and this inner side is not less important, for without it there would be no morality. It provides the dynamic and drive without which the outward forms, the rules and patterns of behaviour, would remain a dead letter. Moreover, if goodwill and social sentiments, mutual trust and sympathy, the reconciling and forgiving spirit, are present, they provide an atmosphere in which it is easier to discover our duties. They will even make smoother the working of even imperfect rules and patterns of behaviour. They will make the right response more likely and without them no response has moral value. Nevertheless, by themselves they are not sufficient; for the moral life needs direction as well as drive. The inner life must find expression in outward and visible forms; for goodwill, however important, does not tell us what we ought to do, as we can see in the difficulty which sincere and honest men sometimes have in discovering what their duty is, and in the ineptitude with which people of goodwill at times do the wrong thing from the best of motives, or even the right thing

at the wrong time, or in the wrong way. But though I recognise
that the moral life has two inseparable and equally important
aspects, my main concern has been with the outward aspect,
for it is the one which has to be primarily considered in dealing
with the nature and knowledge of our duties and obligations ;
and it is the one to which the anthropological evidence is specially
relevant.

In my treatment of it, I have assumed, and I have tried to
defend the assumption, that the main structure of the moral
life, the nature of the moral ideal and the grounds of moral
obligation are in principle the same everywhere and for all
men ; and that, therefore, only a theory which will account for
the moral judgements of all men can be regarded as a satisfactory
ethical theory. But I have contended that, if there is this
identity of principle underlying the moral judgements of all
men, it must be compatible with a great diversity in the sorts
of acts which are regarded as right, and in the states of affairs
which are regarded as good, by different peoples.

I have approached the subject through the study of the
moralities of contemporary primitive peoples, partly in order
to show the wide range of facts for which ethical theory has to
account ; partly because the contrasts between the ways of life
and the moral judgements of different peoples help to bring
into clearer relief the distinction between those features of the
moral life which are absolute and unconditional and those
which are relative to certain cultural conditions or sets of
circumstances ; and partly because I believe that some characteristics which are common to all morality are more obvious in
the simpler conditions of primitive life, just as others become
clearer in the larger and more complex advanced societies.

I have held that the way of life of every people known to
history or anthropology is an attempt to embody a moral ideal,
the elements of which are determined by the desires and dispositions of human nature, and the structure of which is determined by the nature of man as rational and self-conscious and by
the conditions of co-operation between individuals which are
necessary for the realisation of selves in their unitary character.
This unitary character of the self is both lateral and longitudinal,
i.e. the self is aware of itself as the unitary centre of many

desires at one moment and also as a unity persisting through many desires from moment to moment. Because the self has this unitary character, the system of activities or way of life which it requires for its expression and satisfaction must have a corresponding unitary pattern; and because it is a member of a community and has social desires and dispositions, this way of life must be one in which different people co-operate. The demand which this way of life makes on the individual is the source of moral obligation. It presents itself to him as an ought both negatively and positively: negatively, it demands the suppression of desires or systems of desires whose expression would be inconsistent with its pattern; positively, it demands the doing of that which the pattern requires, however difficult or distasteful that may be.

This state of affairs makes possible two different forms of conflict or tension within the self. On the one hand, the individual may be in no doubt as to what the way of life which stands for the good of the self in its unitary character demands; but the demand which it makes may be opposed to his inclinations and desires: the individual knows, or believes he knows, what he ought to do, but he finds it difficult to do it. Here we have one form of moral conflict, the conflict between duty and inclination, between reason and passion, between ' the law of the mind ' and ' the law of the members '. On the other hand, there may be doubt as to what the pattern requires, or even whether the pattern itself may not require modification: the individual does not know what his duty is. Moral perplexity of this kind may arise either because of the complexity of the situation with which the moral agent is faced, or because he is incompletely rational: his personality may be insufficiently integrated and the way of life which is its counterpart internally inconsistent, or the pattern of the latter may make inadequate provision for the expression of some aspects of his nature. In some cases powerful systems of desires, the expression of major interests, in each of which the self is deeply implicated, may be in conflict. This gives rise to dividedness of mind and clashes of deep-seated loyalties, which result in major unhappiness and provide the materials of tragedy. With conflicts of the first kind we have not been directly concerned; our main theme has been the problems and perplexities to which the second kind gives rise and the principle on which they can be resolved.

Though the general form of the moral ideal is common to all men and all moralities, its detailed embodiments, the results of the co-operative efforts of different peoples in conceiving and realising it, vary enormously; and it is these detailed embodiments in patterns of behaviour and systems of institutions which provide the operative ideals in the light of which people discover their particular duties and obligations. The evidence which I have submitted suggests that if we isolate an act or a rule, an experience or a state of affairs, from its context in such a way of life, we take away from it the characteristics which are the grounds of its rightness or goodness, i.e. that no act or sort of act or state of affairs contains the grounds of its rightness or goodness within itself. For we have not found unanimity among different peoples as to the sort of acts which they regard as right, or the states of affairs which they regard as good, as there should be if their rightness or goodness belonged to them in their own right and were apprehended by direct insight. The only exception to this is moral goodness which, as we have seen, has a peculiar character in virtue of which it cannot exist by itself. It would seem, then, that when we try to pass a moral or final judgement of value on an act or state of affairs, we have to look beyond itself. How far beyond it have we to go ? — to motives, to consequences, to context, or what ? The answer, which the evidence with which we have been concerned suggests, is that we have to consider it in the context of a way of life as a whole; but it is that way of life as it appears to, or is grasped by, the individual who lives it and passes the judgement.

The way of life of the society into which the individual is born has been built up over a long period of time, in the course of which its parts have tended to become mutually adjusted, but the adjustment has followed different lines among different peoples. In the case of a particular people, the resulting pattern may be narrow and circumscribed or wide and comprehensive, its parts may be more or less completely harmonised, its provision for the needs of human nature more or less adequate. But, whatever its character, the way of life of his people helps to mould the individual and to determine his interests and ideal. Different individuals may enter into its spirit to differing extents. One may find it on the whole good mainly or even merely because he has been brought up under it and has been formed by it. Another may more or less reflectively grasp its pattern and consciously make it his own ideal; while yet another may build up for himself, on the basis of it, an ideal which may involve a more or less radical modification of it. But unless an individual accepts it as on the whole good, in the sense that he believes that, if all the members of his society were to live according to it, the resulting state of affairs or form of life would be on the whole satisfactory, he will feel no moral obligation to comply with its requirements. He may consider it prudent to do so from fear of punishment or for other reasons, but his conformity will not be moral. It is in the light of such a way of life that final judgements of value are passed. Those acts which fit into its structure are regarded as right; and those which are inconsistent with it, however powerful may be the desire to perform them, are regarded as wrong. Compliance with its requirements from good motives constitutes moral goodness.

I have, therefore, argued that the good life is not good in spots or patches to which the rest of it is mere means, but throughout; that the moral ideal is not a distant end to be reached sometime in the future, but a way of life which can be progressively realised and may be being realised here and now; that the duties in connection with what are called the lower goods are not lower or less urgent duties; that, in fact, morality is not concerned with a separate sphere of activities; that moral duties are not a separate class of duties, duties to be morally good or to improve character as such. Character is improved and moral goodness realised by doing whatever is right in the circumstances, whether it be the humblest domestic duty or ruling an empire, whether it be removing the rubbish that disfigures a street or 'the rubbish that lies in the way to knowledge'. I have thus tried to break down the separation between moral duties, on the one hand, and social, economic, political, religious or legal duties, on the other. In all spheres of life, duties arise and they are moral duties. In all of them the moral judgement is the final judgement. Moral considerations are not restricted to a limited sphere or to the application of a limited set of rules — rules which are usually regarded as mainly negative, kept in a special compartment, and acknowledged in general terms. Morality is not concerned merely with the impartial administration of the law, but also with the justice of the law which is administered ; not just with keeping promises or contracts, but also with the kind of promises which should be made and the kind of contracts which should be entered into ; not merely with telling the truth, but also with intellectual integrity in weighing evidence and reporting facts ; not just with making a return for services rendered, but also with what is a fair return for what services, and so on. It is mainly with regard to the latter of these alternatives that we find differences of opinion between different peoples, whereas most ethical theorists concern themselves mainly with the former which do not normally profoundly stir or deeply perplex the moral agent, and which remain vague and general until they are articulated in a way of life in which they are brought into relation with the latter. It seems to me that the same principle of moral judgement applies to both, and that, in trying to formulate it, we must not neglect the more concrete, complex and controversial issues.

I have also argued that the way in which we get knowledge of the moral characteristics of things, whether of rightness or goodness, resembles the tentative groping, and the growing vision, of the natural or empirical scientist rather than the crystal-clear intuitions and the incorrigible judgements of the mathematician.

Now these general considerations, and the formal structure of the moral life which I have described, apply to all men and all morality, and they are compatible with the enormous diversity which we find in the operative ideals or ways of life, and, therefore, in the particular judgements of rightness and goodness, of different peoples. Is there, then, any test which we can apply to discover whether one way of life is better than another, whether one operative ideal is a more adequate expression of the formal ideal which they are all attempts to embody ?

In particular, can we discover any evidence of progress in this respect from the more primitive to the more advanced societies ? And, if so, along what lines does it proceed and what criterion of progress does it imply ?

If my account of the moral life has been in principle sound, moral goodness consists in loyalty to the recognised or operative ideal. This is possible for every man in every society, whatever its stage of development or way of life may be. Accordingly, with one possible exception which I shall mention later, there has been no evolution or development of morality from the most primitive men known to history or anthropology to the most civilised men that we know, in the sense that the meaning of moral goodness has changed or that it is more possible at one stage or in one society than in another. It is difficult to say whether there has been any progress in moral goodness, in the sense that more advanced people are morally better, i.e. live up to their own ideals more consistently, than primitives; but there is no reason to believe that this is so. To discover how far different peoples live up to their own ideals would entail an enquiry which has not yet been conducted; and, no doubt, there are great differences between different primitive and between different civilised peoples in this respect. It is true that the higher the recognised ideal, the greater the demands it makes on those who acknowledge it, the more difficult it is to live up to its requirements, and, therefore, the less likely it is that people as a whole will do so consistently. It is also true that among some peoples there are more stimuli to moral steadfastness, which make it more likely that they will conform to the requirements of their recognised ideal; but mere conformity is no guarantee of moral goodness. It may also be thought that the nature of the operative ideal of a society may be some indication of the moral goodness of its members, because one condition of developing the insight necessary to recognise a higher ideal is that men should conscientiously perform the duties which they already recognise; while persistent failure to live up to an ideal tends to discredit the ideal itself, so that it ceases to be recognised as such; but, as we shall see, other conditions are also necessary for the recognition of higher ideals. Taking everything into consideration, then, there is little evidence to suggest that the more advanced peoples are either morally better or morally worse than the more primitive.[1]

Accordingly, if we are to find development or progress at all, we must look for it in the nature of the ideals entertained rather than in the consistency and conscientiousness with which they are realised, that is, in moral enlightenment rather than in moral goodness. It seems to me essential, for our understanding of both morality and progress, that we should distinguish clearly between moral goodness and moral enlightenment. Moral goodness consists in loyalty to the operative or recognised ideal, whatever the content of this ideal may be; and, therefore, it does not change. But the content of the ideal itself changes. It may be more or less enlightened, richer and more comprehensive or narrower and more circumscribed, its parts more or less consistent, its provision for the needs of human nature more or less adequate. Therefore the acts in which moral goodness manifests itself and the ends which the morally good man pursues change. We have seen that the general form of every operative ideal is a way of life in which different people co-operate to realise the ends which are dictated by their nature as self-conscious persons. I think we may say that the development which has taken place in the conception of the moral ideal consists in an increasingly adequate grasp of what is implied in such co-operation, of what it means to be a person and of what is involved in membership of a co-operative community of persons.

This development has been mainly along two closely interconnected lines. The one has been an extension of the number of those who are included in the community to which the way of life and the rights and duties which it involves apply, an extension which continued till all men are, at least in theory, included in its scope, and, therefore, entitled to be treated as persons. The other has been a changing conception of the nature of personality and of the relations between persons which are necessary to express this nature, and provide scope

[1] Cf. Gore, *The Philosophy of the Good Life* (Everyman ed.), p. 245; Hobhouse, Wheeler and Ginsberg, *The Social Institutions and the Material Culture of the Simpler Peoples*, p. 254.

for its development. Progress in enlightenment has not consisted merely, as is sometimes suggested, in giving a different
answer to the question ' Who is my neighbour ? ' but also in a
different conception of what is meant by neighbourliness, not
merely in an extension of the group who are believed to share
in the common humanity, but also in a deepening of the significance of what is involved in the common humanity. Indeed,
it may well be that a change in the way of life which is shared
by a group is a condition of the extension of the group who
share in it, and especially of its extension to include all mankind.
There are peoples whose ways of life and scales of value have to
be remodelled to make such extension possible.

Consider, e.g., the way of life of the Crow Indians.[1] Their
way of life is based on principles of mutual helpfulness and
friendly co-operation between the members of the in-group.
Quarrelling and fighting between them are strongly disapproved.
But the whole structure of the group-life, the relations between
individuals within it, the constitution of its societies, its scale
of values, and even the content of its religious visions, were
dominated by the military spirit and the pre-eminence of the
military virtues. This assumed that members of other groups
were to be treated as enemies, and the presence of such enemies
was a presupposition of the whole structure of the way of life.
Extend the principles of friendly co-operation which prevailed
between members of the in-group to their relations to their
neighbours and the whole pattern and scale of values of their way
of life will collapse, as in fact happened when the United States
government forbade them to make war on their neighbours.

Here, then, we seem to have one test which can be applied
to different ways of life to discover their adequacy. Any way
of life whose general structure or scale of value does not admit
of being extended to mankind as a whole, without denying the
common humanity of some men and their right to be treated
as persons, must be regarded as unsatisfactory ; and the more
remodelling it needs to make this extension possible, the more
unsatisfactory it is.

There are other ways also in which development in enlightenment has taken place, and these lines of development condition,

[1] See Lecture VIII.

and are conditioned by, the extension of the size of the group and the deepening grasp of the nature of personality. For a way of life does not grow up in a vacuum. It is developed in interaction with, and in response to, a natural and supernatural environment, and the form which it takes is partly determined by the beliefs entertained about that environment. It is, therefore, liable to be modified not only by the degree of insight into the nature of personality, but also by the extent and accuracy of the knowledge available about the nature of the environment in which life is lived. Accordingly, the development of the conception of the moral ideal is largely the result of increasingly accurate knowledge of matters of fact about nature and man and supernature. And the development in one of these lines influences, and is influenced by, development in the others. For the way of life which is the embodiment of the ideal is a relatively integrated whole in which the different aspects mutually modify, as well as support, one another. We may also get progress in the degree of integration of the way of life, in the adjustment of the institutions which in their interrelation constitute it. Here the line of advance has been from a way of life whose unity consists merely in the functional interdependence of its parts towards one which is rationally coherent. Without such integration, clashes of interests and conflicts of loyalties are bound to occur and to give rise to frustration, unhappiness, and inefficiency in action. Similar results follow from failure in comprehensiveness, i.e. failure to make provision for some of the major needs of human nature, and, in this respect too, progress is possible. In the main, however, it would seem that the way in which progress in moral enlightenment or the conception of the moral ideal has come about is not so much through the development of new powers of moral insight as through the emergence of conditions in which such powers of moral insight as men have can function effectively.

Bearing in mind these general considerations, and in particular the interaction of the different lines of development, let us look a little more in detail at some of the lines of progress in moral enlightenment, see the conditions under which they take place, the principle or principles, if any, on which they proceed, the direction in which they tend, and their significance for further progress.

The increase in the size of the group to whom moral considerations apply seems to come about in part, at least, through peaceful contacts in intertribal trade and commerce, and, perhaps even more, through the conquest of one group by another. Not that either commerce or conquest produces greater moral insight, but they provide opportunities for contact and co-operation, and, wherever such opportunities exist, there is a tendency for men to come to recognise one another as persons, and to take an interest in one another's welfare. In many forms of contact, especially contact which is brought about forcibly through conquest, there are many forces which militate against such recognition, forces which lead to such institutions as slavery or a caste system, under which some individuals tend to be treated as things rather than persons. But the greatest barrier to the mutual recognition of people as persons is ignorance. This arouses fear and suspicion which lead, at worst, to hostility and, at best, to indifference to one another's interests. When this barrier is removed through contact, especially contact which involves co-operation, even if it is in the first instance forcibly brought about, opportunities are created for man's natural interest in man to assert itself.[1] Co-operation tends to be found good, social sentiments develop, and man's natural interest in the welfare of others finds expression.

As I said earlier, it seems to me unnecessary to ask, and impossible to answer, the question, which comes first, co-operation between people, their interest in one another's welfare, or their recognition of one another as persons? All three develop together and mutually condition one another. One cannot develop far unless the others are also present in some measure.

In the process of growing moral enlightenment, direct experience of what is good seems to come first; and, in most cases at least, such experience is a condition of a state of affairs

[1] Cf. " If all men ate at the same table no one would be allowed to go hungry " (R. L. Stevenson).

being recognised as good. Favourable circumstances may produce a state of affairs, a form of life or a kind of relationship between individuals, which is found to be good. Even when this happens, the state of affairs may be accepted as a matter of course, and no consideration may be given to the conditions which produced it and are necessary to maintain it. When circumstances change and the form of life disappears, men may regret the loss and yet do nothing about the matter. On the other hand, the disappointment due to the partial or total loss of what was regarded as good may lead men to make an effort to retain it. This, in turn, leads to some consideration of the conditions which made it possible, and to an attempt to produce them, and it may be to extend the sphere of their application. Even so, there may be little reflective analysis of the principles involved in the form of life, and the conditions required for its realisation may not be disentangled from the concrete circumstances in which they were first given. Reflective analysis, conscious planning of a form of life, deliberate attempts at extending the application of principles, are much later products than the direct experience in which a form of life is found good. Rational justification of a way of life which is essentially rational belongs, like the flight of Minerva's owl, to the evening twilight of reflection rather than to the dawn of direct experience. But the reflective analysis reveals only the principles which were present in the experience from the outset.

The other great barrier to the recognition of other people as persons and to paying regard to their welfare, is lack of imagination, of capacity to put oneself in the other person's place, to realise what he is thinking and feeling. Among all peoples much selfishness is the result of thoughtlessness, of lack of imagination. In breaking down this barrier, the example and the teaching of specially gifted individuals, who are more sensitive and sympathetic to the feelings of others, and have more imaginative appreciation of their position and point of view, play an important part. The great moral teacher is he who opens our eyes so that we come to recognise what we had hitherto been unable to see for ourselves, but which we acknowledge when he points it out. He makes us feel that he knows us better than we know ourselves. But if the insight of our best moments and the impulses to which it gives rise are to survive, they must be embodied in customs and institutions, and become part of our way of life. These act as reminders to us in the days of gloom of the vision of the hours of insight; and they provide stimuli to moral steadfastness when the vision is dim and the impulse to well-doing weak.

Once the moral implications of men's common humanity are recognised and pointed out and acted on by some individuals, others will come to acknowledge what they might have failed to realise if left to themselves. Thus a social conscience comes to be developed; and, if it is embodied in institutions and organisations, even those who have little inclination to respect the common humanity or the rights of others cannot help, from time to time, being reminded of them and even being troubled by their own neglect of them. A social conscience, whether in relation to the members of one's own or another society, is just the inability to be content, however adequately one's own needs, material and spiritual, are provided for, as long as other people are without the conditions necessary for their welfare or deprived of opportunities to develop their personalities. And among the conditions which favour the development of such a conscience, the most important are contact and a vivid imagination.

How these conditions operate we see, e.g., in the way in which the results of the air-raids brought home to many people who ought to have been, but apparently were not, aware of them, the conditions under which some of their fellow-citizens in our large towns were living, and the stimulus which this gave to the formation of a social conscience with regard to such matters; or in the way in which, in the instruction of the young, we try to bring home to them the evils of cruelty to men or animals: we try to get them to realise imaginatively how their victims are feeling. We see the same principle at work in the way in which the intimate contacts between men of different classes and sections of the community, both in the armed and civilian services, during the war produced in many minds a new conception of the requirements of social justice. But such insights are apt to be intermittent and the stirrings of the social conscience to which they give rise tend quickly to subside, unless they are embodied in institutions and social structures which, by their perpetual suggestion, help to form the habits of think-ing and feeling of the individual.[1] Hence the impotence of moral advice and exhortation unless the feelings to which they give rise are canalised and directed into the service of organised institutions, which not only act as reminders to us of our duties and stimulants to perform them, but also provide the machinery by which we can fulfil them. This is specially necessary when the group is large, the members remote from one another, and the means of communications between them few. In such circumstances, it requires a vivid imagination to take an interest in one another's welfare, and especially to weigh the claims of those who are remote with even relative impartiality against the nearer and more pressing interests.

Another influence, which has played a considerable part, if not in bringing about, at least in strengthening, the belief that all men are persons owing duties to one another, is religion and religious institutions, especially those of the universal and mono-theistic religions. Even within the limited group, religion is, as we have seen, one of the great cohesive forces which serve to unite men into a common brotherhood ; but it is also one of the chief barriers which divide groups from one another. When, however, the believer regards his God as the creator and preserver of all men, this has a profound influence in breaking down the barriers which prevent him from regarding other men as persons like himself. It may well be that the recogni-tion of men's common humanity is as much the cause as the effect of monotheism. But whether it be the cause or the effect of this recognition, monotheism helps to conserve and support the belief that all men are persons, and that they owe duties to one another. For the association of this belief with the profoundest emotional reactions and the most deeply cherished convictions of believers in a universal God, acts as a reminder to men of their common humanity and their duties to one another.

Thus, through increasing contacts and co-operation between peoples, and a deepening imaginative appreciation of one

[1] Cf.   " That most difficult of tasks : to keep
                  Heights which the soul is competent to gain."

another's feelings, and with the support and sanction of the monotheistic religions, the group to which moral considerations apply has extended, slowly and intermittently, until, in theory at least, it includes all men.

Consider next the progress which we find in the content of the moral ideal, the changes in the quality, as distinct from the extent, of the common life in which it is embodied, and the ways in which these have altered men's ideas of their duties.

Increasingly accurate knowledge of nature and of the consequences of actions have led to modifications of men's ideas of what they ought to do. For example, once it is recognised that ill-health and death are due to natural causes and not to the malevolence of fellow-men, one barrier to the formation of social sentiments and friendly relations has been removed. Similarly, certain views about the effects of actions, such as that telling the truth to your neighbour will put him in possession of the means to use magic against you, or that the scalps of other people are necessary to make crops grow, make a marked difference to the sort of actions which are considered right; and, so, a more accurate knowledge of the consequences of actions and of their effects on people's welfare plays an important part in the progress of men's conception of the good life.

An even more important effect of growing knowledge is a change in men's ideas as to what is inevitable, part of the human lot, and, therefore, to be tolerated and accepted with resignation.[1] The primitive is apt to regard many of the causes of his frustration and unhappiness as inevitable; and this applies not only to natural conditions, but to many aspects of his social environment. He sees no alternative to them; and he does not think anyone is responsible for them. So the idea that it might be possible to change them does not occur to him.

---

[1] Men do not resent the evils which befall them as the result of natural causes or, to use the legal phrase, of ' acts of God ' as they do those which are due to the intervention of their fellows or even those which they believe could have been prevented by the knowledge and goodwill of other men. Contrast, e.g., the attitude of the farmer to losses to his crops due to drought or storms with his attitude to the same, or even a smaller, amount taken from him by a tax.

Accordingly, his ideal tends to be to change himself into line with them, an ideal of self-discipline and resignation to the nature of things. And this attitude is strengthened when he regards the nature of things as the expression of a superhuman purpose; and especially when he believes that this purpose is good, though he may be unable to understand how it is so. But, with growing knowledge comes an increasing sense of power over his environment, and his ideal tends to become one of mastering and controlling and changing it so as to bring it into line with his desires. Thus, there emerges a new and more conscious attitude to change. The idea of progress takes shape, and men try not only to master and control their natural environment, but also to change their social institutions, if not in the light of a consciously held ideal, at least so as to remove some of the major ills of life.

Now this growing dominance of mind over nature and social structures has resulted in very great gains; for many of the ills which men have been accustomed to accept as inevitable are preventible by human wisdom and goodwill. But the change of attitude may be carried too far. There is a danger that men may regard themselves as completely masters of their fate, set up their uncriticised desires as the directors of evolution, and forget that there is a constitution of the universe to which the proper attitude is one of recognition and acceptance, and into conformity to which they ought to discipline themselves. In particular, there is the danger that, either directly or through their mastery of nature, they may try to control their fellow-men, that they may regard people as objects to be understood and mastered and used for their purposes, instead of recognising them as persons, independent centres of purposes, to be accepted and respected. The danger of adopting this attitude is specially great when people are concerned with large masses of men to whom their relations are largely impersonal and mechanical. An attitude of humility and deference, even of reverence, is becoming in our relations with another personality; for it is something which has value in itself and not just in relation to our purposes; and this attitude is inconsistent with that of mastery and control. I believe nothing is more necessary or perhaps more difficult in the modern world than to distinguish clearly between the occasions on which these different attitudes are appropriate; for without a recognition that there are ideals and values which are rooted in the nature of man and the constitution of the universe, and, therefore, to be accepted and appreciated, the reforming spirit is in danger of losing its direction.

There have been two other lines of development which in part preceded, and which provide a supplement and corrective to, the attitude of mastery and control which is embodied in the idea of progress. The first is an increasing emphasis on the inner life, on motives and intentions and the spirit in which actions are performed. This is the one sense, to which I referred above, in which there seems to me that there has been development in the meaning of moral goodness from the more primitive to the more advanced societies. In the main, the primitive tends to think of moral goodness as doing what is believed to be right rather than as doing it from a good motive. It is not so much that he lays all the emphasis on the external action as that he fails to distinguish as clearly as we do between the external action and the spirit in which it is done, just as he often fails to distinguish between accident and design, or between the unforeseen consequences of an action and those which are deliberately willed. It is true that in relatively small communities, in which there is little difference between the ideas as to what is right entertained by different individuals, the performance of the external action may be taken by a man's neighbours as a rough indication of his motives. It is also true that field workers among primitives give us less information than we would wish about the extent to which, in their moral judgements, primitives take account of motives; and that the more thoroughly primitive ways of life are investigated by trained experts, the more account they are found to take of motives, as we have seen, for example, in Malinowski's account of the Trobrianders, Junod's account of the Bantu, and Hogbin's account of the inhabitants of Wogeo. But when due allowance has been made for these considerations, there is little doubt that most primitive peoples pay insufficient attention to the inner aspect of the moral life; and that one of the most important developments from the more primitive to the more advanced peoples has consisted in the discovery of the inner life and the consequent importance attached to conscientiousness and purity of motives.

The other closely connected line of development has been an increasing appreciation of the individuality of the moral agent as a self-governing, responsible personality, with a right of private judgement and entitled to some measure of tolerance and freedom to conduct his life in his own way. In these respects, there are considerable differences between different primitive peoples, but there is no doubt that among most of them these aspects of the moral life are imperfectly recognised and insufficiently provided for. Just as there is a lack of clear distinction between the inner and the outer aspect of life and a failure to recognise the inner life as the real self, so we find an absence of sharp distinction between a man and his belongings, or a man and his family, or the individual and his group. There is, therefore, a tendency to treat an individual as a member of a group rather than as a responsible, independent agent, and to pay less attention to justice to the individual than to what is believed to be for the good of the group. We must not, however, exaggerate this characteristic of primitive ways of thinking, as is done when we are told that among them there is no sense of individual responsibility or personality: that " responsibility is collective and punishment vicarious ".[1] For, while there is a substantial foundation for such statements in the facts of primitive life, they apply much more to the relations between groups than they do to the relations between members within a group. When we distinguish between these relations, I think we shall find that, significant as are the differences between primitives and ourselves in these respects, they are differences of degree rather than of kind, and that there are analogies to most of their ideas and judgements among ourselves.[2]

It is true that in their thinking of the relations between one group and another, whether the groups concerned are families or villages or clans or tribes, primitives accept the principle of

---

[1] Ginsberg, *Moral Progress* (Frazer Lecture, 1944), p. 24.

[2] Cf. the differences between ourselves and primitives " while sometimes large, and always important, are at bottom differences in degree and not in kind and are indeed . . . superficial rather than fundamental " (Sharp, *Ethics*, p. 172).

collective responsibility more often than our ideas of justice would warrant. They are prepared to let one man suffer for the misdeeds of another. They will defend or avenge a fellow member without too nice a regard for the justice of his cause. They will visit the sins of the parents upon the children. They will take vengeance on one of a man's kin or group instead of on the actual offender. And they seem to be generally satisfied that these things meet the requirements of justice. But, while instances of all these things may be quoted from different primitive peoples, they do not prove that primitives do not recognise individual responsibility. Some writers have an unfortunate tendency to generalise from one or two instances. When they come across one or a few cases in which a primitive people accept, or act on, the principle of collective responsibility in circumstances in which we would not do so, they tend to jump to the conclusion that the people concerned do not recognise the separate individuality of their members at all, that they have no sense of individual responsibility. This, however, is very far from being the case. Indeed, the very writers who indulge in these generalisations often report many situations in which the people about whom the statements are made show a quite keen sense of individual responsibility; and careful observers report both the cases in which primitives do, and the cases in which they do not, show a sense of individual responsibility.

Take as an example the case of punishment. Hobhouse, Wheeler and Ginsberg sum up the results of their examination of the evidence available about more than 650 primitive peoples as follows : " It is just as likely that primitive justice or redress is sought at the expense of the wrongdoer alone as that it will be collective or vicarious ".[1] Peristiany reports that the Kipsigis have a keen sense of individual responsibility in most things, but that in the case of murder they accept the principle of collective responsibility.[2] Similarly, Schapera tells us that among the Tswana the head of the family is responsible for the conduct of its members but that " when a thrashing is deserved,

---

[1] *The Social Institutions and the Material Culture of the Simpler Peoples*, p. 54.
[2] *Social Institutions of the Kipsigis*, pp. 99-100.

it is the culprit who gets it ".[1] The Trobrianders sometimes refuse to exact vengeance for one of their number when they recognise that he had been clearly in the wrong;[2] while other primitives accept the principle of collective responsibility only for the first offence committed by one of their number, and warn the culprit that the offence must not be committed again, and, if it is, they refuse to defend him.[3] The fact seems to be that, even in the relations between different groups, while primitives may have to be content to take vengeance on any member of a group, one of whose members has offended against them, many, if not most, of them much prefer to punish the actual offender, if they can get him.

Thus it is by no means true that, even in the relations of different groups, primitives never recognise the principle of individual responsibility, but their recognition of it is partial and hesitating. In the relations between the members of the in-group, on the other hand, they recognise it to a quite marked degree. In general, we may say that, in the relations between the members of a group, the individual is regarded as responsible for his own acts and blamed or praised accordingly. Action may be taken against him and punishment inflicted on him as an individual; and, in certain circumstances, he may be driven out of the group to face the perils of the outside world and usually to perish. No doubt in some cases his family may be made to suffer with him, but this is by no means always true. But when due allowance has been made for all these considerations, it must still be admitted that, in many circumstances, primitives pay much less regard to the principle of strict individual responsibility than more advanced peoples; and the line of advance has been towards an increasing emphasis on individual responsibility.

Moreover, even within the group, that which is believed to be for the good of the group as a whole tends to be regarded by the primitive as more important than justice to the individual. Accordingly, we find actions which are disapproved but not punished because suitable punishment might disrupt

[1] *Tswana Law and Custom*, p. 50.
[2] Malinowski, *Crime and Custom*, p. 118.
[3] Hogbin, *Experiments in Civilisation*, p. 97.

the group or deprive it of a member. We also find cases in which an individual, who is regarded as less important to the group, is handed over to the vengeance of another group instead of the person who has actually offended against them. Such a person may be either a kinsman of the offender or someone who is disapproved of by his group for other reasons. But, while this involves vicarious suffering, it is doubtful if the group think of it as vicarious punishment.

We find analogies to many of these practices in which one has to suffer for the good of others among ourselves, but we do not think of them as vicarious punishment. We segregate lepers and typhoid carriers and those who have, or have been in contact with, infectious diseases ; and we impose these irksome restraints and restrictions on them, not because we believe they are responsible for their condition or have been guilty of anything morally wrong, but for the good of the community as a whole. We conscript one man in war-time and send him to almost certain death, while we compel another man who wants to take these risks to remain in a safe job, because he possesses some special skill which is of value to the community. In other words, we, too, especially in times of stress and group danger, subordinate justice to the individual to what we think is for the good of the group. The primitives do this on a much more extended scale, though its extent varies from one people to another ; and this is so, in part at least, because times of stress and danger are more common among them. But neither with us nor with them is this inconsistent with the recognition of individual responsibility in other connections ; and, as I said, they too recognise it within limits.

There are two other pieces of evidence that primitives regard their fellow members of the group as independent personalities entitled to consideration and respect. One is their strict codes of etiquette and manners, and their unwillingness to hurt anyone's feelings by infringing these codes. Field workers among most primitive peoples have been deeply impressed by their politeness, their sensitiveness to the feelings of other people, their unwillingness to do anything that would hurt them. The other is that, in regard to all matters which are not believed to affect the safety or the food supply of the group, many primitive peoples allow their members considerable scope for free choice and initiative. And few of them persecute their members for unorthodox beliefs. As long as a person's actions conform to what is believed to be for the good of the group, his beliefs are largely regarded as his own affair. And so, we find sceptics and agnostics as well as reformers and rebels among them; and the former at least are generally left unmolested.

Nevertheless, in all matters of fundamental importance freedom of choice and initiative is very strictly limited. For, in the conditions of life of most primitive people, unity is necessary to survival and unity is apt to be interpreted as uniformity; non-conformity is regarded as dangerous and, therefore, the would-be reformer is apt to be classed with the rebel and treated accordingly. No doubt the most difficult problem with which any people is confronted is that of reconciling freedom for initiative and the expression of creative impulses, which justice to the individual demands, with the requirements of social order, which regard for the common good demands. Every way of life, primitive or civilised, is an attempt to solve this problem; but among most primitives the scales tend to be very heavily weighted in favour of social order and the common good rather than justice to the individual and opportunities for initiative and self-expression.

Whether an individual can effect any changes in the way of life of his people, and, if he can, to what extent he can do so, depends not merely on his personal qualities, but also on the position which he occupies in the community. Specially gifted individuals who are in positions of political or religious authority sometimes bring about important changes; but, in the main, such changes as come about in the institutions and ways of life of primitive groups are not the results of conscious planning; the emergence of the idea of progress in social and political conditions, the attitude of the reformer who sets out deliberately to change the beliefs and institutions of his people in the light of a consciously entertained ideal, is, as we have seen, one of the significant changes in the advance from the more primitive to the more advanced peoples. And this development is not unconnected with increasing respect for personality, for the need for tolerance of individual differences and the desirability of opportunities for initiative and the expression of creative impulses. Here, too, the line of progress has been in the direction of a more widespread recognition of individuals as self-governing, responsible persons, to be persuaded rather than coerced, to be provided with opportunities for developing their powers rather than directed.

The last line of progress which I want to mention concerns the development which we find in men's conception of the supernatural. We have seen that even the most primitive men believe themselves to be in contact with something in their environment which they regard as supersensible, superhuman, or supernatural, something which evokes in them a profound emotional reaction, and to which they consider it necessary to adjust themselves. Here the line of progress has not been towards a greater certainty of the reality of the supernatural, but towards a different conception of its character. Just as we find man, as his insight into himself and his fellows grows, drawing a clearer distinction between the inner and the outer aspects of his life, and tending more and more to regard the inner or spiritual self as the real self, and its values as the highest values; so, in his thinking of his cosmic environment, we find him distinguishing more sharply between the natural and the spiritual, and interpreting the supernatural in more personal and spiritual terms, till in the end he comes to conceive it as a personal or supra-personal being who is the embodiment of perfect wisdom and goodness, a being who is regarded not so much as an external judge or law-giver, much less in terms of mere power, operating on men through hope or fear, but rather as a being whose very existence is a condemnation of moral imperfection and weakness, and arouses in man a desire for moral purity and perfection, a being whose character evokes reverence and loyalty and provides a standing challenge and encouragement to man to try to realise the highest ideals which he finds in his moral consciousness, and to transform himself and his world so as to approximate more closely to their requirements. At-one-ment with the supernatural then becomes his highest ideal, that which calls forth his supreme loyalty.

In this way, religion, as it renews its vitality in the insight of its great teachers, has shown a wonderful capacity for absorbing into itself and putting in a cosmic setting the values and ideals which the developing moral consciousness reveals. The cosmological and metaphysical framework into which the values are fitted may change from age to age, but the reality of the values and the need for loyalty to them remain; and the added significance which religion confers on them provides a support of the moral will and an incentive to right-doing the importance of which cannot be over-estimated. Nevertheless, as Bowman has pointed out, the lesson of history seems to be that " when morality and religion fail to synthesise, morality may hold its own against religion, but religion will have the utmost difficulty in maintaining itself against morality ".[1] Certainly not the least significant of the triumphs of the moral spirit has been the gradual moralisation of the concept of the supernatural, and the line of progress has been towards conceiving the relation of man to the supernatural as a relation between persons, a relation in which the value and dignity of personality is respected and enhanced.

What we seem to find, then, is this. From whatever point of view we consider the progress in enlightenment or in the conception of the moral ideal from the more primitive to the more advanced peoples, it seems to take the form of an increasing recognition of the fundamental importance of personality and of the distinction between persons and things. Increasingly accurate knowledge of matters of fact, and increasing communications and contacts and co-operation between individuals and peoples, provide conditions in which moral insight can function more effectively; and, as it does so, we find men slowly, intermittently and haltingly, but none the less surely, coming to recognise other men as persons, independent, responsible, self-governing individuals. Things we try to master and control and use. Their value consists in ministering to our purposes. Persons are subjects of purposes, not just objects of the purposes of other people. They are separate centres of spiritual life, independent expressions of the

[1] *Studies in the Philosophy of Religion*, ii. 37.

moral consciousness. This characteristic of men as persons is what Temple has in mind when he writes [1] of the moral equality of men, and what the advanced religions refer to when they say that all men are equal in the sight of God.

This moral equality of men is, of course, compatible with many differences between them in other respects. Men differ in physical and mental capacity, in knowledge and experience, in wisdom and moral goodness, and so on ; but they are equal in a sense which is deeper than all their differences. They are all subjects not objects, persons not things, ends not means. They are self-conscious moral beings, having in themselves a principle of self-government which gives them a worth and dignity which entitle them to our consideration and respect. Only as we recognise this do we understand them as they really are. It is this fundamental moral equality of men as persons which is the justification of their equality before the law, equality of civil and political rights, equality of educational opportunity, and so on. The ideal to which the growing recognition of it points is that of a community of persons co-operating as persons. In this ideal we find the criterion of progress in moral enlightenment, the criterion by which we can test the adequacy of different ways of life. This ideal seems to be operative in the minds of all men so far as they are rational moral beings, however dim and obscure their grasp of it and however imperfect their understanding of its require-ments may often be. Its operation is the mainspring of pro-gress, and of dissatisfaction with things as they are. We find it adumbrated in the constitution of the simplest primitive institutions and in the moral symmetry of the principle of reciprocity which underlies all primitive ways of life. At the other end of the scale, it forms the basis of Kant's conception of a Kingdom of Ends and of Christ's idea of the Kingdom of God. The difference which we find between these extremes is twofold, consisting partly in the extension of the group who are recognised as persons, and partly in a deepening of the meaning of what it is to be a person, a deepening which has come about through a clearer grasp of the inner life and of the distinction between persons and things.

[1] *Christian News Letter*, No. 198, supplement.

The principle of which this ideal is the expression I have called the principle of justice or equity. It seems to me an objective or rational principle. The moral equality of men as persons is not something which depends on us, not something which we want or create. It is something which we discover or recognise and have to accept. Our recognition of it may be within narrow limits and confined to moments of insight when our vision is unclouded by passion and prejudice. In such moments we find we have no option but to recognise others as self-governing moral beings like ourselves, with independent lives and purposes of their own, and our natural interest in them and their welfare takes the form of a desire not to direct and control them and impose our will upon them, but to co-operate with them, to provide opportunities for them to realise their purpose and develop their personalities. But if the spark which flickers in such moments of insight is not to die, but to develop into a steady flame, it must be caught and embodied in patterns of behaviour and institutions and a way of life, which will act as constant reminders of it, till it becomes part and parcel of our habits of thinking and feeling and acting, not so much something which is at the focus of consciousness as what forms the background in the light of which we see everything else. Even then, there will be many forces in us and around us which militate against its continued recognition and its realisation, and the effort to be true to it requires a constant warfare from which there is no discharge. There is, however, another side to this picture which is no less important. The real test of the genuineness of our vision in what we take to be our moments of insight is whether the values and principles and ideals which it reveals can be embodied in a way of life in which they can be reconciled with others which we also recognise. The attempt to effect such a reconciliation may mean a more or less radical reconstruction of our accepted way of life and it may also involve a modification of the new values and ideals themselves; but, until we see how it can be done, we have not really grasped the meaning of these values and ideals themselves, and, unless it can be done, they cannot be accepted as they stand as genuine and worthy of our loyalty. The real difference between the genuine vision of the moral

2 G

pioneer and the wishful thinking of the utopian dreamer is that the former can, and the latter cannot, be translated into an operative ideal ; and the reason why it cannot is not that it is too ideal, but that it is not ideal enough, because it has not grasped the inner nature and possibilities of the actual, what human nature has in it to be and is striving to become.

No doubt the individual who believes he sees values hitherto either wholly or partially unrecognised, rightly considers it his duty to work for their recognition and realisation, even if he cannot see in detail how the way of life of his people has to be reconstructed to give expression to them ; and he may be performing a very useful function in his one-sided emphasis on them. But the final test of their validity is their capacity to be incorporated in an operative ideal. And the moral pioneer himself may be unsure of the genuineness of his vision till he has succeeded in persuading at least some others of the worth of the values which he is seeking to realise. He is often acutely conscious that, in pursuing them, he is taking a risk, and that the risk is a moral risk. It is not only a venture of faith, but a venture which may not succeed and may not deserve to succeed, because the insight on which it is based is partial and imperfect. There is such an element of faith in all moral living, but it is specially prominent in the lives of moral and social reformers.

I have already referred to the distinction which is sometimes drawn between two kinds of duty — one concerned with the conscientious discharge of the requirements of existing institutions and ways of life, and the other concerned with the re-moulding of the operative ideal so as to bring it nearer to the formal ideal — and I pointed out that both rest ultimately on the same principle and tend to merge into one another. In a relatively stable society, most of the duties of most people belong to the former class, and the moral goodness of most individuals consists in the conscientious discharge of such duties ; but the best men in every society feel it their duty to do more than the accepted pattern of the way of life of their people requires, or than others have a right to expect of them. Thus such people are already on the way to raising the requirements of the accepted pattern. The reformer who tries consciously to alter the operative ideal so as to make it more consistent, or to embody new values in it, is only carrying the process a stage further. While there is a difference of emphasis between the two attitudes, they may both be found alternating in the life of the same person ; and when duties of the former kind are performed in a spirit of loyalty to the formal ideal, which the accepted way of life is an attempt to express, they tend to pass into the latter class.

In a period of transition such as we are living in today, when traditional values are questioned and established institutions are crumbling, and people are trying consciously to reconstruct many of their institutions and, therefore, the way of life which in their interrelation they constitute, duties of the second kind tend to be much in evidence, and their determination is apt to be a cause of moral perplexity to many individuals. In such circumstances, it is essential that men should examine the foundations of the moral and social order and bring to light the fundamental principle which justifies traditional values and institutions, so far as they are justifiable ; and which points the direction in which they should be modified, so far as they require modification. The principle which our analysis has revealed as the basis of moral and social obligations may be stated, ' Be a person and recognise and treat others as persons '. That, however, is only a formal principle and, before we can understand its nature and requirements fully, we must, as I have already said, try to embody it in a detailed way of life more completely than has yet been done ; but many of its conditions are already clear, and what is necessary is to grasp it more clearly, apply it more consistently, and extend it to the whole range of human relationships.

In these lectures, I have been concerned with the life of man between birth and death with nothing more than occasional side-glances at the cosmic arena in which this life is lived. This is not because I consider metaphysical and theological speculations, of the kind with which most of the lectures on this foundation have been concerned, idle or unimportant. It is rather because I chose as my subject the last, and perhaps the least, though I should contend not the least important, of the subjects prescribed by Lord Gifford, the nature of morality and the grounds of moral obligation; and because I am convinced that these can be discovered by an analysis of the moral consciousness and the consideration of the life of man as a person among persons, without reference to any metaphysical or theological system. If my analysis has been sound, there is one, and only one, thing which is absolutely and unconditionally good, moral goodness, the goodness of conscientiously doing that which we believe to be right and trying to realise that which we believe to be good, and one, and only one, thing absolutely evil, the evil will, the deliberate doing of that which we believe to be wrong, not because we believe it to be wrong, but despite the belief that it is wrong; and this would still be so, and the duty of realising the one and avoiding the other would still be unconditionally binding, even if there were nothing beyond the grave, and even if there were no answer from the universe to man's cry for cosmic support in his moral struggle except the echo of his own voice. Not that I believe that the evidence compels us to take so pessimistic a view of the universe and man's destiny as part of it, a view which, as it seems to me, would make the emergence of a being capable of entertaining a moral ideal and feeling an obligation to realise it in spite of consequences, an inexplicable enigma, and which would deprive many people of one of the main stimuli to moral steadfastness and make it more difficult for them to maintain the warfare against the powers of evil in and around them. For though the conclusions at which I have arrived about the moral life do not seem to me to derive their justification or authority from any metaphysical or theological system, and though they seem more certain than the results of any such speculations, they are not without metaphysical implications. They have to be taken into account in constructing cosmological systems, and, though they are not the only evidence to be taken into account, any system which does not leave room for them seems to me necessarily false. But if we are to use them as data or premises for such construction, it is all the more important that they should themselves be independently established.

INDEX

THE END

PRINTED BY R. & R. CLARK, LTD., EDINBURGH